American Indian Lives

University

of

Nebraska

Press

Lincoln

and

London

Life Lived Like a Story

Life Stories of Three Yukon Native Elders

By Julie Cruikshank in collaboration with Angela Sidney, Kitty Smith, and Annie Ned

#27291099

Copyright © 1990 by the
University of Nebraska Press
All rights reserved
Manufactured in the United States of America

First Bison Book printing: 1992
Most recent printing indicated by the last
digit below:

10   9   8   7   6   5   4   3

Library of Congress Cataloging-in-Publication
Data
Cruikshank, Julie.
Life lived like a story: life stories of three
Yukon native elders / by Julie Cruikshank in
collaboration with Angela Sidney, Kitty Smith,
and Annie Ned.
p.   cm.
Includes bibliographical references.
ISBN 0-8032-1447-2
ISBN 0-8032-6352-X (pbk.)
1. Tutchone Indians—Biography. 2. Tagish
Indians—Biography. 3. Tlingit Indians—
Biography. 4. Ethnology—Biographical
methods. 5. Storytelling—Yukon Territory.
I. Title
E99.T92C78   1990
917.9'1004972—dc20   89-49361
[B] CIP

Contents

Part III ✳ Old-Style Words Are Just Like School: Annie Ned

Preface

Storytelling is a universal activity and may well be the oldest of the arts. It has always provided a vehicle for the expression of ideas, particularly in societies relying on oral tradition. Yet investigation of what contemporary storytellers actually communicate to their listeners occupies a restricted place in anthropology. The growing literature on small-scale hunting societies pays careful attention to their subsistence strategies but less to ideas that seem peripheral to their economic activities. A gap remains in our knowledge about the contribution of expressive forms like storytelling to strategies for adapting to social, cultural, and economic change.

The life stories appearing in this volume come from communities where storytelling provides a customary framework for discussing the past. Angela Sidney, Kitty Smith, and Annie Ned are three remarkable and gifted women of Athapaskan and Tlingit ancestry who were born in the southern Yukon Territory around the turn of the century. Their life stories tell us as much about the present as about the past, as much about ideas of community as about individual experience; they call our attention to the diverse ways humans formulate such linkages. When they talk about their lives, these women use narrative genres familiar to anyone sharing their cultural background but not always clear to cultural outsiders. They may, for example, explain an event by telling a story in which a protagonist suffers complex repercussions because he behaved rashly, a point easily lost on a Western audience, that sometimes confuses hubris with individualism. A written text of their accounts, then, does not unambiguously speak for itself.

Those of us raised in a Western tradition tend to approach life history with certain preconceptions about what constitutes an "adequate" account of a life. The familiar model comes from written autobiography—an author's chronological reflections about individual growth and development, often presented as a passage from darkness to light. Yet this form of exposition is relatively recent and began to appear regularly only after the eighteenth century. Since then it has become so well entrenched, so structured by convention, that it has come to seem "natural" to Western readers and a form not requiring explanation. Gertrude Stein's *Autobiography of Alice B. Toklas* reminds us just how predictable our expectations of this genre are when we approach texts from other cultural traditions and how we make the category a prior condition of perception. Pre-understandings about how subjective experience should be expressed may disappoint a listener steeped in Western categories: in a telling commentary published with his life history of an Acoma Indian man, Leslie White complained that "the autobiography of a Pueblo Indian is about as personal as the life story of an automobile tire."[1] Such thwarted expectations should remind us that autobiography is a culturally specific narrative genre rather than a universal form for explaining experience.

If writing an autobiography implies a solitary exercise, recording a life history is usually a social activity. It is the collaborative product of an encounter between two people, often from different cultural backgrounds, and incorporates the consciousness of an investigator as well as that of a subject. Crapanzano has charged that orally narrated life histories are too often written as though the narrator were addressing the cosmos when in fact narration is occurring in a very specific context.[2] Yet oral testimonies are more than just the spontaneous product of an encounter between an interviewer and a subject: the narrative has symbolic qualities—a kind of autonomous life that simultaneously reflects continuity with the past and passes on experiences, stories, and guiding principles in the present.

This volume results from collaborative research in which the narrators and I each used our own culturally embedded "stories" to interpret the past. The narrative equipment I originally brought to our discussions combined some training in anthropology, considerable enthusiasm for documenting unwritten social history, and a cultural habit of looking for chronology in a life account. Over the years, I have become increasingly attentive to the ways Mrs. Sidney, Mrs. Smith, and Mrs. Ned mobilize traditional dimensions of their culture—in oral narrative, songs, names of places and people—to explain and interpret their experiences. Shared traditions and symbols of cultural identity infuse their life stories; historical verisimilitude plays a less important part. Each of these women has taken an energetic role in determining both the direction of our work and the various forms in which it has already been published and distributed in her community. Under their tutelage my interests have shifted away from an oral history committed to documenting changes in social reality and toward an investigation of narrative forms for talking about, remembering, and interpreting everyday life. Potentially, an oral history attuned to narrative conventions provides an observatory from which to assess the shifting boundary between what we call *history* and what we call *myth*.

The book, like our research, is a product of collaboration. My introductory comments provide some cultural context and a discussion of how each narrator combines traditional narrative with individual experience to construct a coherent account of her life: Then each life story is presented in a way that clearly acknowledges the oral copyright of the narrator—first, Mrs. Sidney's, then Mrs. Smith's, then Mrs. Ned's. A conclusion analyzes some of the recurring themes. Some readers may prefer to go directly to the life stories and return to the background commentary after becoming familiar with the narratives.

Angela Sidney, Kitty Smith, and Annie Ned are accustomed to training children, but it is harder to teach a cultural outsider even the simplest concepts. In the many years we have worked together producing booklets of their narratives and family histories, they have drawn on their life experiences with good humor and penetrating wit to teach me about their culture, about the vagaries of human existence, and about what it means really to live life fully.

The families of these women have been most supportive over the years, and we wish to thank the daughters, sisters, nieces, and grandchildren who have consistently encouraged our work: Ida Calmegan, Richard Craft, Mary Easterson, Carol Geddes, Judy Gingell, Beatrice Hayden, May Hume, Mary Jane Jim, Stella Jim, Wayne Jim, Louise Profeit-LeBlanc, Doris McLean, Edna Rose, Clara Schinkel, Elijah Smith, Walter Smith. And I especially thank my own family—Garry, Lawrence, and Julian—for their patience and good humor during successive drafts of this book.

We all acknowledge the encouragement and support of the Yukon Native Language Centre and particularly thank John Ritter, Gertie Tom, and Margaret Workman from that institution, Jeff Leer from the Alaska Native Language Center, Bill Ferguson from the Yukon Department of Education, and Paul Birckel, formerly Executive Director for the Council for Yukon Indians. Initial funding from the Explorations Program of Canada Council and from the Urgent Ethnology Division of the Canadian Ethnology Service enabled us to begin this work in the mid-1970s. From 1980 to 1984 the Council for Yukon Indians supported the linguistic parts of our work through the Yukon Native Languages Project[3] as we recorded toponyms, personal names, narratives, and songs in Tagish, Tlingit, and Southern Tutchone. Fellowships from the Social Sciences and Humanities Research Council of Canada and the Association of Canadian Universities for Northern Studies made it possible for me to write a longer version of this book as my doctoral dissertation at the University of British Columbia. During the winter of 1987–88 the Scott Polar Research Institute at the University of Cambridge generously provided me with office space and library facilities, and the Explorations Program, Canada Council, with funding for the completion of this book. I am very grateful to Lavonne Brown Ruoff and Kim Vivier for their editorial advice. Ultimately, the book owes much to conversations, over many years, with Catharine McClellan and Robin Ridington.

As agreed by the four authors, any royalties from this book will go to a scholarship fund for Yukon Native students who have an interest in oral history and want to undertake postsecondary education. The annual Oral History Award will be administered by the Curriculum Development Program of the Council for Yukon Indians.

Julie Cruikshank
Vancouver, November 1988

As this book goes to press in late 1990, Mrs. Smith is no longer living. She passed away in June 1989. Mrs. Sidney and Mrs. Ned continue their active lives. Mrs. Ned was awarded the Order of Canada on August 1, 1990.

Linguistic Note

Mrs. Sidney, Mrs. Smith, and Mrs. Ned are all multilingual. In addition to English, Mrs. Sidney speaks Tagish and Tlingit, Mrs. Ned and Mrs. Smith speak Southern Tutchone and Tlingit, and all three women are conversant with neighboring Athapaskan languages. Tagish and Southern Tutchone are both part of the larger Athapaskan family of languages; Tlingit is quite different. There is still scholarly debate about whether Tlingit and Athapaskan languages were once related, because their grammars, though not their vocabularies, are parallel; however, it is not yet clear whether these parallels can be traced to a genetic relationship or to a long history of contact between the two language families.

Accounts in this volume were recorded in English, but clan names, personal names, and place names in Tagish, Southern Tutchone, and Tlingit are retained in the text. I am indebted to linguists John Ritter, Jeff Leer, Gertie Tom, and Margaret Workman for assistance with transcriptions. Despite their best efforts, I am completely responsible for spelling errors and inconsistencies. A spelling system for Tlingit has been developed at the Alaska Native Language Center, and standardized writing systems for Yukon Athapaskan languages are now being developed at the Yukon Native Language Centre. Sounds in Tlingit and Athapaskan languages differ, so the alphabets for these languages also differ. Because Mrs. Sidney is the last fluent speaker of Tagish, linguists working with her have chosen not to develop a separate Tagish alphabet but to use the alphabet of her other language, Tlingit, to write Tagish words. Although this has the advantage of giving Mrs. Sidney's written accounts a certain internal linguistic consistency, her Tagish words are written rather differently from words in other Athapaskan languages, including Southern Tutchone, even when they *sound* very similar.

These are all tonal languages, and a major difference in the spelling system concerns the way in which tones are marked. In Tlingit and Tagish, high tones are marked and low tones remain unmarked. For linguistic reasons, scholars have chosen the opposite strategy for Southern Tutchone, marking low tones and leaving high tones unmarked. Because this system is becoming conventional, I have retained it even though it sometimes looks awkward when a narrator uses words from both languages. Southern Tutchone has another layer of complexity because there are also distinct rising and falling tones; however, so few Southern Tutchone words are used in the text that I have left rising and falling tones unmarked.

I have standardized Tagish and Southern Tutchone in two cases, even though the formal writing conventions differ. The suffix *Maa* (Tagish) and *Ma* or *ma* (Southern Tutchone) appears in some women's names and means, literally, "mother of." The Tagish/Tlingit convention is to write it with a double *aa,* whereas the Southern Tutchone convention uses a single *a:* both are nasalized. In this book a single *a* is used and the nasalization is implied rather than marked. Second, the voiceless fricative ł, usually written as a plain *l* in Tlingit, is marked with a bar for consistency with Athapaskan languages.

Alphabetization

Words in the glossary and index are arranged following Southern Tutchone, Tagish, and Tlingit alphabets, which include consonants not found in English. When words from several languages are combined, the alphabetization may seem unfamiliar. Attention is drawn to the way the following consonants are ordered: ch, ch', d, g, g̲, k, k̲, k', k̲', l, ł, s, s', t, tl, ts, t', tl', ts', x, x̲, x', x̲'.

Names

Individuals referred to in this book are identified by both Native and English names. Around the turn of the century, Tagish, Tlingit, and Southern Tutchone men began to acquire English names like Jim, John, Charlie, prefaced by the name of the geographical area with which they were associated, for example, Hutshi Jum or Tagish John. Their wives are frequently referred to as "Mrs. Hutshi Jim" or "Mrs. Whitehorse Billy." Later, these became family surnames, and their children were given names such as Frankie Jim or Johnny Johns. For consistency, these names are alphabetized in the index so that family members are listed together.

Other men were named to distinguish physical attributes, for example, Skookum Jim and Slim Jim. They are listed under the prefix because it was more likely to become the family name. Slim Jim's children inherited Slim as a family name.

Tlingit and Tagish Alphabet

Tlingit Vowels

Short	Long
a	aa
e	ei
i	ee
u	oo

Tlingit Consonants

Plain stops	d		dl	dz	j	g	g̲
Aspirated stops	t		tl	ts	ch	k	k̲
Glottalized stops	t'		tl'	ts'	ch'	k'	k̲'
Plain fricatives			l	s	sh	x	x̲
Glottalized fricatives			l'	s'		x'	x̲'
Other sounds	m	n	ł		y	w	h

Tone

High tone is marked (v́) on short vowels.

High tone is marked (v́v) on long vowels.

Low tone is not marked.

Source: Adapted from *Tlingit Literacy Workshop,* January 23–25, 1984, pp. 6–7, Yukon Native Languages Project (now Yukon Native Language Centre), Box 2799, Whitehorse, Yukon Y1A 5K4, Canada. The Tlingit alphabet is also used to transcribe Tagish vowels.

Southern Tutchone Alphabet

Southern Tutchone Vowels

High vowels	i	ü	u
Mid vowels	e	ä	äw(o)
Low vowels		a	
Diphthongs	ay		aw

Nasalized vowels are written with a (̨) directly underneath the letters:

į ę ą ų ų̈ ą̈ ąw ą̈w ąy

Southern Tutchone Consonants

Plain	d	dl	ddh	dz	j	g	gw	
Aspirated	t	tl	tth	ts	ch	k	kw	
Glottalized	t'	tl'	tth'	ts'	ch'	k'	k'w	
Voiceless fricatives		ł	th	s	sh	kh	khw	h
Voiced fricatives		l	dh	z	zh	gh	ghw	
Nasals	m	n						
Nasal + stop	mb	nd		nj				
Other sounds				r	y	(w)	'	

Tone

Low tone is marked (v̀) on vowels.

High tone is never marked; rising/falling remains unmarked here.

Source: Adapted from *Southern Tutchone Literacy Workshop,* May 9–11, 1984, p. 6, and *Southern Tutchone Literacy Workshop,* May 22–24, p. 5, both publications of the Yukon Native Language Centre.

INTRODUCTION

Life History and

Life Stories

*Well, I've tried to live my life right,
just like a story.*
—Angela Sidney

One of the liveliest areas of discussion in contemporary anthropology centers on how to convey authentically, in words, the experience of one culture to members of another. Kaj Birket-Smith's suggestion that anthropology originated with a group of tribespeople listening to one of its members tell stories about the strange customs of a neighboring tribe is only half-facetious[1]: questions about how to explain unfamiliar human behavior have probably troubled people from all cultural backgrounds in all periods of history. However, anthropology's claims to provide authoritative interpretations of culture are being challenged from both inside and outside the discipline. Debates about how to represent cultural experience may be partly responsible for recent scholarly attention to orally narrated life stories.[2]

Documenting life histories has always been an approved fieldwork *method* in anthropology, particularly in North America. Until recently, though, such accounts were treated as supplementary material, possibly a corrective to ethnographic description or a way to breathe life into academic writing. Renewed anthropological interest in life histories coincides with increasing attention to analysis of symbolism, meaning, and text. The expectation seems less that such accounts will clarify social structure and more that they may show how individuals use what Sapir called the "scaffolding of culture" to talk about their lives. The present volume is based on the premise that life-history investigation provides a model for research. Instead of working from the conventional formula in which an outside investigator initiates and controls the research, this model depends on ongoing collaboration between interviewer and interviewee. Such a model begins by taking seriously what people say about their lives rather than treating their words simply as an illustration of some other process. By looking at ways people use the traditional dimen-

1

sion of culture as a resource to talk about the past, we may be able to see life history as contributing to explanations of cultural process rather than as simply illustrating or supplementing ethnographic description.

Although the evolution of this project is described in greater detail below, it is worth summarizing the central issue that has interested me most in order to clarify how it shapes the rest of the book. In 1974 I began recording life histories of several Yukon Native women[3] born just before or shortly after the Klondike gold rush (1896–98). As our work progressed, it became clear that these women were approaching our task with a different narrative model of "life history" from my own. My expectation had been that our discussions would document the social impact of the Klondike gold rush at the turn of the century, the construction of the Alaska Highway during the Second World War, and other disruptive events. From the beginning, several of the eldest women responded to my questions about secular events by telling traditional stories. The more I persisted with my agenda, the more insistent each was about the direction our work should take. Each explained that these narratives were important to record *as part of* her life story.

Their accounts, then, included not only personal reminiscences of the kind we normally associate with autobiography, but detailed narratives elaborating mythological themes. Also embedded in their chronicles were songs, sometimes moving listeners to tears and other times to laughter. Their life stories were framed by genealogies and by long lists of personal names and place names that appear to have both metaphoric and mnemonic value. In addition to biographical material, we recorded more than one hundred stories about the origins and transformations of the world and the beings who inhabit it. Thus the essential issue addressed in the following pages is how these women *use* traditional narrative to explain their life experiences.

If a distinguishing feature of these life histories is their inclusion of well-known stories, we have to ask whether they may actually reflect as much about the dynamics of narration as about the workings of society. These women talk about their lives using an oral tradition grounded in local idiom and a shared body of knowledge. A strict notion of biography might treat seemingly archaic mythological tales, place names, and songs as extraneous and omit them from the account. But a recent review of American Indian women's autobiographies identifies these themes as precisely the ones they all share—an emphasis on landscape, mythology, everyday events, and continuity between generations.[4] The genre, in other words, may be more closely associated with conventions of oral narrative than with positivistic evidence about the past.

It is becoming clearer that all autobiography is shaped by narrative convention. Much of the literature addressing this issue comes from studies of women's life stories because they so regularly diverge from the critical ideal of "good autobiography." Jelinek observes that classic male autobiographies tend to be modeled on a heroic literary tradition, projecting an image of self-confidence in the process of overcoming difficulties; women's autobiographies rarely present a coherent polished synthesis, and the form of presentation is frequently discontinuous, reflecting the nature of women's experience.[5] Other writers, analyzing accounts by minority women, point out that their life stories are doubly marginalized—first by male-centered conventions defining what events are significant enough to describe in writing, and second by the position these women have as members of a minority culture.[6]

Orally narrated Native American life histories provide a point of reference for examining whether Native women handle notions of individuality, culture, and gender differently from Native men. Most accounts in this literature document men's lives. Usually they focus on historical events and on particular crises, in either the life of the man or the life of the tribe.[7] Native women's stories differ both from Native men's accounts and from those of non-Native women. The recurring theme is one of connection—to other people and to nature. Connections with people are explored through ties of kinship; connections with land emphasize sense of place. But kinship and landscape provide more than just a setting for an account, for they actually frame and shape the story.[8]

The life stories told by Angela Sidney, Kitty Smith, and Annie Ned contribute to another issue that has been the subject of considerable controversy in both anthropology and history—the extent to which oral tradition can enlarge our understanding of the past, particularly in areas where written documents are biased by the circumstances or conditions under which they were produced. Oral testimonies are very different from archival documents and are never easily accessible to outsiders. They are cultural documents in which much is implicit, in which metaphor and symbol play a role in how ideas are presented. Indeed, there is a longstanding debate in anthropology about whether oral testimonies are statements about the past or attempts to rationalize the present social order.[9] More recently, structuralists have explored the fertile idea that myths are not clear-cut reflections of either past or present, but statements about the human mind. They point to the tendency of myth to invert normative social behavior and suggest that one purpose of symbolic narratives is to resolve issues that cannot be worked out in everyday life.[10]

Such approaches underscore the importance of looking at how oral tradition is *used* rather than focusing narrowly on its factual contribution. These are some of the questions to be considered later in this volume when we turn directly to the words of Angela Sidney, Kitty Smith, and Annie Ned.

* The Cultural Context: Through the Eyes of Strangers

To interpret an orally narrated life story, we need enough sense of the speaker's cultural background to provide context for hearing what is said. One obstacle hampering the analysis of autobiography is the very real human tendency to make implicit comparisons between the account heard or read and one's own life.[11] Our interpretive abilities are inclined to fail, though, when we hear a culturally unfamiliar account, in which we may grasp the general framework but flounder when faced with the particular. Frequently, this is complicated because a narrator believes that the listener understands far more of the unspecified context than is actually the case.

In anthropology it is customary to provide context in an ethnographic overview. This convention has obvious shortcomings. It offers very little sense of cultural experience because it smooths out contradictions in an effort to present a comprehensive picture. There is also the risk that an outsider's synopsis may seem to explain away the subjective reality of the speaker. Its real value, though, lies in providing a framework for hearing a narrator convey some of the richness and subtlety of experience by explaining how normative rules actually worked during her own life.

If we want to maintain a critical balance between "insider" and "outsider" views of culture, it is worth noting the kinds of questions ethnographers originally brought to Northern Athapaskan studies. Inevitably, the issues important to them at the time influenced their formulations just as changing questions in recent years have altered contemporary portrayals of northern cultures. In the late 1950s anthropologists were paying considerable attention to developing worldwide, comparative, cross-cultural typologies of human institutions with the objective of testing hypotheses about social organization. Small-scale hunting and gathering societies played an important role in these classifications. Areas such as the arctic and subarctic began to receive particular attention because they were the last regions in North America where subsistence economies were still self-sustaining.

Attention to the organization of subsistence activities produced valuable empirical data, but this emphasis shaped the accounts ethnographers wrote in predictable ways. Their books tended to treat groups of people who spoke the same language as though they were clearly bounded social units. As least eight distinct languages were spoken in the Yukon: Gwich'in (sometimes written Kutchin) in the far north, and Han, Tutchone, Southern Tutchone, Upper Tanana, Tagish, Kaska, and Tlingit farther south. Mrs. Sidney was born into a Tagish-speaking community, and Mrs. Smith and Mrs. Ned have spent their lives in the area where Southern Tutchone is spoken, but to suggest that they were members of mutually exclusive social or cultural groups would be misleading (Map 1). The intensive fur trade during the late nineteenth century, fueled by the demands of international fur markets, led to considerable blurring of linguistic and cultural boundaries. Yet in Yukon ethnography, titles refer us to "the" Northern Athapaskan Indians, "the" Kaska Indians, "the" Han Indians, "the" Kutchin Indians, "the" Upper Tanana Indians, and so on.[12] For years the debate about the structure of band society dominated theoretical discussions in subarctic ethnography, and it remains the unifying theme of the recently published *Subarctic* volume of the *Handbook of North American Indians*.[13]

As ethnographers began to think seriously about Athapaskan and Algonkian communities, rather than viewing them as evidence for more general theory, they were confronted with individual differences. Firm definitions of band society seemed to evaporate. Every attempt to produce a normative account generated further questions. Individuals within any one group did not necessarily agree when questioned and offered thoughtful but idiosyncratic responses. Ethnographic evidence soon made it clear that Athapaskan and Algonkian bands were *not* clearly bounded units, and most of the recent work has stressed the flexibility of group composition and recruitment principles.

McClellan's fine ethnography of the southern Yukon Territory broke new ground by showing that a broad areal perspective is more likely to yield insights about patterns of human activity than an artificially circumscribed study of a single linguistic group. Her two-volume study, *My Old People Say*, provides the real context for understanding the life accounts included here because she has reconstructed cultural history for the territory where Mrs. Sidney, Mrs. Smith, and Mrs. Ned have spent their lives.[14]

The picture emerging from McClellan's work is one of people adapting not only to changes in wildlife cycles but also to changes in human history. Trade between coastal Tlingit Indians and interior Athapaskans probably began at least two centuries ago. Yet our knowledge of it comes

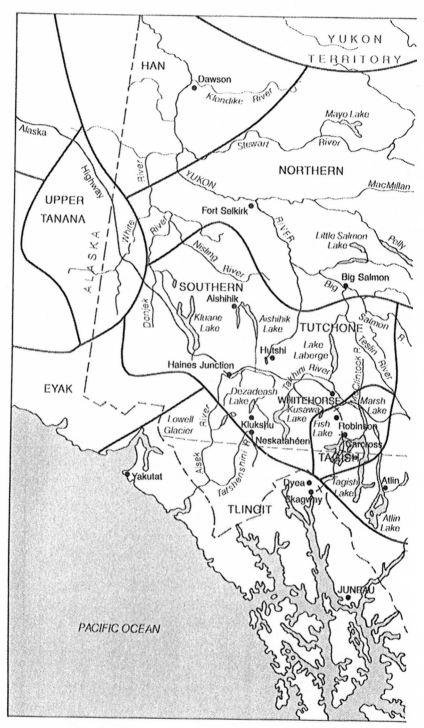

Map 1. Languages spoken in the southern Yukon Territory

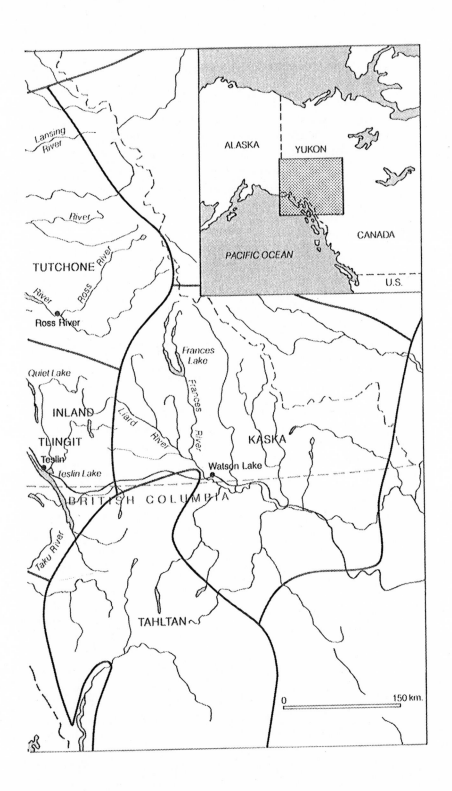

almost exclusively from oral accounts because perishable trade items do not survive in the archaeological record. Originally, coastal Tlingit Indians imported aboriginal trade items to the interior—spruce root baskets, cedar boxes, fungus for red paint, medicinal roots, native tobacco, shells, and obsidian—and exported inland items such as mountain-goat wool, dyes, tanned moose hides and caribou hides, sinew, and raw copper. With the arrival of Russian, British, and American traders on the coast, Tlingits substituted European trade goods and shifted their attention to exporting valuable inland furs. Like tribes all along the western coast of North America, they consolidated their position as middlemen between Europeans and more distant Native peoples by maintaining strict control over trade routes to the interior and over rates and terms of exchange. Tagish and Southern Tutchone speakers in turn became middlemen between coastal Tlingits and Athapaskans farther inland. One way of regulating the social interaction necessary for smooth trade was to establish ongoing trading partnerships between Tlingit and Athapaskan men: Tlingits often formalized such partnerships by arranging for marriages of their sisters to Athapaskan partners in the interior. Other Tlingits, moving inland to be closer to sources of furs, brought their language, social customs, clans, and crests with them and blended them into local cultures.

Mrs. Sidney, Mrs. Smith, and Mrs. Ned were each raised on the inland side of the high-country frontier separating coastal Tlingit and interior Athapaskans, near centers where Tlingits had been coming inland to trade with Athapaskans for years. Each is able to claim both Athapaskan and Tlingit ancestry, and as children they all learned Tlingit as well as an Athapaskan language. But these women were all born within a few years of the Klondike gold rush (1896–98) at a time when their parents were experiencing unprecedented changes. The reputed Athapaskan willingness and ability to adapt to changing economic circumstances was being stretched to its fullest potential during their childhood. As young women, they added English to their language repertoires.

Ethnographers have repeatedly documented the ability of Athapaskan Indians to adapt to changing conditions of life, and nowhere is this clearer than in the southern Yukon. Native people living there were aboriginal hunters and fishers whose technology, social customs, and seminomadic lifestyle were admirably adapted to a subarctic environment. Since resources varied cyclically, family groupings traveled over extensive areas of land during any year in the course of harvesting resources for food, clothing, and shelter. These aggregations were not large: every hunting group needed enough able-bodied adults to provide for the needs of its members, including dependent children and old people, but not so many individuals that a food shortage would endanger all of them. People fished for and dried salmon in summer, hunted game animals and dried the meat in fall, stayed relatively immobile in winter to conserve energy, and began trapping and fishing again in spring. Their movements were never random, and as much as possible they returned to familiar camping places year after year. The group might have eight or ten members in winter, when solitary, large game animals were hunted, but much larger congregations were possible at summer salmon fishing camps or intersections with caribou migrations. Because animal migration patterns sometimes changed, hunters were always prepared to modify their movements when necessary.

Athapaskan social organization has been called "flexible" because of this demonstrated ability to disperse and regroup as seasons and resources required. In the southern Yukon, however, social organization was profoundly influenced by two matrilineal kinship divisions, Wolf (*Ägunda*) and Crow (*Kajìt*).[15] Anthropologists use the term "moiety" (from the French "half") to describe this organizational principle: everyone was born into one of these two groups and inherited the same affiliation as his or her mother. Rules of exogamy were strictly enforced: a Crow could marry only a Wolf, and a member of the Wolf division had to marry a Crow. Disobedience of this rule was considered incestuous and was punishable by death or banishment. Every family grouping, then, was composed of members of both moieties; alliances were repeatedly forged between moieties through marriages, partnerships, and trade, linking people from widely dispersed areas in networks of familiar responsibilities.

In the southern Yukon, where there was considerable Tlingit influence, moieties were further subdivided into clans. Clans are distinct matrilineal subdivisions of moieties but differ from the latter in claiming a common ancestor, as well as distinctive crests, songs, and formal oral histories. Because certain clans are mentioned repeatedly in these life histories, it is worth identifying them and noting their moiety affiliation as well as the areas where they are particularly important. Crow clans include *Deisheetaan* (sometimes called by its older name, *Tukyeidí*), *Gaanax.ádi*, and *Gaanaxteidí* in the southern Yukon; *Kaach.ádi*, associated with Telegraph Creek, British Columbia; and *Kiks.ádi* and *Łukaax.ádi*, both coastal clans. Wolf clans include *Dakl'aweidí* and *Yanyeidí* in the southern Yukon, and *Kaagwaantaan*, an important clan of the Chilkat Tlingit tribe. Some clan names vary for men and women: the endings *-eidí* and *-ádi* refer to men, and *-sháa* refers to women, so that, for example, the female variant of *Dakl'aweidí* is *Dakl'usháa*.

Moiety and clan alignments were expected to guide behavior at such ceremonial events as birth, puberty, and death and on numerous less formal occasions. At death, for example, members of the moiety opposite from that of the deceased took responsibility for mortuary arrangements. Approximately a year later the bereaved clan would hold a potlatch to "pay back" the clan that had done the work. In the Yukon, potlatches supported an effective redistribution system whereby one moiety performed services for the other and was later repaid by it. Because every household included members from both moieties, goods potlatched by one "side" might very well stay in the same domestic unit.

Within any household, division of labor reflected age, gender, and ties of kinship. Generally, men provided and women prepared the food, clothing, and shelter, though any adult was capable of performing the role assigned to the other gender when necessary. At marriage a man initially came to live with and work for his wife's parents for a specified period of time; he would be expected to support her mother and father in their old age. Children were encouraged to assume responsibility early in life and to work with and learn from adults. In a society in which individual experience was particularly valued, elders were expected to pass their knowledge on to younger people, both orally and by demonstration. The special regard for elders as teachers, historians, and sources of authority underlies ethnographic accounts by "outsiders" as well as contemporary discussion by "insiders"—younger Native people concerned about incorporating traditional values into present-day life.

The most striking differentiation between male and female roles occurred at puberty. At the onset of menstruation a young woman was sequestered some distance from the main camp for a period of time varying from a few weeks to many months. During her seclusion her spatial separateness was reinforced in several ways: she wore a moosehide "bonnet" or "hood" that covered her face and much of her body, effectively cutting her off from the familiar world. She was visited only by women and could not see any males except younger brothers; she had to obey strict taboos about food consumption and personal grooming. Older women tutored her in technical skills, such as sewing and preparation of babiche (thin strips of soaked moose or caribou hide), and also gave her intensive instruction about her own powers as a woman and about how to deal with unfamiliar power when confronted with its various manifestations. She worked hard and continuously during her seclusion making and repairing clothes for family members. When the household moved, she and her mother followed behind, relocating at a safe distance when the people stopped to camp. It is worth noting that the oral accounts in this volume contrast sharply with the conventional view that secluded women are ritually "polluted." In retrospect, these women refer with admiration to others whose seclusion was lengthy, possibly because sequestering was so firmly associated with acquiring ritual and practical knowledge unavailable to men. Mrs. Sidney, in particular, expresses regret that her own seclusion was cut short by her mother's illness and by the fact that "times were going ahead."[16]

Angela Sidney, Kitty Smith, and Annie Ned were all born at the close of an intensive period of Tlingit-Athapaskan trade and within a few years of the Klondike gold rush. Coinciding with a world depression in 1896, it drew more than thirty thousand immigrants to a tributary of the Yukon River within a few years, making Dawson City the largest city north of San Francisco. Indians along the route became involved in packing, guiding, and providing food for prospectors; a few years later others became deckhands on riverboats. The Tagish who participated in the initial discovery of gold and the Han at the mouth of the Klondike River were the Yukon Natives most directly affected; each of the accounts in the volume makes particular reference to how the gold rush influenced women's lives. The consequences for Native people living some distance from routes to the Klondike were indirect: the breaking of the Tlingit fur-trade monopoly, the impact of forest fires on wildlife along the Yukon River, the arrival of independent white traders, the expansion of missionary activity, the building of the White Pass and Yukon Route railway from Skagway to Whitehorse, and the running of a riverboat fleet between Whitehorse and Dawson City.

Most whites left the country soon after the beginning of the century. In 1900 the total population of the Yukon Territory had climbed to over 27,000, of whom 3,000 were classified as Indians. By 1912 it had declined to 6,000 Indians and whites; by 1921 just over 4,000 people were reported in the government census. The population remained relatively stable for the next twenty years: 4,230 in 1931, and 4,914 in 1941.[17]

A second "rush," as older people call it, came with the construction of the Alaska Highway in 1942–43. Again, more than thirty thousand men arrived for the construction phase, then left. The new route replaced the Yukon River as the administrative axis of the territory, testing Native adaptability even further. How the highway affected both the longstanding social institutions associated with kinship and the relationship between Native people and land becomes clear in oral accounts.[18]

A striking characteristic of anthropological subarctic literature is the way theoretical models have changed since the 1960s. A postwar emphasis on "modernization" in the 1950s led to predictions that band societies would inevitably be swallowed up by national industrial economies. During the 1960s an acculturation model came to dominate government plans for northern Canada; numerous arctic and subarctic studies, many of them sponsored by the Canadian government, took acculturation as their main theme.[19] A decade later Native northerners were becoming politically vocal about their own views of their society; in the mid-1970s hundreds of Dene addressed the Mackenzie Valley Pipeline Inquiry, and Yukon Indians spoke to the Alaska Highway Pipeline Inquiry protesting that they were not societies in transition, but strongly committed to continuing their way of life in the present. Across the north, attention to land claims has sparked a corresponding interest in documenting cultural *persistence*.[20] Subarctic societies do not seem to be vanishing, despite the prognoses of the 1960s; in fact, they appear to be maintaining themselves against great odds.

There seems to be an unresolved conflict between models of stability and models of change in arctic and subarctic ethnography. Native northerners have been quick to draw attention to shifting fashions by pointing to studies they find misleading; not surprisingly, acculturation studies from the 1960s have come under intense criticism. Multiple life histories offer one point of departure for investigating questions about cultural continuity. Oral testimonies have been called "statements of cultural identity where memory continuously adapts received traditions to present circumstances."[21] Looking at how individuals take these shared cultural traditions—their statements of identity—and how they use them to interpret events from their own experience and then pass them on to succeeding generations may add a different perspective to debates about cultural persistence and cultural change.

✳ Collaborative Fieldwork

The current anthropological interest in life-history writing focuses as much on the process by which accounts are constructed as on the finished product. The direction each collaboration took and the individual editing decisions made with each narrator are discussed in my introduction to each account; here I simply outline issues affecting our day-to-day approach to our work.

Any description of fieldwork occurring over ten years inevitably has the quality of a period piece, reminding us that research occurs in both a social and a historical context. As an undergraduate during the 1960s, I came to a clear, if imperfect, understanding that the cultural activity defining anthropology was fieldwork based on participant observation. Like every other anthropology student, I was jolted by the contradictions in that definition when I had my first opportunity to do fieldwork, in the Yukon Territory in 1968. Returning to graduate school in 1969 at the height of the debate about ethical dilemmas of anthropological research only increased my sense that the methodological goals of observation and participation seemed incompatible, at least in the climate of that discussion. My eventual decision to return to the Yukon to do anthropological research outside a university framework was not uncharacteristic of the times.

By 1974 I had already spent some years living and working in the Yukon and in Alaska. Questions often arose in conversations with politically active Native women my own age about whether anthropology could make local contributions to the north. At the time, we all tended to see anthropology's value as rather narrowly related to historical reconstruction in ways that might prove significant for land-claims negotiations. Several women independently suggested that I might make a substantive contribution by working with their mothers or grandmothers recording life histories in a form that could be distributed to family members. It is important to remember that this was the early 1970s and that the activity engaging these women was political organization, making the task they were suggesting for me one that could be appropriately assigned to an outsider. A decade later, when the conflation of political and cultural issues is clearer, a significant number of Athapaskan men and women are doing their own cultural documentation in the Yukon.[22] In 1974, though, such an exchange seemed to benefit everyone involved: I could learn something about changing roles of women, the older women with whom I was working could produce their own booklets of family history in their own names, and younger family members would be able to put that material to whatever use they saw fit. The notions of "participation" and "observation" could be made compatible within the broader framework of locally based, collaborative research.

Over the years, I worked with a number of women of varying ages, and we prepared booklets for family members ranging in length from twenty to one hundred twenty pages. Three of the older women viewed the initial booklets primarily as evidence that our association might bear fruit; once the narratives were transcribed, typed, and duplicated, these women insisted that there was much more for us to do. Their continued enthusiasm and desire to see their work distributed more widely led to this volume.

Our understanding was always that the material recorded belonged to the narrator. Each woman had her own ideas about how it should be used. In one case we arranged to have narratives typed on stencils and duplicated, and the narrator was able to sell copies of her own booklet. In 1976 a local newspaper (then called the *Yukon Indian News*, now *Dän Sha*) agreed to pay the women an honorarium for the right to publish their stories. Shortly afterward a local radio station made similar arrangements to have some of the women tell the same stories for broadcast. In 1977 the Council for Yukon Indians published one booklet of stories, *My Stories Are My Wealth*, by Angela Sidney, Kitty Smith, and Rachel Dawson. A few years later they jointly published two more books of stories with the Yukon Territorial Government: *Tagish Tlaagú/Tagish Stories*, by Angela Sidney, and *Nindal Kwädindür/I'm Going to Tell You a Story*, by Kitty Smith. As our work became more language-specific, the Yukon Native Languages Project published three more booklets: *Haa Shagóon* and *Place Names of the Tagish Region, Southern Yukon*, both by Angela Sidney, and *Old People in Those Days, They Told Their Story All the Time*, by Annie Ned. Simultaneously, I published preliminary analyses of our work elsewhere.[23]

Over time, my own understanding of our objectives shifted significantly. Initially, I expected that by recording life histories we would be documenting oral history, compiling accounts that would be stored, like archival documents, for later analysis. I was interested in hearing women talk about events chronicled in written documents and records and tried to steer our conversations in that direction. Although the older women responded patiently to my line of inquiry for a while, they quite firmly shifted the emphasis to "more important" accounts they wanted me to record—particularly events central to traditional narrative. Gradually, I came to see oral tradition not as "evidence" about the past but as a window on ways the past is culturally constituted and discussed. My experience was strikingly similar to that recounted by Rosaldo when he began recording oral history with Ilongot people only to be confronted by men and women reciting, with obvious emotion, complex lists of toponyms. He describes his own feelings of bewilderment as he painstakingly transcribed these place names until he came to understand that they embodied a culturally distinct sense of history.[24]

I always brought questions to our sessions, but as I began to take increasing direction from the narrators, the kinds of questions changed. In the beginning I asked about their childhood experiences, about seclusion, about marriage and childbirth, and about how events like the gold rush and Alaska Highway construction had affected their lives. The women would give brief answers to my direct inquiries and then suggest that I write down a particular story they wanted to tell me. Usually such stories involved a bewildering series of characters and events, but with practice I learned to follow the complex plots and to understand that when women told me stories they were actually using them to explain some aspect of their lives to me.

An important part of our collaboration involved jointly reviewing and correcting the transcripts I made from our taped conversations as soon as possible after each session. Older narrators usually responded by listening carefully for a short while, then breaking in to retell the story rather than waiting for me to finish reading it back. Each narrator might tell slightly different versions of a particular story from the others but was so internally consistent that her retelling proved an effective method of checking the transcript.

Initially, I was quite shy about how much technology I should introduce into our work, wondering how older women would react to tape recorders. One day while we were checking my transcript of a particularly circuitous narrative, one woman in her mid-seventies patiently asked me whether I had ever thought of using a tape recorder so I could "get it right the first time," thus dispelling any simple notions I had about the alienating effects of technology. In fact, during the years we have worked together, three of the eldest women were given "ghetto blasters" as gifts from grandchildren and used them to replay tapes we had made. One even invited neighbors in, and we all sat around drinking tea in her cabin and watching the digital strobe light flash as a tape of our interview played. This level of objectifying our work was rather more than I had anticipated, but it certainly demonstrated to me that technology itself was not a problem. When I was able to work with a filmmaker of Tlingit and Athapaskan ancestry, Carol Geddes, recording videotapes in the summer of 1984 and 16-mm film footage in the summer of 1986 with Mrs. Sidney, Mrs. Smith, and Mrs. Ned, I found that I was more inhibited by the technology than they were.

The one codicil to this observation is that the women's response to tape recorders and cameras varied depending on where we were working. They seemed quite at ease with technology when we worked in their own homes but considerably less relaxed when we went to work somewhere unfamiliar (usually a quiet setting selected for its sound-recording potential). Attempts to combine technology with optimal conditions for using that technology present some problems for producing recordings that are simultaneously high-quality and spontaneous.

The issue of transforming oral tradition into written text is a complex one, and a limited resolution of one problem simply raises others. Narrators had very definite views about why they were doing this work and saw production of their own booklets in English for young people as central to our task. I was comfortable enough recording oral accounts of *events* in English but less so when they began asking me to write down traditional *stories* in that language. My discomfort had two sources: first, my reluctance to be diverted from what I took to be our primary goal— the recording of everyday events; and second, my sense that it was inappropriate to record English versions of stories originally learned and told in an aboriginal language because so much would be lost in translation. This inevitable loss in style and form was noted by Boas generations ago, and his observations seem as appropriate now as they were then.[25]

Nonetheless, the context of recording oral tradition has changed from the time when Boas was working. A contemporary narrator working in collaboration with an anthropologist usually has an agenda every bit as clear as that of the ethnographer. Although enthusiasm for Native language instruction in Yukon schools has been growing during the 1980s, it is still the case that all Yukon Native children begin school with English as their first language.[26] These narrators want to produce booklets that their grandchildren can read. Their own childhood instruction came either from observation or from oral tradition, but they recognize that children now learn from books. Mrs. Smith explained her motives for recording her stories with reference to a great-grandchild: "Well, she's six years old now. She's going to start school now. Pretty soon paper's going to talk to her!" Schools teach things totally outside the experience of elders; stories, on the other hand, recreate the life cycle. Women see their books of stories as a connection between the world of tradition and the schools' "paper world" and feel that, thus legitimized, the stories should be part of the school curriculum.

Another reason they recorded stories in English reflects the developing relationship between each of the women and myself. Our collaboration has been and continues to be a source of enormous enjoyment for all of us. Storytelling does not occur in a vacuum. Storytellers need an audience, a response, in order to make the telling a worthwhile experience. They have patiently trained me to understand conventional indigenous literary formulae so that I can *hear* stories told mostly in English sprinkled with place names, kinship terms, clan names, and personal names in Tagish, Tlingit, and Southern Tutchone. Telling stories in their own language to someone who cannot understand the subtleties is like talking to a blank wall. Furthermore, they are excellent teachers, and when they tell me a story, they do so to explain something else to me. The whole rationale for telling them disappears if I cannot understand what they are trying to teach.

With the growing interest of younger Yukoners in reclaiming their Native languages, the problem of translation has troubled me sufficiently that I have spent a lot of time working with Gertie Tom, a Northern Tutchone woman trained by linguist John Ritter to write her own language. Mrs. Tom, in turn, has taught me enough of her Northern Tutchone language that I can recognize and transcribe words in Tutchone and neighboring Athapaskan languages. Much of her own work involves recording elders in the Tutchone language, then carefully transcribing her tapes. Then she and I begin a scrupulous word-by-word translation of the story, and when we have completed that we rework our verbatim translation into standard English. Gertie Tom has recorded dozens of stories, many of them long and complex, and the process of learning from her as we translate has been endlessly fascinating. However, I reluctantly admit that the careful English translation we arrive at still seems to both of us to be vastly inferior to the original story. The spare prose of English flattens the complexity of Athapaskan verb forms, and the finished product lacks the flavor of real telling which emerges in a narrator's own energetic translation.[27] Texts transcribed in original languages, like those Gertie Tom produces, are critical for the study of language, but if no one else is trained to read them, writing them can be a lonely exercise. The elders with whom I have worked provide their own English translations. Their English is lively, colorful, and highly metaphorical. Although there is undoubtedly loss in form and style, the narrators are at least able to retain their own rhythm and idiom, their own expressions, the nuances of their unique narrative performances.

One aspect of storytelling that *does* seem to survive translation is the way narrators use stories to explain a particular point they are making. It is this sense of stories as explanation that I have tried to capture here by alternating accounts of personal experience with traditional narratives. By arranging the life histories this way, I am attempting to show two things: first, how each woman is using stories to explain events in her life, and second, how each brings special narrative skills to the construction of her account.

Some comments about editing are necessary. The following texts are distilled from approximately one hundred sixty hours of tape-recorded dialogues with these three women—ninety hours with Mrs. Sidney (with whom I have worked longest), forty hours with Mrs. Smith, and thirty hours with Mrs. Ned. I have transcribed each of these tapes, but the accounts are edited for length, simply because the verbatim transcripts are too long for a book-length manuscript.[28] For the same reason some of the lengthier traditional narratives previously published in booklets by the narrators (cited above) have not been included here. Others have been excluded because narrators requested that they be left out or because they deal with sensitive current events and issues and name living people.

The transcripts are also edited to bring together materials recorded in many different sessions and over many years as one continuous narrative. I have ordered the account using a chronology that is roughly the one each woman instructs me is the "correct" way to tell her life story, beginning with her parents' genealogy, followed by her husband's genealogy, leading eventually to her own birth. In each case the narrator enters her own life story only well into the account, with a discussion of childhood, then puberty, then marriage, then various incidents from her mature years.

The only consistent editorial changes involve personal pronouns, subject-verb agreement, and subject-object order in a sentence. Gender distinction is irrelevant in Athapaskan languages, so "he" and "she" may be used interchangeably. This is sometimes confusing in English, so I have substituted a noun for a third-person pronoun if the referent is unclear, quite often the case in stories with several active characters. Speakers of Athapaskan languages frequently remark that their language and English are "backwards" because in Athapaskan languages object precedes subject; I have reordered this sequence if it clarifies the meaning just as I have standardized subject-verb agreement where there is ambiguity. When it seemed helpful to add words for clarity, I have placed them in brackets.

Converting spoken conversations to written text also raises questions about the "texture" of oral narrative. Hymes, Tedlock, and Toelken have devised experimental written forms that attempt to capture a sense of the actual performance.[29] Breaking lines to correspond with a pause by the narrator—and indicating longer pauses or topic changes by the addition of a blank line—seems to reproduce the emphasis and cadence of the spoken word more accurately than does conventional paragraphing. Native women who know the storytellers and have read various versions of the text say that they find it easier to "hear" the speaker's voice when reading this form. But as a written style it may be better suited to poetry and to traditional narrative than to discussions of experience. Here I have retained something closer to paragraphs for sections Westerners normally associate with autobiographical accounts and have distinguished the explanatory stories by using phrases and breath groups. Throughout,

I sometimes use a dash (—) to punctuate a phrase when a period seems too abrupt; ellipses (. . .) may indicate a longer pause or an incomplete thought.

I have not included my own questions in the body of the text, partly because so many of these accounts are told as sustained narratives. None of the women appreciated being interrupted, and usually they interpreted any request for clarification as a sign of flagging attention. Once I started using a tape recorder, I discovered that most intrusions were unnecessary because my questions would be clarified when I transcribed the tape. It seemed more appropriate to bring any remaining questions to the beginning of our next visit. This illustrates a difference between interviews, in the way we use that term, and oral tradition, in which storytellers take it for granted that they won't be interrupted.

Numerous other problems are involved in writing down oral tradition, and they are familiar to anyone who has done this kind of work. Does a written version suddenly come to have an authority that makes it the socially "correct" version to the exclusion of others? As we see in this volume, different narrators tell stories differently, and it is important to stress that no version is "better," "worse," more or less "correct" than another: the differences reflect individual talents and interests of different storytellers. Does writing down oral tradition make it seem less urgent to continue *telling* stories now that a record exists? The resurgence of interest in storytelling during the 1980s in the Yukon suggests that younger women are looking seriously at ways to revive storytelling both with their own children and publicly.[30]

These life histories all come from women, and comparable accounts from men would obviously be valuable. Over the years, I have had discussions with several older men about doing this; in each case we worked for two or three sessions and then the man suggested that I really ought to be working with his wife or his sister. The kinds of long-term collaborative working relationships I have developed with older women are simply not socially appropriate for me to have with older men. For similar practical reasons male anthropologists working in this area have relied heavily on men to teach them, though they have not considered it necessary to comment on how this might bias their accounts.

We turn first to Mrs. Sidney's account of her life, then to Mrs. Smith's, and finally to Mrs. Ned's. An introduction to each account provides basic linguistic and cultural information a narrator would expect a listener to have. It summarizes some of the events described, identifies some of the narrative themes, and interprets how each narrator uses stories to explain events. It also discusses the nature of the collaboration between each narrator and myself and how that affected the text we produced. A reader, though, may prefer to proceed directly to the narratives and to return to these framing sections after the stories are familiar. The clearest ethnographic instruction for reading the accounts comes from Mrs. Sidney. "Well," she commented one day after we had finished recording, "I've tried to live my life right, just like a story."

PART I

My Stories Are

My Wealth

ANGELA SIDNEY

✳ Introduction

Angela Sidney describes herself as a Tagish and Tlingit woman of the *Deisheetaan* (Crow) clan. Her uncommon ability to step back
from her experience when she explains her culture or her language to a
novice makes her life history an exceptional cultural document. Part of
her talent lies in her capacity to understand the kind of context a cultural
outsider needs to be taught before that person can actually begin to hear
what she is saying. How she developed this skill becomes clearer in her
account of her life.

Born in 1902 near the present village of Carcross in the southern
Yukon to *La.oos Tláa* (Maria) and *Ḵaajinéek'* (Tagish John),[1] she was given
the Tlingit name *Stóow* and a second Tagish name *Ch'óonehte' Má*. A
prospector passing by on the night of her birth came in to warm himself
at Tagish John's fire, and when he saw the new baby he remarked that she
looked like an angel, so she was given the English name Angela. This
child and her four-year-old brother Johnny were the beginning of a new
family for the couple: a few years earlier during the height of the Klondike
gold rush, they had lost all four of their young children in an epidemic.

Angela's mother became ill during the same epidemic that took the
lives of her children, and although she lived to be elderly, recurring
illnesses forced her to spend a great deal of time close to home. As the
eldest daughter, Angela looked after her mother, and she used their time
together to question her about family and clan histories, traditions,
songs, and stories. In this way the child absorbed normative rules about
social behavior for potlatching, puberty, marriage, and childbirth. Her
disappointment when her own experience never precisely matched the
"old ways" may have fostered her growing ability to recognize contradic-

21

tions between what people said *should* happen and what actually happened.

The timing of her birth gave her ample opportunity to observe such changes. Her Tagish grandparents and parents had become involved in intensive trade with coastal Tlingit in the late 1800s; some Tlingit women had married Tagish men, introducing Tlingit customs and language into their inland Athapaskan families. Her Tagish uncles are credited with the discovery of gold that set off the Klondike gold rush only six years before Angela's birth.

A recurring theme in Mrs. Sidney's account is her preoccupation with evaluating and balancing old customs with new ideas. Her childhood disillusionment when she was not given a potlatch name and when her puberty seclusion was cut short is matched by equal regret that her father removed her from the mission school before she had learned to read. Her youthful marriage to George Sidney followed customary arrangements; however, under pressure from a member of the Anglican Church, she later agreed to add a church wedding. As a child caring for an invalid mother, she learned about traditional healing; as an adult, she expanded that knowledge by studying a medical textbook her brother bought, and she became an unofficial nurse in her community during the epidemics that accompanied the construction of the Alaska Highway. She raised her children so they would understand old ways without being "too old-fashioned." When her son served overseas in the Canadian army during the Second World War, she bought a radio so she could follow daily reports of progress "at the front"; when he returned home safely, her welcoming gift to him was an ancient Tlingit song. Her immediate concern in the late 1980s is to reconcile orthodox spiritual beliefs with a potpourri of religious ideas introduced to the Yukon during her lifetime. She uses narratives as a point of reference for discussing all these issues.

One of the changes occurring during her childhood was the extremely rapid demise of the old Tagish Athapaskan language, initially exchanged for Tlingit, the language of trade. By the late nineteenth century a number of Tlingit-speaking women had married Tagish speakers. Mrs. Sidney also recalls the names of Tagish women who, in turn, married men farther inland; such marriages may partly account for the gradual abandonment of the language. She remembers speaking and hearing Tagish until she was about five years old and then speaking only Tlingit, and later English. One of her more extraordinary accomplishments is her recall of Tagish

Mrs. Angela Sidney, photographed in Whitehorse in July 1988. She is holding a replica of her Deisheetaan Beaver clan crest. Photo © 1988 by Jim Robb–Yukon.

language eighty years later: when she uses the term *den k'e,* which means literally "Indian way" or "the people's way (of speaking)," she is referring to the Tagish language and is distinguishing it from Tlingit. Tagish is of particular interest to linguists because it is more closely related to relatively distant languages south and east than to neighboring downriver languages. This fact is not easily explained, but it makes Tagish a key language in any attempts to reconstruct linguistic history in northwestern North America. Mrs. Sidney is the last fluent speaker of the language, and linguists working with her have commented on her exceptional ability to analyze the meaning of words in Tagish and other nearby Athapaskan languages.[2] Her claim to both Tagish and Tlingit ancestry means that she identifies herself sometimes as Tagish, sometimes as Tlingit, depending on the context.

Mrs. Sidney repeatedly demonstrates a command of metaphoric language when she uses stories to explain her life experiences, particularly when she explains Tagish and Tlingit customs to outsiders. For example, her *Deisheetaan* clan owns the Beaver crest, and she compares that crest to the British flag, her Beaver song to a national anthem, and another clan song to a hymn. But she is equally perceptive when applying metaphor to unfamiliar cultural customs. In 1986 she was awarded the Order of Canada for her remarkable combination of community service and scholarly contributions. She enjoyed her trip to Ottawa and appreciated the sense of Canadian ritual at its most formal. Describing the ceremony to an elderly Tlingit friend a few months later, she pointed to a beautiful framed photograph of herself standing in Government House with Jeanne Sauvé, Her Excellency the Governor General of Canada, explaining, "This is me, getting the Government's pin, and this is the Government's wife, giving me the Government's pin."[3]

* Narrative Text as Collaboration

When Angela Sidney and I began working together in 1974, she showed no hesitation about defining the terms of our work. She understood that family members wanted her to record the story of her life and that I was a willing secretary and an eager student, and she had very clear ideas about how we should proceed. I had specific questions for her, too, mostly about how her life differed from her mother's and how events like the gold rush and the construction of the Alaska Highway had affected women's lives. During our first six months working together, we produced a one-hundred-twenty-page typewritten booklet for her family. It

contained a very abbreviated version of her clan history, a brief discussion
of puberty seclusion, a short account of her marriage, and more than one
hundred pages of traditional narratives. My initial concern was that this
collection of narratives rather inadequately represented our objective of
recording life history.

This disparity between our definitions of life story made me reassess
my approach to our interviews: Mrs. Sidney seemed to be ignoring the
questions I was raising, yet her patient efforts to direct me with stories
added a bewildering variety of characters and events, some from historical memory and others from a timeless repository of myth. We agreed to
begin each session by my reading back to her a transcript of our previous
interview and together making corrections, additions, and deletions.
There were always aspects of the interview I hadn't understood, and my
questions arising from the transcript would propel our interview in a new
direction, usually culminating in Mrs. Sidney's telling of a story to explain
a particular point to me. By the time we had recorded enough stories to
produce two booklets[4] I had a clearer sense of how her narratives *did*
indeed reflect back on the original questions I had been asking her about
her life.

A certain amount of editing occurred while we were correcting transcripts. Mrs. Sidney had a sharp eye for her audience and occasionally
asked me to eliminate references she felt others "might not like," usually
comments having to do with whether particular clan responsibilities had
been properly carried out. Because I made verbatim transcripts, she also
noticed her tendency to end sentences with "I guess," which she asked
me to delete whenever it suggested uncertainty on her part. One of her
objectives was to develop booklets demonstrating unambiguous ethnographic authority, a point she emphasized by regularly naming the person from whom she first heard each narrative.

In 1980 we began a rather different project, recording and mapping
Tagish and Tlingit place names on topographic maps. During that summer we traveled by car, boat, and railway to locations where Mrs. Sidney
had lived and traveled. We discussed events that had occurred there,
people who had camped there, stories that were set there. Sometimes she
had not visited these places for more than forty or fifty years, and they
looked physically different from her memory of them because vegetation
had changed so much. Often it was difficult for her to remember the
name of a place until she actually saw it again, and naming those places
had the mnemonic effect of recalling events that had occurred there. As
we continued mapping, she attached specific stories, songs, and events to
features of landscape.[5]

Virtually every place we located and mapped also led to discussions of individual people in some way associated with that place. We began compiling separate lists of Tagish and Tlingit personal names and from there went on to assemble extensive genealogies and clan lists.[6] This aspect of her work had a noticeable effect in her community, where many young people are now giving their children Tlingit and Tagish names from the appropriate clan. Old names are also appearing on recent gravestones. A much-abbreviated version of her genealogy (figures 1 and 2) includes those individuals actually discussed in the following account.

What became clear in our separate projects—recording stories, place names, genealogies—was Angela Sidney's view that we were gradually building the framework for constructing a comprehensive life story. Initially, recording stories or place names or family names might provide the theme of a particular session. But as she became confident that I was grasping the building blocks she was providing, more and more of our discussions began turning to her own experience. When we returned in the summer of 1985 to the task of seriously reviewing events in her life, I understood how very much I was relying on the scaffolding of narratives and names she had already provided.

As our acquaintance deepened over the years, we spent long periods of time together, sometimes working and sometimes just visiting. We traveled within the Yukon but also to a conference in Vancouver, and another time to a storytelling festival in Toronto where she was an invited speaker. During our travels together we have had long conversations about aspects of her life not included here: the topics in this book are ones she identified as important to write down.

Some of my editing may seem more problematic. Mrs. Sidney told many more traditional stories than the ones recounted here, most of them published in her booklets, cited above. The stories included here were selected to make the link between narrative and life as unambiguous as possible. I recognize that this is a specific intervention on my part determined by my desire to maintain a consistent theme at the center of what is written. I believe, though, that this theme—that narratives continue to explain experience even in the 1980s—is the same issue concerning Angela Sidney.

✶ Narrative as Explanation

The shape of this account reflects both Angela Sidney's abilities as a teacher and storyteller and my sense of how she is using stories to ex-

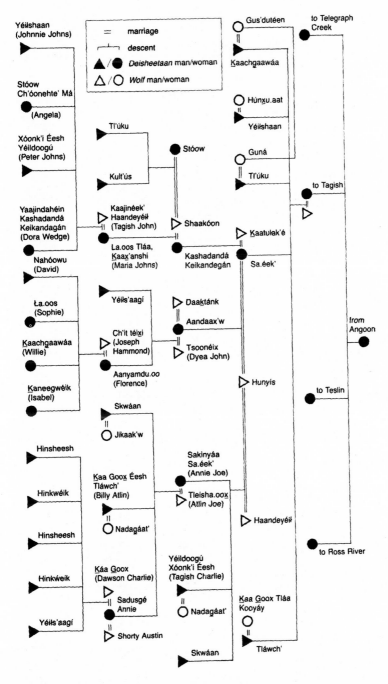

Figure 1. Partial family tree of *Deisheetaan* ancestors
of Mrs. Angela Sidney

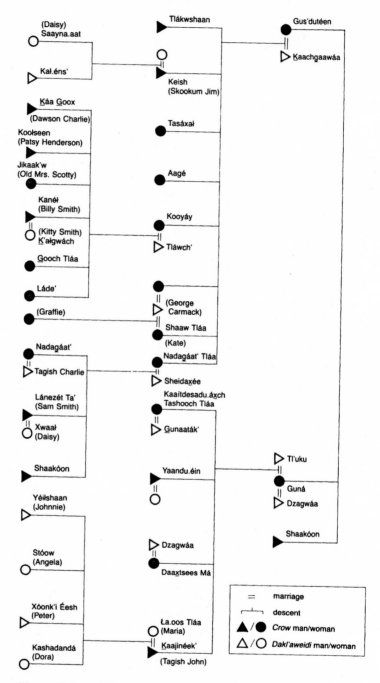

Figure 2. Partial family tree of *Dakl'aweidí* ancestors of Mrs. Angela Sidney

plain her life. Her story is presented here in seventeen sections. Odd-
numbered sections approximate a conventional Western understanding
of life history and include events she either experienced herself or heard
about from older people; beginning with family history, they are edited
for chronology moving through childhood, puberty, and marriage to
middle and later years. Even-numbered sections are traditional narratives
she also wanted to record as part of her life story; though she actually told
many of them before discussing her own experiences, the sequence in
which they appear here reflects the way she later refers back to them to
explain various events in life. The format of alternating sections gives us
some appreciation of her "bifocal" perspective on her life.

Angela Sidney employs slightly different narrative conventions to discuss childhood from those she uses to talk about her adult years. She
reviews her early years with reference to the lives of others, commenting
on her own experiences briefly and in the third person. She pays particular attention to recounting long and detailed narratives that were part of
her education, implying that the lessons they convey are self-evident.
When she describes her years as a mature adult, though, she adds more of
her own experience and then refers back to traditional stories she has told
earlier to explain or illustrate specific points. By the end her own experience becomes the narrative line, reflecting her assertion that she has
indeed tried to live her life "like a story."

In Section 1 she specifies a formula for using traditional narrative to
talk about the past: there is a correct way to tell one's family history, one's
Shagóon: first, you tell your mother's clan history, then your father's, then
your husband's. Clans trace descent through the maternal line and claim
a common history, exclusive ownership of a pool of personal names, and
specific rights to crests and songs and territories. She has recorded her
Shagóon on several occasions during the ten years we have worked
together, sometimes emphasizing the songs, sometimes the stories, sometimes the names of deceased clan members. This set of narratives broadly
establishes the notion of "self" in time and place, defining for her where
her life begins and specifying the ties binding clans rather than individuals.

Because descent is traced matrilineally in the southern Yukon, it is not
surprising that the presentation of her mother's Deisheetaan Crow genealogy (Section 1) is more elaborate than her father's Dakl'aweidí Wolf
genealogy (Section 3). What is more significant is the way she describes
her father's Dakl'aweidí history almost as an extension of her mother's
Deisheetaan clan.[7] This does not mean that "Father's people" are less
important than "Mother's people"; the foundation of their marriage was

the set of reciprocal and ongoing obligations established between their two distinct clans and moieties. The convention for naming ancestors is biased to one's mother's side, so the details are recalled through maternal linkages.

Mrs. Sidney goes on to describe marriage patterns that reinforce bonds between clans rather than between individuals. At the death of a married man, for example, his brother or his sister's son or someone socially equivalent would ideally take over the responsibility of looking after a widow; similarly, if a woman died, her sister or sister's daughter would customarily marry the widower. These conventions, called *levirate* and *sororate* by anthropologists, ensured that no one was left without a spouse and that alliances between clans survived the deaths of individuals.

If Sections 1 and 3 account for a *specific* social order, Section 2 accounts for a *general* social order. These stories are told widely throughout the southern Yukon. They explain how the world began—how the ambivalent trickster/transformer Crow brought the sun, moon, and stars to the world, and then created people and taught them social customs; how Game Mother gave birth to game animals at the beginning of time, establishing their common bond with humanity; how the axis of the world shifted so that day and night, winter and summer, animals and humans could coexist. Consistent chronology is not a feature of these stories, and they work together as parallel texts rather than as sequential accounts.

Mrs. Sidney introduces her mother's family by precise genealogical linkages, but she is more inclined to discuss her father's family by telling stories (Section 4), particularly when she begins to explain the unprecedented changes that occurred during his lifetime. Although the idiom may be unfamiliar—a shaman who dresses in women's clothing and flies through the air, a frog who appears as beautiful women, a baby whose cry brings good fortune if precise rituals are followed—the events described all occurred at the end of the last century to people a generation older than Mrs. Sidney. In this section she also uses stylistic conventions that become familiar in the rest of her account. We learn that certain images foreshadow narrative complications: dangerous, ambiguous animals characteristically have "eyes like the moon" and appear from "between two hills"; animals disguised as humans reveal their true nature by sleeping on the opposite side of a fire from humans. Both historical and fabulous characters speak their own lines directly, lending immediacy to their conversations.

The first story in Section 4 concerns her father's stepfather, *Dzagwáa*, a

shaman who used all his powers to divert a monster that was tormenting
the fishcamp. Three more stories dramatize events associated with her
uncle Skookum Jim and her aunt Kate Carmack, who were involved in
the initial discovery that triggered the Klondike gold rush. Popular accounts of the gold rush single out Skookum Jim as a man radically unlike
his contemporaries, an Indian who "longed to be a white man—in other
words a prospector. He differed from the others of his tribe in that he
displayed the white man's kind of ambition."8 Mrs. Sidney's account
emphasizes not the exceptional man but his social context: his acquisition of a Frog spirit helper, his encounter with Wealth Woman, or
Tl'anaxéedákw, his exemplary assumption of responsibility for his sisters.

Mrs. Sidney enters her own account (Section 5) only after the overriding importance of kinship and stories has been established. Her description of her birth pays particular attention to how she acquired her three
names—in Tlingit, in Tagish, and in English. The two *Deisheetaan* names
given to her were identical to those of her maternal step-grandmother,
Stóow (Tlingit) and *Ch'óonehte' Má* (Tagish): a child named after an adult
usually receives all the names belonging to that person, including English
names. When she talks about her childhood, it is often in the third
person, as in a normative account: for example, "when she's a kid, they
train girls that way." She interjects her own reflections about how she
used to listen to adults talking and how she puzzled about the meaning:
"I always listened to what they're talking about; I always know it. After
company goes, I asked her [Mother] questions. That's how come she told
me all that."

A theme of matching old styles with new styles of learning begins in her
childhood account. Shortly before Angela's birth, the Anglican Church
had established a mission at Carcross, where it set up a residential school
known as Chooutla school. Angela expresses ambivalence about school:
she and her friends were excited about going there until they learned that
they would be punished for speaking Tlingit. However, when her father
decided to withdraw her after less than two years, she was distressed
because she had not quite learned to read. She continued to teach herself
by studying books she found, and she remembers her sense of triumph
the first time she sounded out a long word, "SUPERINTENDENT," on her
own.

Stories from her childhood become incorporated into Mrs. Sidney's
discussion of events from her early years (Section 6). One tells about the
old woman who holds up the world: her brother and father used to
evaluate this story, her father insisting that the story proved the world was
flat and her brother demonstrating centrifugal force by swinging a bucket

of water above his head to argue that the world was round, like a ball. When she describes the time her mother and father became separated in the bush and later found each other, the words of relief she attributes to her father are reminiscent of those Fox spoke in the story of how people lost immortality: "I wish dead people would come back like you." A longer story in this section, Moldy Head, illustrates the folly of human arrogance; much of the dramatic action centers on how humans learn appropriate ways to negotiate with the animal world. Whenever I ask her what it is that children actually learn from these stories, she replies by repeating the story for me. The messages, she suggests, are implicit, self-evident; the text, she would argue, should speak for itself.

If personal names and clan names provide a framework for talking about the distant past, place names seem to have a similar function for remembering and talking about more recent events (Section 7). Mrs. Sidney recounts her family's annual movements between 1912 and 1915, from her tenth to her thirteenth year. Toponyms simultaneously root her travel accounts to a sense of place and tie events to chronological time. Traditional stories she told earlier now become attached to landscape features. Even the travels of Game Mother, Fox, and Wolf explain the origins of names (Section 8).

In 1912 and 1914 Angela remembers the last big *Daḵl'aweidí* potlatches being held (Section 9). She repeatedly emphasizes that her perceptions were those of a child who did not at the time fully understand how she fit into a social context, interjecting, "I'm only a kid, too, myself," "here I was, running around," and "I was just a child . . . I was just beginning to realize things." Her account suggests that the onus was on a child actively to learn what each of the greetings, exchanges, songs, and dances meant rather than on adults to provide elaborate explanations of each component. One of the most significant features of a potlatch is the public reaffirmation of kinship ties, and in her descriptions of these two potlatches, personal names provide the framework for describing events, just as place names provided the mnemonic for childhood travels.

The formal description of the invitations, the official welcome, the dancing, songs, and ceremony, the placing of gravestones, and her childhood speculations about the meaning of her place in all this contrast sharply with her self-portrait, a few pages earlier, of a plucky, independent child playing in the creek with her friends, lying on a cabin roof with her cousin singing songs, making mud-pie wedding cakes (Section 5), or helping her brother construct a family Christmas from ideas they had acquired at residential school (Section 7). Her deep disappointment at the last *Deisheetaan* potlatch (probably held in 1906 or 1907) that there was no living *Deisheetaan* elder to give her a potlatch name remained for years: "I took it hard," she says when her friend Daisy (from the *Gaanaxteidí* clan) was given a name and she was not (Section 9).

At the 1912 potlatch Angela heard for the first time a particular song and story that she tells here (Section 10). After naming the singer from whom she first heard it, she tells how the song was made by a woman whose adopted "son" (a giant woodworm) was killed by her uncles. This reminds her of her *Deisheetaan* Beaver song, told at the beginning of her life story and retold here to put the potlatch song in context: both refer to tragic consequences that followed when a nonhuman son was adopted and raised by a human woman.

Angela's intellectual struggle to strike a balance between the old ways and the new becomes an increasing preoccupation as she gets older. Her puberty seclusion was not taken as seriously as it would have been a few years earlier. The customary "bonnet" had been prepared for her, but it was given away to someone else at the 1912 potlatch. Though people certainly had time to prepare another one for her, no one did so: instead, they gave her a flannel one. All the necessary customs were observed, but her mother was ill and finally one of her aunts insisted that Angela be removed from seclusion to help: "People don't believe in that nowadays," she says. "Times are going ahead," she says to my mother. "What foolishness! Why are you keeping her in jail when you're not well. You need help!" So they took her long hat off, but Angela always felt somehow cheated by the minimizing of the ritual (Section 11). She says that the tent where she was secluded should have been given to her father's sister—her opposite-moiety aunt—but instead it was given to relatives she considers genealogically more distant just because they happened to travel past at the time and needed a tent.

The three stories in her explanatory Section 12 all have as their central character a young woman who is just reaching marriageable age; in two the girl's seclusion is an important part of the plot. The stories explore some of the implications of a woman's changing status and powers at puberty.

When she describes the transactions surrounding her own marriage, Mrs. Sidney gives a skillful depiction of the roles of various kinsmen: the lengthy formality of the negotiations, the expectations and actions of various older relatives, especially opposite-moiety aunts. She reconstructs dialogue showing her deferential behavior to her suitor—"I have to talk respectable, not crazy, like nowadays"—and his statement of intentions to her father—"my father sent me to you people to help out." ("Well," she comments, "the old people understood.") The tension between observing old traditions and making way for new ideas persists. Her husband was older: she was fourteen and he was twenty-eight. They addressed each other by "old-fashioned" terms: he called her the appropriate Tlingit kin term, which translates as "my father's sister (of the opposite moiety)," and though she recognized that he was being respectful, it embarrassed her when he used the English translation "auntie" because "he used to say that even amongst white people! Gee, I don't like that! I get shamed. It's old-fashioned! I used to say, 'Why do you say that in front of people? You know they're going to think she married her own nephew. White people don't understand!'" After all the appropriate negotiations were completed, the families held a feast to celebrate the union. Her father spoke to the couple, and again it is his comments about old and new ways which she reconstructs: "I don't want you fellows to have a hard time. Maybe you came to us for your aunt, so you fellows stay together. Don't be too old-fashioned: I'm not old-fashioned. A long time ago, people work for their wife a long time. But I'm not like that. I don't believe in it."

Shortly afterward a staunch member of the Anglican Church Woman's Auxiliary who had taught Angela briefly at residential school paid her a visit and told her, "You're not supposed to be like that. You've got to get married in church!" Angela protested that her husband wouldn't like the idea, but the matron, undeterred, accosted George on his way home from work with threats: "You've got to marry her white-man way. I raised that kid!" The church wedding seems a drier affair than the original marriage, with attention focused on whether the bride and groom had the "correct" clothing: her parents did not attend, so the minister, bride, groom, Angela's cousin Sophie, and "the white ladies" were the only ones present (Section 13).

Meanwhile, there is an ongoing sense that little changed in her life after her marriage: she and her husband lived with her parents, she played with her younger brother, and she cooked and kept house as she had since her childhood: "I still felt like a kid even though I was living with Old Man. . . . When he was gone during the day, I played. . . . I was still a kid yet." The reflecting stories in Section 14 dramatize the new decisions a woman may have to make in her role as wife, particularly if marriage removes her from her mother's people.

Section 15 gives us a portrait of rural Yukon social life in the twenties, thirties, and forties. We learn how the missionaries directed their attention to altering practices associated with birth and death, both critical aspects of women's lives in a small Yukon community. She describes the horrifying effects of influenza epidemics in 1920, coinciding with a

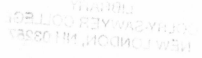

worldwide epidemic, and again in 1943, accompanying the construction of the Alaska Highway. The increasing medicalization of birth and death also becomes an issue, as does her enormous sense of loss when the doctor consulted her husband, not her, about her health and she underwent surgery without even knowing that it would mean she would be unable to bear more children.

Possibly the most poignant use of a traditional story links Sections 15 and 16. When World War II ended, her son sent a telegram from Europe announcing his return. She began planning his homecoming at once, estimating the number of days it would take for him to travel across the Atlantic by boat, across Canada by train, up the west coast of the country by boat, and inland to the Yukon on the narrow-gauge White Pass and Yukon Railway. She arranged a party to welcome him and as a special gift she gave him the song of Ḵaax̱'achgóok, a Tlingit song and story given to her Deisheetaan clan long ago by another Crow clan, Kiks.ádi, to settle a dispute. The story tells how a man became lost at sea; using the sun as a navigational aid and locating its position at the summer solstice, he was able to chart his way home a year later.[9] Once home, he had to come to terms with the ways life had changed in his absence. Mrs. Sidney's husband's admiration and praise of her ingenuity for devising such an appropriate gift especially pleased her. His respect for her abilities grew, and after he became chief of the Carcross village, he sometimes asked her to represent him at important meetings.

A final section, 17, indicates how she explicitly continues to use stories to think about events in her present life. First, she describes her visit to Angoon, Alaska, at the age of eighty-two. This is the village where her Shagóon began and the location to which her Deisheetaan crests, songs, and histories are traced. The visit was a tremendously exciting opportunity for her, and she reports it here in fine ethnographic detail, linking it with the narratives that appear in Section 1. The trip provided her with an opportunity to discuss her Shagóon with people who shared her context for understanding the details and who could contribute a different (coastal) perspective. Several days were spent comparing versions of stories and discussing their implications. Coastal people were able to answer a question that she says had always puzzled her, by explaining why Raven had two heads. She, in turn, was able to explain to them why she has a "split-tail beaver"—with two tails and six legs—on her drum, because they didn't know that story. The narratives she knows continue to be as important as ever to her understanding of who she is.

A second narrative documents events leading up to a potlatch she held in 1984 to place a stone marking the graves of her brothers and sisters who died in the 1898 epidemics. She describes her research, which began in earnest after her trip to Angoon. She formulated her plan and then consulted with an appropriate Tlingit elder from Klukwan, Alaska; he responded by telling her a story about a similar incident from the past. Combining his story with her own knowledge of family history, she reviews how the children died and how the original graves were washed away, and outlines her careful preparations for the potlatch. Much of the discussion refers back to the story of her mother's life (Section 3).

A third narrative shows her continuing intellectual struggle to integrate traditional understandings with modern ideas. In the last few years, Mrs. Sidney has become actively involved in the Baha'i faith. She has paid a great deal of attention to reconciling her present beliefs with the shaman-istic ideas she learned from her parents, uncles, and aunts, and with her own longstanding membership in the Anglican Church. Her account has a splendid coherence, and as usual, she makes narrative connections between events in her past and present life.

The structure of this account remains collaborative. By ordering it this way, I am inevitably interpreting what I believe Mrs. Sidney is saying. In her account she provides her own culturally grounded explanation of her life: first, by furnishing the necessary scaffolding to make her account accessible to outsiders, and second, by drawing contrasts between nor-mative expectations and actual events in life, using narratives to explore those contradictions. Because she is a keen observer, she tends to reflect on the differences between the way things "should be" and the way things are. Sometimes her ideal point of reference is contemporary and other times it is "old-fashioned," but she is always weighing the balance. She consciously uses stories as part of this process, trying to resolve the contradictions she observes by referring back to narratives. She repeat-edly comments on the significance of traditional stories in her own life and her hope that even if the social meaning of narratives changes, as it must, they will continue to be important to her descendants. "Well," she concluded one afternoon, "I have no money to leave to my grand-children. My stories are my wealth."

1 ✳ Our *Shagóon*, Our Family History

First I'll tell you our Shagóon, *our family history. This is for our family to know. The way you should tell your history is this way: first, my own history—that's the same as my mother's in Indian way—then my dad's, then my husband's. I'll start with Deishee-taan history. That's my own people.*

✳ *Deisheetaan* History

One time, long ago, a chief of the *Deisheetaan* nation—that's us—came in from Angoon. That chief's family sailed up Chilkat River: they stayed there with Chilkat people and dried fish for the summer, maybe for two months. When they're going to head back, here that Chilkat chief's son has fallen in love with that *Deisheetaan* chief's daughter! Well, they got married, Indian way. Her father and mother are from Angoon—her father is a chief, too. She is a *Deisheetaan sháa,* that means a *Deisheetaan* woman.

Her children grew up around Taku River. [When they were grown] her three girls married [inland] to Tagish, to Teslin, to Telegraph Creek. One married to *Dak̲l'aweidí* here, in Tagish; one married to *Yanyeidí,* in Teslin; one married to Telegraph Creek: they call themselves K̲aach.ádi instead of *Deisheetaan* at Telegraph Creek, so we've got relatives there, too. Some people say there is a fourth daughter married into Pelly Banks, near Ross River: they use our *Deisheetaan* names up there so they must be related to us somehow. That's how we came to this country. Now hardly any of us are left here.

When those daughters got married, people put out moose skins for them to walk over to their husbands. Just think how many moose there must have been in those days! Then they potlatched those skins off to Wolf people. And then they killed three slaves.[10] Those girls are all Crow.

Deisheetaan owns Beaver: just like the British have a flag, we have Beaver, and we have our own songs—they belong to us. This is the story about it. They say there was a little lake behind Angoon. Beaver owned that place—a beaver lake. Here, one time, somebody saved a little beaver and *Deisheetaan* people raised it. When it got big, that chief said to let it go. But Beaver dammed it up, they say—he dammed up the creek, and   37 when he did that, it raises the lake. He made tunnels all over the place, under the town. And when he slapped his tail and when he dived, the wave from that goes into the tunnel. And one time the town sank . . . caved in . . . too many holes. He made a great wave which drowned most people. That wave just about washed out Angoon.

So those who survived made a song about Beaver. The words of it are:

Who was smart enough to stop [advise against] this city at the
    sandy beach?
Are you going to save your Crow?
Is that why you're crying about it, Wolf, dear Wolf?

We own that song: it's like our flag.

I want to talk first about my mother's family. My great-grandmother is named *Sa.éek'*—she was born at Klukwan. *Sa.éek'* had three daughters from three different husbands: my mother's mother *Kashadandá* was the first child—she was born at Log Cabin, *Men Ch'ile Táh*.

Sa.eek' was married to two brothers and they both died. Before the second child was born, *Sa.éek'*'s husband *Kaatulak'é* was dying, so he called the men together and he asked for one of them to look after his wife. The one that took over was his nephew—his sister's son—his name was *Haandeyéil*, the same name as *my* father. *Kaatulak'é* said to his nephew, "I don't want my child to be born without a father. You stay with her right away." Grandma Hammond was the second child—sometimes they call her Mrs. Dyea John, or Mary John; her Indian name is *Aandaax'w*. She called that *Haandeyéil* "Daddy" even though *Hunyís* was her real father. The third child was called *Sakinyáa*. Later they made a potlatch for that child, and they gave her the second name *Sa.éek'* like her mother.

Then Tagish Charlie was the next child—his Indian name was *Xóonk'i Éesh*; later they gave him a second name, too—*Yéiłdoogú*. Tagish Charlie guided White Pass builders [when they built the railway from Skagway to Whitehorse]: he's my mother's uncle. He is *Deisheetaan*. They always mix it up when they talk about how those boys found gold: they say Tagish Charlie was with them, but he wasn't. The one who found gold with Skookum Jim is Skookum Jim's own nephew, Dawson Charlie, brother of Billy Smith and Patsy Henderson. He's *Dakl'aweidí*. They always make that mistake! They say that Dawson Charlie and Tagish Charlie are the same person. They are not! They are not even the same nation![11]

The last child of *Sa.éek'* was a boy named *Skwáan*. He died when he was young and never had a white-man name.

Those people I'm telling you about are all *Deisheetaan*—*Deisheetaan* owns Beaver and is Crow. *Deisheetaan* owns Carcross: *Tukyeidí* is part of

Deisheetaan. Those *Deisheetaan* who married in this way, after a while they got children. That's the time they claimed this country. It was the women who came up here, who married up here, but it has to be a man who claims the country: I never heard of a woman claiming it. It's always in a man's name, but it's still our land. One nation owns it, not one person alone. We all own it. And we've got song like that, too, just like national anthem. All nations have got their own songs. You should not sing songs that belong to other nations. But stories are different—you tell what you know. I tell them, and the way I tell is what I know.

In my time, Skookum Jim's father was the one that claimed Carcross for *Deisheetaan.* *Ḵaachgaawáa* was his name, and he was *Deisheetaan* nation. *Naataase Héen* is the Tlingit name for Carcross, *den k'e* is *Todezáané.* The oldest *Deisheetaan* should claim Carcross now—that's my brother, Johnny Johns.

To tell the truth of it, I met someone last summer [1980] from coast people. I told him that I'm *Deisheetaan sháa,* from Angoon. "Oh, my," he said. "My great-grandmother told me, 'Two women went that way, inland. Two or three. They got married inland!' Now I'm glad to meet you." He shakes hands with me. I know now the truth that coast people are our relations.

---

* *Daḵl'aweidí* History

Now I'll tell about my dad's side.

My dad is *Daḵl'aweidí:* *Daḵl'aweidí* owns Killer Whale and is Wolf. Tagish *Daḵl'aweidí* came from Telegraph Creek—that's where they were staying—at *Taltan.* *Tal* means a platter, Indian way, [in] *den k'e; tan* means "it's laying there." *Taltan*—*tal* laying there—"it's all flat." That's where my father's people were. That's their *Shagóon,* they call it, their history.

They had some trouble down there over a woman—that's why they parted, why they moved away. They floated down the Stikine River to Wrangell. They were close to salt water when they saw a glacier coming down—just touching the creek, like this. You can't go across in front of it. That glacier always falls down, makes a noise.

So they landed above it and started to talk about it: "How are we going to get further down? That glacier might fall down and get us all killed!" So they don't know what to do. They didn't want to go back to *Taltan* because they made trouble with each other. That's why they're moving out. Finally, two old men decided to go—to try it. Two little old men, ready to die, I guess. "Send us through it. We're old now. We're no good to you people. If we die, you won't miss us much anyhow." That's what they told the rest of the younger people, the rest of the people. Those two little men had a boat of their own, so they must have gone under the glacier. I wish I could get up that way and find it!

When they're ready to take off, they made a song: "Shove it out now!" This is the song they pushed them out with. They remember it [still]— that's the song they separated on. My father's people used to sing it if they're going to make a potlatch. I remember they sang it in 1912 when I was a little girl—I was ten years old that time. They sang it just before they're going to spend money at that potlatch.

Those two men were going to make a sign if they got through safely. Here, they made it through! So they made a sign—what kind of sign I don't know—they made a sign when they landed safely on the other side of the glacier! So the rest went through, too.

When they reached Wrangell they camped on a gravel beach. That's where they got their name—*Daḵl'aweidí*. That's what they called them- selves now—I don't know what their name was before.

Before they started out again, they made another song: "Way out to the sky I aim my boat." Then that group split three ways: some went out to deep water, and some went to Yakutat. [The third group] came up the coast and went up Chilkat River. They landed up there, and then they cut across country by Bear Creek Pass, and they landed in Tagish. That's where they make their home.

That's how my father's people landed in Tagish: therefore, they have got people in Telegraph Creek, too. It's *Daḵl'aweidí* who own Tagish: they were the first to make their village here. That name passes through women, but the woman stays in the husband's ground. My aunt, Mrs. Bert Dennis, told me about this.

Some *Daḵl'aweidí* went overland—over the mountain to Pelly [River] or Ross River or someplace. Those people tied a string around their belt—that's supposed to be people's life—it keeps them safe. Here, their leader was walking ahead and he saw big feathers. They say they were just like loon feathers. Loon feathers are always green—pretty, they say. He should have known better! They were lying right in front of him, and here he just kicked them out of sight. Kicked them away!

When he kicked those feathers, a big thunderstorm came on top of them. Some of them were hurt badly. A lot of them were killed. That was thunder[bird] feathers he kicked![12] Then their boss made a song for the people who survived. My father and his people used to sing that when they made a potlatch.

Old Man Dickson from Ross River—he's from those people. In 1942 I
met Old Man Dickson in hospital—he told me his name. "You people use
our names," I tell him. "You must be our people."

"Yes, I'm your people," he said.

✳ *Yanyeidí*

Now I'm telling my husband's story.

My husband's people are *Yanyeidí:* they separated, too, from Taku
River, them. That's what Kitty calls "Old" *Yanyeidí*—they are the ones that
landed at Nisutlin Bay and that's why they own Nisutlin.[13]

They drifted down Taku [River]. They came to that place, to a little hill
that looked just like *Kaax* eggs—sawbill duck eggs. There was nothing
growing on it—just bare—that's why they called it that way.

When he went down the river, the leader landed there. He had his
slave with him and he told that slave, "Pack my drum up on top of the
hill." That slave was scared to pack that drum up. "Oh, he's going to kill
me now"—that's what he thought, but he had to do what his master told
him. So the slave did that, took his drum up there. And then he came,
that bigshot chief and the rest of his nephews and their wives came, too—
and here instead of killing him, that chief told that slave, "Drum it. Hit it."
So he started hitting it. He started to drum, and here he [the chief] made
this song for that separation: "My good country, I'll never see it again."

And then he set that slave free. And when they got to Taku harbor,
they're going to camp. That's the time he told his nephews, "Pull those
young cedars and make a cabin." So they made a little cabin, *Yanhít,* a little house. That's why he called those nephews *Yanyeidí,* because they
camped under that cedar *Yan,* that cabin. The chief—bigshot—says,
"We're going to change that name. We're *Yanyeidí* from now on," he said.

I don't know what kind of name they had before: they gave themselves
that name when they separated. That bunch went to Teslin—I don't
know how they came up: they came up lately, not so long ago. *They made
a song, too. I know those songs.*

My husband, George Sidney, is *Yanyeidí:* his mother is *Yanyeidí sháa,*
that means *Yanyeidí* woman. His father is from Taku, from Juneau. George
is Jimmy Jackson's first cousin. George Sidney's grandmother, *La.oos,* was
married to a rich man with fourteen slaves: he was so rich that he had a
big boat which you needed a stepladder to get into.

That's all three nations I know that separated from different places.

2 ✳ How the World Began

"You tell what you know.
The way I tell stories is what I know."

✳ The Story of Crow

One time there was a girl whose daddy is a very high man.
They kept her in her bedroom all the time—
Men tried to marry her all the time, but they say no, she's too good.

Crow wanted to be born—he wants to make the world!
So he made himself into a pine needle.
A slave always brings water to that girl, and one time he gets water
    with a pine needle in it.
She turns it down—makes him get fresh water.
Again he brings it. Again a pine needle is there.
Four times he brings water and each time it's there.
Finally, she just gave up—she spit that pine needle out and drank the
    water.
But it blew into her mouth and she swallowed it.
Soon that girl is pregnant.

Her mother and daddy are mad.
Her mother asks, "Who's that father?"

"No, I never know a man," she told her mother.

That baby starts to grow fast.
That girl's father had the sun, moon, stars, daylight hanging in his
    house.
He's the only one that has them.
The world was all dark, all the time.
The child begged for them to play with.

Finally, the father gives his grandchild the sun to play with.
He rolls it around, plays with it, laughs, has lots of fun.
Then he rolls it to the door and out it goes!

"Oh!" he cries. He just pretends.
He cries because that sun is lost.

"Give me the moon to play with."

They say no, at first—like now, if a baby asks for the sun or moon you
    say,
"That's your grandfather's fire."

Finally, they gave it to him.

One by one they gave him the sun, moon, stars, daylight—
He loses them all.

"Where does she get that child from? He loses everything!"
That's what her father says.

Then Crow disappears.
He has those things with him in a box.
He walks around—comes to a river.
Lots of animals there—fox, wolf, wolverine, mink, rabbit.
Everybody's fishing . . .
That time animals all talk like people talk now—
The world is dark.

"Give me fish," Crow says.
No one pays any attention.
"Give me fish or I'll bring daylight!"
They laugh at him.

He's holding a box . . . starts to open it and lets one ray out.
Then they pay attention!
He opens that box a bit more—they're scared!
Finally, he opens that daylight box and threw it out.
Those animals scatter!
They hide in the bush and turn into animals like now.
Then the sun, moon, stars, and daylight come out.

"Go to the skies," Crow says.
"Now no one man owns it—it will be for everybody."

He's right, what he says, that Crow.

After Crow made the world, he saw that sea lion owned the only island
    in the world.

44 The rest was water—he's the only one with land.

Angela The whole place was ocean!

Sidney Crow rests on a piece of log—he's tired.
He sees sea lion with that little island just for himself.
He wants some land, too, so he stole that sea lion's kid.

"Give me back that kid!" said sea lion.

"Give me beach, some sand," says Crow.

So sea lion gave him sand.
Crow threw that sand around the world.
"Be world," he told it. And it became the world.

After that, he walks around, flies around all alone.
He's tired—he's lonely—he needs people.
He took poplar tree bark. You know how it's thick?
He carved it and then he breathed into it.

"Live!" he said, and he made a person.
He made Crow and Wolf, too.
At first they can't talk with each other—
Crow man and woman are shy with each other—look away.
Wolf is same way, too.

"This is no good," he said. So he changed that.
He made Crow man sit with Wolf woman.
And he made Wolf man sit with Crow woman.
So Crow must marry Wolf and Wolf must marry Crow.

That's how the world began.

❋ Game Mother[14]

This is the story of how game animals used to be.

This Game Mother, she's just an ordinary woman like us.
She got married to two young brothers. She had two husbands—
    brothers.
They stayed together I don't know how many years and they never
    have a baby.
They never travel—she doesn't want to travel around.
Just stay one place all the time.

When fall starts to come her husbands always make snowshoes for her.
The oldest one gets his snowshoes done first—then the youngest one.
She wouldn't work on it either.
Every time they finish, they wrap that snowshoe up in nice cloth and
     give it to her.

Here she always put it in back of her pillow and said to it,
"You undo yourself."
She didn't want to travel with it.
Here in the morning, it would be all undone so next day they'd start
     another one always.
And then the youngest one made snowshoes for her . . . same thing.
She always put it in back of her pillow:
"You undo yourself."
And in the morning it would be undone.

I don't know how many years they were like that—just stay in one
     place.
Oh, they get tired, I guess, those boys.
But she never got tired.

And here she started to grow, bigger and bigger and bigger like that.
And she wouldn't go anyplace, wouldn't travel around.
She was just so big.

Springtime, that's the time when animals are born.
She told her husbands,
"It's no use because I'm no good to you people.
You'd better go on your own.
Just leave me right here.
But make a better housecamp for me."
That's what she told them.

"If you want to, you can watch me from a long ways away,
From on top of the mountain."

Anyway, they left.
They hated to go, but they had to go anyway.
They watched, I guess, all the time.
I wonder what kind of fieldglasses they got, eh?

The first thing they know, moose was born:
As soon as those husbands go, those animals came out!

Moose had grizzly teeth, too, they say—
She called it back and she took those teeth out.
She showed moose what to eat—willow.
Bull moose came with a horn.
"Leave your horn once in a while," she told him.
"Don't use it all the time, just in running [rutting] season."
Then she told moose to lick salt in her ashes.
That's why they lick mud all the time, looking for salt.
They call it "moose lick."

Caribou came next—first bull and then cow.
Bull caribou came with horns, too, so she told him the same thing.
"Leave your horns once in a while.
Don't use them all the time, just in running season.
Just then you use it," she told them.
And she taught them to eat moss.

Next sheep came, and she taught him to eat grass.

Then came grizzly—she tried to call him back to take his teeth out,
   but he wouldn't come.
She couldn't get it!
"I'm going to use these teeth to get even," he told her.
"You're taking everything from us."

"Well, don't be mean to people," she told him.
"Remember that you came from people."

After grizzly, came wolf.
And after wolf, came goat.
Everything came from her!
She gave them a meal right away, as soon as they came, to teach them
   what to eat.

Finally, rabbit came out last.
And he started eating branches off her campfire—
That's why in wintertime rabbits eat pine tree branches.

Those animals started staying around her place, just around her.
They don't know what she eats—what she lives on.
She stayed for one whole year.
Finally, the next year, she got tired of them.
They make too much noise, eat up everything—all the grass around
   her place.

So she made a big swing for them, a trampoline.
She called it *akeyí*, that's *den k'e*, Tagish language.
She made big sport day for them because she's going to leave them.
Falltime, she made it from bull moose skin.
There's no moose before that! Where she got that, I don't know!
Anyway, that's the story—it was bull moose skin.
She put it up right in the middle of Bennett Lake.
It had four strings:
One went to Grey Mountain, *Takaadí T'ooch'*—that means "Charcoal
    mountain" in Tlingit.
One went to the mountain behind Chooutla school, *Métáatl'e Shéch'ée:*
That means "wind on the forehead" in Tagish language.
One went to Fourth of July Mountain: *Médzíh Dzéłe'*—that means
    "caribou mountain"—
And one went to that mountain we call *Chílíh Dzéłe'*—"gopher
    mountain."

They walked out on that line that ties the swing.
The first one to come is moose—even that narrow, they walk on it!

Bull moose sings his song first:
"What is this they put out for me?
I'm walking on it, look at me."

They say he stepped through the skin he's so heavy.
Then the cow comes—then the calf—each one has its song.
That calf can hardly stand up!

Then the caribou came with its young one—
By that time, they had young ones.
Then came sheep—all that were born, they sat on the swing.
Then wolf came and sang his song.
Then came the rabbit song. He says,
"My brothers always do that for me.
They chop down trees and give me food
And I always play around with it."

After she got through with that skin,
She told them she's going to part with them now.
"You go all into different countries.
Go!" she said.

Somebody was watching all this from way back there.
His name is *Tudech'ade*[15]—

That means "duck head feathers" in Tagish language.
He saw when she parted with them.

She didn't go very far—
Right to that *Chílíh Dzéłe'* at Carcross.
She camped there—that's where she slept.
They call it "grizzly bear mother's camp"—*Xúts Tláa Ta.eetí.*

Next day, she went to another mountain.
On top of the mountain, you see there's two big dips.
At the first camp she wasn't comfortable in that bed.
So she moved a little way from there to that Lanning Mountain,
   Kwákah Dzéłe'.

From there she went to Teslin—Three Aces, they call that mountain.
Right there they said there's a little bridge leads to a little mountain.
At that mountain they say there's a dip there, too—
Green grass grows around it.

From there, I don't know . . .
That's as far as I remember.
My father died in 1920, but he told me all these stories before that.

✳ How Animals Broke through the Sky

One time the sky used to come right down to salt water.
Here the animals lived on the winter side. It was cold!
Squirrel always came amongst other animals, crying all the time.

One time they asked her,
"What are you crying for?"

"My kids all froze up again."
Every now and then her children, her babies, all froze up.

So they went to a meeting, all the animals: they are going to try to
   poke a hole through the sky.
They are on the winter side and they are going to poke a hole through
   the sky so they can have summertime, too.
Summer is on the other side.

So they gathered together with all kinds of people—they're animals,
    though—
Bloodsucker is the one they picked to go through that hole.
He poked that hole and then different animals went through.
Wolverine is the one who made that hole bigger—
He went through pulling a dry moose skin—made that hole bigger.
That's how they all got through.

Now they are going to steal good weather.
They went to a high person—he's got all the weather—the hot air,
    cold air,
He's got flowers and leaves.
So they took all that—they stole it when people weren't home.

But there was one old man there.
He went outside—took his blanket outside and waved it around his
    head.

"Get wintertime over there and summer over here.
Don't go away for good," he told them.
He kept them from taking summer completely away.

That's how, when winter goes for good that's the time we get summer.
Then when summer goes back to the south side, that's the time we get
    winter.

He waved his blanket and said,
"Don't go away for good," he told the weather.
"Go back and forth."

Those two worlds were side by side—winter on one side, summer on
    the other.
On one side were winter animals—on the other, summer animals.
They broke the sky down, and after, it went up.

After they got it across, they bust it—the summer bag.
Pretty soon, snow melted—they got leaves,
They had all the leaves tied up in a balloon.
Then they bust the balloon and all the summer things came out.

3 ✳ My Parents

*"We're pretty smart, we're doing this.
This is long before my time and yet I know it."*

✳ My Mother

My mother was named Ḵaax'anshee; her white-man name is Maria. She's
Deisheetaan sháa—that means she is a woman of *Deisheetaan* Nation.
Now I'll talk more about my mother's people.

That *Deisheetaan sháa* who came inland had daughters, and *they* had
daughters. One of those daughters was *Sa.éek'*. She was my grandma on
my mother's side, and also on my daddy's side because her brother was
my daddy's father, *Tl'úku*.[16] I heard my mother and my daddy talk about
their grandmother.

I never saw *Sa.éek'*, but I knew two of her daughters, Grandma Hammond, *Aandaax'w,* and Annie Atlin, *Sakinyáa*.[17] I never saw my mother's
mother, either: her Tagish name was *Kashadandá*; her Tlingit name,
Keikandagán.

She died when my mother was six or seven. My mother had no sisters
after that. She died going through that pass from Millhaven, going
through to West Arm. There's a little creek comes down—they call it
Rosebud Creek—that's where they climbed up right on top of the mountain. She was carrying her baby, my mother's sister. Here that baby died
five days after her mother—that baby must have starved herself, my
mother said. Well, of course, they burned people that time I'm talking
about, and they brought her ashes back to Carcross. This is my mother's
time I'm talking about.

That fall that her mother died, my mother went down Taku River with
her aunt, *Sakinyáa*. She went down in falltime. My mother was raised by
her aunt that one year. In springtime they came back, and here, her father
was staying with *Stóow* already. That *Stóow* was Tagish Charlie's sister, my
mother's mother's half-sister. *Stóow*—her husband had died, too—and
people said, "You fellows just go with each other. Who's going to guide
you fellows? You fellows just help yourself, enjoy yourself together. Your
husband died, and his wife died, and they're your people."

And they talked to my Grandpa *Shaakóon:* "This is your people's wife,
too. And you're her people's husband. Might as well be you people stay together." That's what they told them. That's why they stayed together. So *Shaakóon* married a Tagish lady, *Deisheetaan.* So that's all my mother stayed with her aunt, just that part of one year. My mother said she was only one year without a mother. From then on, she called *Stóow* "Mother": *Stóow* is the one that died at Indian Point, *Ta Tígi.*

✳ My Father

My father was *Kaajinéek':* his name in English is Tagish John. Later they gave him his second name—*Haandeyéił,* "come on crow" [or "hither, crow"]. He was a *Dakl'aweidí* [that is, Wolf] and *Deisheetaan yádi:* that means "child of *Deisheetaan"* [or "child of Crow"]. Now I'll talk about my father's people.

My daddy's mother, *Guná,* was sister to *Shaakóon,* my mother's daddy.

My daddy's daddy, *Tl'úku,* died at Quiet Lake. *Tl'úku* was a brother to *Sa.éek',* my mother's mother—that's why my father took the news to *Sa.éek'* when his father, her brother, died. People burned the body in those days—they would bring the ashes and bones back in a blanket or whatever they've got. Then they put them away in the spirit house, and then they had a party in the springtime. People came together to pay the people who've been handling him. Wolf people carried back my father's father, because he is Crow. After *Tl'úku* died, *Guná* married *Dzagwáa.*

Aandaax'w—Mary—was the daughter of *Sa.éek'* and was my daddy's cousin. When they were kids, they traveled around together all the time. Whenever my daddy used to tell a story, he always said, "*Aandaax'w* was with us." They grew up together like partners because my daddy's daddy traveled with his sister, *Sa.éek',* and her husband: those brothers-in-law were partners. They were all together when that animal came to them [see Section 4].

My daddy's mother, *Guná,* died in 1898 or '99. They were in Skagway and my daddy was freighting—that's the time his mother died at Bennett. The old people can't go over the pass so they stayed at Bennett. She was never well for six years, never walked for six years. In those days people lived in brush camp, and people packed [carried] her when they moved; in wintertime they used a sleigh.

Well, my father was in Skagway when they brought the news his mother died. So Tagish John and Tagish Jim and other *Dakl'aweidí* went over to Bennett. They [*Deisheetaan*] burned her—those were the days they burned people—and they had a cup of tea. They never really had a good party for her till they came back from Skagway, falltime. Then they brought the bones back to the spirit house in Tagish—they brought them back in a trunk: they gathered up the bones and ashes and brought them back to Tagish. That's all my mother told me about her.

My daddy had a twin sister, and they both grew up. After their mother, *Guná*, died, his twin sister married *Dzagwáa*.[18] She was Bill Bone's mother.

My daddy's other sister married *Yéils'aagí*. When he died, and when *Gunaaták'*'s wife died, she "took over" because it was their people—*Gunaaták'* was Marsh Lake Chief. They never had kids together. That auntie, *Tashooch Tláa*, had a son, though—*Tashooch*.[19] They claim that she was single, too, long after her husband died—that's why she never had another child. But *Gunaaták'* [already] had a daughter: she's the one my auntie raised—Mrs. Whitehorse Billy—my aunt raised her since she was two years old.

Tagish women married to all parts of the Yukon—I think that's why now they want Tagish people at that elders' meeting, because we went everywhere:[20] my father's sister *Tashooch Tláa* married *Gunaaták'*, Marsh Lake Chief; Jimmy Kane's mother married to Champagne; *Tatl'èrma*, Kitty Smith's mother, married to Dalton Post; Jenny Dickson married to Ross River; Tagish Jim's mother's sister married to Mandasaa, Laberge Chief. I remember my mother said, "How come you people call yourselves like that [use Tagish names]? Go back to your country, Marsh Lake! You just like to use our names but you don't want to go back to your country," she told them. But I guess that's why they want us at that meeting.

My daddy was maybe thirty when he married: my mother had just become woman. Old-timers got kids married right away. They tell them, "You're ready for marrying now. You've got to get married."

In 1898 Mother was in Skagway. Mother lost four kids—all at one time: one was six years old, next were two girl twins, then one other girl. They are buried at Dyea, under one house in Dyea. My mother got that 1898 sickness, too—measles—and it made her blind. The doctor and the bishop told her not to sew because she would damage her eyes more.

After that, they came over the Summit and found Atlin. Johnny was born that year, 10th of July, 1898. After Johnny, there was one girl died between Johnny and me, and then me, Angela—I was born in 1902. My Indian name is *Stóow*. After me came a girl named Dora, who died later, then David, who died 1929, then Dora, born July 29, 1916—her real name is Alice Dora, but we call her Dora.

4 ✳ Stories from My Parents' Time

"My father died in 1920,
But he told me all these stories before he died."

✳ *Dzagwáa*

My father told us this story.

He said when they were kids—ten or twelve years old—he and my
   mother's aunt, Mrs. Dyea John, *Aandaax'w,* were pals.
They used to run along and get water—play around all the time.

And here, all of a sudden, dogs begin to bark in the night always.
People never used to have a lot of dogs—
Maybe one family got just one dog—they never used to have big
   bunch of dogs.
They miss salmon, too, when dogs bark.

So finally, Tagish Jim's father, *Yéiłshaan,* told my daddy's stepfather,
   Dzagwáa
"What's your doctor [shamanic power] for?
Go find out. Find out what's doing that.
Is that a person, or what is it?
Is it an animal stealing fish?"

He said, all right, he's going to try to find out.
So he made doctor one night, and he sees that it's an animal doing
   that.
"It's not a human being," he said.
So he watched for it, watched for it.

The next night he said,
"It's going to come . . . huh, huh . . .
Its mind comes here already . . .
It's going to come again . . ."
So he told those people exactly where to sit down and watch for it.
"It's going to come over there, right there.

You fellows watch that all the time."

And in the meantime, he made that arrow—the head of that arrow is
bone.

He put his paint on it and he told *Yéiłshaan* to watch for it.
He gave that bow and arrow to him for him to shoot it.

He knows just when it's going to come. He said,
"His mind comes here already."
That's the time he told them to watch for it.
Him, he's at the camp—he's sleeping all the time.
After those people went to watch, he lay down again—
He sleeps—put his blanket over his head.
"Kids have to keep still," he said.

My father said they put the kids to bed while the sun is still up yet.
Those kids got to go to bed—never run around.
Nobody runs around—just lay still one place.
But he's making doctor.

Pretty soon, all at once, it started to get dusk but you could still see
good yet.
All of a sudden it just came out of a kind of valley between the
mountains where an old water bed came out—
Little creek down at the bottom—
But it's got shoulder on it—it's steep, too.
Here that thing just came out and he's just watching the camp, just
looking at the camp.
All of a sudden that *Yéiłshaan* took a shot at it with his bow and arrow.
And it's just gone, like that.
Just gone.
Disappeared.

Well, they watched for a while, I guess.
That Indian doctor said,
"He shot it all right, but it took off with the arrow.
There's a little arrow sticking into him yet"—
It's just the spear of the arrow, you know:
They put the arrow somehow on a stick
And when the arrow goes through, the stick just falls off but the bone
stays inside.

He watched all the time, that Indian doctor, *Dzagwáa.*
Never eats—never eats anything.

Other people ate early in the morning and late in the evening.
But that Indian doctor is just sleeping all the time—
Watching . . .

Pretty soon . . . "Aha," he said.
"It's coming back to its mother.
And oh, his mother feels sorry—that animal died after it came back to
    its mother.
Now his mother is going to come here, she's starting to come."

It's going to come, so everybody keeps quiet, keeps still.
Here, the next night, it's going to come.
"You fellows watch between the mountains."
I wonder what in the world that could be?
Couldn't be that big . . .
I would like to see that place at Quiet Lake where they looked, at Big
    Salmon.
They said it was between the valley, like that.
Here it comes out.
Something just like towards Tagish, I guess, between mountains.

Here all of a sudden in the evening he said,
"Here it's coming, it's coming.
Watch that place up there, you fellows—[pointing]
Watch up there. It's going to come out."

So people watch it.
The kids are all in bed.
The women are all in bed, too, with the kids.
Just that Indian doctor—that *Dzagwáa*, his name—my father's
    stepfather—
And her, that animal's mother.

Pretty soon . . . "I'm going to meet it,"
He said that when it came out.
There was a light just like a moon, they say—
Just like the moon, her eyes between those mountains—
Two lights there, it seemed just like two moons.
And he said he's going to meet it.
So he went.
He's gone.
My father's stepfather, whole thing, gone—just like he's flying!

And he told those people,
"When I'm coming back, you fellows stand like a **V**,
Like a *shal*, like head of a *shal* [fishtrap]," he said.

And *Yéiłshaan*, oh, he's the one!
He don't believe in Indian doctor, don't believe him.
He [*Dzagwáa*] said to him:
"You stand right there and try to catch me."
And his feet are that far off the ground! [two feet]
He's flying, they said.
"If you don't catch me, I'm going to go round the camp and come back
    the same way again.
Then you try a second time.
You try with your bare hands first."
He gave them willows and a little tree top and his mitts.

He said, "You switch me with this one.
Switch me with it if you can't catch me."
That's what he told them.

The first time, he went dressed just like he was, and that thing said to
    him:
"Why are you coming to me with dirty clothes?"
So he came back to camp and he wants clean clothes.
And nobody had clean clothes, I guess—only his wife, that's my
    father's mother—
She had a brand-new dress.
Well, they thought she [the spirit] wouldn't mind it.

So he used that dress—it's homemade, you know—sewed by hand.
He put that on and he went to meet it again.
It just stayed there in one place right there—
I guess his doctor tied her up there, too.
He went again.

You could hear, they said, from the camp.
Just like something roaring—You know . . . "RRRRRRRRR"—
That's when she's talking to him, I guess.
And here he's coming with that dress.
And again, she didn't like it.

"Why are you coming to me with a dress?" she said.
"I want a man, not a woman."

So she did that to him: [indicating tearing]—
Here that dress just ripped right from the neck right down to the
     bottom.
That's what happened to him the second time.

Well, he went right back again—he went home.
"I'm going to lead her the other way," he said.
"Lead her past the camp, lead her farther on."
And soon he's gone again.

Well, he's coming back—it's just like he's flying in the air.
And that *Yéiłshaan* couldn't catch him—
He tried to grab him, I guess, but he couldn't catch him.
And here he went around the camp.
And he came back the same way, second time.
That's the time *Yéiłshaan* switched him with those willows—
The little tree top and his gloves, that Indian doctor's gloves.
And he just dropped right there.
That's the way they catch him again.

And the third time he went.
That's the time he led her down the other way.
Everything quieted down after that, after he led her past the camp.
She took off the other way.

This happened at Quiet Lake, head of the Big Salmon River.

That Indian doctor stayed in bed for pretty near a whole week
To get straightened out again.
His name was *Dzagwáa*, Billy Bone's father, my father's stepfather.

✳ Skookum Jim's Frog Helper[21]

To start with, Skookum Jim's family built a house there in Dyea.
People used to go there long time ago before Dyea was a city.
They had only one store there.
They stayed there all the time, Skookum Jim's family.
In falltime, the ground is getting frozen already.
But it's coast, you know, that different climate.

Here, he went to bathroom outside.
When he's coming back, he hears something making a noise.

"Whoo . . ."—just like sand pouring down.
So he stopped and listened.

Here there was a ditch alongside the house where they dig up the sand
     and put it on the moss for roofing.
That's what they used, long time ago.

So he went to the edge and he looked down.
Sure enough there was a big frog—coast frogs are bigger than these
     frogs, you know.
Long way from water, too, they said.
Here it was trying to jump up and trying to get back but it fell down.
Kept doing that, I don't know how long.
Gravel fell down with him—that's what's making the noise.

Anyway, Skookum Jim saw it, so he looked around for a board.
Here he found a board and he shoved it down that hole
And then that frog crawled on that board.

So Uncle Skookum Jim lifted it up.
He lifted it up and carried it and took it down to the creek—
There must be a creek there—this is Dyea.
So anyway, he left it there.
He let it go.

And about a year or so after,
Here he got kicked in the stomach by a drunkard man.
And it got festered—oh, he was sick, they say.
It happened somewhere around wintertime—
He was so sick he couldn't move anymore.
And here that sickness broke open to the outside.

That's when my mother was looking after him.
Well, he's my daddy's cousin—their mothers were sisters.
My mother's got three kids—four altogether with my oldest brother.
And she's got one baby and twin girls, four altogether.
My mother was looking after them.

Skookum Jim's wife and my daddy,
They go back, pack stuff [for prospectors].
They're freighting over the summit toward Bennett.
They get paid for packing stuff: flour, soap, everything like that.
And that's what my father was doing.

My mother stayed home and looked after the kids and my uncle,
   Skookum Jim.

Here one morning in June, his stomach broke out.
Sun was way out already when my mother heard Skookum Jim calling
   her:
"Mrs. John, Mrs. John, Ła.oos Tláa, Ła.oos Tláa.
Wake up. Come on."

Well, she got up—she's a young person.
She jumped up and went over there.
"Look at this thing here!"
Well, he was too hot—it was just burning, that sore place.
So he had his blanket way up and his shirt way open
And he pulled off those bandages because it was too hot.
He wanted to air it, open place.

And here he feels something tickling him there—
That's why he looked down.
Here it was a frog licking that sore place.
That's what it was that woke him up.
My mother saw it and then she just got a board or something and put
   the frog on that.
It never jumped, too, nothing, just stayed like that.

Well, my mother used to have silk thread and beads and stuff, too.
She was good then—she wasn't blind then.
They gave that frog silk thread and some beads.
They put swan down feathers all around him, too.[22]
Then she took it down to the creek and left it there.

That's payment for Skookum Jim to that frog.
They paid him.

And here two or three days after, he started feeling better
And that started healing up, too.
So it healed up good in no time—just in a week or so.
He's all better and he's able to walk around good again.

I don't know how long after that he wants to see his mother—
His mother lives at Carcross.
Naataase Héen, they call it in Tlingit,
"Water running through the narrows."

Tagish language, they call it *Todezáané*,
"Blowing all the time."
He wants to see if his mother is okay.
It's getting to be falltime—
The ground is frozen already, but no snow yet.

So he went through the pass here [route of the present Tagish road]
Shásh Zéitígí, "grizzly bear throat," they call it.
They call it that because north wind's always blowing through—
It's open there, too, just like down a throat.

Through there, he went to see his mother, down in Carcross.
And here he camped halfway around the first lake [Crag Lake]
Just right in the middle.
There's a camp place there all the time—brush camp—
And here he camped there.
He slept there.

That's the time he dreamed nice-looking lady came to him—
Gee, she's just pure—just like you can see through her,
Just like shining, gold shining.

He said that lady told him
"I come for you,
I want you to come with me.
I come for you now.
I want you to marry me," she said.

And my uncle said,
"No, I can't marry you.
I got wife already.
My wife and children are in Tagish."
That's what he dreamed he told this lady, he said.

"Well," she said,
"If you can't go with me, I'll give you my walking stick."
So he took it.
He tells her, "Thank you."

"You saved me one time," she said.
"I was almost starving and I was just about going to die.
And here you saved me one time.
And I'm the one that saved you, too, when you were sick.
When you were sick, I saved you.

I helped you.
I medicined you.
That's why you got better."
That's what that lady's supposed to tell him because he dreamed that.

And that lady told him when she gave him that walking stick:
"You're going to find the bottom of this walking stick.
You're going to find it this way."
So he looked at it, and gee, everything is shining, looks like gold.
"Look this way," she said, pointing to Atlin. "Look this way."
He looks and sees just like a searchlight coming up.
"That's not for you, though; that's for somebody else.[23]
You go down this way and you're going to have your luck,
Your walking stick" [indicating down the Yukon River].
That's what that lady is supposed to tell him.

When he woke up in the morning,
Here there was snow on top of him, about a foot deep, they say.
It snowed that night.
I guess he slept in an open place.
He didn't sleep under anything.

After he ate breakfast, he went down to Carcross.
He got to Carcross that night.
And his mother and those people are all fine.
It's all okay.
That's after his father died, I suppose; they never mention his father
    when they tell this story—they just say his mother.
Some of her grandchildren are staying with them.
She was fine—nothing wrong—lots of wood—lots to eat.
Everything.

So he just stayed one night, and then he started back.
He camped on the way back, too.
Then finally he got home.
He thought he was gone four days.

When he got there they tell him,
"What kept you so long?
You're gone eleven days."

Well, after that he forgot about his dream.
About a year later, though,

That's the time he went down Yukon River.
He didn't think any more about it
Until he went down the river and found gold.

✳ Good Luck Lady

When people go to Skagway,
They always camp at that little lake back of the section house at
    Bennett [on the White Pass Railway]—
It's too little to have a name, that lake.

They were camping there in the lakeside when they heard that baby
    crying—
Skookum Jim heard it—then Dawson Charlie heard it.
Here they got up to go after it.
Patsy [Henderson] went with them—he went a little way, but he got
    scared, started crying—he was still a kid yet.

"Crazy me," he tells us later.
"That's why I never get rich."

And they tried to chase it around—around the lake.
It kept disappearing.
That's why their money didn't last after they found gold.
They found money all right, but it didn't last.

The night was pitch dark.
You know September, how dark it gets at nights?
And you know how bushy that place is!

Grandma Hammond, *Aandaax'w*, said she heard that baby, too.
She heard it, but she never tried.
She thought it was her sister coming, and here, no!—nobody showed
    up.
So when it quit, she started to cry—she told us herself.
That's around Bennett.
But she used to make money like everything, sewing, you know.

My mother said they went to Ptarmigan Mountain, back of Tagish.
K'asmbáa Dzéłe' in Tagish language; *X'eis'awaa Shaayí* in Tlingit.

In the evening they went to bed.
Fire started to go down a little bit.
They didn't have tent or anything—it was just open—
They got a fly tent, though.
They dried some meat.
All of a sudden, at nighttime, baby started to cry.
"Waa, waa, waa," and they hear that mother making a noise.
They got up, sat up, told each other,
"You hear that noise?"
My brother Johnny heard it.
That's why he's lucky all the time.

✳ Discovery of Gold

In the first place, he wasn't looking for gold.
Skookum Jim went downriver to look for his two sisters
Because they missed them.
They were gone two years already—
No telegram, nothing.
He doesn't know if his two sisters are alive or not.
That's why he thought he'd go down the river, too—
To see if he can find his sisters, *Aagé* and Kate.
They were strict about that kind of thing, the old people.

He took his wife and his two nephews—
Dawson Charlie and Patsy Henderson.
My father was going, too, but they turned back at Lake Laberge.
My father turned to my mother and he said [looking back]
"See that *Chîlîh Dzéle'*?" And she started to cry.

"Why are you crying?"
"I'm just thinking about your poor crippled mother, and your sister
   and my mother.
Who is going to cut wood for them?
Who is going to help them get water?
They're sick and crippled and helpless."

And so my father and mother turned around and went back—
Otherwise they might have found the gold, too.

Angela   But maybe it was just as well . . .

Sidney   All those men who found gold split up with their wives . . .

When they got to Klondike River,
That's when they started to dry salmon.
And that's when they came to George Carmack's camp.
Well, Kate and her husband were drying salmon, too—
They've just been living on fish, but they're starting to get hungry for
     meat.
They decide to go hunt, go shoot the game.
At the same time, they're prospecting, too.
When they got to Bob Henderson's place,
He talked to George about it, but he said they couldn't stake,
"Because you've got two Indians with you."
So they came right back, other side—they made fire then.
Patsy's home, I guess, looking after the women and the camp.
Here, Skookum Jim just saw this shiny thing sitting on top of a rock.
So he picked it up and looked at it.
It was a nugget worth fifty cents.
He looked . . . looked . . .

"George, George, come down.
I'll show you something."

"That's gold!"

They pan in a frying pan, find nuggets everywhere . . .
"We found our fortune now!" George said.
They started staking right away.

They say that after Dawson Charlie found that gold he poured nuggets
     into the coffin. And he said,
"My sons, I gave them hard time, trying to rustle for this gold."
So he thought he'd put some gold away with them.
That's why he did that.

And Skookum Jim, too, he poured some gold on his sister, Susie's
     mother.
One bag he poured, whole thing, into their coffin.
His sister died while she was traveling over the summit.
All of a sudden, I guess, north wind started to blow.

The girl fell down—well, what's she going to do? Her mother can't
    leave her!
She fell down, too.
They were still alive when somebody found them.
But after they brought them into the house,
That's when they died.

5 ✳ Childhood

"I know what I know because my mother taught me . . .
After company goes, I asked her questions.
That's how come she told me all that."

I was born on January 4, 1902. My mother says it was four days after New Year's Eve, and we think it is 1902 because that's what it says on my baptism card.

This prospector, George Dale, was mining down at Coal Creek— *T'ooch' Lutú*—below Carcross town in wintertime. Here, New Year's Eve he wants to go to Carcross, I guess. So after he got through working, he walked there on the ice. About two o'clock in the morning, he started to make Carcross—he saw lights. It was a *cold*, cold night, he said. And here the only light there was in my father's house, my father's place—my father Tagish John's place. And he knocked on the door, and here my father answered.

He turned to the heater and he got warmed up. And my father said, "Well, my wife got a little baby girl. That's why I was keeping the fire burning." Them days there were no houses yet: they were living in tent frame. He's got tent frame—boards on it, bed, and everything. There is curtain between: one side they as a kitchen; other side they use as bedroom.

So he asked George Dale, "Would you like to see the baby?" And George said okay. So he brought me out—I guess it was me—and he showed me to George Dale. George Dale looked at the baby: "Oh," he said, "that baby looks so sweet. Just like a little angel."

And that's how come I got my name Angela. He told my father, "Call her Angela. She looks like a little angel. And when she is going to be baptized, let me know. I want to be her godfather because I'm the first person she saw." That's why he claimed me.

Year 1917, that's the time I was already living with my husband. Well, we just got married in July and this was in August. He was working on section. One time he was coming home from work and there was a party going on where that George Dale rented a house. The boys called him in—so he went in, and then they introduced him around and told George [Dale], "This is George Sidney, Angela's husband."

"Angela who?" George Dale inquired.

"Angela John, used to be."

"Oh, my," he said, "that's my godchild." So anyway, he shook hands with George, and he told George that he was supposed to be my godfather and everything.

After a while, George came back and I asked him, "How come you're so late?"

"The boys up there invited me in for a drink. And you know what? I met your godfather."

"My godfather? Who's that?"

"George Dale," he said.

"Aw, go on. How in the world you know he's my godfather?"

"He told me himself."

I didn't believe it, so I asked my mother about it. And my mother said, "That's right, that's right. About two weeks later, we took you to the church. Somebody took you off my arm and held you. So it must have been George Dale. White man, anyway." So he's the one that gave me this name, Angela.

When I was born my mother must have had a nurse, but she didn't tell me who was with her. I told you they partitioned that tent frame off—my dad wouldn't have been in the same room. Somebody must have been with her, but she didn't tell me who was her nurse.[24]

You've got to give kids a name as soon as they're born. Otherwise they get lost—their spirit gets lost—that's what they claim. I've got two names: Stóow for my grandmother—my mother's stepmother—and Ch'óonehte' Má. My mother gave me a little dog: Ch'óonehte', they call it—that's how I got that name, Ch'óonehte' Má, "mother of Ch'óonehte'." That Ch'óonehte' means "deadfall" tree: "Deadfall Mother," they say. And Stóow, my grandmother, had the same name—she had a dog named Ch'óonehte', too.

Some women have two Indian names. They get one when they're a baby, and another one when they make a potlatch for her brother. When you give a child a name, you can only use a name of someone related to you. Every nation [clan] has its own names, and you have to use the right name. Sometimes a baby is given the wrong name, and that causes fights.

My mother had lots of babies: four died before Johnny, including those two twins. Let's see . . . she had my oldest brother Willie. Then she had three girls—all buried at Dyea. Then she lost one at Dasgwaanga Áayi—Squanga Lake—that's after they came back, that's after Johnny. . . . Johnny was born 1898, then one died at Dasgwaanga. They started burying people before that, I guess; they brought her back where the graveyard is at Tagish, anyway. Then me, I'm the next girl to this one they brought back from *Dasgwaanga*. Then I had another sister—Dora—we lost her 1912, her. Then my brother David was born 1905 or '06. And Pete was 1908 . . . I remember I was in school then, and one afternoon my aunt Mrs. Austin came. She got us out of school for the weekend, and she told me, "You've got a new brother. You got another brother." Here it was Peter. I was really happy to see that baby anyway!

Then six years after Peter, she had another baby, a girl—she lost that one, too, when she was four months old. I've got a picture of that baby, too. And then no babies after that until six years after, my sister Dora, the one that's living. Her first name is Alice and her second name is Dora. But I missed my sister—the one next to me that died in 1912—I missed her so much I started calling the new baby Dora. Pretty soon *everyone* started calling her Dora. That's her second name: Alice Dora is the way she was baptized.

I guess my mother took it hard to lose those babies—she must have taken it hard, but what can they do? Nothing! She never talked about it, not in front of me. She just told me about it.

But I remember when my sister Dora died—the first Dora—*Kaneeg-weik*. My mother used to cry every now and then, summertime. And I missed my sister so much I used to cry myself. I used to wander off some afternoon when I see two girls playing together, dolls and stuff like that, and me I've got nobody to play with. I used to cry quietly to myself. When I came home, though, it used to be nobody knew when I was crying . . . Boy, when I found out my mother was going to have a baby, I used to pray, "Let it be a girl, let it be a girl." And here she happened to be a girl! But I didn't play dolls with her anymore! I played babies with her!

In my mother's time, Indian way they say, if they put wolf droppings around your waist when you become woman, then you won't get babies. But some people get babies just the same—they say they did that to *Nadagáat'*, but she had babies just the same. They did that because her mother used to have a hard time. They also throw a puppy down your dress so you could have your babies quick like nothing—I remember my auntie, my father's sister, did that for me. My mother's dog had puppies, and when those puppies were first born—their eyes closed yet—she called me and my sister and she threw those puppies through our dress down to the bottom. That's so I wouldn't have hard time when my babies started to come. Year 1910 she did that.[25]

They used to nurse babies all the time. Then, after a while they gave them rabbit's brain or gopher brain to eat—anything soft. They boil it and soften it and feed the babies. They begin that even younger than one year old—until the next baby.

When a baby is born, he sleeps with his mother and father until the next one. My mother sure used to get surprised when she sees baby sleeping alone in a crib. She said, "*Tlaagóo!* Surprise!" Claps her hands like that. "Is that what they do? Nowadays people let their babies sleep alone? My days it never was like that. People always sleep with their babies!"

My mother used to tell me that my aunt used to tease me after the first Dora was born. "Did you get kicked out? Did your sister kick you out?" And I was supposed to make a sad face and say, "Yes!"

They used to teach kids to behave themselves. Girls—they had little jobs to do, too—they try to teach them to sew. I don't know how old I was when my mother told me to make moccasins, told me to sew my own moccasins. She gave me a new pair of moccasins and told me to sew it, told me how to start it. And here I started gathering it. I guess I gathered too much, or not enough, and here my moccasin was just crooked, like that. And I showed it to my mother. "Look! It looks funny!" I told her. One side had hardly any gathering. She told me to undo it, then start all over. Then finally, I got it right. That's when I was eight or nine years old.

I don't remember ever getting spanked. Of course, my mother gets after me, gets mad at me once in a while. But my father *never* did.

I know what I know because my mother taught me—I was alone with her, don't know how long. I was ten years old that time my sister Dora died—she was eight years old. When we're in the bush, well, I'm alone with my mother. Sometimes I could hear them talking—I listened to what they're talking about; I always know it. After company goes, I asked her questions. That's how come she told me all that.

They spoke Tagish language all the time. Us kids, we talk Tlingit—don't know how come. Mom and Dad spoke Tagish lots of times, to each other, and my mother said when I was really small I used to talk like that, too. But as soon as we got a little older—four or five years old—we started talking Tlingit. Our cousins—David and Willie and Sophie and Isabel Hammond—they're Tlingit: they don't talk Tagish language. Every once in a while they would come up to Carcross and we got all mixed up with them, and we talked Tlingit. In the first place, we are Tlingit, you see: our ancestors got married into Tagish.

They used to teach us with stories: they taught us what is good, what is bad, things like that. I remember they always told us this story: There's supposed to be an old lady—or an old man—sitting at the water hole. And you tell kids, "Go and knock the old lady down, or the old man down." Early in the morning, they give you a bucket, and if you knock that one over, well, then, that's your money, your future. But there's no old lady or old man there, of course. Those kids go every morning to get water, look for it. It's never there. Gee, I sure laugh. "I run down to the water, never see an old lady," they say.

Well, it's supposed to be like that, you see; knock that old lady down and your money comes in easy. If you're lazy, then your money is lazy, too; you won't get it. That's why lazy people don't have money.

The old people thought the earth was all flat—my father used to argue with my brother about it. My brother used to tell him: "No! The earth is round. It's like a ball."

"Nah!" my father said, "it can't be. Those two ladies down below are supposed to be watching the world. They're the ones looking after the world. If it's round, going round, how come the water stays one place all the time? Shouldn't the water leak out some way?"

My brother said, "You fill a bucket of water and make it go round. See if it comes out!" He won't believe it—they argue with each other. My brother put water in a bucket, made it go round, and found it never comes out. "That's the way it is," he tells him.

When I was a kid, we traveled lots. I went to Chooutla school twice before I stayed there for good. Even then, we didn't stay there for very long, because my father took us out of school when I was ten. That was because my sister died there, so my father blamed the school because they didn't get help soon enough. He took me and Johnny out of school—Johnny was in the fourth grade then, and I was in the first. I was just going to pass that spring! After that, my father never allowed me to have pencil and paper. He thought I would write to boys, I guess.

But I learned reading from books. I used to babysit Lilly Henderson, and she had a storybook. I used to just study and practice the words—the first word I learned myself was "SUPERINTENDENT." Here I just spelled it out, spelled it out, and finally I figured out what it meant! So I can read even big words. But I don't write.

I must be seven years old when we went to school first. I remember we used to go just to morning class—that's the time we only went to school four hours a day. Before grade 4, you go to school in the morning; after grade 4, you go to school in the afternoon. There was me, and there was Daisy (Smith), and one boy Tony—Ginny Thomas's son—used to go to school in the morning. We learned some little writing, some reading. I don't know that part of it much. All I know is we used to play in the yard in the afternoon, the three of us. The rest of the time, we packed wood, packed water, sewed patches, darned socks—things like that.

The school used to be in Bishop Bompas's house: they used half the

house for classroom. Then, year 1911, that's the time they started building that school, Chooutla school, and they finished that fall.

When they were building it, we went there for a picnic one time. They were working there, and we went down to the river—digging bear roots.[26] And one girl called, "Oh, Dora fell in!" I started looking to see what happened—and here they were fooling me! And me, I missed a step and then I was the one that fell in. The kids grabbed me and pulled me out, and they said, "What did you see when you fell in the river?"

"Well, I saw the heavens open." How quick I think! "I saw the heavens open but they pushed me back. You pulled me out, I guess!" They laughed, those kids, thought it was lots of fun. They knew I was joking, I guess, that's all.

In the falltime, when the school opened, we went over in October. When we first went over to that Chooutla school, all those kids got off the cars, horse teams—we all started running around the Chooutla school first. Oh, boy, lots of fun! We thought it was a good place we're going to stay. But that's the time we found out we couldn't even talk even to our brothers! We got punished if we did. And we weren't supposed to talk Indian, Tlingit. There were three of us: my cousin Sophie and my sister Dora and me. Daisy [Jim] she never went back to school again; one year was good enough for her! She never went back. She told them about the school, I guess, and her father and mother didn't want to take her back anyway. Anyway, this was about year 1911.

I just went to second reader—I came out in May. That's when I remember my daddy was building a house, and they were putting a roof on it. Daisy and I were down there—and we climbed up that house and lay on top of the roof, and we were singing songs up there. That's the time Tagish Jim [Daisy's father] and my daddy went to West Arm, Millhaven, hunting, falltime, mid-October.

The earliest time I'm talking about is 1910—I can't remember when I was much younger. I remember we were staying across Ten Mile on that island—they used to call that island "Tagish John Island," and later they started to call it "Old Scotty Island"—it's right straight across Ten Mile. I remember that time—that's year 1910. I remember my father was fishing and we were staying on that island. I remember we used to play getting married. I don't know how in the world we ever thought of that! We made mud-pie wedding cake—how in the world I knew those things I'll never know!

Brother David was there . . . brother Peter was walking around by then . . . my auntie Mrs. Austin's two boys were there—Pete and Edward.

We were fishing for my aunt Mrs. Austin's husband—Arthur was his name, but they used to call him "Shorty." And I remember we got a visitor—my father's nephew—my father's sister's son and his wife. They were coming back from Marsh Lake. They came—they landed. Well, I guess they knew that my father was living there and they wanted to see him.

We were staying at Scotty Island—across from Ten Mile. I was just a little girl—I must have been smart . . . well, I heard my mother talking and I remember her asking, "How is Mrs. Tagish Jim?"

"She's okay."

And I remember my mother asking, "She never get her baby yet?"

And she [Mrs. Bill Bone] said, "Yes, she never get her baby yet. She's just about falling over backwards now, bent backwards." I didn't even know what they were talking about. How could she be bent backwards and never get her baby yet? I used to wonder about it . . . After a while, I found out, of course; when I got grown up, I knew.

6 ✳ Stories from Childhood

"They used to teach us with stories
They teach us what is good, what is bad, things like that . . .
Those days they told stories mouth to mouth.
That's how they educate people."

✳ How People Got Flint[27]

Bear was the only one that had flint one time.
There was no flint, they say.
People were having a hard time—sometimes fire would go out, you
   know.
Mice are the ones that really got it.
They say Bear tied it under his tail where he had long hair under there.
So one time, mice tried to get fur from him.

"What are you doing?"

"My kids all froze up on me," Mouse said.
"I want some of your fur."

Well, get it from under my tail. There's lots."

So he did. In the meantime, he chewed that flint off.
The bear noticed it right away, but Mouse threw it to the animals.

First, Fox ran with it.
Oh, he crossed two valleys and here Bear couldn't catch him.
Finally, Bear gave up.
Fox threw it down to a big rock and here that flint broke up.
He threw the pieces around, and said,
"Go all over the world.
People need you.
Make lots of flint for people."

And it did fly all over the world.

Oh, Fox waited to see if Bear would come.
No, he never came.

73

So Fox started to backtrack.
Here he came to a little lake and he got dry rhubarb—
Hollow in the middle.
Then he went down to the lake and shoved that rhubarb stick in the
     lake
And it came up.

"I wish that when people are dead, they come back like this," Fox said.

But that Bear was sleeping pretty close to him, and he heard it.
Here he picked up a rock and threw it in the water.

"I wish that when people die they would be like that.
Let them die like a stone," Bear said.

He was mad.

"Oh, Grandpa, I didn't know you were there.
I guess you're right."

If he didn't do that, I guess people would come back.
That's why when they die, they die for good.

✳ The Old Woman under the World

There are two old ladies down below who look after the world.
One is supposed to be sleeping;
The other one holds up the earth with a pole.
When she shakes it, that's when there's supposed to be an earthquake.
That old lady there with the pole is supposed to be Death.
She always argues—she's the one who always says,
"Let people sleep for good when they go to sleep.
Let them die."

That Death Woman wants to kill people before their time.

But Sleep Woman says,
"No!
Can't you see how my boss put a good pillow for me to sleep on?
And you want me to let her go to sleep for good?
No. No—I won't do that."

Those two old ladies—
One is Sleep Woman, the other is Death Woman.

_____

❋ Moldy Head—*Shaatláax*

One time there was a little boy who lived with his mother and father.
People dry fish—that's how they rustle for food.
If they do that, they don't have much hard time in winter when it's
    hard to rustle for game.

And so this little boy always cried for food in the evening,
Before he goes to bed his mother always gives him dry salmon, head
    part.
Here he tells his mother,
"How come it's always moldy?"
He gets disappointed, throws it away.
"It's moldy."
Anyway, his mother gave him another one again, always.
Every now and then, like that, it's moldy.

But he said something wrong against the fish spirit.

So the next year, they go to the same place—
That's where they dry fish.
They were there again.
Here, his mother was cutting fish.
And you know how seagulls want fishguts all the time?
Here he set out a snare for that seagull.
Set out a snare to catch him.

Anyway, that toggle wasn't very strong or very big or very heavy.
And seagull started to drag it out.
That little boy started running after it.
He ran in the water to try to catch it.
Pretty soon, he fell in a hole.
He caught it, I guess, but they couldn't save him.

And here right away the fish spirit grabbed him—they saved him.
And when the fish went back to the ocean, they took him.
But for that boy, it seemed like right away he was amongst people.

They got a big boat, and they took him with them down to the fish
country.
They came to a big city, big town—
Oh, lots of people run around, kids playing around.

One time they're playing outside and the little boys see fish eggs.
He starts to eat some.
He doesn't know what those people eat—he never sees them eat
anything.
Here, he starts to eat fish eggs.

Here, someone called out Shaatláax, "Moldy Head."
They call him that because he used to call fish moldy.
"Moldy Head eats someone's poop," they said.
Here it was fish eggs.
Oh, by gosh, right away he gets shamed!
When the kids come home, they tell older people about it:
"Moldy Head eats people's poop."

Next morning, adults tell them,
"Why don't you kids go play around that point, play ball.
While you play, you catch fish.
But when you eat it and when you cook it
Don't let anything fall in the hole, that cooking stick hole, where they
put the stick in to roast fish."

So they make fire and one lady sees fish and clubs it and cooks it for
him.
Now and then when he gets hungry, they do that for him.
In the evening when they come home,
Here that boy never came home until last.

They told him,
"Throw the bone and skin and everything into the water,
But don't let anything fall in the cooking stick hole."
He threw everything in the water except that one eye.
It fell in the cooking stick hole.
They didn't see it—the lost eye.
So when they came home, that boy has got one eye missing.
He came back to life again, and he's missing one eye.

The parents tell him to go back—look in that cooking stick hole,
See if there's anything there.

So they went to the playground,
And sure enough there is fish eye there.
He picked it up and he threw it in the water.
And when he came back, all of a sudden
That boy has got both of his eyes back.[28]

Finally, springtime started to come.
Everybody started to get ready to go up the river again.
That boy stays with those people that adopted him first and they all go
   up the river again.

They come to that same place—"Hee hut, hee hut," they pole upriver.
That's how come they know where to go:
They say when the fish go up the river
Their great-great-grandmother is at the head of the creek.
And that's why they go up to visit the great-great-grandmother, that fish—
They come back to the same place.

Here he sees his human mother—
His mother is cutting fish.
He goes close to his mother.
Just the same, his mother never paid any attention to him—
It was just a fish to her.
I don't know how many times she tried to club that fish
But it always takes off.

So finally, she tells her husband about it.
"How come that one fish always comes to me and just stays right there
   all the time?
But after when I go back to see him, that fish is always gone.
Why is that?"

"I don't know why that is.
Let's try to kill it," he said.
"You know we lost our son last year.
Could be something. Must be something.
Let's try to catch it, okay?"
So they did. Anyway, they got it.

And here she started to cut that fish.
And here that fish had copper around his neck
Just like the one that boy used to wear all the time.
And that's the one when that lady started to cut his head off,

She couldn't cut the head off.
So she looked at it good.
Here she saw this copper ring on his head.
So she told her husband right away,
"Look at that. What's this here?"

And her husband said,
"Well, you know, our son used to wear a copper ring all the time
    around his neck."
Yes, they remembered that.

So they washed it good.

And then they took it home.
There's an Indian doctor there, too.
And the Indian doctor said,
"Put it in a nice clean white skin."
Old people used to have lots of that.
They put it in a nice clean skin,
Covered it with down feathers.

Then they tie it way up to where the smoke goes up,
Smokehole.
That Indian doctor told them to go fast for eight days.

So people fasted for eight days.
That Indian doctor said,
"If you see feathers blow up,
Then you take it down quick."

So they put the body up there,
Fasted for eight days.
That Indian doctor sang all the time.
They were singing, too, I guess—
Got to help the doctor sing.

Finally, on the eighth day, here they see the feathers blow up.
They take it down quick.
Here that little boy comes to life again, in human's body.
They brought him back to life.

That's how they know about fish.
That's why kids are told not to insult fish.
And kids are not to play with seagull because that happened.

7 ✳ Childhood Travels, 1912–1915

After our daddy took us out of school, we traveled around all the time. When I got back home, we went around in the bush with our family. The first year, we stayed at Black Lake and Millhaven Bay—that's the winter of 1912. My father used to go farther away to trap, but by now he was getting older, and also there's us kids to think about. Johnny's always with my father that time, helping him. Me, I learned to make skin, set rabbit snares then. Mother's a great hunter—put up gophers, rabbits. Mostly women trapped; men get big animals like moose, caribou.

This is 1912 I'm talking about, when we went up to Black Lake—*T'ooch' Áayi*. We traveled around the shore, hunting for moose. From what I remember, we stayed under that gray mountain—*Taaghahi*—until Christmas, and then we moved to Millhaven. And from Millhaven, we went up to Black Lake. Then, almost at the end of March, we started coming back—back to Carcross or Tagish. That summer we didn't go to Marsh Lake.

That's the time my daddy and mother almost lost each other! Here one time my mother went through the shortcut and my daddy went round the point. That's where halfway down he looked back and couldn't see my mother. So he went back, and when he was on the other side he couldn't see her either. He hollered and hollered, and my mother finally answered. When he found her, that's the time my father just burst out crying.

When they got home in the evening, my mother said, "Why were you crying?"

"Well," he said, "I think about how I wish all the dead people would come back again like that. I never thought you were living—I thought that you were drowned. And when I saw you, I couldn't help but cry. I think about how I wish all the dead people could come back. That's what I think. That's why I started crying."

And then they asked my brother, Johnny, "What would you do if we drowned?"

And Johnny said, "First thing I would do if you fellows didn't come back is take my sister and my brothers back to Carcross and put them in [residential] school." And here he was only fourteen!

And my father said to him, "That's a good idea. It's okay. It's good. You're smart all right."

79

"And then I would come back and look for you fellows then. I'd get a helper, too," he said.

That's the time Johnny he got a hundred grouse . . . I forget how many it's supposed to be—maybe seventy-five. And here it was a dollar a grouse! Mrs. Watson bought all that grouse for the school. And Johnny got all our Christmas outfit with that.

That's the year Johnny made Christmas, 1912. My dad and mother told him what groceries to get, and then he bought Christmas presents. He got a little doll for me because Mr. Watson used to have toys, and he got some things for the boys—I don't remember what. And he got a pair of stockings for my mother. Me, too, he got a pair of stockings. And for my father he got big German socks and tobacco—chewing tobacco. My mother doesn't smoke, so she didn't bother about smoke or anything.

Then he hung that bedsheet over the ridgepole, and he told us kids to go on the other side; and on his side he started hanging up our stockings: "Make sure your stockings are clean," he said. He told us before, so we washed our socks and they were dry by the time we're supposed to hang them up. We watched him through that curtain he put up. It was a bedsheet he put up, and we could see his shadow right through it!—We laughed at him! Then after a while, we got to go to bed. Well, they blew out the light. Here, early in the morning, we wake up quick. "Santa Claus been here last night!" And here we were watching him all the time!

We had learned about Christmas in school—Johnny bought a chicken or something, and he told me, "If you make a cake we could have Christmas dinner." Well, I didn't know how to make a cake! All I could think of was molasses.

"We could make molasses cake," I told him.

And he said, "That sounds good: you bake the cake and I'll cook the dinner." Well, we cooked that dinner together. That was the first time we made Christmas!

The first time we stayed at Marsh Lake was year 1913. We had our cousins there—Johnny played with Frank Slim—I played with Annie Slim—Peter played with Susie Slim. Here one time Peter and Susie stole our clothes while we were swimming and we sat in the water all afternoon because we've got no clothes! Nobody around. It's far off to camp, too. Those kids went home! Annie's father was the one that reminded them. "Where's your sisters? I cooked some fish heads. It's going to get cold! Call them now!" Here we saw Peter and Susie sneaking down the hill! "As soon as we get hold of you . . . !" we hollered. When we came home, they asked us where we've been, but we weren't allowed to swim, so we didn't tell them.

They let Sophie (Hammond) stay with us because our great aunt, Mrs. Dyea John—her grandma—was going to go to Skagway. Sophie used to tell me after we got friendly her mother used to say to her, "You're going to see your sister, *nishemb'e'e*."[29] "And I used to be curious to see you," she told me. Sophie was with us that time, 1913. That fall, after salmon were dry, we went up the lake. We went on the mountain, back of Judas Creek. We killed some moose, dried some moose. Whitehorse Billy and my brother Johnny and Frank Slim went to Whitehorse to sell meat. Us, we went across to *Kooshdaa Xágu*, "otter beach." We landed there, and we came to a mountain on the other side. Down at that sharp-pointed mountain is where we dried meat—my father killed four or five moose there.

Well, there were *lots* of families! There was our family and Whitehorse Billy's family—old Mrs. Sheldon was with Mrs. Whitehorse Billy because her husband went down the river, working on the telegraph line. That's how he always spent the summer while Mrs. Whitehorse Billy dried meat, dried meat. She's got dogs of her own—when anybody takes dry meat ahead, they take her dog, too. People used to help each other, those days—not like now. When they take meat ahead, they pack it ahead in dog packs. That's how we always get meat down the lake—and we bring it back to Tagish.

We came back to Carcross, 1913, falltime. When we got back, my aunt—my father's sister, Mrs. *Gunaaták'*—was sick. That's why we didn't go anyplace, just spent the winter in Carcross. Nineteen thirteen falltime she came to stay with us; that New Year's Eve, she died.

Then my mother got sick again—she always used to catch cold in her eyes. That's the time I was supposed to be cooking supper: I cut up the meat and put it in the pot, and I started peeling potatoes. And I heard my father say, "Quick! Hurry up. The meat is almost done and you're fooling around with potatoes yet!" And here I put the potatoes in, skins and all! They're washed, though. And my brother Johnny and the boys—David, Pete, Edward, and Jimmy Scotty—called me "dirty cook" because I cooked potatoes with skins on. They gave all us girls nicknames, and that was mine.[30]

Then in springtime, 1914, we went to Whitehorse after my aunt died—in March or April we went to Whitehorse. We stayed in Whitehorse almost two years, till 1915. We hunted there—my brother hunted foxes and stuff like that.

That's when I used to sew undershirts. My mother used to get a big pile of calico—they call it—flannelette. She cut out undershirts and underpants for the boys, and I sewed them by hand all the time. Finally, I got really used to sewing—that's how come my father bought me a sewing machine. It's still in the family yet, still in Carcross. Year 1914 he got that sewing machine for me—I don't know how much he paid for it.

[This is how he bought it:] My father, and Big Salmon Jim, Tagish Jim, and John Joe, went down the river. Their nephew got killed at Little Salmon or Big Salmon and they wanted to see about it. On the way down, they say, [they saw] a black fox take its little ones to water. So they landed! They chased the young foxes up on top of the mud bluffs and my father and those men caught the young foxes—and the mother, too, I suppose. They caught them. [Those foxes] stuck their heads through the mud bluff crack, and they caught them by the back of the neck and they threw them in a gunnysack. Just when they got back to the boat, here the steamer *Whitehorse* was coming up the river! They stopped the steamer, and John Joe went back to Whitehorse with it: he sold those black fox pups, their mother, all, and then John Joe divided that money four ways. That's the time my father bought a sewing machine for me. Then he bought a gun for my brother Johnny out of that fox money. This was year 1914, sometime in July or August.

That's the time we went to Marsh Lake: we stayed with my uncle Slim Jim there. Slim Jim had a great big house—it's got a bedroom, everything. They used to stay in the bedroom, and we'd stay in the front room—great big house. People used to live together, those days, no trouble, nothing! . . . kids mixed up together. Slim Jim built that house himself. That springtime—May or something—we went downriver—down to Steamboat Bend, they call it, down below Whitehorse. And Taylor and Drury gave Big Jim the wood contract for their boat, *Kluane*, the steamer boat. It took all their freight down the river, down to their stores and up to Teslin.

I remember my father and Big Jim were cutting wood—my father made a little wagon out of a tree. We hauled wood, us kids, me and my brother David. Brother Johnny helped them to cut wood, and we would run back and forth from where he's cutting wood, down to that riverbank. That's where they would pile the wood when they were finished—I don't know how many cords they put up. When we came back to Whitehorse, that's the time my father and Big Salmon Jim and Slim Jim and John Joe went down the river.

That's when they sent me to my uncle Patsy Henderson.[31] He wanted somebody to babysit for them, so they sent me back to Carcross and I babysat [his daughters] Irene and Lily. Lily was a year old then—I must

have been twelve, that year, 1914. They sent me back to Carcross on the
train—Uncle Patsy paid my fare; and when I got to Carcross, I got on the Galena—that's the second time I went on the boat Galena—and they let me off at Ten Mile, Tsuxx'aayí—that "moose corral point." They put out what they call the "gangplank," and I got off at Ten Mile.

Well, they [Patsy Henderson and his wife] had fox ranch at New Ten Mile—they used to call that place. They had foxes—they had lynx—marten. I looked after those kids while they ran their nets, ran their gopher traps. They had to rustle for their fox food—they got fish and gophers for their foxes. So I babysat for Mrs. Patsy while she ran her nets and fed the foxes and stuff like that.

Then, after a while, I came to Tagish with my great-aunt, Annie Joe. I went to Tagish with them and stayed with Daisy Smith's father and mother for a week or so—two weeks—I guess. Tagish Jim killed black foxes, too. He caught black foxes and he sold them to Sam Chambers, the postmaster. He caught eight black foxes, and when he got the money for them, he bought a gas boat! That boat used to be called Caribou—it's got its name written on it. They went to town to get that boat, and here Sam Smith came back with him—Sam Smith was his engineer—he started the boat. "Coal-oil boat," Tagish Jim used to call it . . . Tagish Jim had the first coal-oil boat, but now they call them "gas boats."

So they were going to take me in that boat to Marsh Lake, to my father. And when we got there . . . tuk, tuk, tuk . . . boy, that was something great! Here, when we got to Marsh Lake, my uncle Slim Jim was already there. We were ahead of my father; he was still in Whitehorse. Tagish Jim didn't want to leave me, but I stayed anyway. "Him, too, he's my uncle, too. Slim Jim is my uncle, too." So I stayed. They didn't want me to, but just the same I stayed.

"What's your father going to think if I just let you go anyplace? Your father is going to get mad if I let you go."

"I want to stay and wait for my father." So I stayed at Marsh Lake, and two days later, my father came up.

First, my brother Johnny walked to Marsh Lake with dogs and said my father and mother were coming behind up the river with the boat they had bought in Whitehorse, a lumber boat. There were shipyard people making lumber there—one man built and sold boats to people going down the river on their own, so my father bought a boat and came to Marsh Lake with it. We went up the river, up the McClintock River to fishcamp. I knew my cousin Annie Slim—I remember I just felt like I was home while I was there!

We traveled back to Whitehorse that fall with Slim Jim and the rest.

After January, we moved up to Fish Lake³² where my brother was trapping with Whitehorse Billy. A little ways above Fish Lake there's another lake there—my brother called it "Muskrat Lake"—gee, lots of muskrats. My aunt Mrs. Whitehorse Billy trapped rats there all winter. We stayed around Whitehorse that winter again.

In Whitehorse, above the town is that Moccasin Flats or Whiskey Flats or whatever they call it. There were lots of people there. Susie Fred's mother and father were living there—and so we spent the winter there with them. My brother said it was too far to travel from Whitehorse to his trapping place, so we all went up there to Fish Lake and pitched tents. And after fox season closed, that's the time we went back down to Whitehorse. There was nothing to stay up there for. They were hunting foxes above Fish Lake, don't know how many miles.

I helped my mom get water and stuff like that, and if Daddy's out, us kids got wood. The wood was always there, though, but we would pack [carry] it in—we always packed in the whole thing. Then we played getting wood; we would saw it with a little saw . . . I was going on to thirteen—I was thirteen already, I guess.

One time I was walking around—there was a little creek there and great big willows. I just broke them out, some of them—I didn't have an ax. I took a sleigh, too, I guess—it's hard to remember now—got dry willows for wood, just breaking them out. Boy, I had the sleigh loaded! And one little boy—my aunt Mrs. Whitehorse Billy was looking after that boy—here he came to me and said, "Why did you get lost? Everybody's looking for you!"

"What for?" I say.

"Well, they thought you got lost." Anyway, he helped me push the sleigh—here my sleigh was just loaded with willow, with dry willows, some great big ones. I broke lots out, too, and then my brothers went there with me and got another load—that much willow I broke down! It's hard to get wood there, high in the mountains, way up.

Sometimes I would hunt just for fun, I guess. Trap gophers with a snare. I didn't really have to rustle for anything—my brother Johnny already went with my father. That's the year he killed a moose—oh, he had already killed moose when he was eleven years old, up at Little Atlin, 1908. In those days my father and brothers sold meat to the school to earn some money.

All women worked on skins, those days: women trapped around while men hunted. Then they made fur—when a woman fixes skin, then it be-longs to her and she can trade it. Most women don't hunt big animals—

my mother did, though. One year when she was still well she got fourteen caribou!

Women with lots of children stay at fishcamp instead of traveling. They rustle for food there—net fish, set snares, make dry meat. Sometimes a visitor kills a moose for them—they are never left without anything: if a newly married woman goes with her husband, she fixes skins along the way. Me, I never hunted much, don't know why—not interested, I guess. But my sister Dora, gee, she kills just about anything—mountain goat, caribou, wolf—I don't know if she ever killed bear or wolf. My daughter Mabel was a good hunter, too.

My mother was a good rustler—she's always out with my father. We stayed in Carcross one time—I forgot what year. We got left way out down the mouth of the Carcross River. She rose early in the morning and came back while I was still sleeping yet, me. 'Specially, I used to be sleepyhead. She already came back and cooked breakfast. That's the time she started hollering for us to get up. And then after we had breakfast, she goes to set rabbit snares—she's got rabbit snares she had to run. One time I was ahead of her, and I saw rabbit hanging up there [on a snare]. "Look, Mamma, somebody hangs rabbit for you," I tell her.

"Yeah? Who do you think hung rabbit for me?" That was her snare.

Nineteen fifteen, we finally came back to Carcross—springtime, in May or June. That's the time I finally became a woman in May, this time of year.

8 ✳ Stories and Place Names

✳ Fox Helper

This man was Wolf [moiety].
People always put up meat in summertime—
They cached it up high, made a good cache.
Then they went back down the lake in falltime to get fish.

After they finished fishing at the head of Tagish River—
They call that *Taagish Tóo'e'* in Tagish, *Taagish Héeni* in Tlingit—
Right up here, they floated down in a boat.
They had a little torch made of kindling.
They tied it to a big stick—that's the way they made light.
They can see down to the bottom of the water.
They had a spear; they fished with it.

After they finished fishing, they went up on the mountain to get their
   winter food.
They went up to their cache.

They have two little girls.
They got up there, made camp—*Shaashuhídi*, they call it, Tlingit
   way—Mountain House.
They've got a camp up there already.
They call that place *Núsтséhé Dzéłe'* in Tagish language,
Naasgas'éi Shaayí in Tlingit.
That means "fox mountain," because that's where fox came to them.

Every year they go up there because they've got a house,
It's open on both sides, but it's a house.
If they come year after year to one place,
That's where they put the house.
Both sides are open, so they can come in from both sides.

In the evening they made a fire
And they told those two little girls to stay home.

"Don't leave the camp.
We're going to get to the cache—
We're going to bring our meat back."

Here, when they came to the cache, something had stolen their cache!
Everything is gone!
Hardly anything there—just a few little things.

So they came back.
They told those two little girls there is nothing there—
No gophers, no groundhogs.
That's the head of the river, up this lake toward that big mountain.

Those little girls said, "Somebody came to visit us.
He's got a foxtail tied on the back of his hat—nice man."

"What did he say?"

"He said he's going to come back later on
When our father and mother are here."

So they don't know who is that.
They're ready, though—here he comes.
Nice red jacket—nice red foxtail hanging behind his hat.

"My brother-in-law," he said.
He happened to be Crow and he's speaking to his Wolf.
"From here, you go.
You get down the lake from here.
You go to that *K'aa' Deitl'óoní*—that means "where arrows are tied up
     in a bundle."
That's Tagish language: Tlingit is *Chooneit Wusi.axu Yé*.
Now they call it "Frying Pan Island" because it's sometimes joined to
     the shore.
It's across from Ten Mile, *Tsuxx'aayí*.
"Put bait in the water.
From here on, you go . . ."

They call that mountain behind that place *K'aa' Deitl'óoní Dzéle'*;
Chooneit Shaayí, Tlingit way.

He's the one, Fox, gave Indian names to all those points on Tagish
     Lake.
They still use them, Indian way.

It was Wolverine stole their cache—
That's how come they have no grub.
But Fox gave them luck.

"From here you go:
You go to *K'aa' Deitl'óoní* and put hook in the water.
Then you're going to catch fish.
From there, you go up the lake—next place, same thing.
Pretty soon it's going to be springtime—you'll pull through.
Me, I give up."

That man camped with them—camped across the fire.
Here, next morning, there's just hair stuck to the snow,
So they know it's red Fox.
And he had a red foxtail—that was his own tail.
It looked like he had a red tail tied to his hat.
Early in the morning, he's gone.

✴ Wolf Story

This story happened here, at this head of Tagish Lake someplace.

Some people didn't put up much food.
They started to have a hard time in winter.
There were no rabbits in the country—hardly any grouse either.

The man hunts every day—
Keeps the family going somehow.
They've got a little bit of grub, but they're stingy with it.
They eat just a little bit at a time.
He hunts, hunts, hunts, but he kills nothing.
Finally, he hunts up this way, toward Carcross there, someplace,
    behind that big white rock.
Up toward Ten Mile, *Tsuxx'aayí.*

There's a big rock there on the beach.
That's where this story happened.
Ḵaax̱ Teiyí—"sawbill duck rock," they call it in Tlingit,
Tsós Tsei'e' in Tagish language.
There's another story that that rock was once a man who married a
    woman:

There was some trouble in their marriage—
He moved away and became this rock.
Anyway, this is where it happened.

Back of that Ḵaax̱ Teiyí is a big meadow—open place there.
Here, he came by snowshoe track, on round-headed snowshoes.

So he thought, "Gee, could be somebody is helping me."
That's what he thought.
Sure enough, not far, it started to get dark.
Here's a big campfire in front of him.

Soon that man told him to come in,
And here across the fire—he made a camp for him and he camped
     there, by campfire.
In the evening, that's the time he told him:

"I'm Wolf. You're my brother-in-law:
I'm the same people as your wife.
I killed all those caribou for you. You can have it.
And I give you my snowshoes, too."

That's how come these people have those round-headed snowshoes—
That's where they got it.
"I'll give you my snowshoes, too.
From now on, your luck is going to change.
You're going to have good luck.
But look after my snowshoes good!"
And he gave him his bow and arrow.
"I'll give you everything that I use to keep myself going."

It's just like his gun, I guess.
None of these people had bow and arrow—
It's just like his gun.
None of these people had guns.
Before this, they killed animals by snares.

That's how they got bow and arrow from Wolf
And how they got snowshoes.
That's how it started.
Of course, they had those sharp-pointed snowshoes before.
That's the only kind they had then.

"Tomorrow, you go home—take a load home.
I'm going to leave you in the morning and you can have all that meat."

Early in the morning, that man woke up, got up,
And here there was no fireplace there.
It was just like he had been seeing things.
His camp was the same
But where his brother-in-law slept was just like a wolf slept there
Right in the snow.

Anyway, he got up, made fire, got warmer,
And he went over to where those dead caribou were supposed to be.
He fixed them up and took them home.
And he thought to himself,
"Maybe Wolf camped up this way."

So he just took enough for two or three days.
They've got to take enough to get their strength back.

He buried that meat,
Put it all in one pile and buried it so it would be safe.
He came back to camp,
And he told his wife everything.
They stayed there two or three days
And then finally they went there.
And here they had enough meat to last to springtime.

From now on his luck changed.
He starts to kill moose, started to kill game.
At the same time, he had bow and arrow and snowshoes to help him.

9 ✳ Potlatches

Crow people had potlatches at Beaver House, and Wolf people had potlatches at Killer Whale House. When they had potlatches in the fall, they had people from both these houses. They used to have two nations: if Wolf people make potlatch, they [guests] all have to be Crow—Laberge Crow, Dyea Crow, Crows from everyplace. And if Crow people make potlatch, it's got to be Wolf people—*Kaagwaantaan* from coast and *Dakl'aweidí* from here.

They had two potlatches when I was a kid—one was 1912, the other was 1914. I was at both of them. That 1912 one was in Carcross; the other one was in Whitehorse, though—Wolf people again. They were both [given by] Wolf people. From there on, they never had potlatches, no big potlatches anymore. They had tea all right after the funeral, and something after they put up the fence, too, but that's not the same thing.

In 1912 Wolf people put a stone on Dawson Charlie and on his sister, *Gooch Tláa.* And [they also put a stone] on John Bone's wife and on Tagish Jim's brother at Marsh Lake. That one—Marsh Lake John, they call him—his name is *Gooch Ooxú,* Indian way. Tagish Jim made a spirit house at Marsh Lake for his brother Marsh Lake John in 1910: then he made the potlatch in Carcross in 1912. All three were *Dakl'aweidí,* so *Dakl'aweidí* people made this potlatch to pay back *Deisheetaan.* That's the time they got people from Champagne, Laberge, Whitehorse, all. They had to go get the Crow people. Tagish Jim and Dawson Johnny went to Champagne, invited all the people.

They say when you invite somebody, you're supposed to sing: "I'm coming to get you." You've got to name the person who you want. Then you go around to the next village, [and say] just the same: "I'm coming for you."

And after they finished [inviting people], they started back walking. They came all the way to Carcross, and people asked Tagish Jim, "How soon are people going to come?" And I guess he told them. I can't remember all that—I was only a kid, too, myself.

Pretty soon the potlatch people came. We heard guns shooting across. On this side Patsy [Henderson] and Tagish Jim and all of them were running around, getting guns. They started shooting, too. That's to answer, that they are shooting. They were shooting on this side, too [north side of Nares Lakes]; and here they went right up to the sand cut here. And finally, they walked across the bridge and down to the Indian village.

Then they made a fire at Dawson Charlie's house. That's where they were going to make the potlatch, at Dawson Charlie's house, Wolf House[33]—that's where all the potlatch people stayed, in Dawson Charlie's house. And here I was running around! They took that picture in front of Skookum Jim's house: people from Champagne, they had to dance; Carcross people, they danced to welcome the people. They danced—they made speeches—I can't remember the speeches, though, I'm only a child, me, too . . . I had a little button blanket that time—my mother put it on me.[34]

That's how they welcomed the people. It was a good life, too: people used to enjoy it. I don't know how many days they stayed. Anyway, they opened that Dawson Charlie's house for visitors. There's a big heater stove there, and a cook stove there. And then whoever gives the potlatch has to finish getting the wood. They got the wood ready there for them, things like that. I didn't understand much. I just thought there was lots of fun going on. Later on, of course, I knew what it was all about.

Then—I don't know how many days later—they took that stone down to the graveyard and set it up. Crow people are the ones that had to do that: they put up the stone. They put the stone up on Dawson Charlie and put a fence around his sister, *Gooch Tláa*, Mrs. John Bone. Here, they tied ribbons all around it—handkerchiefs and ribbons and ties; they tied ribbons and ties and everything around the fence. Then Crow people had to take them off, whichever ones they like. And here that Paddy Smith, Mrs. Johnny Ned's first husband, he came with the potlatch people as [to represent] Mrs. Ned because she can't come—she's got two kids, Roddy and Elijah. The next time I saw her, two years after, she had another baby. She had three boys when I saw her, 1914.[35]

That's the time people started to go back.

It all stopped after 1915, because . . . well, no more old people, just a new generation, no more old people. The new generation didn't bother about it, I guess, that's all. If anything happens on our side [*Deisheetaan*], though, we always make tea after the funeral. When my mother died, when they put up her fence, they made tea after that.

My mother sang those [potlatch] songs and I learned them. Just when she sings—I listen to her; then I asked her to sing so I could learn them. Brother Johnny can sing, and I can sing, but not brother Pete and not my sister Dora—not so much.

The last *Deisheetaan* potlatch that people gave in Carcross was when they put up Tagish Charlie's stone. They gave names to the ones that are supposed to be the grandchildren: Daisy Smith was named *Kudewugoot,* "go in the den for good," and they named Daisy Mason and Bill Bone's [future] wife, and someone else. You have to name your great-grand-children on your same side.

I was just a child, six or seven. I was just beginning to realize things. When they were naming Daisy, I took it hard. "How come they never named me?" I said.

"It's too close," they told me. "It's got to be Tagish Jim's kids, and Skookum Jim's girl."[36] When they gave Daisy that name, *Kudewugoot,* "go in the den for good," it's because they're not going to make a big potlatch again, because there's no older people. That's right, too.

And I remember when they took down that *Kéet hít*—Killer Whale House—1912 or 1913, falltime. Tagish Jim tore it down after all the Wolf people died. Tagish Jim only, because he was always living here. There were lots more Wolf [people], but the old people were all gone. He tore it down and rebuilt it on *this* [west] side of Tagish Narrows.

And fall 1911, Uncle Billy Atlin tore the Beaver House down. He moved the lumber to the head of the [Tagish] River. They rebuilt it there because he was looking after live foxes [there]. My brother, Johnny Johns, had two live foxes there, too, so he helped him rebuild it.

There were no more potlatches in the Tagish houses then. Everybody moved to Carcross.

10 ✴ A Potlatch Song

When they made that potlatch in 1912 in Carcross, I was ten years old at the time. I heard Mrs. Tagish Jim's mother sing this song— she's Wolf, you see. She's a Wolf woman and this was potlatch for Crow.[37] Another time I heard Mrs. Patsy (Henderson) sing it when her daughter died. See? That's why they could sing it. It's just like a hymn, I guess.

I'll tell you the story of why they made that song.
It's about the girl who raised that worm at Klukwan.
She's *Tukyeidí shóa*—Crow woman.
In the wintertime her uncles—her father's nephews—
Were splitting wood outside.
And here she was watching them, jumping around, playing.
Here when they split that wood a worm fell out of it, a woodworm—
I guess it was frozen—
One of the boys gave it to her.

"Well, I found a son for you"—that's what the uncle said to her.
So she picked it up and she took it in the house
And she thawed it out.
Well, after it got thawed out,
It came back to life.
Here she started to feed it grease with her hands,
Feed it anything, I guess.

She let that worm suck on her breast—
Here it started to grow, started to grow big.

And here she wouldn't come out of her bedroom.
She's always in her bedroom all day long sitting down, never coming out.
And sometimes she sings.
Her mother always hears her singing in there:
Her father is the one that got wise to it.

"What is that?
Why is that she won't come out?"

When she came out, too,
As soon as she finished eating she just went right back into her room.
And here she sings that song:

"My son has got a face . . ."

This is the song she sings for that snake all the time.

And then she's got another song for when they killed him—
That one is the funeral song—they call that one funeral song:
Anybody can use it when they want to.

They made a spear when they found out.
Her mother through the crack . . .
She watched her when she's singing this song.
That's the time she saw it—
They say that worm's face is as big as the moon.

Well, when they found out good what it was, they went to a meeting
    about it.
All her uncles and her aunties and all—[wondering] what they're
    going to do about it.
They're going to kill it or something.
That's how come they made a law.

Her aunties, her uncles, sent for her to make gopher robes.
Here, she went down to her aunties,
Started sewing those gopher skins together—just in one day, she
    finished it up.
She went home.
And here those boys and people weren't quite ready for it.
They made a spear and stuff like that,
And here she came home.

Next time her uncles put marten skins in the water.
That one took a little bit longer than the gopher skins to sew.
But that time, halfway through, when she was sewing those things
    together,
She heard this noise.
Every time they speared the snake they hollered,
"Whoa, whoa."

And that snake makes a noise, too—
Just like nails knocking on each other [claps].

And she knew right away.
She heard it right away.

"Ah, Ah, Ah, *Aҳ Yéet(k')*, my son, my son!"

She just dropped everything and she ran back home—
Here they had already killed that thing.
They say that it was so big that it made a tunnel under the house.
She talks to it and it understands her.
They tell that worm,

"Come on out. Your mother wants you."

That's how come it started coming out.
From the bedroom, it crawled inside, crawled all out.
They started killing it—and they killed it.
And when she came back, that worm was already dead.

And she just cried.

"Burn it!" she said.
"I want you fellows to treat it just like a person,
Like a human being, because it was my son.
I adopted it."

That's why they wrapped it up in a button blanket and they burned it.
That's the time she sang this song.
She made this song while the worm was burning up.

"My son, my son,
I hear the noise."

That's like that *Deisheetaan* story
That's *Tuҟyeidí sháa*—Crow woman, too.
That happened in Angoon;
That's our country.

They say there's little beaver pond
And that's where that little beaver was
And that's where she saved that little beaver.
From there, she raised it.
And that little beaver got big, swimming around there.
And in the meantime he was making tunnels under the city;
Here and there he made a den.

And here when he swam around,
And when he flopped his tail like that
The water just rushed up and down those tunnels.
It did it so many times the ground was getting weak and weaker
And finally, one time, the whole town sunk,
All caved in from those tunnels.

That's why they made this song.
Whoever was saved, he's the one who made this song.
And he said,

   "Who is going to advise
   To stop making a city on a sandy beach?"

People sing this song when they make a potlatch.
It's *Deisheetaan* song, but any nation could use it.
They could say,
"My song," or "my father's people's song."[38]

11 ✳ Becoming a Woman

They put me away when I first got like that. My mother told me, "Don't hide it or it's bad luck. Tell right away." They put me outside, away from camp. You have to wear a bonnet—mine was a fancy flannel blanket. I was going to have broadcloth—they had it already—but they potlatched it away in 1912. So they didn't get another one in time. They could have! They had time! I didn't get that way till 1915. Spring, 1915.

"When you get like that, don't come into camp," they say. So that morning I woke up—something was wrong. So I stayed. They sent someone to look for me—Isabel [Hammond] came. "What's the matter with you?" she asks me. She looks at me. "Are you woman? Come home!" I'm embarrassed—don't say anything! I'm shy.

Isabel went back to camp. Then Grandma [Hammond] came out—she checked me and then she went back to get things ready.[39] Then Mother came. She led me farther away—I was away from camp, but not far enough away, I guess, still too close to camp. She put me under a tree and left me. It takes time for them to get things ready. All that day I didn't eat anything.

Next day they brought me a new five-by-seven[-foot] tent and put it over me. All that day, too, no food. For two days I didn't eat.

The third day, that bonnet is ready. Somebody—I forgot who—packed it out over a stick, carried it to me. My three brothers are supposed to try to shoot at it with bow and arrow—my brothers David and Peter and my cousin Willy—brother Johnny's away that time. That's what they're supposed to do, but I don't know why.

People [women] came to where I'm sitting. They brought the bonnet, put the tent over me. Then they gave me water in a baking-powder cap. Two times they gave it to me—they spilled it on purpose. I'm not sure why they're supposed to do that . . .[40]

I heard kids—then little kids came. They gave me a dish of food—I took one bite and then gave it to the kids. I'm supposed to do that so I won't be stingy with food when I'm older. Also it teaches me not to be hungry—that's why we never ate breakfast yet today. After those first two days, they fed me two times a day, morning and evening.

When you're there, they teach you how to sew. Then they give you all you can to do—the whole town gives you sewing! You can't eat fresh

meat or fish while you are there—they smoke it a little bit and dry it. And
no fresh berries or it makes your menstruation strong [painful] because
berry juice is like blood.

All that time, you have to sit with your knees doubled up—that's "to
hold your family's life": if you stretch your legs, you shorten that life. You
can't peek out from under that blanket—it's a whole blanket, that bonnet. I had a flannel one—it's sure hot! This was springtime, May.

You're not supposed to scratch your head—you're supposed to have a
bone attached around your head, but they didn't do that to me. But they
did tell me not to scratch that time.

Your mother is supposed to help you, but my mother was sick, so my
mother's aunt helped me—Mrs. Dyea John. That's Grandma Hammond.
When that bonnet was on me, she visited me once a day. One of the girls
stayed with me all the time. There were three *Deisheetaan* girls in that
camp—me and my cousins Sophie and Isabel: Isabel brought my food.
Sophie was one year younger and she stayed with me for a while. After a
while, after that period is over, they allow younger brothers to come and
visit.

We had to move camp when I was like that—we moved in June—we
had to move to the head of Tagish Lake. I had to leave that tent over my
head when we moved: I can't see anything! Mother leads me after
everyone else leaves, me last. When we got there, I got out of the boat and
Mother put up the tent for me, away from camp.

After I came out of that tent, they gave that tent away. It sure bothers
me! Mrs. Frank Sidney brought a moose shoulder for Father. "We've got
no tent," they say, "just fly tent. We got no tent to go back with."

And here my father said, "Let's give them that tent." Well, of course, my
mother said okay, so they gave it to them. And here it should have been
for my aunt, Mrs. *Gunaaták'!* It should belong to *eshembe'e',* my father's
sister—things weren't even divided up yet. I stayed in it one month
already, but my tent was still up yet. Gee, I sure was sorry when I found
out! They should give it to Wolf people who are *close:* should be they give
it to Mrs. *Gunaaták'*—my father's sister—or to Aunt Susie—Billy Atlin's
wife, or else to Mrs. Jimmy Scotty. Instead, they gave it to distant Wolf
people.[41]

When they take that bonnet off, you have to learn "outside work." Me,
I was only out for two months because my mother wasn't well. It was too
soon! Mrs. Patsy Henderson was out for one year! They took off my
bonnet after two months—they pulled it off because my mother was sick
again. My brothers were having a hard time. Aunt Susie took it off.[42]
"People don't believe in that nowadays," she says. "Times are going

ahead," she says to my mother. "What foolishness! Why are you keeping her in jail when you're not well. You need help!" She took me back to camp, and right away I began to cook for our family. I still had to eat dry food that time, just till that fall.

In the old days, there would have been a party when I came back, but we had just two families at the camp then. Just my mother, Aunt Susie, and their families. I guess that dinner that night was sort of a party . . . After I came back to camp, they told me and my brother we can't look at each other or talk to each other now.[43] "Why?" my brother said. "You want me to be bad friends with my sister? She's my sister!" I couldn't talk to him until after I married.

Boys have to be trained, too, the first game they kill. People get babiche [made from thin strips of soaked moose or caribou hide], twist it with swan down feathers, and make four bands—two garters for around the leg and two armbands. They use those garters to hold up mukluks, and they use one for each arm. Then a boy is not supposed to be lazy—boys have to get wood and water and things like that. If they're lazy, then they'll be lazy, too, when they grow up. That's why they use down—feathers—so they could be light. I don't know how long they wear that thing. Then at the end when they put it away, they put it away where the wind can shake it all the time, those armbands and those garters. When the wind shakes it like that, it means that a person will not be lazy, not heavy—light, like down feathers. That's their first meat, what they kill first.

It was 1915 when I tanned my first moosehide. Well, I saw people do it—just as soon as you are ten years old your mother makes you sit down and watch people—not like nowadays. First, I cut the hair off with a little sharp knife. Then I fleshed it and scraped it with a sharp bone—tangwat is the name of that bone you use to flesh it. Then I kept fooling around with it.

That fall, I started sewing. They had police barracks and a telegraph office [at Tagish]. Police used to stay there—lineman, too, and here one of those linemen wanted moccasins. That same fall, I tanned it, smoked it—everything—that yearling moose. My brother got the order: "outside moccasins." Here I sewed those moccasins, put on canvas top. That lineman needs them when he goes on the line. Pretty soon that lineman wants mitts. Gee, I made more than twenty dollars that winter! My brother sent for a suit for me. A little blue suit! That's 1915.

We stayed at the head of the river that fall. Then November we moved to Little Atlin. They went way up to Frying Pan Island—K'aa' Deitl'óoní, they call it. My father and mother moved, and I stayed with my auntie,

Mrs. Austin, *Sadusgé:* she wasn't well, so they told me to stay with her and they went without me. Then they stayed at *Kídeeténe',* "where the trail comes out." They didn't come back till springtime.

We went back to Carcross early, because my father's cousin, Skookum Jim, was sick. We went to Carcross in April and we stayed there all spring until he died. [His daughter] Daisy used to call me, daytime, to sit with her father—during the night, she watched him, nursed him. When Skookum Jim got sick, Daisy came back to look after him, 1916.[44] Nighttime, she looks after him; daytime, she asks for me always. She tells me to watch Uncle, give him water—it was just like I was babysitting when I used to sit with him.

After he died, she stayed about one month—then she went back. She wasn't married then. She used to say she'd like to get married into this country. But there was no man [of a Wolf clan]—Jack *Shaakóon* was the only one who was single. "I wouldn't mind staying with him," she said. We told that to Jack *Shaakóon.* "Who wants to marry a white lady anyway?" he said. "She acts too white lady too much." So she went back to Seattle; after that, she got married. She passed her motherhood by the time she got married, though—that's why she never had children.

I saw her grandmother in Haines one time, and she asked about Daisy. "She used to be your people, your sister. She died amongst you people. One of you fellows might as well name one of your kids after her." But we never did, not one of us. We never used anybody's name [from another clan]. We used our own names all the time. *Saayna.aat* was her name.[45] Nobody knows how Daisy died, but her husband brought her back to Carcross. She wanted to be buried beside her father in Carcross.

12 ✶ The Stolen Woman (1)

✶ The Dog Husband[46]

This story happened on the Stikine [River].

A middle-aged man and his wife and daughter camped one place—
That's because they were too old to travel around.
She's quite a young girl, that daughter.

Whenever she went out, a dog sits in the doorway—
They live in a brush camp there—
She jumped over the dog all the time; sometimes kicked him away.

"Get off, you old dog.
Who likes you?"

Finally, they moved someplace—I don't know how far away they
    moved,
But that dog doesn't go with them.
"Go back and get my dog," that father says to the girl.

The girl goes almost close to the camp.
Just near the camp, a pretty young fellow meets her.
"Marry me. Stay with me," he says to her.
"Let's dry meat, then see your mother and father."

They camped the other way, off the road.

The next morning, they go hunting.
They kill moose first time!
Then they moved back to where they killed that moose—
It's hard to pack, so those days people moved their camp to where they
    killed moose.
They started drying moose, do that all the time.

He told her,
"Don't throw your bones away.

Just throw them across there, not far."
Next morning, those bones always disappear.
They kept doing that.

Another time, he went to hunt caribou.
She heard a dog bark, "Bow, wow, wow"—that's how it sounds.
She looked and saw her father's dog.
He had a string around his neck, a string her father made:
That's how he catches animals, makes snares for them.
She finds that out, and she wants to know how to kill him.

That evening, her husband came back.
He's got meat now, caribou this time.
They move again, dry meat, throw the bones.

One night she wakes up. Here her husband is gone!
She hears a dog chewing something.

She waits a while, looks around.
She sees her father's dog across the fire, chewing bones.
She just waits; she's anxious, I guess.
Not long after, that dog stops chewing.
She hears the dog shake.

Soon her husband comes in again, all clean.

"Where did you go, husband?" she asks.

"Oh, just out, just out to pee."

That girl fixed skins the way people do.
Next morning she went out to fix her skin—
She's got a pole to hang the skins she's fixing.
She's got a long one, light enough to handle.

That night, she throws bones out again—pretends she falls asleep.
He tries to move around, to check if she's asleep.
She pretends to be asleep.

He went outside.
Then he came back inside—a dog!
He started chewing.
She sneaked up quiet—hit that dog on the head with her pole.
She clubbed him to death.
She killed him!

"What are you doing, wife?"

"I'm killing you!" She threw him in the fire.

Finally, she traveled out, back to her father and mother.
She found she's going to have a baby—
She had eight puppies that time.
What's she going to do?

They start to grow up, too.
That woman and her mother always go out hunting.
She leaves those pups—it's their home, eh?
When she finally comes home, the house is all messy—
Puppies leap around.

Finally, that woman and her mother decide to watch to see what makes
    that mess.
They look back—see those puppies turn into kids!
They find out what is happening!
When those kids lie down, before their mother and grandmother come
    home,
Those kids turn back to puppies.

"How can we make them turn to person for good?" they think.
There's only one female in that litter.
There's seven boys, one girl.
Those women make seven clothes for boys and one dress for a girl.
They pretend to go out.

Those puppies turn into kids, play around.
Then their mother runs in:
"You stay that way!
You're human, not pups!"
Their grandmother comes in, too.
They put clothes on them.

That's why, long ago, dogs talk.

Eight months later, they're grown-up people.
They grow as fast as pups.
They do anything all the time, just like pups.

Finally, that daughter turns into woman:
Her mother makes a bonnet for her.

They move away from the old people's camp.
She got tired of those kids, those boys.

Those boys are good hunters.
One time, they see a goat across the river, coming down from the
    mountain.
Three of those boys go down the river near the girl's camp.
Two stand there, one stands down below.

"Go after that goat," one says.

That boy slipped in the water.
His sister pulls up her bonnet, looks at them.
Right then, they turn into stone.
A girl like that is *never* supposed to lift her bonnet up!

Then she looks at her mother: her mother turns to rock.
Then she looks at herself: she turns into rock.

On the Stikine River, there's three rocks.
They call them the Three Sisters—that's those boys—

Don't know why they call them "sisters."
That girl and her mother, they're there, too.
Those rocks, one looks like it's lifting up its bonnet.
Three look like human beings.
The spirit of those boys went to Dogrib.
That's why Dogrib people talk like people here.

That's all happened on Stikine River—it's a true story.
Those grandparents told that story—that's how we know it.
Lots of things used to happen like that.
Why not now, I wonder?

✳ Star Husband[47]

A father and mother had two daughters.
They travel around in the bush, drying meat, camping out here and
    there.
These two girls talk a lot and play at night—
Don't sleep quick.

One night one said, "Gee, I wish to marry that red star."
The other one said, "Gee, I wish to marry the blue one."
They talk away like this.

Next morning, first thing, they found themselves in another country.
Both of them have got husbands—they're sleeping with men.

One of them when he walked away looked kind of blue.
The other one looked red.
"You wished for us," they said.
So they found out that they are stars.

Their husbands are good hunters.
They go out every day—bring in moose, bring in meat.
Those girls stay up there—must be quite a while,
Tanning moosehide, making babiche.
From the skins they tan, they make big thick winter mitts and
    leggings.
That's what people used to wear.
They made quite a few of them.

Finally, though, they get lonesome for their mother and father.
They made up their mind to run away.
The only way they could run away, though, is to dig through that sky.
That's what they plan.

Their husbands said,
"What are you doing with all those skins?"

"Oh, we boil them and eat them," they told them.

They make babiche string—I don't know how many tons of it.
They get together their thick leggings and mitts.
Finally, they find a big rock, then start to dig.
Then they tie babiche around the rock and they start to let it down.
Go down, go down, go down.
Finally, they could tell it landed someplace.
After they were sure it landed safely, the youngest one went down first.
"When I get down, I'll pull the string."
They tied the other end to a tree.
She takes quite a while going down.
Finally, the oldest one feels the string move, so she went down next.
Here it was on top of a big flat tree.

They stayed there—don't know how they're going to get down.
Here, they are sitting over an animal trail.
Every day when animals go by, they say,
"Pack us down, Grandpa."
"No," each one says, "I don't climb trees."
Then another one goes by—moose, caribou—
They all say they can't climb trees.

Finally, at last, Wolverine was coming along.
First thing they did was they whistled at him.

"Oh, oh. What's that?" he said.

They kept whistling at him.
Finally, he sees the girls up there.

"Grandpa, pack us down and we're going to marry you," they tell him.

"Okay," just that quick he got up there—
Brought them down, both of them.
Right there, they camp.

Next day, he goes hunting.
Oh, they stay there for a while, I guess,
But then they said they're going to run away from him next.
So when he went down hunting in the morning, they took off.

It was right close to where their father and mother were staying.
Must be they stay in the same place yet, I guess, kind of hoping those
    girls might come back.
They don't know what happened to them:
They're staying there because they thought they might come back.

Before they left, they kicked their garters off—
Four garters—each had two.
They made a snare of them, put it in four places.
They told those four strings,
"Whistle at him when he comes back."
They figure he's going to keep running back and forth there among the
    garters.
That's to slow him down, I suppose.

In the meantime, they got back to their father and mother.

✳ The Stolen Woman

My aunt, Mrs. Whitehorse Billy, told me this story.

A man and his wife and their two boys were out hunting.
They had a daughter, too, and that daughter was living outside.
She had her bonnet on.

War came upon them.
Her mother and father were killed—both of them—so she threw her
    bonnet off, herself.
Two boys found her, two brothers. They asked her,
"Were you like that?" [secluded for the first time]

She said, "No,
I was out here because I'm going to get my month's sickness again."

But anyway, they kept her.
They took some dry meat and then they told her,
"Are you alone?"

"Yes, I'm alone now that my father and mother are gone."
She didn't tell them she had two brothers—
She's smart.

"Well, who gets meat for you?"

"Well, people kill moose for us and we go there and dry it.
Long ways people.
You can't tell where they are."
She hid it [what she knew].

They all go away, go back to where they came from.
They traveled all day, and then they come to a big creek from the
    mountains.
But she wouldn't go across it: she just sat down.
They put up a bridge—they chopped down a tree.
And she just sat down saying,
"I always fall in the water when I go over a bridge.
I don't want to go over."

She's sure smart, that girl.

Those two brothers are going to stay with her [and be] her husbands.
They met quite a few of their people.
One of those boys packed her across:
That's her husband-to-be.

While she was getting close to the camp, here she picked some
    cranberries.
She picked some up and then she put them on her legs
To make it look like she had her month's sickness.
One of those boys saw it.

"What's the matter? Are you like that?"

"Yes," she just lies, you know.

That night they gave her a big pile of moccasins to patch.
One slept one side; another slept on the other side.
She just patched those two boys' moccasins and then she stepped over
    them.
People were sleeping all around them to make sure she won't get
    away.

She stepped over them and ran as fast as she can back to the creek.
And she went in the water, up the creek, where moss falls over.
She watched the bridge from there [from her hiding place].

Sure enough, the sun was up already, and people started to come.
But those boys were looking for her—
All those others were looking for her, too,
But they didn't study very hard.

"Maybe she fell in the water?"
They looked down in the water, too.
They looked down the creek—pretty soon it started to get dark.

She looked out: no more people.
She came out of her hiding place and started to run back.
Here she met her own two brothers, going after her, I guess.
They told her to go right straight home,
And they went after those people.

After running around for that girl, those people slept in.
That older brother had doctor
So he put sleep on them.

110   They killed them—they clubbed them to death with sheep horn
Angela   club—
Sidney   They killed them all off except those two who saved her.
And here those people never got up.

When they got back to camp,
Here her mother was scraping skin and her daddy was cutting meat.
He had brought them back to life.
She's sure surprised.

13 ✴ Getting Married

"I stayed with Old Man year 1916.
Well, I was still a kid yet."

After I came out from under the bonnet, I went to Atlin with my aunt, Mrs. Austin, *Sadusgé*. They [*Sadusgé* and her white husband, Shorty Austin] were going prospecting, head of the lake. Her boys were going to stay in Carcross with her mother, and she took me to Atlin with her, year 1915. Here she got sick, so we stayed in Atlin.

My aunt used to talk to me about George Sidney: "If I see my nephew, George Sidney, I'm going to throw you at him!" And I used to think, "You marry him yourself!" but I never said it aloud, though. George's father was her cousin, too, so she called him "my nephew."[48]

I was shy to George when I first saw him. I used to talk respectfully to him: I used to say, "my nephew," "*Eshidaa*."[49] They taught me to talk that way to show respect to people. My old man [husband] used to call me "*Aχaat*": that means "my auntie [on the side of] my father's people" in Tlingit. Here, he used to say that even amongst white people! Gee, I don't like that! I get shamed. It's old-fashioned! I used to say, "Why do you say that in front of people? You know they're going to think she married her own nephew. White people don't understand!"

"Well, you *are Aχaat*, Indian way," he tells me. His father, Jim Sidney, was *Deisheetaan*—that's why I'm *eshembe'e'* to him Tagish way; *aχaat*, Tlingit way.

The Sidneys are Teslin people—they were at Johnson's Crossing that year, 1916. George was staying with his cousin, Jimmy Jackson. My father sent word to him and told him, "If you're going to Teslin, you better come this way. I want to see you." He was working longshoreman in Whitehorse. Whitehorse Billy called him up, "Come on for supper. I've got moose ribs." So after he got off at five o'clock, he went there. Whitehorse Billy was staying in Whitehorse, in tent frame—and so George went up there for supper. Whitehorse Billy had campfire outside, moose ribs boiling and cooking, I guess.

After they finished eating, that's the time my father's niece, my aunt, Mrs. Whitehorse Billy[50]—*Gunaaták's* daughter—said, "My uncle, Tagish John sent word to you. He said for you to go back to Teslin now, by Marsh Lake. That's the word my uncle sent to you."

"Okay, well, how am I to go to Marsh Lake?"

And her husband, Whitehorse Billy, tells him, "Well, there's Pelly Jim: he's going back to get some grub tomorrow. Get in touch with him."

So he did. Early in the morning, he got sugar, flour, everything. He's got little tent, too, five by seven [feet]. And here he saw Pelly Jim. "Can I go back with you to Marsh Lake?"

"Okay, I'm going back to Teslin—I'm going to work my way back that way."

"I want to see Tagish John—that's how come I want to go back with you." And that's how he got to Marsh Lake.

When he saw his father and his mother and his aunt, he told them Tagish John wants to see him. And his father told him after a while, after he thinks about it, "What does Tagish John want to see you for? Maybe he wants to give you his daughter or something like that." Before George leaves, his father tells him, "Go. Whatever he wants you to do, just do it. It's okay." That's how come he came directly to us. This is fall, 1916—that's how come he stayed with us.

Well, I kind of didn't like it—he's a stranger to me, you know. But when my father and mother told me to give him a cup of tea, to feed him, stuff like that, I had to do what my mother and father said. I never ran around like kids nowadays! As long as he's Wolf, I'm supposed to be his aunt; I'm Crow. He calls me "Auntie." And me, I have to call him "my nephew" when I feed him. "Eat, *Eshidaa*." I have to talk respectable, not crazy, like nowadays. That's Indian law—as long as I'm Crow and they're Wolf, they have to call me "auntie." So I gave him tea. He came nighttime with Pelly Jim and that bunch.

When he first came to us, he talked to my mother. He said, "My father sent me to you people to help you out with things." Well, the old people—they understand right away what he meant. I wasn't surprised. They had talked to me about him, long time ago. That's when I told you Mrs. Austin—*Sadusgé*—used to tell me about him. "You marry him yourself," I used to think, but I never said it out, though. "You marry him yourself!" I used to think that way.

When Old Man came to us, first year he stayed with us, he put up meat behind that *Chookanshaa,* behind Jake's Corner. He put up a cache there, way up high. We dried meat there, and he packed it all up. That's when he started to go with us. Well, my father and mother let me stay with him right away as soon as we came back to the main camp. He didn't want to make him work too hard for nothing.[51] "You might as well stay with him. He wants you. That's why he came to us."

They made a big feast for us: just us—my father and my mother and

the baby Dora and me. Oh, they talked things over with my aunt *Sadusgé*
already, I guess. "Let them stay together." They made a nice big dinner. Up
on the mountain and back of Jake's Corner—*Tlo'ó K'aa' Dzéłe'*, they call
that mountain. That's when we got through drying meat, I guess. We
were going to put meat in the cache, next day.

That's the time my father talked to him—made a big supper for us and
talked to both of us. He talked to George and told him, "I don't want you
fellows to have a hard time. Maybe you came to us for your aunt, so you
fellows stay together. Don't be too old-fashioned: I'm not old-fashioned.
A long time ago, people work for their wife for a long time. But I'm not
like that. I don't believe in it." And he made me sit by him where he's
going to eat. That's the way they made me stay with him.

That night—he's got a little tent outside he's sleeping in it—us, we just
stay in a brush camp, pull fly tent over it. I was sleeping with my mother.
Instead of going to my bed, they told me to go to the tent. "Go with him. Go
in the tent." So I took my blanket and I started to make my bed in there.

"What are you doing?" George asked.

"Well, my mother told me to sleep in this tent . . . sure looks like it's
going to rain . . ."

"Yeah?" he said.

After I fixed my blanket, he pulled my blankets. "Come sleep with me."
And we started fighting and laughing over that blanket. And pretty soon I
forgot about sleeping alone!

Now. You know it all. Everything!

But one of the school women, W.A. women[52]—her name was Mrs.
Watson—she used to be my teacher in the school. She heard about me
being married. So one day I had a visitor. Here it was Mrs. Watson—her
maiden name was Thompson—"Miss Thompson," we used to call her.
Oh, she was so kind, she loved me up and everything. And then she told
me, "I understand that you are married."

I said, "Yes."

"Did he give you a ring?"

"Yes, he gave me one—his own ring—one time when we went to
cache."

"Are you married in church?"

I said, "No."

"Well, you know what?" she said. "You're not supposed to be like that.
You've got to get married in church!" Well, I told her I didn't mind, but
my husband wouldn't want it—not to get married in church.

"Why?" she asked me.

"Well, I don't know . . . he's pretty shy, I guess."

"Where is he?" she tells me.

"He's working on the section."[53] Sure enough, she watched for George when the section crew came home.

"I understand you're married," she told George.

"Yes, Angela Johns."

"Well, you know you've got to get married."

"We are already married, Indian way. It's just as good, isn't it?"

"That's not good enough," she told him. "You've got to marry her white-man way. I raised that kid!" she told him.[54]

My Old Man said, "Why? What's the difference?"

She said, "You see that Church of England?" That church was sitting on skids already, ready to pull across. It was too far for the kids to cross from Chooutla school, so they moved it across to where it is now. Mrs. Watson said to my husband, "You see that Church of England sitting on skids? It's not going to be moved unless you get married. You've got to get married first."

George just gave up. Gee. "Okay," he said.

Then she came over one night and asked me what I'm going to wear. I had a Sunday dress—it was kind of blue. Well, blue was good, I thought—but no. Here the W.A. gave me a cream-colored linen suit. She brought it down. She asked me what kind of shoes I've got. I've got nice white canvas shoes and a cream-colored hat with a black band. All that! And she gave me pearls to wear on my neck. She told me everything I should wear.

She asked George if he had a suit. He had a nice gray suit—when he first came to Carcross, he spent the winter in Whitehorse cutting wood, and when he sold the wood he bought a suit for himself—bought it for a celebration. He left that suit in Whitehorse with the Second Hand man, and that spring after we came he wrote to that man about it. And the Second Hand man, he sent it up by train. So she told George, "You wear that." That was 1917.

My mother and dad couldn't come to that wedding—just me and George and Sophie, my cousin. Then there were the white ladies—Mrs. Watson and Mrs. Johnson and the others. So Mrs. Watson gave me away. We got married in Carcross. We were married twice. I was glad about it in the end.

After I started staying with Old Man, he got a job on section. My father and mother had to leave me then to be with my husband in Carcross. There was hardly anybody in Carcross that fall—just me and my husband, and my aunt Kate Carmack, and old *Hunxu.aat*—Tagish Jim's

mother—and my uncle Billy Atlin, and Jimmy Scotty. They used to call
me "Carcross Chief" because I stayed in Carcross. I used to give them
lunch anytime, give them lunch or supper.

My father and brother sold meat to Chooutla school that time. Mr.
Johnson was principal of that school that time. He said, "The kids eat
meat at home. Why shouldn't they eat meat at school, too?"

George was supposed to go back to Teslin that fall—he wanted to send
word to Teslin people. But here that fall he started going into the mountains, killed moose for us—for my parents, too—started going round
with us instead of going back. And he never did go back to Teslin till later
on, maybe two years. I stayed with him all that fall.

All winter we lived together with my mother in one big tent, twelve by
fourteen. We had our own little tent—we got stove in it. But wintertime
when it gets cold, we just wanted to cut wood for one place, so we stayed
with my father and mother that winter in that twelve-by-fourteen tent.

Us kids, we cut wood. Well . . . I still felt like a kid even though I was
living with Old Man—I was just like a child then! When he was gone
during the day, I played. Oh, I was still a kid yet, played around, rustled
around. One time when he's gone, my little brother Peter was with me,
and we set gopher traps on that *Chílíh Dzéle'*, that Carcross mountain. We
caught some gophers and cooked them for supper. When Old Man came
back he said, "Where did you get that from?" he asked me.

"What do you think I did?" I told him. "We went out gopher hunting!"
Oh, he was surprised. He was proud of me!

George and my brother Johnny would go out trapping, sell meat once
in a while. And they started buying everything half and half—partners.
My father didn't have to think about anything! In the falltime, they've got
a big pile of grub. When grub comes, they're the boss![55] The first year we
stayed together, my old man killed twenty-two lynx and my brother
killed eighteen lynx. Old Man bought a bottle of whiskey, to show
respect, and gave it to my father—*and* all the grub. They're the boss of it!
Nowadays people don't do that anymore.

Christmastime, my brother and my Old Man came to Skwan Lake—
Skwáan Taasłéyi. They killed some moose and roasted moose head by the
campfire. We caught a great big fish, and my father cooked that for
Christmas dinner. He invited Grandma Hammond—*Aandaax'w*—and
our cousins Isabel and Willy and my daddy's cousin Susie and her family.
Mrs. Dyea John—she stayed with Hammonds when she was getting
old—they're the ones that started calling her "Grandma Hammond." But
her real name is *Aandaax'w*, Mary John, Dyea John's wife.

Of course, we didn't know much about Christmas. But that's the time he taught us peace songs: he taught us this song and told us stories, and that's our Christmas fun . . .

And then they went out to get moose, and my uncle went out with them to get meat. Here they got up in the morning and my uncle said, "It's snowing hard, and gee, the stars are out!" So my brother looked up, and here the tent was on fire! That's how come they could see that—the snow and the stars.

14 ✱ The Stolen Woman (2)

✱ The Woman Taken by Lynx[56]

One time, a man and a woman were traveling.
People always travel around and put up meat for winter.

You know how eagles make their nest on a rocky cliff where no one
    can get to it?
People used eagle feathers to sew with—
They split them and they do fancy work with them, just like they do
    with beads now:
Like porcupine quills, like moosehair.
They dye them—cranberries for red color,
That moss that grows on tree limbs for yellow . . .

She ran out of eagle feathers. So her husband told her,
"You let me go down that cliff there.
I'll get some eagle feathers for you."

So they untied their pack string.
He tied it around his waist and then he went down and she held it
    from up above.
It was babiche string—they braided it like rope.
That's how they made string long time ago.

"When I want to come up, I'm going to pull like that," he said.
"Then drag me up again."
That's what he told his wife.

So she lowered it down, went down to get eagle feathers.
In the meantime, while she was sitting there, her husband never pulled
    that string.
Here somebody came to her—a nice young fellow—
Gee whiz! Pretty-looking man.
You know Lynx has some pink on his face?
Here, that boy told her he wanted to marry her.

"No, my husband is down that cliff," she said.

"Let him go, let him go," he told her.
And he started to drag her away.

There was a big rock there and she put that string around it and tied it up.
That's the way she let it go.

Then Lynx dragged her away from there—not very far, I guess.
"Oh, this place is good enough"—great big tall trees there.
So he made camp there, and he married her.
But he's got his camp on the other side of the fire.
He always sleeps on the other side, across the fire.

He went out hunting—here, he would only bring back lots of rabbits
    all the time.
She skinned rabbits, skinned rabbits, put it up to dry all the time.
He brought back lots of rabbits.

I guess where they are is not very far from that rock cliff.
So one time, here her husband tracked up that track.
He was tracking that Lynx.
Here, he came to her, daytime.

Her husband told his wife,
"What are you doing here?"

"Well," she said, "that man packed me away, that's why."

"What does he do?"

"Oh, he kills lots of rabbits for me, all the time."

Her husband asked her,
"Well, you want to stay here?
Do you want to go back with me?"
"I want to kill him," he was thinking.
"You fool him," he told her.
"Put blanket across the fire.
Pretend the wind is blowing so I can sneak up there."

In the evening, she put a blanket across there.

She told him,
"What for you sleep here?
Why don't you sleep on this side with me? You wanted me."

"It's not March yet. I can't sleep with you yet," he told her.
You know lynx mating season is in March.

She talked cranky to him.
"What is this you bring to me all the time?
My hands are just getting rough from skinning those rabbits.
My husband used to kill nice fat moose all the time.
You—you kill nothing but rabbits!
My hands are getting rough from rabbit blood."

"What do you mean?" he asked her.
"That's animal, too. Rabbits are animal, too.
What's the matter with you?"

That night, she put blanket across.

He said to her,
"What are you hanging that blanket for?
What do you think?
Do you think I'm not good enough to kill anything?
You put that blanket up there so I won't see something?"
He got wise to her.

"Because the wind is blowing this way," she says.
"It smokes up."

Here, just while she was saying that, that man, her husband shoots an
   arrow right here [base of his neck].
From behind the blanket, that's the way he killed him.

When that arrow hit him, he jumped up, saying,
"I'm going to be lynx."
Here he ran up that tree.
Not very far later, he fell off.
That's how they know it's Lynx who stole her.

He died, and he turned to lynx when he died.

✳ The Stolen Woman

One time there was a man who was camping with his wife close to a
   lake.

He went out hunting, but she stayed home.
You know how when they become a woman they wear a bonnet?
She was wearing her bonnet yet.

All of a sudden, somebody came.
He started asking her questions, how come she's staying there.

"My husband went out hunting," she told him.

"Your husband shouldn't leave you," he said.
"Come with me."

"No, I don't want to do that.
I love my husband—I want to stay."

They argued for a while,
Finally, he grabbed her and started to drag her away—
He threw her bonnet away, and dragged her.
There was a little trail going down to the water—
That's how her husband found her—by following this little trail.
All the time that man is dragging her, she grabs at little branches and
    breaks them.
By the time they get through, it's just like there's a big road down to
    the water.

He put her in his boat, then floated around until her husband came
    back.

Finally, her husband came back.
He came to the water, and here she was in the boat.

That man who took her took an arrowhead.
He tied a little strip of gopher and loon's head to it with babiche
And he threw it to her husband.
"Here, this is for your wife. I pay you."

"No," that man said,
"I want my wife. You can't pay for her!"

That man started to go, started to row.
The husband started to follow, too.
Paddle, paddle . . . keeps going, going . . . don't know how far they go.

Finally, they came to a place where they say a point of land in the lake
    lifts up.
And that man went under it, to the other side.

Well, that husband can't go under it—
On the other side was winter. Snow.

From there, where that point lifts up, that husband had to turn back.

It took him two or three days to get back to camp.
He dried up some meat and then he went to look for his brothers-in-law.
He had told that man [who stole her],
"She's got lots of friends.
Don't think we won't come after her!
Don't think you're going to get away with it!"

Ah, that man laughed at her husband.
"You won't come after us. You can't!"

When that guy who took that woman got past that point, he put up
    his boat.
He followed a trail with that woman and caught up with his people.

Meantime, her husband gathered up her brothers and his brothers.
They're going to follow.
They go to the cache and get dry meat for their food.
They travel along the shore.
When they come to that point, here it lifts up and they go under it.
On the other side, here it was really deep snow.
There was an old trail there, so they started to follow it.

Here, there were two little old ladies camping there.
They've got a little trail to the water and they've got a fishhook, fish for
    ling cod.
Every day, they catch two or three.
They cook them all.
They had enough to supply people who went by.

Just the husband went up to them.
"Did you see my wife walk by with someone?"

"Yes, we heard there was a girl from a different country going by with a
    bunch."

"How long ago?"

"Quite a while ago, but you can follow this old trail," they tell him.
"Every evening late in the evening,
Your wife always goes back along the trail to get wood."

He went back to his gang.

One of them went back just to listen to those two old women, in case
   they say anything.

One said, "My son used to go out to hunt early in the morning, just
   before daylight breaks."
The other one said, "My son used to go out a little while after when the
   daylight really breaks."

Both those women wished their sons would get away before anything
   happens:
They know these men are going to make war on people.

Then those men followed the trail.
Sure enough, they start to catch up to people one evening, don't know
   how many days after that.
They just hear somebody chopping wood up ahead of them.
Just that man, that husband, went to where they hear that chopping.
Sure enough, it's her.
Just when she lifts the wood she is going to pack home, he grabs it.
She pulls, she turns around—here it's her husband!

He starts to ask her questions.
"Your uncles and your brothers are all with me and so are my uncles
   and my brothers.
We have run out of food.
Can you get some for us?
We're going to make war, but your uncles, your brothers, we are all
   hungry.
We've run out of grub."

"Okay, I'll see what I can do.
I've got food in my skin toboggan, too."

"Well, try to get some."

She had a stone ax, like old time.
And he cut the string that holds the ax on the handle—cut it off.
"Tell your mother-in-law you broke that string, ax string.
Then you can take the string off the toboggan."

She went home without the wood.
She told her mother-in-law, "My ax string broke."

"Well," her mother-in-law said,
"Take the string off your skin toboggan and fix it."

"Okay," she pretended to fix it.
Then she stuffed that dry meat under her arms.
She stuffed willow branches into that toboggan to make it look full.
Then she went out to her husband to give him that food.

Again, they pretended that babiche broke off that ax.
She came home again, told that mother-in-law,
"That string is broken again.
Maybe mine is not strong. Maybe yours is stronger."

"Go ahead and help yourself," her mother-in-law said.
So she helped herself to her mother-in-law's toboggan.
She took lots of meat under her arm, under her blanket—
They used blankets in those days.
Again she breaks willow branches, stuffs her mother-in-law's toboggan.
Then she went to her husband again.

"What do they do?" her husband asked.

"Well, when the hunters come back,
Everybody always goes to bed early," she tells him.

"Where is your husband now?" he asks.

"They're both out hunting."
She's got two brothers for husbands.

"When they come back tonight, play with them.
Make them tired out so they will go to sleep."

"Okay." She brings that wood back.
Her husbands come home.
After they eat, she starts playing with them, playing with them.

The oldest one said,
"Don't bother me; I'm tired."

So she started playing with the youngest one.
He said the same thing:
"I'm tired. What's wrong? You never did that before.
How come you're doing that?"

"Oh, I just feel like playing."
Then she went out for a little while.
She listened for what her mother-in-law is going to say.

Her mother-in-law comes in and says,
"My sons, I love you, boys, used to be.
My sons, I don't know what is wrong with your wife.
Your wife is acting very strange.
Her ax string broke . . .
She came and took a string from her toboggan
And when she went out, she looked big to me.
And then she came back and told me her ax string broke again.
So she took some off my toboggan.
And the same way, she looked very big when she went.
Be careful, you boys. Sleep light!"

"What do you expect, Mother?
It's a long way to where that woman comes from.
Nothing but lynx droppings around here—
That's all there is, lynx."

"Well, just the same, you look after yourselves good," she tells them.

And finally, they went to bed.
The woman's husband had told her,
"Sleep with your clothes, and don't tie up your blanket."
See how smart he is?
"So you can jump out if they grab you;
They're going to try to grab your blankets."

When that young wife heard them, she just jumped up.
They just grabbed her, just grabbed her blanket.

She jumped up, went outside.
In the meantime, they both got killed—the whole camp, everybody got
    killed.
And that old lady who said, "My son goes out before daybreak,"
Sure enough, he was gone.

When they do that, it's bad luck to start to eat right away.
They have to take scalps first—then they wash their hands—they tend
    to the dead.

They did that all during the day.
Then one or two followed the trail to get that boy who went hunting.
When he came back, he was dragging white caribou, they say—must
  have been reindeer—
They killed him, too.
Then they had fresh meat, that caribou.

Finally, they're through everything and they start to go home.
So they have lots to eat.

On the way home, they came by those two old ladies' camp again.
Those old ladies dig a tunnel in the snow.
That husband took a walking stick, and shoved it in the snow.
Then, when he took it out, there's blood on it.
Those two old ladies made nosebleed and make it look like they are
  killed.

So they let them go—they left them some meat—then they went on.
Those two old ladies could tell when they are gone.

They came to their boat, paddled to the place where the point lifts
  up.
It was summer on the other side.
They came back to their own camp.
From there, they are home.

They say that point doesn't lift up anymore.
When a woman first becomes a woman one time, she looked at that
  point.
That's why it doesn't lift anymore.

✴ How Mrs. Dickson's Aunt Came Home

This is a true story about how one woman came all the way from Pelly
  Banks, home to Tagish.
This was before my time.

Mrs. Jenny Dickson, who lives in Ross River, came from Tagish people.
Her grandmother married in that way.
I think it is her aunt who did this.

Long time ago, people camp at Marsh Lake,
Down near where John Joe lives, they put up meat.
When snow came, they went to Pelly.

One winter they started coming back.
Then those people got sickness:
One woman's father lost his wife and children, too.
When he was strong enough to travel, he went back to Pelly.
He left his daughter with his older sister, in Pelly.
She just lived with them—
He came back home alone.

The following springtime, people meet [for trade].
One man wants her for his wife, so he took her right away.
He already had one wife—that older wife gave her cloth to make a
    dress—gave her skins to make moccasins.
Then they went to the mountains.
That daughter made her mind up she's going to run away:
She had her own sewing kit.

The older wife said to her:
"You pack one of my babies for me."
"No," [the younger one] said. "Even my own sister didn't ask that.
Is that the only reason you want me?"

They went ahead—she said she would follow.
She sees pieces of big stick, burning, fire at the end like charcoal.
She picks it up.
She traveled on windfall so they can't find her tracks.
She had no matches—she blows on that fire to keep it going.
She does that all the way she walks to Marsh Lake.
It's summer.

She had snares with her.
In morning, she sets rabbit, gopher snares.
At night, she builds a little fire.
Finally, she came to an empty old camp at Marsh Lake.
She's lonely—tired.
She sees that camp where kids chopped wood last fall,
Sees where her mother scraped skins . . .
She cried.

She dreamed at night. Her mother said,
"I kept your fire going.

Now you are close to your camp, close to your people.
I'm going to leave you."

Next morning, that fire is out.
From Marsh Lake to Tagish, she traveled without fire.
She made it through, though.

15 ✳ Marriage and Children

I got in family way 1917. Gee, isn't that lucky? I was lucky I never got like that before! Peter was born April 13th. My mother and Daisy [Smith] helped me. Oh, they talked to me . . . I wasn't sick long. I felt funny—told Old Man I didn't feel good. My stomach aches:

"You're sure it's your stomach?"

"How would I know?" And finally my water broke and he found out what's wrong, and he sent for my mother.

That was at Tagish—therefore, Pete owns half of that "Tagish John Rock." That's the way they do it: Pete put a claim on that Tagish John Rock, because Wolf people claim this Tagish River.[57] John Atlin was born at Tagish, too—head of Tagish River. And Pete was born at head of Tagish, too, in April.

There were no hospitals in those days. People lived in one house— that's why they used to make a little camp back of the main house, back of the main camp. The woman is there by herself: when she starts to get sick—when they know she's in labor—they take her there. Well, of course, [other] women watch her. They drive a stick alongside of her so she can hang on it. There are two sticks, straight up and down: she is lying on her back.[58] Sometimes a woman lies on her side and she has the stick just on one side: she holds the stick and she pulls on it. Sometimes women have a rope and they can pull on it. And sometimes those women who are helping put a stick at your foot so you can kick on it—or a log or something, so you can push and your foot won't slip. And, of course, they hold her knees, hold the lady's knees so she won't wriggle around too much, and she won't hurt the baby.

People are fighting for two lives: fighting for the mother, and fighting for the baby. That's why. If she is Crow, then Crow ladies are with her— her mother's got to be there. And sometimes if there is a Wolf woman [in the camp], they ask her: of course, they have to pay them, just like a potlatch. Some rich people do that, or some respectable people, or whoever thinks they respect themselves or something.

After the birth, you break off the soft tops of young trees and you get Hudson's Bay tea, and you mix it and boil it. That's what they use right away: she drinks it. It cleans out her stomach, and it goes to her breasts, I guess. It's good for the baby, too.

If it's a boy, they take that afterbirth, and they take it out to the bush. They put it up in the tree and let camp robber [Canadian jay] eat it: they say that will give him luck so he'll become a good hunter. Girls' afterbirth, they put in a gopher nest, bury it in a gopher den, and then they become good gopher hunters. And for girls, they take gopher bum [anus] and cut it off and make a little ring so they become good gopher hunter. That's what they do with afterbirth. Just lately they started burning it, lately when white people started coming around—white people or the minister—missionary. *They're* the ones that started changing everything. From then on, they start changing everything—burning the afterbirth. They never did that before!

Same with burying people. They used to burn them: wherever they died, they burned them. My father's brother died at Quiet Lake—they must have burned him there and brought back his ashes. They must be in the little spirit house.[59]

Pete was four months old when we went to Teslin. We went to Teslin for one year in 1918. George's parents would write to him all the time: "Come back, come back, come back to fix your mother's grave," they told him.

"Go," my father said to him. That's why we went back, why we went to Teslin. I had only one child then. There used to be a trail where there's a highway now, and we followed it. We walked to Johnson's Crossing and we built a boat to go to Teslin. We stayed there one year—the next fall, we came back. Good thing we come back, too, because my daddy died that spring, 1920.

My husband's father had two wives—George's mother was that second wife, the youngest one. Even though that first wife was her full sister, she was still mean to her. So George's mother left: she took off from there and coast people took her. She said, "There's lots of men in the world, lots of men in the country—no use making trouble over one man." And she took off.

Those Tlingit people took her to their camp, and then in Juneau they gave her to Edgar Sidney instead. She spent three years in Juneau and then she got kind of lonesome for her country, so Edgar took her back to Teslin again. He was Coast Indian—he never saw a rabbit before in his life![60] They just stayed there. Well, she's got her own home now—she's not scared of her sister anymore.

Nineteen nineteen, Old Man was unlucky. He never killed anything all winter. No fur, nothing!—just one mink, I guess. That was bad luck, that one. First, I got chicken pox, and here George got it. They went out hunting and George got sick and they had to come back. Then in springtime, beaver season closed. In B.C., beaver season was open.[61] That's the time my brother-in-law came with us, John Sidney.

My father was sick—that's why Old Man left us, at the head of the Teslin [River]. He left us there at Johnson's Crossing. But Frank Sidney stayed with me and that John Sidney, too, stayed with us. He stayed there because somebody had to watch out for us. That winter they found gold someplace around close to Liard, I guess. They staked the place out and Old Man staked, too—that's why we had to stay. Then we didn't go back because he was going to work that claim. Instead of that, he got sick, the flu. His ear ached for pretty near one whole month. So when he started to get better again, he said, "Let's go back to Carcross. No good here!"

That fall, we walked back—Frank came with us, too. We never made any money; we just went back flat broke. When we got back to Carcross, we started to sell meat right away; that's how we got our groceries. We put in the winter in Carcross. That's fall, 1919, I'm talking about.

Year 1920 was the flu.[62] March, 1920, my daddy was living yet. There's a coal boat landed in Skagway. All the longshoremen quit! They went on strike. So White Pass gathered up all the section men on the line and they took them down to Skagway. That's the time the crew got sick—Sam Smith is the first one who got it, they say. Then *Shaakóon*, then everybody. Flu! They got that sickness from the coal boat—somebody had flu and everybody got it. Maybe that's why those longshoremen quit anyway! All the crew from Whitehorse got sick. The hospital was full . . .

They were going to take George to the hospital, but he didn't want to go, just him alone. "Supposing something happened to me alone here?" That's what he thought. So he just went back, went back, went back with the rest of the crew. Instead of going to Whitehorse, he got off at Carcross, went back home. Then he sent word to me—he told Frank Slim to tell me to come back to Carcross. "Leave everything there," he said.

I had a big pile of wood, too. I gave it all to my uncle, Whitehorse Billy. He was sickly, too—he'd had double pneumonia the spring before— never got better yet. So we took that wood all down to them. I packed everything up and I got somebody to take my stuff to the train and I came back. Good thing I did, too—that's the time my father died.

We lost my father the last day of March. He was good right to the end—used to run a net every day. That flu got lots of people. We lost the baby first before anybody else got sick. There's a doctor at the mission. Lots of people died in that flu—my father died; Mrs. *Shaakóon* lost a baby; I lost one. My son Pete and my little sister Dora never got the flu—I wonder how come . . . Lots died in Atlin, too.

My auntie, Mrs. Kate Carmack, died, too. I remember my father came back when she died: he came in the evening and my mother was very

sick, and he was starting to get sick. Here he came in and told my mother, "My cousin, my sister—*Shaaw Tláa*—my sister's light is on." And here he broke down and started to cry . . . and then just two days later he died, him, too.

They leave the light on as long as the body is there—some people sit and sing funeral songs. The people that visit have to smoke. You treat them with smoke like that and sing some songs—cigarettes, tobacco, snuff—that's how they entertain people when they come and visit. That's the time they choose the people to work for them, too—like who is going to be pallbearer, who is going to dig the grave—stuff like that. [They do it] through that smoking and singing songs, funeral songs. I was there when they asked Old Man to come and visit the dead—it's just like visiting. Everybody is there, sitting around him. It's the side who loses that person that has to decide who does the work: they're the ones that chose the people.

Before my time, they say, when somebody died they put up a stick and put black around it. That's how they know if somebody is dead in that camp; that's the message they give. They put that man's clothes on—tie them to the stick. That's how the other people know who the stick belongs to.

From there on, we *really* went alone—we had to go alone. [Until then] we were always with my father and mother, you know . . .

Year 1920, muskrat went high—six dollars a skin—muskrat skin. So my Old Man and Sam [Smith] went back to Teslin, way up the Nisutlin River to someplace where he knows there used to be lots of muskrat. He *could* have stayed at Little Atlin—could have stayed here and hunted rats. People don't know! You always do the wrong thing, and later you see where you made mistakes. They had no business going there! He could have hunted muskrat around Little Atlin. Instead of that, when they came back, rats went broke—it was only two and a half dollars the trader paid! Still, we made our grubstake for the summer.

That summer we stayed right in Carcross. My mother wasn't very strong yet, after the flu, so we had to stay in Carcross. After my father died, my mother stayed with us for six years. Then Billy Hall's father stayed with my mother after that. Six years she stayed with us. While ice is still there yet, we came down to fishcamp—Mother, me, and [Sam's wife] Daisy Smith and her grandmother—it's this side of the Narrows at Carcross. It's easy to get fish there. So we stayed until Old Man and Sam came back.

Then, when they came back, we moved to Carcross. He got a job on section. Every summer, he used to work—pretty near every summer: I think he just missed two or three summers. I stayed in Carcross [when he worked for White Pass and Yukon Railway].

We would go out trapping in the fall, to *Dasgwaanga* or Little Atlin. Then summertime, we came back in April or end of April, and he started working right away. They always kept a place for him. People asked, how come they do that? Well, they know he's a good man. After we came back, he's got a job next day, starts working next day.

I used to get up six o'clock in the morning—he'd leave home by seven o'clock—then he doesn't come home till five o'clock in the evening. Six o'clock we have supper. That was ten hours a day and he only got three dollars and ninety cents. And yet we used to save money. And nowadays people want ten dollars a day! They get the weekends off, too! That started after George got laid off.

Look how long I lived with Old Man and never got water! He packs water, and if he's going to go away for a short time he gets water, wood, everything ahead. I never hauled water or cut wood. I hear some people say the [Indian] woman is the one that cuts the wood and packs the water all the time. No, not me! He used to say, "My mother never packs wood or gets water, so why should you?" Well, his mother was married to Old Man Edgar Sidney, and Edgar Sidney was raised in school, you know—Sitka school. Well, he learned white man's ways, everything. And George learned it from his stepfather—that's why he didn't allow us to cut wood.

Then in year 1923 or '24 we went out hunting at Marsh Lake. When he's not working section, he gets license to get meat and sells meat. Every week he's supposed to bring in two quarters for the school—for the Mission school. Down at Marsh Lake my uncle Whitehorse Billy used to sell meat. He sold it to Pete Burns's butcher shop. Then, of course, when the season opens in September, they quit their work and tend to their own drying—stuff like that.

Year 1923 is the year they started building that Marsh Lake dam, in August. Here he went down and got a job there, cutting wood for camp. They started to cut wood there and they sawed wood by hand—imagine! Then everybody got laid off in the fall, except him. Well, he asked for a steady job.

"You think you could help the carpenters?"

"I guess I could. I could drive a nail." So he got a job with the carpenters.

He said the carpenter work was down at the bottom. You don't see anything from up on top, he said. First they block the water up. Then they make the sections. Down at the bottom is where they really work. He worked all winter—oh, he had a good job. Boy, he used to work like everything!

Year 1924, falltime, that winter, he took the mail from Carcross to Atlin. They just go to Moose Arm, used to be: they've got a camp there—a roadhouse, they call it. When they have a passenger, they camp there in that roadhouse. And he worked on telegraph line one time. I don't think anybody else ever did that—work on the telegraph line or be a mail carrier—he used to go working—work, work, work, all the time.

Other winters, we were out, until 1935. Then we started to stay in Carcross for good. That's after Mabel went to school. We didn't feel like going in the bush after those kids go to school. And Ida went, too, a little bit.

Old Man worked on section year-round until 1963. Then they laid him off, and he got his pension right away. His unemployment [benefits] started, and that's for one year. Then they told him to go back to work for three months, and he can draw [benefits] again. Ah, to heck with it, he said. He didn't want to work again after laying up that long. After his unemployment [money] finished, that's the time his pension started.

Altogether we had seven kids—Pete and Mabel and Ida. I lost three boys and one girl—all just babies, too, just little babies yet . . . I had seven children, altogether.

You notice those kids how far apart they are? It's because I lose the middle ones. They say when you're having babies it's not as bad as miscarriage. When I had my first miscarriage, I didn't even know it. We went to Atlin and the German measles were going round. Here my son Georgie who was two and a half got sick on us. Two or three days later I started to get sick, too—I got headache. We started from Atlin and got as far as Taku.

I had my miscarriage there—I was sick all night. When we left Atlin, we walked over the portage. We got our boat and went to Indian Point. That's where my aunt, Mrs. Bill Johnson, met us. Here I set traps with Mrs. Johnson, and then I got worse that night. By morning, I couldn't get to my traps. My husband picked up the ones he could find, and we went on to Golden Gate. I was sick all night, too, the second night. Then we took off that morning and we landed at Ten Mile. There's a point there called *Gáanuuláa*. That's were Alec McLeod was living, and Mrs. McLeod. And Mrs. McLeod said, "You'd better take her in. There's something wrong. Is she in a family way?"

I didn't know I was in a family way . . . "How could I be? I had my sickness not so long ago."

"But you are," the doctor told me. "Come back in six weeks."

But before six weeks I miscarried. It happened when we were going around Scotty Island. After that passed, I felt good . . . no more pains. And when we were coming across Windy Arm, I woke up. My husband had a coal-oil lamp. First thing I woke up, I saw that light swinging back and forth. I spoke to my old man: "Where are we?"

"Crossing Windy Arm now. Don't move. Just stay still." When we got to Carcross, he told me, "Just stay in bed for a while. I'm going to make a fire." Finally, he made a fire and he took me home. He held onto me one side, led me home. After he put me to bed, after everything was ready, he just broke down and cried.

I said, "What's the matter with you?"

He said, "Boy, you don't know what I went through. I thought you weren't going to speak to me. I thought you were gone."

I don't know how many I lost that way . . . I lost one child after each one I got—that's why Peter is almost four years older than Mabel. Then I lost another little girl after Mabel. And then I got Georgie and I lost one after Georgie, a boy. Georgie used to tell me, "Mamma, I want a brother."

I'd tell him, "You've got a brother."

"But he's older than me. I want one younger than me," he said.

I said, "Never mind. You had one, but God took him back from us."

"Why did he do that?"

I'd tell him, "I can't tell you why, but it just happened. Don't think about it," I'd tell him. Then I had Ida, my last one. Ida was a year old when I had my operation. Even so, if I knew what it was about I wouldn't have let them do it . . . But I didn't know. The doctor talked to my husband. "What do you want, your children or your wife?"

"My wife," he said. "I love my children, but the ones I've never seen, I can't help. I love my wife. I'd rather be without them." So they decided. My husband is the one who signed the papers—I didn't even know what they were going to do. I can't have any more children . . . I never found out till long time after.

I used to blame the Old Man for it. "It's all your fault!" I said.

He said, "I love you, that's why. We've never seen those children. We don't know them. You've got to fight for the ones we've got now." So I believed him. I was twenty-seven years old the time I'm telling about when I had my operation.

That's why I adopted that little girl, because I was thinking of babies all the time. But I lost her, too, 1943. When the army came in, there was lots of sickness—dysentery, spinal meningitis . . . I lost her then.[63] Her name is Beatrice, and that's how come my granddaughter has that name—she has the same Indian name, too. We took her to the army doctor, but he said, "We've got no license to practice in Carcross. We can't look at anybody. But if you bring her here, we'll look at her." So they took her, but they said she had to go to Whitehorse, to the hospital.

And here we caught the midnight train—and me alone with her. She died the next day around eleven o'clock . . . I never slept the whole night. When we got to Whitehorse, I got taxi which took us to the hospital. The doctor had phoned Whitehorse anyway—they came to see her right away. I stayed with her until about eleven o'clock next day. And Isabel came. I told her, "Beatrice is very, very sick." I got tired, very sleepy, and she told me, "You better find someplace to sleep. I'll stay with her." So I went to Mrs. Laberge Billy's place. And I just got there and Isabel came behind. "She's already gone . . ."

That time when the army came I was the only nurse. I borrowed a doctor's book from Johnny: he bought it when his wife was ill. I would get called out nighttime—for anything. There was no doctor, no nurse—they called me instead. So I did the best I could. But still they died—Daisy [Smith] lost two children, all one hour between them. Daisy Sheldon's sister died of dysentery. Johnny Taku died—that's Andrew James's brother—I guess John James was really his name. And my little Beatrice Sidney died in 1943.

After the Alaska Highway came, everything stopped—kids go to school . . . they don't talk Indian anymore. [Even when I was a kid] they didn't allow us to talk Indian in school; otherwise we get punished. We can't talk to our brothers, too.

Everyone bought cars after the highway came. Old Man and I had a Model T before that, but now everyone got them. They ordered cars through Matthew Watson. People sneaked around with cars—the army had that rule: civilians couldn't use the road. The highway was patrolled, too; they didn't allow people to park on the road during the war.

My son Pete was in the war: I got Old Man to get little radio so we could listen to hear where they're moving the troops so we would know where he is. Five years he's gone—just like that Kaax'achgóok story I told you [see Section 16].

Finally, it's getting over, war. Pete sent a message: he sent a letter home, airmail. He said, "Dear Mom, I'm booked for Canada. Tomorrow I'm leaving." The letter came in two, three days. I knew what date he wrote the letter. We start counting the days . . . we gave him five days to cross the ocean. He's coming back on the *Queen Elizabeth*, "the new one," he said.

When he landed in New York he sent a telegram again: "Landed safely in U.S.," he said. From there, we counted the days again. We gave him four days to come to Vancouver . . . From there when he gets on the boat, we counted [the days] again. We give him four days to land in Skagway. From the time he got on the boat from Vancouver we're counting the days again. Well—*I'm* the one counting the days—I don't know if the rest do.

And finally, one night, George asked me, "What are we going to do?"

"I'm going to invite everybody for dinner. I want a bottle of rum," I said. Those days Indians are not allowed to get whiskey. Anyway, we got the bottle of rum. And I invited the chief, Patsy [Henderson], and his wife and all the people—my brother Johnny and his wife, and my brother Peter and his wife, too.

So George asks me, "How are you going to serve it?"

"Well," I said, "after everybody sits down, after they're all ready to eat, I'm going to open the bottle of rum and give everybody a shot. And then I'm going to sing that *Ḵaax̱'achgóok* song." See? We call that Pete's song. That's how come. And my Old Man said, "Gee, I didn't know you were so smart to think like that! That's *good* idea!"

Ḵaax̱'achgóok is supposed to be *Kiks'ádi*, but they say they made war on us *Tuḵyeidí*, us *Deisheetaan*. And after, they captured his brother for a slave—it happened to be his brother they captured—and that's his song. And when they were straightening everything out, that's the time he gave us that song—his song. He gave it to us in place of his brother. That's why we use it. That's why *I* use it! That's why I gave it to Pete when he came back from the army, because he just went through what happened to *Ḵaax̱'achgóok*. He drifted away in the ocean, but finally he came back. I asked all about it, too, before I find out how that song goes.

Patsy told my mother, "It's not you fellows' song, that song. You can't use that song."[64] He asked Johnny Anderson about it, and Johnny Anderson said, "No, it's not *Deisheetaan* song." Well, that's right, it's *not* our song, but he gave it to us in place of his brother. And we sent his brother back, too, on his side, see?

Old Man was chief of Carcross after Patsy [Henderson] died. He was chief for three years. One time when he was chief they started talking again about separate schools for Indians. George talked against it: "How come? Before when those kids go to mission school, they were shy toward white people. Now they aren't shy. Who wants to get old style again? Not me!" I agreed with him. He told me to say the same thing, too. He said, "Supposing a bomb dropped amongst us here. Our Indian blood and white-man blood is going to get mixed up then! Who is going to gather up the white-man blood from the Indian blood?" Nobody answered him! He said, "I think it's good kids all mixed up together."

Another time they talked about moving Carcross village. Old days in Carcross, *Deisheetaan* people lived where the village is now, and *Dakl'aweidí* were across the river. In Tagish, *Dakl'aweidí* lived where the campground is now, near the graveyard. *Deisheetaan* had their summer houses on this side, where I live now.[65] Now in Carcross, Indians are all on one side. They don't boss themselves: government bosses them around all the time!

One time before Old Man was chief, the government wanted to move the village. There was a meeting in the village. He didn't want to go there: "You talk as good as me. You go." So I did. They wanted us to sign a paper to see how many want to move the village. They said they're going to have water running—everything. Everyone agreed. Then I said, "No! I don't want to sign it! I'm not going to move down there anyway. I'm not living in the village. I live across the river."

And they asked me, "Why don't you want to go down?"

And I said, "Because I already heard that story. The Whitehorse people are moved way below town. They said they were going to have running water in the house and bathroom in the house. Where are they going to get the water *from* in Whitehorse?" I told them.

And they said from McIntosh Creek.

I said, "They said they were going to run a bus free. People going to run back and forth to the store. Right today there is no taxi going to the village yet.[66] I never see a free bus running back and forth. It's going to be the same here—just watch, it's going to be the same. That's why I don't want to sign that paper. And George told me not to sign. He's not feeling good—he has a bad cold. That's why he didn't come up." That's what I said.

And so they put it off. The next week Patsy said, "Throw that paper out! Just fix these places up better. They're not going to move Carcross Indian village." That's why they didn't move it.

George got sick in 1969—cancer, they said. The doctor sent him to Vancouver. I remember when I went to see him there—July—that was my first trip to Vancouver. July. Gee, I sure was surprised when it got dark at night! I *never* saw that before, never in July!

They wanted to give him that operation, like they gave me. But he said, "No. If God wanted me to have tube in my stomach, he'd put it there himself." That's what he said. I sure didn't like it, me either, when they did that to me. But nobody asked me. They just did it.

George died in 1971. Old style, one of his nephews should look after me after he died. Like I told you about that *Sa.éek'*, my great-grandmother—before her husband *Kaatułak'é* died, he said to *Haande-yéił*, his nephew, his sister's son, "I don't want my child to be born without a father. You stay with her right away." So that nephew, *Haandeyéił*, moved in. But they don't do that anymore, not now.

George used to tell me, "If any one of my nephews asks you, you just give yourself up." That's what he used to tell me. But they don't do that now. Nobody asked me.

And long time ago, people used to give away what their husband owned—tools, everything, to his people. They used to do that. Even me, I did that when I lost my husband. I took a trunk—we bought that trunk from my brother Johnny Johns—he bought that trunk in Seattle someplace and he brought it back. My sister, Dora, packed up my old man's things—all his clothes, everything, and we took it back to Teslin that same fall. That same fall they're going to make tea for my old man. Frank Sidney brought that fence for him and put it on his grave. And Frank Sidney said they wanted me and Dora to come.

So Dora and I went up there—I forget who took us. I gave that trunk to him, full of my husband's clothes and everything. The only thing I kept was his guns, because he told me who to give those guns to—his snowshoes, too. I brought the trunk into Frank Sidney's place, and I guess he distributed it amongst them. After the party, we came right back. The only reason I never let his guns go is because he told me who to give his guns to—he told me to give his "twenty-two" to Melvin because our *Deisheetaan* boys are the ones that used to look after him. When he was getting old, he couldn't hunt anymore—can't do anything no more. The boys used to keep up hunting for us, give us meat, stuff like that.

Nowadays we don't care if we've got no meat, 'cause there's always meat in the store. But old people are not like that. Every falltime we used to get a month when he's working on section—he worked on section for thirty-five years. I've got a railway pass forever, used to be. After he was gone, I only used it once.

16 ✳ Ḵaax̱'achgóok

I was ten when I heard this story first.
My auntie, Mrs. Austin, told me the story first time.
Later I heard my father tell it to the boys.
This is that song I gave to Pete.
I'm going to tell how we claim it.

This is a true story.
It happened on salt water, maybe near Sitka.
It goes with that song I sing—I'll tell you about it.[67]

This man, Ḵaax̱'achgóok, was a great hunter for seal.
He was going hunting at fall.
He has eight nephews on his side, his sisters' sons.
Ḵaax̱'achgóok is Crow and so are those boys.
They all went out together in a boat.
Early in the morning, they left.
Fog was down low on the ocean.
He's captain: he sat in the back, guiding that boat.

He heard a baby cry that time, "Waa, waa."

"Stop. Listen. Stop that, baby, now!
Don't you know this is Ḵaax̱'achgóok's hunting ground?"
He listened quite a long time.
Here it was baby seal crying.

That's bad luck.
That voice even called his name, Ḵaax̱'achgóok.

So he told his nephews that's bad luck:
"Let's go back."

They came back that same evening.
He brought up his boat, paddles, spears, and he tells those boys to
    chop it all up.
"I'll never hunt again."
He knows it's something. It's bad luck to hunt now.

139

After that, he just stayed home, I guess.
Anyway, he didn't hunt anymore that one year—
Stayed home all year until fall.
Maybe he goes out a little bit, but he never hunts.

Finally, someone else killed sea lion.
They invited both those two wives of Ḵaax'achgóok.
When those wives of Ḵaax'achgóok came back, he asked the youngest
   one,
"Did they give you any fat? Any fat left over they give you to bring
   home?"

"No, just meat," she answered.

Then he asked his older wife,
"Did they give you any fat to bring home? Any left over?"

"No, no fat, just all meat."

"How come they're so stingy to not give you women any fat!"
He thinks maybe his luck will change.

Next morning he asks his older wife,
"Go ask your brother if I can borrow his boat.
I want to go out just a little ways.
Want to borrow boat, spear, hunting outfit.
I'm lonesome—tired of staying home."

She goes to her brother.
"I want you to lend my husband your boat, spear, your hunting outfit.
He wants to go out just a little ways.
Not far."

"Okay," he says.
"The boys will bring it over later this evening."
He's got eight boys, too—
That's Ḵaax'achgóok's wife's people, Wolf people—they call them Killer
   Whale on coast—
That evening they packed over a brand-new boat—dugout.
Spears, oars, everything in there already.

Ḵaax'achgóok tells those wives,
"You girls better cook up meat in salt water for us."
Next morning, those boys get water ready in sealskin.
Cook things.

Then, when they are ready, Ḵaaxʼachgóok goes out again.
Not far, north wind starts to blow.
You know north wind blows in falltime?
Ḵaaxʼachgóok thinks,
"Gee, we should go back while it's not too rough.
Let's go back," he tells his nephews.
They turn around.
Right away, that wind came up—they row and row.
Soon waves are as big as this house.

Ḵaaxʼachgóok is captain: what he does, the rest of the boys do.
He throws his paddle in the boat.
Those boys do that, too.
Ḵaaxʼachgóok pulled up a blanket and went to sleep.
Those boys, too, they sleep.
They went the whole night and the next day like that.

Towards the second morning, Ḵaaxʼachgóok woke up.
He feels the boat not moving, but he hears waves sucking back.
He pulled the blanket down and looked.
By gosh, they drifted onto an island—
Nice sandy beach.

"Wake up, you boys. What's this I hear?"
It sounds like when the wave goes out, goes back.

Next oldest boy looks up, too.
"Yes, we're on land," he said.
"Well, might as well go on shore."

Those boys run around.
They see a leaf like an umbrella—
It's a stem with a hole that is full of rainwater.
"Frog leaf," they call it.

"Eh, save that [fresh] water."
Each has his own sealskin water bag.
He looks around.
"Take your time.
Go back and see if there's a good place to make a fire."
They found a good place, sheltered from the north wind.

"Let's go there."
Big trees around there.

They make brush camp out of bark.
They carry that bark with them in boat.
Just that quick they had camp put up.
Look for wood—lots of driftwood.
"You boys are not to run all over. We'll check all around first."

On the south side of the island, there's a rocky point.
All kinds of sea lions, seals, all kinds of animals.
When they're on rocks, the tide is out.
He thinks that's the best time to club them.
That's what they did.
Each boy made a club.
They killed off as much as they needed—
Sea otter, sea lion, seal.
Not too much—just what they can handle.
He told them to look after that meat good.

Some people say he was there over a year—
Some say till next spring.
He dreamed he was at home all the time.
    "I gave up hope, then I dreamed I was home."

That's the song I sing for you.
I'm going to tell you about it and tell you why I can sing it
And why we call it Pete Sidney Song.
I'll tell you that when I finish this story.

That man, Ḵaax'achgóok, he always goes to northwind side every day.
He goes out on the point—never tells anyone.
He marks when the sun comes out in the morning—
Marks it with a stick.
In the evening, he goes out again,
Marks a stick where the sun goes down.
He never tells anyone why he does this.
He just does it all the time.
Finally, that stick is in the same place for two days.
He knows this marks the return of spring.
Then the sun starts to come back in June, the longest day.

In the meantime, he said to the boys,
"Make twisted snowshoe string out of seal skin.
Dry it; stretch it.
Make two big piles.

One for the head of the boat, one for the back of the boat."
Finally, when the sun starts back in June,
He sees it behind the mountain called *Tloox*, near Sitka.
In June, that sun is in the same place for one, two days.

He tells those boys just before the end they're going to start back.
Tells those boys to cook meat, put it in seal stomach.
Once they're out on the ocean, there's no way to make fire
So they've got to cook first.
They prepare ahead.
Sealskin rope is for anchor.
When the sun goes back again on the summer side, they start.

"Put everything in the boat."
He knows there's a long calm time in late June when the sun starts
     back.

No wind—
They start anyway.
They think how they're going to make it.
Those boys think, "Our uncle made a mistake.
We were okay on the island, but now we are really lost."

Row, row, row.

Finally, sun came out right in front of the boat.
Evening, goes out at the back.
Ḵaax̱'achgóok anchors the boat and he tells those boys to sleep.

I used to know how many days that trip took—it's a long time,
     though.
I was ten when I heard this story first—
My auntie Mrs. Austin told me the story first time.
Later, I heard my father tell it to the boys.

Sun down.
They anchor the boat when it goes down on the steering side.
Next morning, the sun came out same way at the head of the boat.
He knows what is going on—
They're right on course.
They keep doing that I don't know how long.

Finally, one time, just after the sun goes down,
He sees something like a seagull.

When the sun comes up, it disappears.
Evening sundown, he sees it again.
Four days, he sees it.

The second day he sees it, he asks,
"What's that ahead of our boat? Seagull?"
They think so.
Where could seagull come from in the middle of the ocean?

They camp again.
It gets bigger.
Finally, it looks like a mountain.
They don't stop to rest anymore!
Four paddle all day—four paddle all night.
Their uncle is their boss: he sleeps all day, I guess. Don't know.
Finally, they see it.

Early in the morning, Ḵaax̱'achgóok's oldest wife comes down to cry for
    her husband.
That youngest wife they already gave to another husband.
Finally, all of a sudden, she sees boat coming.
She quits crying—she notices how her husband used to paddle,
Same as the man in the boat.

She runs back to the house.
"It looks like Ḵaax̱'achgóok when he paddles!
Get up! Everybody up!"

"How do you expect that?
It's a whole year now.
You think they live yet?"

Then he comes around the point—
People all pack around that boat.
They took him for dead—already made potlatch for him.

So he gave otter skin to everyone who potlatched for him.
Sea otter skin cost one thousand dollars, those days.

Then he sang songs he made up on that trip.
He made one up when he gave up the oars.

  "I gave up my life out on the deep for the shark."

That song he gave to Ḡaanax̱.ádi people.

Then he made up a song for the sun who saved him:

"The sun came up and saved people."

He made that song during winter
And he sang it when he made a potlatch.

Then that song he sang,

"I gave up hope and then I dreamed I was home."

That's the one I sing.
Deisheetaan people, we own that song,
Because long before, our people captured *Kaax̱'achgóok*'s brother.
When they started to make peace, he sang that song and gave it to us
    for our potlatch.
Then we freed his brother. That's how come we own it.

That's why we claim that song.

17 ✳ Thinking with *Shagóon*

"Well, I've tried to live my life right,
Just like a story."

✳ Travels to Angoon

Well, they talk about us, those people in Angoon. They never see us but they know we're up here from way far back. They know part of them are up here. They've been calling us, "Come back, come back." They want to see us.

And so the boys—my sister's sons—got hold of the idea, Mark and Les, and Mark went to work and started going about it. That's how come we went—it didn't cost us very much but gas. They got the money some way, and the rest of them went on "teaching," for Baha'i. We had prayers every time we meet and any place we go.

And we went from Whitehorse. My daughter Ida and I went to Whitehorse to do our washing, stuff like that. First thing we know, Mark phoned us. "Get ready! Are you ready? We're going on that Angoon trip." My gosh sake, we just had to get ready. Four o'clock they're going to pick us up. "Take your sleeping bags. Just whatever you need, your clothes."

Well, I got extra clothes with me all the time—the only thing I didn't have was my sleeping bag. So I just thought to myself, "Oh, gosh sakes, I need a new one anyway." So I bought a new one that day. And on top of that, I never used it!

So anyway, they picked us up at four o'clock. We got to Haines—I don't know what time—it was dark already, dark when we got there. But we stayed with somebody—friends—Baha'i friends, I guess. They found out the boat was six o'clock in the morning. That lady we stayed with took us to the boat—at six o'clock we got on the boat; we landed in Auk Bay around ten o'clock.

We met somebody at Auk Bay—they knew that we were on the boat. The others went to town. Everybody left me because they know I can't walk around fast like them, so I stayed right in the boat. In the meantime Mark and that girl phoned. When we were in Auk Bay they went ashore and phoned. I know because I asked, "Where's Mark?" And they told me,

"They're phoning. They went ashore and they're phoning." And here they were phoning Angoon Chief! I didn't know. Pretty soon, they all came back again. We stayed about two hours in that Auk Bay and then we went again, we pulled out: that girl that met us went with us to Juneau.

We pulled out of Juneau about twelve o'clock and we stayed on that boat till midnight that night. Then we went off to Hoonah. I didn't get off—nobody got off there—they just stayed there one hour. It was getting dark already.

Then we pulled out of there and we went to Teneki—they stayed at Teneki one hour, too. And from there we all went to bed then. It was dark—nothing to see. Might as well go to bed!

After we left Teneki, we got to Angoon—midnight. And here the chief met us there! He brought somebody with him—there were two cars there. Ida and I stayed with the chief; he told us he's got only room for two—he's just got beds for two. The rest went to hotel, I think. There was my brother Johnny, and Mark, and my sister Dora and Mabel. We wanted to take my son Pete, too, but we couldn't catch up with him—too short notice—we couldn't take him.

The very next day was Sunday. First thing I get up in the morning, I said right away, "I want to go to church." So they took us Presbyterian Church. Then in the evening we went to Salvation Army Church. And, of course, they had meetings [Baha'i] in the afternoon. We prayed, everything.

And Monday afternoon, we were invited to the hall. Ida knows [the name of] the hall—they made lunch for the elders: all the Angoon elders were invited and we were invited, too. We had lunch there. Oh, of course, people talked—they introduced us to the rest of the people. They said we were long-lost relations. And I talked about the Beaver—how we own Beaver and everything. I told them the story I know, our *Deisheetaan* history. And they told the same—yes, they know all that story, same story. But they don't know how we got there. My daughter said, "We never had any trouble. We never separated through trouble. We just married into this country. That's how we're Inland Tlingit."[68]

And that Monday night they invited us to the hall—the community hall. We're all invited there, and they sat us at the head of the table. The chief told us to use our costumes—it's just lucky we had them! I took my costume to Fairbanks and left it right in Whitehorse—that's how come I never took it back to Tagish, so I just took it to Angoon. And all of them had their vests: my sister Dora had hers, and my daughter Ida—she bought one; my daughter Mabel bought one, too, and Mark had one—his mother made him one—and my brother had his. And I took mine, too.

A funny thing happened: my drum quit working. Got flat on me. I had to borrow the chief's drum to use it.

Here, they danced for us, those kids. They came in, came in, came in dancing. Then—where we were sitting at the head of the table—they came right in the middle in a circle in front of us. Even little kids about two or three years old! They said "Welcome home" to us every time they go by. Each one of them going by, they said "Welcome home" to us! Isn't that something? Even those little tiny things! They went dancing right by us and went right out.

Well, this is Monday. Then Tuesday, there was nothing going on. And Wednesday, the Angoon elders made tea for us again, and then the chief told us, "On Friday night you fellows, you Inland Tlingit, you got to make tea for us, too," he said.

We said, "Sure, we will, we will."

He said, "I don't know what we're going to do about the Indian food. These Angoon Ravens are going to help you people. You fellows can just buy the fruit and vegetables—potatoes and stuff like that. And the fruit salad, and the juice, the cookies, apples, oranges. Stuff like that."

And that Wednesday, when the Angoon elders made tea for us again, when they were finished they started collecting money. I don't know how much they collected now—three or four hundred dollars, I guess it was. My daughter Ida knows how much it was. It sure came in handy when we were buying the food. Oh, of course, we kept some—we collected again and put it in for the food. Wasn't that something? The chief told me that's why they put up the collection—I didn't know what it was for—I thought it was all finished. Here he came to me and gave it right to me. He said, "This is for you fellows, for your welcome home!"

The next day he tells me, "Friday is the time you fellows are going to make tea for Angoon people. So I'll give you fellows advice. You fellows do that, too. It won't be right if you fellows never do anything." But we *were* planning to make tea, you know—we were planning to "open the house"—that *Deisheetaan* House at Angoon. But here that house we really wanted to open burned down. It burned down quite a while ago.

I showed them the picture I had of the Angoon house—they were sure proud of it![69] They said: "That's the one that burned down." That was *Deisheetaan* House: *Deishuhít*, they called it—"end-of-the-trail house." And that Beaver—I always tell you about that Beaver song—well, they know that story. They said where that beaver trail comes out, that's where they built that house. And they call it *Deishuhít*. That trail is still there: they use it as a public trail now, she told me, that Beaver trail.

It was Killer Whale people—*Daḵl'aweidí*—who made a tea on

Wednesday night, so *Deisheetaan shdá* helped us make the party Friday night. They told us how they came to call that place Angoon. The really old name of the place was *Xutsnoowu*—that's the way my mother used to call it—just lately, I hear "Angoon." They said *an* is "town"; *goon* is "cold water." They've got cold spring there—that's *goon* country: "cold spring-water country." *Xuts* is "grizzly bear"; *naawú* is "den": "grizzly bear den." That's a big island.[70]

I told them about that Beaver story and how we came to this country—they didn't know *how*—all they knew is that we went to this country, but they didn't know *how* we went into this country: we got married into inland people. They used our names, too. They sure were surprised: they sure were glad to find us. "Our long-lost relations!" they call us.

The chief took us around there, showed us the houses—the Wolf House, the Killer Whale House. And they told us about this Raven having two heads; I always wondered why it was like that—they told us that when we were having trouble amongst each other, we separated—we split the name. *Deisheetaan, Tukyeidí, Ǥaanax.ádi,* and *Ǥaanaxteidí* were all one. And here they made trouble, so they separated. They never separated to different country, they just separated, just like their flag or something. They stayed right there, but they split the head of the raven.[71]

But they know nothing about that split-tail beaver and they asked me how come I've got that split-tail beaver on my drum. It's a doctor that saw that through his medicine: he says that beaver sits behind the dam, and that's why the dam doesn't break down. It won't break down unless all the beaver are killed off. I told them about that story and how come I've got it on my drum. And I've got split-tail beaver on my shirt, too.[72]

Raven is supposed to own Dog Salmon, too—that's why you see some of them with Dog Salmon on their shirt; that Angoon chief told us we own it.[73] Raven is supposed to be Eagle's wife—Eagle and Raven are husband and wife.[74]

Up here in this country, killer whale and timber wolf are supposed to be brothers—their father is *Deisheetaan* and their mother is *Dakl'ushdá.* Wolf and Wolverine are brothers-in-law: Wolf is married to Wolverine's sister. Fox is Crow, too—*Ǥaanaxteidí* owns that fox. Moose mother brought all the game into the world, but we don't know what she is.

The money they gave us, we used when we made tea for them that Friday night. But we kept some as a souvenir.

Well, the next day was Saturday and we were free—we were going around town visiting people. Wherever we went, we had prayers—and, of course, we made tea and we sang songs. My brother Johnny talked, and I talked, too—talked how we left that place and everything like that.

We walked around to the stores and stuff like that . . . Midnight Saturday night, that's the time we left. We got on the boat again.

Well, the next day we got to Juneau early Sunday morning. We slept—that's the only time I used my eiderdown, when we were sleeping on the boat. When we got to Juneau we stayed overnight. Somebody took us in again—that night we were invited to a potlatch dinner, and I asked those people, "Do you fellows have potlatch dinner every Sunday?"

And he said, "No, that was put up for you." They were making potlatch dinner for us.

Then we stayed overnight there. Early in the morning, they took us to the boat—bigger boat. I don't know what time the boat left . . . eight o'clock, I guess. Then we got to Haines around two o'clock, I think it was, and we stayed there until four o'clock. We started shopping around, running around. The girl we left the car with met us at the boat: she brought our car down, and we met some people because they knew we were coming back that day.

And then we came back to Whitehorse, that night. It got dark on us before we even got to Dezadeash.

✳ The Potlatch at Dyea

Well, people used to go down to deal with those Coast Indians. They used to go down after beaver season closed in springtime; then they would go down to Dyea. Then they would go over the summit—they've got a little boat—everybody's got their own boat to cross Lake Lindeman, I guess, and when they got to the other end, that's the time they would go over the summit and down to the coast, to Dyea.

My mother and father were there one time—I don't know what year it was—anyway, 1898 days—that's the time they went down there. And they lived down in Dyea for three years, she said. The reason they stayed there is because she lost all her children there—three girls and one boy.

My mother tells me my oldest brother was born at Pelly Banks—someplace around there. She called that place *Jamalooga*, Indian way. His name is *Yéilshaan*, too, just like the one we've got now: my brother Johnny Johns. The boy was six years old, my mother said. The twins were *Sa.éek'* and *Sakinyáa*: they all died by German measles and dysentery—everything was going around when the stampede was going to Dawson. White people came and brought their sickness. Oh . . . lots of kids died off, they say, in Juneau and all over. My mother said the baby died first . . . then the others died—I guess that's why my mother didn't feel like coming

back. They stayed there in Dyea for three years. Anyway, my mother said
that my father's cousin—Skookum Jim's oldest brother—was sick. And
they can't leave him!—that's my father's cousin—they can't leave him—
so they stayed there. That's how come she lost all her kids.

The same fall, they went up into the mountains around there and dried
some goat meat. They killed goats and groundhogs and stuff like that—
they just did what they used to do up here in this country. So when all the
meat was dry they went back down to Dyea. Of course, someone else was
looking after his cousin, I guess [while they hunted]—that's why my
mother went with my father. That's the summer my mother lost all those
kids. They made a big spirit house on them.

My mother's aunt, Mrs. Dyea John, *Aandaax'w,* had a son, too, one boy.
Well, he died, too, and then another one—that's two boys of Mrs. Dyea
John. The next one was David Hammond's oldest brother—well, David
Hammond's brother is my mother's cousin. And then they lost my
mother's brother—his name was *Tl'úku*—I don't know his English name.
And *Aandaax'w* built the spirit house. Of course, my mother and them
helped get the lumber and everything. Those kids are the only ones that
had a spirit house on them, she said.

And then—I don't know what year it was—we went down to Skagway, my sister Dora and me. We went down and Mr. Matthew took us to
Dyea cemetery. He wanted to show us his daughter's grave: that's how
come we went there. And since my mother had told me about the spirit
house, we looked for it and we found it. It's okay—nothing wrong with
it . . . but it was close to the water bank there. Well, it was all right, I saw
that spirit house; I knew that my sisters were there, my oldest sisters.

And then another time we went down again—my daughter Ida and I
went down and we went to the cemetery and that spirit house was still
there yet, but the roof was kind of caving in. Not very long after, we heard
about the cemetery washing out—landslide, I guess.

Then about the year before last, we went down again. Ida and I went
down to visit the cemetery and here we could see that there's no spirit
house there—nothing! We just saw something swimming around the
grave. Just close by we saw the lumber piled up there. Maybe it caved
in—maybe it washed out . . . we don't know—but if it washed out, I
guess the lumber wouldn't be there.

And then when I came back I started thinking about it, thinking about
it all the time. Gee . . . there's no mark on those kids. And if my mother
was living, I bet she'd do something about it. I thought that way all the
time. And pretty soon, I started thinking about it *all* the time.

I always travel around. I went down to Haines and visited Austin Hammond . . . Well, that's my cousin David's [Hammond] cousin . . .[75] So I asked him. I told him all about those kids had a spirit house on them, and I told him it's washed out. And I told him I want to put a gravestone on it. "Do you think it would be all right if I do that? Just to put a mark on those kids? Just to know that they were there? That our people were there?"

And he said, "That's okay. I think that's okay. There's nothing wrong with that," he said. "Just to know that they're buried there." And he told me a story about it:

> There's two boys lost on Douglas Island.
> That's at Juneau. The island near there.
> They call it Douglas Island.
> Two boys—brothers or close relations—got lost.
> And no one could find their graves, their bodies.
> They didn't find their bodies till I don't know how long after.
> People gathered together and they talked about it.
> They said, "Might as well be we put a stone there,
> Just put a stone anyplace," they said.
> "And put their names on it.
> And that way people will know they *were* there.
> They were lost there, someplace."
> That's going to be just like that if you do that!
> There's nothing wrong with it, he said.

And I told him: "Well, you happen to be our cousin by my cousin David, anyway." He calls us "sister," and I asked him and he said, "Go ahead, if you want to do it, do it. You could do that." That's how come I started thinking about it.

So I talked to my daughter, Ida. I talked to just my family first, and they said "All right." We collected money first for it and we sent out—I've got the address in Vancouver where I bought my husband's gravestone and we wrote to them. And I told them to send us a catalog. And they [family members] drew by hand two or three different kinds of design. And then we said, "Okay," and we went for it.

That's last spring . . . early this time of year we started. And here we never got it till just two or three days before the party was to go! We told Dora we're going to have a party on the seventh of October. And here just two, three days before that we got a letter. "The gravestone has landed in Whitehorse." So I sent Henry to go and get it for me. We gave him the papers and everything and he went to get it. He paid the freight on it and brought it back. Well, we already set the date on what day we were supposed to be down there.

So we went on the seventh of October—we went early in the morning. Who all I notified—my brother and the rest—they all came down there—even William and Winnie and Agnes. And we made a party. In the meantime, I wrote to Austin to come to stay with us, to come and visit us in Skagway. He never did, because he was busy other ways, going to meetings.

But anyway, we rented the Legion Hall: that's where we got the party. The boss of the Legion Hall I knew already—my husband used to know him, so we rented from him—tables and chairs and everything were all there—all ready. And that's where we had our party.

And that day when we all got down there, it was raining like everything! And while it was raining, I just prayed and prayed so it could clear up. And sure enough, it cleared up. It stopped raining for an hour or two and we took that stone over there. We got my daughter's husband Henry to fix up the base and we put it up.

Of course, I told some stories there—I talked to people. And we sang some songs. We sang Beaver song: that's our song, the *Deisheetaan* song we sing all the time. And then I talked to people the best way I could—I don't know much about how to make a speech, long time ago, the old way. But anyway, I talked to people, all the Wolf people who were there.

The people buried there are these: my mother's brother is the oldest one, *Tl'úku*. And the next one is my mother's brother, *Nahóowu*—I don't know the English name. And then there's Johnny's namesake, oldest one, *Yéiłshaan;* and then my three sisters—the first girls were twins, *Sa.éek'* one of them, *Sakinyáa* the other. And then the baby, too. Well, that's three girls and their brother and my mother's two brothers. That makes how many now?—that's six. And then there was Grandma Dyea John—her son, his name was *Yéiłs'aagí*—I don't know his white-man name, that one. And then David Hammond's oldest brother. And then Mrs. Austin's two boys. And we put that many names on that little stone—it's just a little stone, though. But we just want to know how many of them were there.

People used to go down to Dyea always all the time before Skagway—go back and forth from Tagish to the coast. It was just like going to the store—that's the only place they used to get their outfit, like flour and sugar and tea and stuff. They get enough stuff there for one whole winter's supply.

But it's not only my people [*Deisheetaan*] buried there: my mother's father—his name was *Shaakóon*—that's his Indian name, *Shaakóon*—he's buried there, too. And that Skookum Jim's oldest brother, *Tlákwshaan*—

he's buried there, too. That Lucy Wren—her grandma and her aunt, that Susie. I don't know how many Wolf people are buried there. My mother only told me her father's buried there, and that Susie, and Susie's sister.

And not only that! My mother's got a cousin born in Haines—her name was Mrs. Dennis. We heard about that one, year 1910. My mother got a telegram saying she's very sick, but nobody went down. Anyway, a year or so after that Mrs. Austin and Grandma Hammond went down there to visit grave, I guess, and the people that put her away, they put her away with her own money. She gathered up money for herself, I guess because she was living away from her people. The reason that she never came back was that her husband died there, too . . .

Anyway, altogether us *Deisheetaan* collected up a thousand dollars for that potlatch. Of course, the money we collected up, we paid for the food—everything. And the freight. And the telephone. It's not all my money: it's the kids', all of them—my sister Dora's got three boys. Then there's her daughter Annie. Then there's me and my own daughter Ida and my brother Johnny and the boys. Anyway, it costs us a thousand dollars to fix up that grave.

✴ Reflections

Well, I'm going to tell about this Baha'i Religion. Everybody looks down on it, and I don't think it's right. Everybody! There's lots of people came into the country and they talk about Jesus, about God, all the time. What about Oral Roberts?—he gets messages from God. What about Father Divine? Well, that's why I think Indians are like that. But we call it Indian doctor.

I

They tell about that old man—his name was Major—there were no English people in this country, that time. My mother saw him when she went to Pelly, long time ago.[76] And she says nobody knows about Sunday, Saturday, or anything like that. But he used to call it *Linday*, that means "Sunday." *Linday K'esku* means "little Sunday." That means "Saturday." But I guess he can't say very good and he said Sunday as "*Linday*," *Linday Tlein*, that means "Big Sunday." I guess that was white-man name, but he can't say it very good. He tells about it's going to be the last day, someday. So he said, "It's not going to happen right away. It's going to be long time yet," he said. "And," he said, "that animal is going to have nine legs. A nine-legged animal is going to be our food," he said.

And that's the one us Indians think maybe that's Baha'i. That Baha'i
assembly has nine points. That's what we think. That's what it is. And he said, "If the people believe and live my way, I'm going to be very, very old. But if the people don't accept me, God will take me away."

Well, nobody believed things like that, that time, I guess. They say he was very old when he passed away.

Well, nothing like that happened until Baha'i people started coming here, telling about things like that. That's why we think—my family—we think maybe that's what he meant. Because there's no animal got nine legs. And he said, "That's going to be your food, isn't it?" It's just like food.

So there's lots of us joined in. I think I was the last one joined in because I'm Anglican. All of my kids joined the Baha'i. That's why I joined in, me, too.

Well, my husband is gone thirteen years, fourteen years now. Well, finally I gave up—I gave up and I joined them, too. It's fifteen years now since my husband went away. And he was with me that time. He wasn't feeling very well one day, and my sister Dora came down for me. They were staying up in my brother's home—she came down for me and she told me, "They're going to have Fireside at my place. Are you coming up?"

And I asked her, "What's that mean?"

And she said, "Just a prayer, but they call it Fireside."

And I said, "Okay." I told my husband I'm going up there. And he said, "Okay, okay," he said. "Pray hard for me." He was in bed in our bedroom—we were living in the other house. "Pray hard for me."

So I went up with Dora. After everybody at that place met, each one of us had prayers. And then after prayers they had a cup of tea and everything like that. That was what they called "Fireside." And I don't see why people turn it down.

II

Then another one, another story. I saw that man, though. He's *old* man, though. They call him *Małal*; I don't know what his English name is. That's his Indian name. And he tells people—"This ground is going to burn all over, all over." This is 1908—no, 1912 it was. I *saw* this old man, too: he was Indian doctor. One night he was singing: he made Indian doctor. In the morning, he told people: "This place is on fire all over." And people thought it was the flu. That flu was going to come in 1918, or whenever, when lots of people died. That's the one he talked about. That's just like fire, all. "Lots of people are going to die. But if you pray to God all the time, you're going to pass through this fire." In 1918,—'19,—'20, there was flu. Lots of people died.

That's the time my father died, too, 1920, Carcross. And Mary Phillips, and my father's nephew Billy Bone. Look how many people died just in Carcross! My mother was very sick, but she pulled through, and I got sick, too, not very much, though. All! Everybody except my son Pete, and Edward's girl, Alice. Just those two kids never got sick.

But late July they got a different kind of sickness. Their whole body was just full of pimples, red. Both of them [the children], their eyes got like that, too, and so did Pete. When my father died, my auntie's husband, [Shorty] Austin, he went to the police and told the police: "What do you think about our Indians dying off? Why can't you do something about it?" he told police. And that policeman he went and he talked to the missionary and here they drove us all up to the bishop's with horse team, to that house. That Bishop Bompas house is still standing yet. And here that's where one old man took over, looked after us.

See that? Me, my mother, Mrs. Ginny *Shaakóon* and her husband *Shaakóon* and their baby—oh, they lost their baby, too . . . And we stayed there until we finally got better. Then we went back.

That's what he did for us that time, that missionary. They opened that Bishop Bompas house and put in a bed for us and everything. That's where we all stayed. And that old man, Scotty they called him, he's the one that cooked and everything. Of course, somebody came in to clean up the house during the day until we all got better again. Then we all went home.

That was the old man who said, "This world is on fire." That's the sickness. He sees it like fire. And when he died, before he died, he says he's going to come back again. "Tie your dogs a long way out from the camp," he tells people. But you know nowadays people don't listen to each other—he was sick, badly sick, and they thought he was crazy, I guess. "In four days I'm going to come back," he said.

Here, on the fourth day, those dogs started to bark all over. They hear just like somebody's singing or something. That was what the dogs were barking at—the dogs chased that spirit away again. That's what they say. That's what I heard about him, that old man. *Małal,* they call him.

III

I was very sick in 1935. Flu was going around again. It started fluing again and I was very sick in bed. Oh, I was sick! I thought that I was going to die. I was seeing things, too. Anyway, I started to go someplace. I wanted to go with that man, whoever he is,[77] and he said, "No. No, you go back. You're not going to go. There's no place ready for you. You have to go out and preach the gospel. And then there'll be a place for you after you preach the gospel." That's what he said to me.

Anyway, I got better. I often think about it. Now I'm going to Old Crow with my daughter to talk about the Baha'i teachings or something. Well, I don't know very much about the Baha'i. But my daughter tells me, "I guess that's the one that's coming true now, your dream." She tells me I'm going to go.

And then another time I got sick again. Always when I get sick I see things like that. Nineteen seventy-two, I got sick again. Nurses, they ask me, "Do you know where you are?"

"Yes, I'm in Cloudberry Saloon," I said. I don't know what that means! I used to hear my sons, George, especially, say that. And here I was in the hospital. But what made me say that, I don't know.

That time, too, the sun was over this way. Towards the sun there's a ladder coming down—a big golden ladder. It's just gold, shiny like everything. It came down, and I started to go up that ladder. I just took one step. On both sides there was a person, both sides standing there. And they told me, "No, it's not for you. Go over that way, over this way where the sun sets." And so I looked that way and here I saw a church, same as that, golden, shining through just like it was sunlight. "You've got to go there first, and then you'll be ready to go."

So Ida and I talked about it. Maybe that's the church. When I told them this dream they said maybe that's Baha'i Church. Maybe. And that's why I joined in, too. I think it told me to go to that church. And then I heard somebody say to me, "You're not going to die. You're not going to die yet. Until you start going to that church all the time." That's what they tell me. So I think that's that Baha'i temple, that's what they mean. Because it's all shining. I saw up in the sky something, just like the sky opened. Somebody stuck his head out like that and he's a kind of dark-looking person, and his head was just like a turban with a tassel on it. That's what I saw first, and then that church bell was ringing. And then after that, all those things came to me.

When I did wake up, I started feeling better. After a while, I got all right. It's six days I was unconscious. Six days. On the sixth morning I woke up. Nothing wrong with me. They let me stay in—I don't know what kind of place—I had to have a mattress on the floor where I was sleeping. I never ate or drank water for six days until I woke up good. They gave me food all right, but I don't think I ate it. They took it away again. Then on the sixth day, I woke up, just like there was nothing wrong with me. And the doctor found out I had blood poisoning. I had a little scratch on my forehead and that's the one caused blood poisoning. That's how come I pulled through . . .

IV

Year 1910, I see everybody got crosses made out of Golden Eye Eagle feathers. They made crosses, and everybody wore them if they were going out hunting, anything like that. And they say that's what Major told them to do. I was about nine years old and I asked my mother, "What's that for?" And she said that's what old Major told people to wear, to use when they go out hunting, so they would get their game easily and things like that. Nothing would bother them. That's what she told me at that time. I just thought of that now! I guess it was a cross. I guess that's what it was. At that time I never thought of it, see?

That's why when my husband told me to go up to the prayer, he told me to pray hard for him. He told me, "Anything can help as long as we pray! We don't have to turn anybody down." That's the way they believe, I guess. Anyway, Jesus said, "When two or three are gathered together, I am in the midst," he says. That's why I go to anybody that's praying. Don't care what kind of people they are. I was good Anglican. I used to go to W.A., go to Easter Sunday, World Day of Prayer. But now I'm old and I'm helpless and I've got no way to travel around. Except my daughter takes me anyplace . . .

When I think about that Baha'i faith, it just brings back remembrance of that old Major, what he said. I think about it . . . And I think maybe Baha'i is going to be the leader. That's what I think. That's why I joined it. But still Baha'i never told us to quit going to church. It's just that I'm so far away from church I guess people think I don't like it anymore. I sure like to go to church, keep up my old religion.

But my mother used to like praying. Boy, she used to pray, pray, pray. My father used to tell her, "Stop! Save some for tomorrow. Tomorrow you're going to pray again." That's what he used to say to my mother.

I often say that I don't know very much. I read my Bible all the time. I don't understand it, but I keep praying all the time. It's just my prayers that keep me going, and the people that pray for me.

And that Major talked about it. He said there's going to be one leader. That's the time you fellows expect the last day. "Going to be one leader," he said. "And then you expect the last day."

Well, everybody knows it's going to be the last day sometime.

PART II

My Roots Grow

in Jackpine Roots

KITTY SMITH

✳ Introduction

Kitty Smith was born in approximately 1890 somewhere near the mouth of the Alsek River at a coastal fishcamp she calls by the Tlingit name *Ǥaax'w áa yéi daadune yé*. Her father, *Tàkàtà* (his English name was Pardon), was a well-traveled and literate man whose Tlingit mother had married inland to the Yukon. *Tàkàtà* had attended school in Juneau, Alaska, but he and his family were making their headquarters on branches of the upper Alsek River by the time Kitty was born. His *Daḵl'aweidí* ancestry made him a member of the Wolf moiety. Kitty's mother, *Tatl'èrma*, was a Tagish Athapaskan woman of the Crow moiety who grew up farther inland and to the east, around Marsh Lake. Kitty's parents had met in the course of Tlingit-Athapaskan trade, and *Tàkàtà* brought *Tatl'èrma* and her father *Shadanaak* to live with his people at Dalton Post.

Mrs. Smith never knew her real father because he died when she was only a few months old, but her father's parallel cousin and classificatory brother, Pete, took the customary responsibility of marrying the young widow. Two years later, Pete died, too; then a third brother, Paddy, married *Tatl'èrma*. Kitty's childhood recollections of her mother were of picking berries with her, "a nice girl, she was" (figure 3).

A tragic event in 1898 had enormous repercussions for the lives of members of the Marsh Lake Crow moiety. Four Athapaskan men, one of them Kitty's mother's brother, were accused of killing a prospector. They were quickly arrested, taken to Dawson City, and tried for murder: two died in the hospital, and two others were hanged the following year. Northwest Mounted Police Reports treat the case as an example of "Indian unrest" which was quickly subdued.

159

Kitty's mother was "called home" along with all the other Marsh Lake Crow men and women: two of her uncles—her mother's brothers— came to get her with the news that her own mother was in deep despair following her son's arrest and no longer wanted to live. Paddy's family refused to let *Tatl'èrma* take Kitty with her, possibly because she was the only offspring of their three sons' marriages. When *Tatl'èrma* arrived back at Marsh Lake, it was at the height of an influenza epidemic, and she became ill and died without ever seeing her daughter again.

During Kitty's childhood her father's Tlingit family focused consider- able attention on affirming her high status. They held a potlatch at which she was given special names. She was taken on trips down the Alsek River to the coast when her father's family went to see the "big doctor" there. She was given a lengthy puberty seclusion, and her first marriage was formally arranged by her grandmother. Her entire account of childhood is based in the Dalton Post region and emphasizes her Tlingit ancestry.

A pivotal point in her life occurred when she and her first husband separated. Although she does not discuss the implications of her decision to leave, such an act must have flown in the face of clan arrangements backing up the alliance. At the same time, she also made the decision to live with her "mother's people"—her mother's mother, *Dúshka,* and her mother's brother, Albert Allen—entering the extended network of rela- tionships based at Marsh Lake. From that time on, her account is situated exclusively in this region and she identifies herself with her inland Athapaskan family.

Mrs. Smith's stunning success as an independent trapper must have set her somewhat apart from other women of her generation in the early 1900s, yet she insists that she was essentially "old-fashioned" in her deference to her Marsh Lake grandmother. Her second marriage was a satisfying one, a solid partnership in which her contribution to family income, food production, and childrearing was substantial; quite often she initiated economic undertakings supporting other family members. She never talks about those years as an extension of a life as wife and mother, but rather discusses husband and children as an extension of her already active and busy life.

Storytelling has always been important to Mrs. Smith as a critical way of acquiring knowledge. She grew up absorbing Tlingit traditions, learned Athapaskan (Tagish) stories when she came to live with her mother's family as a mature woman, and has taken an interest in "white-

Mrs. Kitty Smith, photographed in Whitehorse in the summer of 1988. Photo © 1988 by Jim Robb—Yukon.

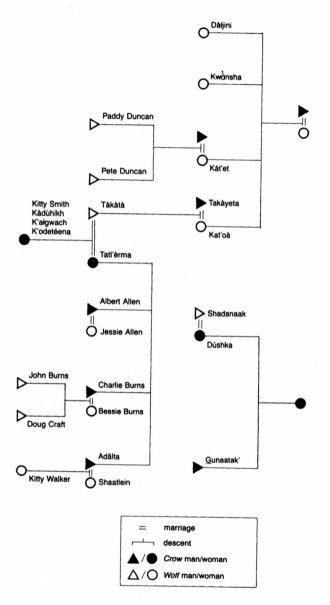

Figure 3. Partial family tree of ancestors of Mrs. Kitty Smith

man" stories during her adult life. She treats storytelling as absolutely

central to conversation and has been interested in stories I could tell her, prompting me with ones she has heard about "Paul Bunny" (Paul Bunyan), to whom she gives an Athapaskan name meaning "he hits the sky," and a variation of Grimm's "Salt Mill" which she recasts as an Athapaskan narrative. To a large extent, her evaluation of other people (including myself) is based on their storytelling abilities.

Her account indirectly explores the nature of the ethnic boundary distinguishing Tlingits from Athapaskans and the implications of bicultural ancestry. This has been a significant question in her own life, because she was raised with Tlingit traditions but her adult life has been spent in the Athapaskan interior. Three ethnic categories appear throughout her account: she uses "Coast Indians" or "salt-water people" to refer to Tlingits (even Inland Tlingits); "Indians" to refer to Athapaskans; and "white man" to refer to all other ethnic groups. Defining one's ethnic identity in areas where cultural boundaries are ambiguous is a complex issue: Athapaskan speakers, now elderly, faced this dilemma in their dealings with Tlingits during the last century much as younger Yukon Indians confront it now in their dealings with Euro-Canadians.

Mrs. Smith knows that she is one of the oldest living people in the Yukon. Some members of her family estimate that she is already more than one hundred years old, although her accounts of events in the early 1890s from the perspective of a child suggest that she is probably now approaching a century of experience. Increasingly, she considers it important to make a record of her memories about the past for younger people. Her own statement about what constitutes ethnographic authority sums this up: "My roots grow in jackpine roots . . . I grow here. I branch here. . . . I'm the oldest one. If I don't remember more, then nobody does. So other people shouldn't talk about what they don't know."

✳ Narrative Text as Collaboration

When I first met Mrs. Kitty Smith in the winter of 1974, she was some years past her eightieth birthday and was living in a canvas wall tent fifteen miles north of the town of Whitehorse, just off the Alaska Highway. "The government" had built her a house in town, she said, but it was cold and drafty and altogether unsuitable for her needs. She was much more comfortable living independently here with her wood stove and her hides for sewing and her things arranged as she liked them; her granddaughter lived in a house nearby if she needed any assistance.

Our habitual afternoon visits that winter occurred in temperatures that regularly plunged to minus 35 degrees Celsius, and I soon came to agree that she was right about the comfort of her tent. The limit to our visits was determined by the amount of time my aging vehicle would stand, unplugged, before refusing to start. Mrs. Smith was much amused by this and took every occasion to remind me that dogs were better than cars for winter travel in the subarctic.

Our acquaintance began when her granddaughter suggested that I might usefully write down her grandmother's history so that family members could have their own history book. Mrs. Smith agreed that this was a fine idea, but rather like Mrs. Sidney, she began by responding patiently to my questions about her early life and then shifted the focus of our visits to record a seemingly endless number of lengthy traditional stories.

A distinctive feature of Mrs. Smith's narrative style is her masterful use of dialogue. Initially, I found it difficult to follow stories in which long portions were rendered as conversation. In these narratives, multiple unidentified characters often carry on debates to which each contributes in turn. Furthermore, much of their dialogue may involve reporting conversations they have had with *other* characters (where each part is again taken by the narrator), and characters' individual thoughts as well as their words may be presented as dialogue. Under Mrs. Smith's expert instruction I learned how she uses this technique to explore conflicting points of view by taking the parts of successive characters and creating discussion among them; she is as likely to do this in accounts of her own life as in traditional narratives. Her manipulation of dialogue provides her with considerable scope for creativity. It is unlikely that she is recalling conversations exactly as she heard them, and even if she were, they were carried on in a different language; yet her English versions convey just the right level of humor, irony, questioning, and concern to bring the events to life.

A few years later Mrs. Smith reluctantly moved to town to live in a house in the *Kwänlin Dän* village within the city limits of Whitehorse, the territorial capital. By now almost ninety, she expressed an interest in teaching me Southern Tutchone names of places she knew near Whitehorse. My bringing maps to her house was inadequate for us to accomplish this task: she couldn't remember the names unless she could see the places, she said, much less explain their location to me. So we began our travels to areas where she had traveled and trapped with her second husband, Billy Smith.

A particular problem arose in my attempts to check transcripts with

Mrs. Smith, and this became clearest once we were recording place names. Whenever we worked together, I tried to transcribe the tape within twenty-four hours and to return as soon as possible to check it with her. Being far from confident about my linguistic abilities, I isolated the Tlingit and Southern Tutchone words, phrases, and names she had included in her account and asked her to repeat them so that I could check my transcriptions with a linguist. Despite our best efforts, this proved impossible. Inevitably, she expressed delight that I seemed able to understand—or at least repeat—names and phrases she had taught me; but instead of saying them again she either launched into the story from which they had been extracted or recited a bewildering array of *other* names associated with it, enjoying the fact that I could now recognize places she named in Tlingit or Southern Tutchone. Repeating a list of disembodied place names was not a meaningful activity; instead she talked *about* the names. Names, like stories, are rooted in context.

During the time we have worked together, we produced a booklet of family history and two booklets of stories for wider distribution.[1] The challenge in our collaboration has been to pull together various narrative elements to reflect minimal Western expectations about life history while showing how, in her view, traditional stories provide a precise, reflective way of accounting for a life well lived. If Angela Sidney gives the impression that she uses stories to build a cultural scaffolding for framing her *life* experience, Mrs. Smith seems to use events from her own experience as the framework for presenting the relevance of her *stories*.

✳ Narrative as Explanation

Mrs. Smith's account appears in twelve sections, with odd-numbered ones containing materials we conventionally associate with life history (family history, childhood, puberty, marriage) and even-numbered sections presenting narratives reflecting back on those accounts. She rarely talks about her own life for more than a few minutes without interjecting an explanatory story; when she returns to her personal experience, she composes her account in a way remarkably parallel to the narrative she has just related. For example, reflecting on her own experience, she draws on some stories with female protagonists (see Sections 8, 10, and 12) to explore a limited number of specific, complex issues in women's lives over and over again from a variety of perspectives. There are stories of conflicting loyalties a woman experiences between affines and consanguineal kin; stories about the choices women make at the age of marriage; stories about resourceful, quick-thinking, and talented women whose cleverness saves others' lives; and stories in which the primary relationship is between a clever grandmother and a loyal grandchild.

Mrs. Smith does not present a formal *Shagóon* but rather tells her family history and her husband's family history as a series of narratives about events she remembers from childhood. She begins by noting her father's high status as a literate man of the *Dakł'aweidí* Wolf clan. Through him, she traces her ancestry back to four important Tlingit sisters who married inland from the coast.[2] The eldest, *Kat'oà*, was her father's mother, the woman who raised her.

Overshadowing all other aspects of her *Shagóon* (Section 1) is the story of the deaths at Marsh Lake which so greatly influenced her mother's family in 1898. It is significant, though, that she discussed this event in detail only after we had begun recording place names in the vicinity of Marsh Lake. Characteristically, she uses narrative to explore conflicting versions of the story.

Briefly, two Indian people died from poison when they used arsenic they found in a baking-powder can to bake bread. Mrs. Smith knows that there are two versions of what happened. Prospectors sometimes used arsenic to refine gold, and some people say that it was deliberately put in the can to poison Indians: "Well, they're just bad friends for Indians, I guess. They try to do things, I guess." But others say that the Indians found the can at an abandoned prospectors' camp and took it and that their deaths were accidental. She also articulates that view: "Somebody found that can, some white-man place. A little baking-powder can . . . An old lady found it—an old lady just like me." She doesn't offer a judgment but uses the narrative to reflect on the incident from both perspectives.

Customary Indian law dictated that members of the victims' moiety (Crow) take steps to avenge the deaths, if not against the individuals actually responsible, at least against representatives of their moiety or clan. The debt could be discharged and hostilities ended either by a formal payment from the offending clan to the bereaved clan or by the death of someone of equivalent status. One white prospector was shot and another wounded; it is unclear whether the two were actually linked with the incident or whether they were seen as appropriate clan representatives of the newcomers. In addition to the dramatic conflict in legal codes, the incident had a profound demographic impact. Marsh Lake was directly on the most popular corridor to the Klondike goldfields; many of the Marsh Lake Crows who were "called home," including Kitty's mother, fell victim to the waves of influenza just reaching the southern Yukon.

After Section 1 sets the stage for Mrs. Smith's own life experience,

Section 2 provides parameters for understanding that experience by outlining the origins and transformations of the physical world where her *Shagóon* occurs. Mrs. Smith tells many other stories about how the world originated and acquired its present shape, and these have been published in her booklets, cited above. Included here are part of her Crow story and her discussion about the continuing significance of the Game Mother story: its reminder that game animals and humans are interdependent.

When Mrs. Smith talks about her husband's people (Section 3), she is referring to her second husband, Billy Smith. She discusses his family with reference to a singular event, which she tells as a story. Billy Smith, a child at the time of the Klondike gold rush, was a nephew of Skookum Jim and a brother of Dawson Charlie, two of the men credited with the initial discovery of gold. Like other women from the southern Yukon who tell this story, she heard the details from her husband's maternal aunt, Kate Carmack, and retells it from Kate's perspective. According to Mrs. Smith, Kate made the whole expedition possible because of her skills as a competent and efficient woman.

Kate had gone down the Yukon River with her white prospector husband, George Carmack. After a whole winter with no news from the couple, Kate's family became concerned. She was the second of Skookum Jim's sisters to vanish downriver with a white prospector, and Jim did the responsible thing (in a matrilineal society) by setting out to find his sisters. The rest of the story unfolds the steps by which they accidentally made the discovery leading to the Klondike rush. Like the story of the deaths at Marsh Lake, this account is told and retold because the events so profoundly influenced the lives of Tagish people.[3] Much of Mrs. Smith's account, though, focuses on the aftermath of the discovery. Following his financial success, Carmack arranged to have his and Kate's daughter sent south to the United States without her mother's knowledge. This callous removal of a child from her mother's matrilineage was still deeply troubling to women in the community of Carcross when I first heard this story in the early 1970s. Kate died in the worldwide influenza epidemic that struck the Yukon after the First World War.

When I began working with Mrs. Smith, I hoped to draw on her century of experience to get some perspective on how women's lives had changed in her lifetime. She responded by redirecting our discussion a generation earlier in time to the changes experienced by her mother and by Kate Carmack. Both were probably born between 1870 and 1880, and both were faced with clear but difficult choices about conflicting loyalties. Their own extended kin group had certain expectations about their responsibilities; these expectations conflicted with those their husbands had of them. *Tatl'èrma* had to leave behind a husband and child when she returned to help her mother. Kate was abandoned by her husband George, who then abducted their daughter and took her to Seattle. As a child, Kitty learned from these stories about the contradictions and conflicting expectations women faced; as an adult, she experienced similar conflicts with her own decision to leave a husband and shift her residence to her "mother's people." Her preoccupation with this theme even allows her to invent a culturally appropriate episode in the Kate Carmack story, giving the white prospector, Carmack, a sister living in Carcross who offered to take in the abandoned wife.

Other stories she tells (Section 4) permit her to dramatize examples more extreme than those normally encountered in life. Put simply, marriage poses an inevitable conflict for women: on the one hand, it is important to retain strong links with one's own parents, brothers, and sisters after marriage; on the other hand, marriage demands new loyalties to a husband and his people. The women in the two stories are forced to make clear choices about whether to ally themselves with their husbands or with their brothers.

Section 5 introduces her own birth and emphasizes the high status she inherited from her father's Tlingit family and their determination to make her name "high." She quotes her stepfather's words to her as a child: "You're not cheap, my daughter. You come from a high place. I don't want somebody to laugh you down. No! High name, we got it. That's our daughter, you!" When Kitty was ten years old, her family held a potlatch to raise her status: she was placed on top of the pile of guns and blankets and was given a new name: *K'odetéena.* Then, one by one, the gifts, including a valuable beaten copper purchased from Yakutat, were distributed. A child's status was bound up with the relative position of her birth within her own lineage and moiety, but she could also be made "noble" if her father's lineage held a potlatch demonstrating its economic strength. One way to raise a child's status—more common for a girl than for a boy—was to hold a feast on her behalf and give away furs.[4]

As the pressure of prospectors on the Chilkat trail intensified, Tlingits tried to replace their waning trade monopoly by claiming the right to be packers, charging high rates to import essential supplies. An enterprising trader, Jack Dalton, brought in horses capable of carrying far more goods than a man could and established his own post near the old trading center *Neskatahéen* in 1894. Mrs. Smith is the only surviving elder from this time who can give an eyewitness account of Dalton's activities. She remembers his arrival first with horses and later with cows he proposed to drive to Dawson City to feed the miners. People were initially terrified by the "big dogs," but her grandfather had seen horses in Juneau and her grandmother had seen cows and the two were able to explain what the animals were. She recalls snatches of conversation from those days: one of the traders insisted that she should drink milk, a suggestion that annoyed her. She describes the system of tokens Dalton used at the post, the buildings he constructed, and refers to a brief marriage with a Southern Tutchone woman.

Mrs. Smith spent most of her early childhood at Dalton with her paternal grandmother and her grandfather "Scottie," who was made a constable by the Northwest Mounted Police in 1899.[5] Her account, though, remains tinged with sadness about her mother's death: she remembers particularly her sense of loss that she had no siblings: "Pretty hard when I was a little kid—no brother, no sisters."

She also traveled a good deal as a child. At least once she made the dangerous trip by boat down the Alsek River to Yakutat with her grandparents and others and learned the names of places along that river and the stories about the surging glaciers animating that landscape. These stories appear in Section 6 as a significant part of her childhood legacy. Glacier stories illustrate the idea that the landscape is active, changing, and alive, rather than inert. Though recognizably of this world, glaciers also seem to symbolize that nether region explored in so many traditional stories, where the world is perpetually winter and ordinary reality is inverted. Such narratives make dramatic use of nature to reflect on culture, enmeshing human activities and behavioral taboos in a living and active landscape.

Like Mrs. Sidney, Mrs. Smith tells the story of "Moldy Head" when she talks about her childhood, as an illustration of the consequences of human arrogance. Her use of dialogue to create two points of view—one human, one animal—reinforces the importance of maintaining a dual perspective in one's dealings with nature.

Kitty Smith was secluded for four months, as befit a young woman of high status, and she attributes her long life to the fact that everything was done just as it should be. Her description of the customs associated with seclusion is presented almost entirely in the third person, a normative account rather than one phrased in terms of her experience. She describes how a young woman's bonnet was decorated with beads or porcupine quills to make it attractive, how a young girl's fingers were wound with string into which down was twisted so she would sew expertly, how she drank only from a swan-bone drinking tube so that water would not directly touch her lips. After her own seclusion, her "long hat" was cut up and given to members of the opposite moiety. Then her grandmother held a potlatch for her, distributing blankets, food, and calico to opposite-moiety relatives in order to affirm the young woman's new status. They planted a tree for her "so I would grow straight," and the following month, a second tree. In her view, contemporary young women remain unprotected for their transition to adulthood and old age because they no longer undergo seclusion. "Schoolgirls, I could fix them! . . . Lots of young people are like old ladies. Schoolgirls get *old!*"

She contrasts the traditional idea of training with that received by "schoolgirls" both in her own day and now. She attended school briefly, but as soon as her stepfather saw her acquiring habits he considered rude, he withdrew her. She repeats his conclusion: "We lived before. We didn't read. We didn't go to school. We're living!" She didn't send her own children to school either, and regular comments about schoolgirls in her account indicate that she is disinclined to change her opinion of this kind of education.

The two stories in Section 8 shift the emphasis to a woman's changing status at puberty when she is "ready for marriage." The drama in each story concerns ways the coming alliance should reinforce, rather than sever, ties between a marriageable woman and her mother or grandmother. In Mrs. Smith's version of "Star Husband" the husbands are exemplary sons-in-law, bringing provisions for their wives' parents. But the girls miss their parents and their mobility so much that they devise a way to escape, making mitts, pants, and babiche, and digging a hole in the sky, climbing down to earth, and returning home.

> You think we're going to stay here when we don't see our daddy?
> When we don't see our mamma?
> When we don't see our sister or brother?
> It's pretty hard—you people up there stay just one place.

And they gleefully report their escape to their mother:

> We got husbands.
> We married that star!
> That's where we've been. But we came down on a string.

The action is less dramatic in the story about Wolf Helper, but it portrays, from a mother's perspective, the ideal cross-generational behavior expected from a daughter and a potential son-in-law, behavior strikingly parallel to that we learn Kitty and her second husband, Billy Smith, displayed toward Kitty's grandmother.

"Well, he's going to marry you, that man," said her mamma.
"We're safe now. No more hard times!"
. . . They don't eat fish no more.
Just like woodpile, grub!

Her description of her own two marriages is pivotal (Section 9) because her point of reference shifts away from her father's people on the upper Alsek drainage to her mother's matrilineage based at Marsh Lake. Her first marriage was arranged by her paternal grandmother: her description of that union emphasizes her own extraordinary skill as a trapper and her husband's general incompetence as well as his philandering ways. She purchased the things he wanted, like a horse and buggy, but his negligence led to an accident and the buggy turned over on her, resulting in a serious back injury that required surgery. According to her account, just before she was to go to the hospital, he abandoned her. Her mother's brothers came to her assistance and signed the necessary hospital admission forms; at that point, she says, she made the decisive choice to leave her Dalton Post people and move to her mother's Marsh Lake family. This was the beginning of a deep attachment to her other grandma, her mother's mother, *Dúshka,* and from then on she says she deferred completely to her, telling her uncles, "I'm going to sleep at my grandma's back. Grandma's my boss now!" She continued to show unusual skill as a trapper, earning eighteen hundred dollars that first winter with her grandma and sending her mother's brother a bottle of rum as a statement of her economic self-sufficiency.[6] This success caused quite a stir, and by Christmas her reputation had spread and suitors were beginning to appear.

Despite her spirited independence, she stoutly maintains that she was conservative in her deference to her grandmother. Her grandmother shared the view advanced in some of the stories that a daughter's (or granddaughter's) marriage should strengthen, not weaken, ties between matrilineally related women, and she put her foot down when the question of a "white-man" husband arose. The dialogue Mrs. Smith uses to recount these discussions suggests that her grandmother saw any potential alliance as a contract between herself and a suitor: "Grandma, she don't want no white-man husband! 'I don't like my grandchild marry white man. No, sir, not me. . . . I've got enough white men. . . . She's just the same as my wind, the air I breathe.'"

The marriage negotiations among Billy Smith, Kitty's mother's brother's wife, and Kitty's grandmother provide a splendid example of Mrs.

Smith's narrative skill at reinventing dialogue. By her own account, she maintained an air of detached disinterest in the proceedings. Her grandmother agreed. Her mother's brothers agreed. Billy Smith made arrangements to build and furnish a house. And when everything was ready, Kitty and her grandmother moved in.

Mrs. Smith described her second marriage as a solid and productive partnership, but her views about marriage as an ideal state are more ambivalent and are expressed in the ways she tells the stories in Section 10. She persistently and methodically explores various perspectives on the woman alone. Characteristically, such a woman is placed in a circumstance in which independence is forced on her and she must think her way out of a difficult situation. Frequently, the plot revolves around a woman who is "stolen" away from her human community and taken to an unfamiliar world where she manages either to escape or to send help to her human relatives. In other cases, she is abandoned because of some real or perceived misdemeanor and is forced to provide her own living. Usually, such a protagonist is able to turn the tables by not only surviving but also providing for the economic well-being of other people.

The first story, "Mountain Man," is most directly patterned on her own experience of being confronted with independence and then taking complete responsibility for looking after and deferring to a grandmother. The second is an account of a woman who was abandoned by one group, survived on her own, and was welcomed into another community. The third is a well-known story of a "stolen woman" who is taken to another world and then helps her human relatives take revenge on her captors.

Section 11 gives a vivid picture of life in the southern Yukon in the 1930s and 1940s. Mrs. Smith discusses her years at Robinson with Billy Smith, the births and deaths of children, and the coming of the Alaska Highway. Her husband acted as a guide for highway construction crews, and she talks about how familiar they both were with the trail he blazed. People were surprised to meet Black American soldiers, but she defined them as "just some kind of white man" and was particularly impressed by their religiosity. She describes her own entrepreneurial success when she enlisted her daughter to sew and her husband and son-in-law to sell warm mitts and mukluks they made. One time her son-in-law went to the airport wearing Kitty's gopher-skin coat: departing soldiers offered him eighty dollars for it, so he sold it. The next time this happened, her husband was wearing a caribou-hide coat she had made him. "How much?" asked a soldier. "Five hundred dollars," replied Kitty's son-in-law and was amazed when the soldier produced five one-hundred-dollar bills. So Mrs. Smith bought a truck for her second family just as she had bought a horse and buggy for her first.

The construction period was an exciting time, but the aftermath was painful. First influenza, measles, and other diseases caused deaths; then tuberculosis forced people, including Mrs. Smith's daughter, into the hospital in Edmonton for years, while things changed at home in their absence. Some women were abandoned by soldiers and reared their children alone.

Mrs. Smith never remarried after her husband died, although she talks about how her remarriage would have occurred in earlier days. Her husband urged her to marry again when he was dying, but she said no, she preferred her independence now that she was older: "I tell him, no. 'I can't take men no more. I can make my own living.' Should be you're on your own. Nobody can boss you around then. You do what you want. My grandchild can look after me."

Mrs. Smith's most recent reflections have to do with her own close and affectionate relationships with her many grandchildren. In many of her stories the major bond is between a grandmother and a grandchild. In one story she explicitly compares the protagonist and his grandmother with one of her own grandsons and herself: the boy in the story was the first one to receive a message that white men, *K'och'èn*, would one day come to the country. Another story continues the theme of the woman "thrown away," but in this case the protagonist is an old woman whose loyal grandchild insists that if she is left he will remain with her. Together they kill a giant, copper-clawed owl that lives in a glacier and emerges to terrorize people. Glaciers were understood to be the dens of giant animals; if the animal could be killed, the glacier would melt.

Mrs. Smith also talks about how difficult it is to outlive all one's friends, and she discusses reincarnation: her husband promised to visit her after his death, and she and women friends have speculated about how he might accomplish this. She also talks about how very much she misses her women friends and names them, all Athapaskan friends she made after her second marriage. She sings a song she made for them, for women of the Wolf moiety, her classificatory "sisters-in-law," and then translates:

> Where are they gone?
> How tough to sing alone.
> They all left me.
> Where are they gone now, all?

How much power do you people think I have?
You left me.
You don't think about me, back this way.
All my friends, where are they gone?
I'm going to be there someday.

Anthropologists have tended to treat life histories of women as a way of presenting the "woman's point of view"; by this they often mean her description of relationships with spouse and children. Mrs. Smith's account certainly does not do this, at least not in any conventional way. Despite her assertion that she was conservative, or "old-fashioned," she barely discusses her first husband and tended to dismiss my questions about him as trivial. She focuses on her travels, her observations, her remarkable success as a trapper, her economic independence, and her friendships with other women. The way in which she does present a woman's view is more complex and relates to her use of stories to explore women's roles. The priority she gives to grandmother-grandchild relationships suggests that not only gender, but also age, influences the way she shapes her narrative: it is possible that had she been describing the same events and telling the same stories half her lifetime ago, at the age of fifty, her emphasis might have been different.

1 ✳ Our Family History

*"I'm going to tell you which way Indians live
And what way this ground we call it."*

My mamma's name is *Tatl'èrma;* she's Crow. Her white-man name used to be Mary.

My daddy's name was Pardon—*Tàkàtà:* he's *Dakl'aweidí,* Wolf. He stayed at Juneau school, Daddy. He's educated. When he came to Yukon, people would say [to anyone who had received a letter]: "Show it to Pardon. He's going to talk to it. He's going to tell you what it says here."

"What does it say here?" they ask.

"You got letter?"

"Yeah, that man sends letter." Well, he reads it. *Tàkàtà* his Indian name, my daddy. He's *Dakl'aweidí,* Wolf. Pardon is his name, though, white-man way. They called him the name "Hume" when he stayed at school.

My grandma's name is Ginny—*Kat'oà*—that's my daddy's mamma. That's Coast Indian name. But they married to Yukon, lots of them—all sisters, four sisters. This one, Grandma, is the oldest, *Kat'oà.* The next one is *Dàljini,* they call her. This [next] one is *Kwànsha.* The last one, *Kàt'et,* Paddy Duncan's mother. Four sisters. Four girls. These names are *heavy:* those are potlatch names. They had a potlatch that time they made those names. They put stuff right there, all they're going to give [away].

My daddy's daddy, Scottie, they call *Takàyeta.*

My mamma's people, though, they're not Coast Indians; they're from Marsh Lake. My daddy's side are all Coast Indians. His grandchild got to go that way. We claim Klukwan, see? Us, Crow. All Coast Indian names they've got it.

They named my mamma, too, when she stayed with my daddy. They gave her Coast Indian name. She says my dad met her on a trading trip at Marsh Lake. When he saw that Marsh Lake woman, he married her. My grandma, *Kat'oà,* saw my mother and liked the look of her—nice-looking woman, I guess. They paid them blankets, paid them guns. Then [my Marsh Lake grandpa] gave his daughter, and my mother stayed with them for good. They go back, go back to Dalton Post, to Haines. That was before I was born, I guess. After white men [started] coming, *they* took Indian women and married them, too. Well, the same thing with Coast Indians, I guess, long time.

175

My mamma's daddy came to Dalton [Post] and stayed there. When his daughter married to Dalton Post, she said to her daddy, "You got to come here, stay here." As soon as my mother married there, that grandpa came there, too, that old man, so they could look after him. After my mother went back to Marsh Lake, he didn't leave. He stayed till he died there. My daddy treats him good. That's why he wanted to die there.

My mamma's daddy had a high coast name—*Shadanaak*, means just like "get up." It's a high name. His white-man name is John. My mamma's mamma came from Marsh Lake. Her Indian name was *Dúshka;* her white-man name was Mary. Pardon Kane's wife is my grandma's namesake—*Dúshka* is her name, my grandma.

When I was a little girl, Daddy died, when I'm a little girl, three months old. They made him get up when he was going to die, made him get up and look at me. He told them, "Don't let her go. Don't let them go. You fellows raise my daughter. Pete Duncan, you marry my wife." Then, after that, Paddy Duncan's brother, Pete, stayed with my mamma. They had no more kids after they married. I didn't know my [second] daddy, Pete Duncan. He died when I was two years old. After that my mamma stayed with Paddy Duncan, and Paddy Duncan stands for my living.

[My mother left because] they took my mother's brother down to Dawson when he killed white man. That's the time they took my mother's brother down, my grandma's son. You know that Marsh Lake? They kill white man, they say—you heard about it, I guess. Well, white men are just bad friends for Indians. They don't want Indians to come close, I guess. They try to do things [to keep them away], I guess. I don't know . . . I don't know *what* they were doing. It's just a story going that way. I don't know much about it, see? This is my mother's people, my mother's mother's son. That's why my mother left me. She heard about it, and she left me. She didn't want her mother to feel bad. That's why she left me.

But they couldn't let me go, nothing! My daddy's brothers—the two of them—Paddy Duncan, Pete Duncan, they're going to raise me. My daddy's mother is going to raise me.

She came back to Marsh Lake that time the rush started. Dawson was just full of white man! Nobody knows what kind of sickness Indians got. They just got sick. *Lots* of people died at Marsh Lake. That's the time she died, too. That's my mother's name that my daughter's oldest daughter has, *Tatl'èrma.*

I don't know what happened . . . Indians don't know . . . I guess something was wrong. I don't know . . . Somebody found that can, some white-man place. A little baking-powder can. An old lady found it—an old lady just like me. People have got flour. A young fellow was staying

with his grandfather. They've got flour and, well, they ask for baking powder. "This looks like the one that cooks bread." Well, nobody can read, you know.

They cooked the bread. It raised the bread, too! Then they gave it to the dog, first time. But the dog died too slow; that was the trouble. Then the boy died, and then his grandpa died. They use that stuff to make gold, they say. That's why I guess they did that.

Used to be they didn't kill people for nothing, long time ago. When they get over it, then they're friends together. This way, however many people died, they're going to pay them. Then they're good friends again, see? Sometimes two chiefs, three chiefs—they kill them to make it even. Then they make a big party. They make a big song.

Well, her mother wanted her. Her son is going to jail. They hanged him up, that time they took him. Somebody came to get her, Dalton Post.

She couldn't take me. No, no, they can't let her take me. My daddy's side, they want to raise me. They want to raise me high, my daddy's people. His grandchild has got to go that way. We claim Klukwan, see? Us, Crow. That's why she can't take me. I knew my mother good, though, I knew her. Oh, gee, I was about that big, me [about five years old]; I used to go with her to get berries, blackberries. I went with her. Ah, nice girl she was.

Two men came to get her: Big Salmon Jim—he married my mother's people. He came to Dalton Post and he said to her, "Your mamma wants you. You come! They're going to take her son down to Dawson to jail." I don't know how many people they took down to Dawson . . . four people, I guess. John Joe's brother, too. John Joe's got a picture, used to be. He showed me one time—they're wearing chains, you know.[7]

My grandma's got no power, my mother's mother. She's got no power. They took her son. She wants to jump in the river, she said. That's what they told my mother. That's why somebody came to get her. My mother's brother came there, and another man, her sister's husband, Big Salmon Jim. They got her. "Your mother's no good. She's going to jump in the water," they say that. "Your brother goes to jail." So they took her. That's where she went. But she can't take me—I never saw her again. At the same time, lots of sickness was going round, you know. She died—just one year she stayed there—at Marsh Lake. Everybody died. Lots of people died when white man got mixed up. All different kinds of sickness, I guess.

When news came about her Marsh Lake brother, my mother didn't want her mother to feel bad. That's why she's got to go. She was going to come back . . . but she didn't come back. I guess she was going to come back, but that spring everybody died.

So I had no sisters. I've got no one behind me. My mother's got just one girl. If she had stayed alive, I would have brothers, sisters. So I have no sisters. Just me, alone.

When her son was hanged, my grandma said, "I don't know if I can forget it, that Whitehorse River way. I wish they'd throw me in the water when I die so I could follow down. My son got lost that way." That's her son who died. They hanged them up . . . Three, four people died for that man. Well, they don't know, that time . . . They don't know policeman business.

2 ✳ Origins and Transformations

*"These stories are true stories,
How this ground came to be."*

✳ How Crow Made the World

That Crow, he's like God: this is how he made the world.
Long time ago, animals were all people.
That was before they had light.
One time they were all out fishing.
Fox and Bear were fishing there—they talk like a person.

Crow comes up.
"Caw! You sleep, you fellows.
If I make daylight, you're going to be scared," he said.
Crow says that. He's really an Indian, though.

People say, "You know that man who's got it? Sun?
That's his daughter's place in there.
He keeps her there, just like old time.
You can't get that kind," they told him.

That big poplar tree right there is rotten inside.
He takes that inside off, throws it beside there.
He throws that tree in the lake, goes in the lake.
He doesn't know where he's going.
He can't die, that Crow, can't get killed.

"That man where he stays, he's got that sun,
That's the place I want it: I want my boat landed there."
That's what he said.
He made a song about that—I know that song, too.

Nighttime . . . Gee, big house there.
Looks just like it's got a light on.

He got out, walked around.
He sees where that big water [stream] running down.

179

He just thinks . . .

Kitty
Smith

He turns himself into a little [piece of] dirt—puts himself right there [in the water].

"I wish she wants to get water . . ." he wants to see that house now.
"I wish that woman wants to drink water."

That lady comes to get water.
Just like a dish, that pot [she carries].
He goes into that pot, goes in like a little dirt . . . he stays there.
She goes in [into the house].

Gee, it shines, that house!
Light in there. Big one! Two.
Right there . . . and right there [pointing].
That's where he throws that light.

He thinks, "What am I going to do?"
That girl is a young girl.
What do you think he did? He went in that cup!
That girl started to drink the water and she swallowed him down!

Just in two weeks, her stomach got big, that girl.
No man here—nothing!
Her mother tells her husband,
"Our girl is going to have a baby.
Where does he come from, that baby?"

"I don't know," he said.

Just one month now she starts to have that baby, gets sick.
He's rich man, that man, that daddy.
Puts everything underneath.
That baby is going to be born on top![8]

Crow thinks, "I'm going to be born-on-top baby:
I wish they would put some grass under me . . ."
That's what he thinks. He thinks for that lady's nurse,
"Get grass, get grass."
That girl is getting tired now.
That lady [her nurse] says,
"I'm going to get that grass. Good one.
I'm going to fix it underneath."

She did it just right then.
It's soft—just like a feather pillow. He's born there.
It's cold. Indian climate is cold, see?

Little boy.
Ah, gee, he sees his grandma.
"Ah, my little grandchild!"
He did that with his eye [winks]. Bad kid!
"Why did he do that?" she asks her husband.
"He did that [winked] with his eye."

"I guess he's playing with you," he told her.
"You see now?
Hi, little baby!
You're going to laugh, you," he told him.

Just in one week, he started to walk.
In two weeks, he's that big [pointing to a three-year-old].
He runs around . . .
Up there are those big ones, the moon and the sun.
Those are the ones he's going to throw.
He starts to cry for that moon.

"Take it down, Mamma, I want to play with it."

His grandpa said,
"I don't want that baby to cry.
Take it off. Let him play with it. He can't lose it."

He rolls it around, I don't know where he put it.
Maybe he swallowed it, I don't know, but he got it!
They look around all over. Lost!
Just that old sun is left there now.

After about one week, he started to cry.
He cried and cried . . .
He's got that moon, though, someplace he's got it.
He cried and cried and his eyes just about slipped out!

His grandpa said, "Take it off.
I don't like my grandchild's eyes that way."

So he played around.
He's going to get away now with that one.

They open someplace—smokehole—when that house is hot.
They've got a lady working there, you know.

"Say, lady," he tells her, "open that. It's too hot."

"You feel hot?"

"Yes," he says.

She opens it . . . He's going to get out that way.
They should put that sun away now!

[Claps hands] Gone!

"Where's that little kid?"
Someplace he falls down, they think.

Crow is thinking about his boat, rotten one.
Just uses it for a boat. He's going to go in it soon.
"I want to be at that fishing place, down the bay," he said.
Don't know how long he stayed in that boat.
"Whew, whew," he paddles.

There's that place. They're fishing yet!

[He gets out.]
"I'm going to make daylight, you people.
Just quiet now," he said.

"Aw, you got no light, you got no sun," they tell him.
He's got them now!

"What do you think I'm going to do?
The best way, I'm going to throw it in the sky.
It's going to stay there."
He throws that moon the first time.
"Stay there for good," he said.
After that, he pulled out that sun.
He threw it, too.

Everything [all the animals] run into the water.
Just one little boy, one little girl they still walk on four hands.
They want to walk that way and he grabs them.

"You're going to walk on two feet.
You're not going to walk on four feet.

I've got two feet, I walk," he said.
He grabbed those kids, one little girl, one little boy.
"I'm going to raise you," he said.
"Sun up there now, daylight now."

Some of them go into the water,
Some of them go into the woods.
They run away.

Two kids only, he saved, one little girl and one little boy.
"You're going to have twelve kids," he told them, that girl,
"This one is going to marry you.
You are going to have two feet: you're not going to walk like that.
Your hair is going to be this way, and your hands."
He showed them.

"No more.
That sun is going to stay for good.
This ground turns, but that sun stays in one place—moon same, too.
That sun does not move, he just stays there."
That's what he said, that Crow.

Those kids, he made them grow.
In the morning, he made them get up, those kids.
He rubs their backs to make them grow. Funny, eh?

Then he gets grub for them.
"What grub am I going to get?" he said.
He brought them grub, gave them some kind of fish.

That Crow, he does everything, teaches everything.
Which way they're going to kill fish, he teaches.
Fishtrap, he makes it; hook, he makes it.
My grandson read that Bible for me—pretty near the same, I think.
He's Jesus, I guess. God, maybe.

✳ Game Mother[9]

In my mother's daddy's time, one man saw Game Mother.
This is just a little while ago, in shotgun time.

I heard this first time when I was a little kid.
My mamma's daddy knew this man: he threw away game for nothing.
Shoots game, then throws it away.
He does this all the time.

One time, Moose came to him and picked him up on its horns:
He dropped his shotgun right then.
That moose carried him away;
He can even sleep right there on those horns.
He carried him across the lake, across to the other side.

A woman was standing up outdoors.
A woman—she's not old, nothing—that's Game Mother.
She stands up, she laughs.

"This is the man you wanted, Mamma?" he told her.

"Yes, that's the man I want.
Come on in." She talks Indian.
Inside the house, she's got campfire.

"You do too much.
Me, I made my kids for you," she told him.
"You use too much.
When you need it, use it, but you throw away for nothing!
What are you doing that for?
You're going to stay with me one month.
I'm going to teach you."

That grub box, she's got it yet.[10]
She opened that box, cut one side that goat.
She cooked it, fed him;
Pretty soon it's one month.

"My son [Moose] is going to take you back."
She gave him lunch, cooked meat.
She told her son,
"If he needs water, take him to a water place.
You take him home to his wife and kids."

He keeps going, keeps going, across the water to his wife and kids.
Comes to camping spot—it's September.

"My mamma told you everything you've got to do right," Moose told
    him.
After that, that man told people how to hunt meat, how to eat,
All she taught him.

This is a true story.
This one happened.

3 ✳ My Husband's People

"Kate Carmack tells me all that.
They just go look for her.
They're not looking for gold!"

✳ Skookum Jim and the Discovery of Gold

Skookum Jim, *Keish,* is my husband's uncle. Dawson Charlie, that's my old man's own brother. Billy was too young, he was too young to stake when they found Dawson. Patsy went and Billy wanted to go, but he got left. Nobody knows that time what is gold anyway—Skookum Jim didn't know either. But his brother-in-law, George Carmack—he knows.

George Carmack, he comes from outside, from California. But he came to Yukon—he wanted to see Yukon, you know. He didn't have much money; his partner was a rich man, though. They went to Fortymile [River], near Dawson. That's the place that George Carmack's partner quit him. What do you think of that? George Carmack came back, walked all the way from Fortymile. He's sure doing good! He came back, and that's how far he made it—to Carcross, Tagish.

In Tagish, there were lots of people—Indians. They knew some white men. Skookum Jim's sister was young girl, that time. George Carmack said to Skookum Jim, "How about I'm going to marry your sister? Then I'm going to be like Indian." Well, it's all right. "You're going to teach me trapping. You're going to teach me everything." He doesn't go back anymore to Skagway, nothing.

Well, they live there, they're doing good. Somebody comes to him: "I'm going to pay you. You come down[river] with me." That's good luck, that one! His wife went with him—Kate Carmack. They go downriver, way down to Dawson, way down to Fortymile. They work there. That other man broke his leg. They took him to doctor. Well, he can't do anything now; he gave George Carmack money, about five hundred.

So . . . they live one winter, Kate Carmack and him, her husband. He's got wife. He's all right! She does *everything,* that Indian woman, you know—hunts, just like nothing, sets snares for rabbits. That's what they

186

eat. I know her: that's my auntie, Kate Carmack, my old man's mother's sister.

Skookum Jim worries about his sister, you know. "Oh, my. Going to get lost. Don't want to get lost, my sister." That's what he says; he talks about it all winter.

Dawson Charlie tells him: "I guess we go down to look for her. We're going to bring her back," he tells his uncle.

Billy, though, Dawson Charlie's brother, he's the same size as that grandchild who looks after me: "Billy, I want him to look after me here." His mother, *Jikaak'w*, says that. He kills game already, Billy, does everything. "You can't take them all to Dawson, that way. It's good enough that Patsy goes," his mother says. She's Dawson Charlie's mother, too.

They fixed their boat. As soon as the ice goes out, they go down. They take lots of grub from Skagway—they don't think they're going to find their brother-in-law. Finally, they were going to go back, talk about it. "We're going to go back, all of us, in this little boat. Easy, we make it."

Here, the same time, George Carmack tells his wife the same thing: "We're going to go back."

One lady, Dawson people, gave them fish. She cut it up, Kate Carmack—that's how they lived there all winter. They got sugar, I guess, down there at Fortymile store. Kate Carmack kills rabbits, lynx, does that way. She's got one little girl now, Graffie.

Springtime now. They're staying at narrow place. You can see boats from there: "August, we're going to try it—we'll make it back." They fix some dry fish—everything. They're going to go back. Kate Carmack sews, she looks around: "Gee, boat coming . . . new boat, too . . . coming this way." They've got a little camp, you know. She tells me about that, Kate Carmack. There's a bed right there . . . fixed it just that way. Somebody gives them moose skin—they put it underneath. They're even got stove. "They're coming onto shore."

George is cutting a little wood. He gets up.

"Ha!" Patsy sees his auntie.

Kate hollers for her husband, George Carmack. "Come quick!" she says.

Skookum Jim is there—Dawson Charlie—Patsy Henderson. George runs down, grabs Skookum Jim. Gee, it's his people! Yeah! They're going to go back now. Going to go back. Going to look first for bull moose. They got lots of grub—I don't know how long they stayed there.

Patsy nearly got shot there, too. He's working on that gun: he's going to clean it, but a shell is in it. He doesn't know it! This time everybody knows everything, but that time, not much. It doesn't go through, though, just on top. Fortymile doctor was there. They're going to go back pretty soon now.

Dawson Charlie says, "We want to kill moose here, to make it dried. Then we'll go back. That way is good. Some hungry people tell me that way is good."

George said, "One man he killed us moose. That way we're pretty good." His wife is kind woman. Dawson Indian, I guess.

They hunt now. Nighttime, they came back. It's dark, too, they said. Skookum Jim, he's got a light—a candle. He got a can, put it in—that's the kind they've got. Dawson Charlie, he shot a bull moose, so they cook meat—big eat! They fall asleep—they eat too much!

Skookum Jim wakes up: Carmack is sleeping, Dawson Charlie too, Patsy too. He wants a drink of water . . . He tells me this, you know . . . He's got hat; he wants to drink with that one. The teapot is full of tea. That's why he goes down, puts his hat in the river that way. He see something up there . . . "Is that copper?" He drinks water, looks again. Same big as beans, you know—bigger than beans . . . heavy.

He takes off. He doesn't know gold much, Skookum Jim. Nobody knows much gold. But George, he knows! He goes back. Dawson Charlie wakes up. "I found something," Jim tells him, Indian way. "Don't know what is that. What does it look like?"

"Copper," he [Charlie] says.

"Make George wake up now—it doesn't look like copper. Heavy, too." George wakes up.

"You wake up good?"

"Yeah."

"What is that, this one? That creek I found it."

"That's gold!" Where's their sleep now! That tea is still there. They don't drink much, though! "You see now gold!" George tells them—runs down to creek.

Kate Carmack tells me all that. They just go look for her. They're not looking for gold!

When they got back to Carcross, George got another girl. She made him crazy—a white lady. He quit his wife, Kate. George Carmack has got sister. That sister's husband tells my auntie, Kate Carmack, "Your husband got another woman. If you want to use your money, you can stay with us." Some days he comes back, stays two or three days. Then . . . gone. That little girl Graffie [their daughter], he gets grub for her. Then he goes again. She knows something is wrong, his wife. Her brother-in-law tells her.

George put his clothes in suitcase. He took that little girl, his daughter.

One man tells him, "I'm going to help you if you want to go back. Go in a boat from Carcross." Dawson Charlie stays there. Skookum Jim stays there. They look for gold again. George wants to go back [to Seattle]. "You go down to that place in the morning. I'll meet you at that place," man tells him. He does that. Goes down, drinks coffee . . . takes his suitcase and puts it in the boat. Then the boat goes—I don't know how many days it gets to Skagway . . . They never came back.

My auntie, Kate Carmack, stayed in Carcross till she died, flu. She didn't get her money, her share, though. She can't know—can't read.

Billy, my husband, used to be Skookum Jim's bodyguard. He's got a gun and he guards the boat for Jim when he's got gold. He got crazy, Skookum Jim, you know—shouldn't be like that. His wife quit him . . . If your husband he finds gold, shouldn't quit him. Dawson Charlie's wife same like that—married white man—Shorty Austin. Mrs. Patsy [Henderson] told me, "You fellows are crazy. What you want to change your husband for?" Lots of women did that, run off with white man.

4 ✳ The Dangers of Distance

✳ Story of Dǫ'

This is true story.

One man was a good man, but people didn't like him.
I don't know why, but people wanted to kill him.

He had a nice bow and arrow, everything nice . . .
Knife, club, horn, bow and arrow . . .
That's why they wanted to kill that man.
Sometimes twenty people tried, but they can't kill him.
He's smart, that man.
When he goes to sleep, he sleeps with his feet where his pillow is.
He's got a club.
When people come there, he gets up quick, kills them.
He's a pretty smart man.
His name is Dǫ'.

One time his grandchild, his daughter's own child.
Married to another place, moved away from her people.

He stayed in one place, though, Dǫ'—he didn't travel around.
She wanted to get away, though, from those people.
She got ready: she's got lots of brothers, three brothers and one sister.
They stay in another city [camp].

One time her husband came back in a skin boat.
He told her,
"Don't go near the boat. It's leaking hard.
I'm going to fix it."
I guess he rides around all the time.
"Don't go to that boat—I'm going to fix it."

Used to be he didn't ever say that . . .
All night she didn't sleep . . .
He's got lots of company, three brothers.

She went to that boat. It's covered with brush:
That's how they used to hide boats.

"What do they do that for?
They didn't bring anything . . ."

She looks . . .
Right under that brush is her brother's head!
Then another brother's head: she saw them both.
That woman's husband did that!
They were hiding them.
They were going to skin those heads there.
Oh . . . she thinks . . .

When she came back, her husband asked her,
"Have you been to the boat?"

"No, you told me not to go to the boat.
I can't go there."

"I'm going to fix that boat.
I'm going to take off.
I'm going to sew up that leaky place."
I guess they packed those heads away someplace.

That girl thought about it.
"I don't know what I'm going to do.
I've got to see my grandpa."

That's her mother's father, that grandpa.
She went there: I guess all the time she sees him.

She told her grandpa,
"Do you know what they did?
They've got my brother's heads, both of them."

"Well, yes," he said.
"War was there. Your sister is the only one who is safe.
She was pulling snares that time it started.
They cleaned up [killed] all the people in that camp—
Just your sister went back to your mother's place.
Her brothers got killed, too.
We're going to go. You stay with me, grandchild."

They camped two days.
They go now.

Her grandpa went with her.

They went in the morning, and her grandpa and her hid on the shore.

That girl threw stumps in the water—threw lots of things in the water.
She made it look as if caribou had gone there:
Then she ran to her husband's place,
"My, I just missed them!
Look at those caribou.
They're just thick in the waters up that point!"

Already she fixed [slashed] every boat.
Quick, they go now.
Sometimes ten people in one boat. Another boat, another boat.
They go.
When they go to deep place, they sink.
Everybody gets drowned.
That Dǫ' now clubbed the ones that got saved.
And she told that mother-in-law,

"Why did your sons do that to my brothers?
What did my brothers do?"

"Well, I don't know."

"How do you not know. Don't your sons tell you?
How is it that they killed my brothers?"
She doesn't believe her.

Then Dǫ' came in.
"Do you want to kill me, too?" that girl asked her mother-in-law.
Her grandpa is there. That woman can't get away.
He's got doctor, I guess, that Dǫ', some kind of medicine.

That old lady hollered.
"Ah . . . her grandpa came with her!
Try to save your people. Try to kill him!"
Crazy!

They want to kill him, the ones that got saved.
Pretty near everybody got drowned, though.
That girl's husband got drowned.
"Chase him in the water! Chase him!"

He ran to the water.
They turned around on the shore.

Some of them fell in the water with cramps.
He clubbed them in that lake.
When they ran away, they fell down with cramps, too.
Both men and women had cramps in their legs.
They just fell down. Can't do anything.
He cleaned them all up, those people.
Just his grandchild was safe: she's the one who made this story.

They didn't kill that husband's mother either.
They told her,
"You're going to live by yourself.
I'm going to go back with my grandpa to my mother."
Well, she can't say anything, that old lady,
She just sat down there.

"You can dry the meat of those ones who got killed.
That's what your son did to my brothers.
You live on that. They're all killed down there.
You dry that one."

Well, they're gone.
Do' takes her back to her mother's place.
He stayed on an island, him.
Wintertime, people came, wanted to kill him.
He's got strong rope, you know.
When people try to get away, they get cramps, fall down.
He clubbed them that way.
That's what he did.

---

* Naakw: Devilfish, or Octopus, Helper

Some Coast Indians, brothers, were going to an island one time.
They told their brother-in-law there are lots of eggs there—
He's married to their sister.

"I want to go.
I'll go with you.
Your sister wants to eat some eggs," he told them.

"All right. Come on."
They took him.

194 There are four brothers and this one, that lady's husband.
Kitty They keep going, keep going.
Smith Pretty soon, now, island.
Gee! He sees island now—ducks, everything. Lots of eggs.
He picks them up.

They got wood. They cooked them.
He ate eggs, too.
That time, he put some aside for his wife in a net basket.
He filled it up, put it in the boat.

Just when they finished eating, those four boys ran off,
Jumped in the boat—
They let that brother-in-law go.

"Ah, they're just playing with me," he thought.
"I'll sit down here. It's all right.
I'm going to eat eggs."

My goodness, they left him. Don't come back!
It gets dark now.
When they get home, his wife asks them,
"Where is your brother-in-law?"

"Down on shore. He saw something.
We let him go—he'll come back.
He wants to look for porcupine."
That's what they said.
They lied: they put him on that island.

Well, he stayed there.
He lived on eggs, he cooked eggs.
He put out snares for seagull.
I don't know how long he was there.

His wife asked her brothers,
"What's the matter? He doesn't come back."

"I don't know."

He stayed there.
One time he saw a boat.
He lay down.
He should have stayed down until they landed,

But they saw him.
His brothers-in-law came back.
As soon as they saw him, they took off. They went back.
Bad people!

But he's living there—he snares seagulls.
He's got fire all that time—lots of drift logs there.
He stayed there . . . stayed there . . .

He got up one morning.
Boat was there!
Nobody in it, though.
He went to see it. He didn't go close, though.
That man is coming his way.

"Gee, what are you doing here? How long you stay here?"

"Well, my brothers-in-law came here to get eggs.
We've got eggs, and they let me go here.
Pretty near two months I stay here," he told that man.
"But those birds that lay eggs are all gone now.
They fly away.
No eggs there no more."

But he's living, though.
Those seagulls are coming there—that's what he lives on.

He talks to him nice,
"Where's your place?"

"My place is up there."

"Oh, my!"

That man went to his boat. He had dry fish.
"You like this kind?"

"Yes!" He's happy now.

"Get in the boat.
I'm not going to take you right to your city, just close."

Right here is the city . . . right here is a point.
Right there, he let him go: he landed at that point.

"You know your place?"

"Yes, I'm going to walk there."

He sat down there until it got dark.

It's pretty near August now.

When it gets dark, when people are sleeping, that's the time he wants
to get home now.

He goes home.

They closed that door: his wife's room is behind that door.

"Who's that?" she asked him.

"Me!" Gee, it's a long time since he got lost.

She got up. She came out to him.

Some people were sleeping there.

They go to her room.

She asked him, "What did they do to you?"

"They let me go on that island."

"But they said you went on shore,

That you went to get porcupine on shore.

You don't come back,

So I guessed grizzly bear killed you.

They tried to look around for you on that shore.

People looked around."

"No, they left me on that island."

"Which way did you come back?"

"Oh, some way I got help."

He doesn't tell her, though, that somebody brought him.

"Some way I came back."

He slept there.

In the morning, that lady got up, started cooking.

Her husband slept.

She cooked something and took it to him.

One week, they stayed that way.

He's getting better now, you know—he was pretty thin, I guess.

He's getting stronger.

That's the time his brother-in-law came, the youngest one.

"We're going to look around that way.

If bear killed him, we can find his bones," he told his sister.

"He got off at that point:
'Sometime I'm going to kill porcupine on that shore,' he said.
'I'm going to walk back.'
Something must have killed him, I guess."
That's what he told his sister.

His sister didn't answer back, just kept quiet.

"You want me to go with you?" she asked.

"We're going to take a boat."
They think he's dead on that island, I guess.
"You can't walk that far."

"All right."

She hides her husband.
They're gone.
All four she sees them—gone.

Well, nothing there.
They look all over for the bones—nothing.
"Well, I guess something ate him.
Should be bones here."
Nothing.
He had a knife with a string on—he forgot it there.
Just that one they find—I don't know what kind of knife—
And they came back.

Everyone was down on the shore trying to get clams when they came
    back.
The youngest brother sat down beside his sister.

"No, we didn't find him.
If something killed him, we should have found his bones.
But nothing there."
He said that.

That time her husband came out!

"What place did I get off?" he asked them.
Gee, he ran outdoors, that boy.
He told his brothers, I guess.
"That man came back!
I was talking with my sister and he came out!"

They get scared now.

That husband and wife were going to sleep when that man [who
helped him] came to the door.
He told his wife,
"This man brought me."

"What are you going to do with those people?" that *Naakw* asked.

They asked the sister,
"What should happen to them?"

That sister said,
"If you go to that island, keep away from them.
They're going to stay there.
You take their boat," she told that helper man.

"All right."

When they hunt, they go to that island, too.
Those boys go again to that island again sometime.
"I don't know which way he came back . . ."
They talked about it, sat down.
"You see . . . he slept right here . . .
He had a pile of wood here . . .
I don't know which way he came back."

They start to go back.
No boat!

"Where's that boat gone? Did you tie it up?
No wind.
Where has that boat gone?"

"You fellows are crazy," that youngest one said.
"I told you, 'Don't let him go.'
You let my brother-in-law go right there.
There's no wind: what would take this boat?
Something is wrong now. We're going to stay here.
That's you people's fault.
Where's that boat now?
You tied it up, you said. No wind.
How quick is gone that boat!
Should be that boat floats around," he tells them.
"You see it now?"

Well, they camp.
They don't know what they're going to do.
Nobody knows that place, I guess.
And, they sleep.

That youngest one hears something—grunt, grunt.
Just like dog chewing, you know.
He wakes up—gee, they're all gone, his brothers . . .
Big thing chewing.
What's he going to do? He sat down there, watched him.

"You leave me alone, me."

"Huh," it said. "Why did you fellows let people go here?
That's why I'm going to eat you people."
He's got six legs, that one, some kind of salt-water thing.
Naakw they call him, coast language—
They say he catches everything.
All he cleaned them.
Just one man he left there.

"You're going to stay here, you," he told him.
He's living there until the end.

People knew they got lost.
They talked about it, I guess.
That man and his wife went to the island.
He's just pretty near bone now, that brother.
Just about fell down.
They found him there.

"Where's your brothers?"

"Something ate them up."

"How come he didn't eat you?"

"Well, I guess because I faced him, that's why I guess he didn't eat me.
Naakw came here." That's what he said.
"He's the one who ate us."

"You threw me away.
That's why it happened."

I guess that's the kind of thing that took him back home, *Naakw*.

His sister and her husband put him in the boat.
They brought him back.

That's because that brother's wife told them,
"Why don't you look around that place where they used to get eggs?"
That's where they found him starving on top.
They brought him back.
His wife went down to see him—
He's just like a little baby, just bone.
They brought him inside.

That man said,
"I told them not to,
Just the same they let my brother-in-law go."
He said that, that man.
That's what happened. We got it, that story.

Should be they didn't do that!
There's a government island now, they say, way out on the ocean.
Seal Island—right full of seals there.
When Paddy Duncan told me that story,
Even then he told me, "It's Seal Island now."

5 ✻ Childhood

"Schoolgirls, who knows this?
Me. I could fix them!"

I was born a long way from Haines, on salt water, at a place where they dry fish eggs—that's the place where I was born. It's got no name now, but Coast Indians call it *Gaax'w áa yéi daadune yé,* "place where they gather herring eggs."[11] It wasn't on a river: it was on the coast, salt water.

They put in some posts down on salt water that time to dry fish eggs. Then they tied up brush right to those posts. Sometimes there are twenty posts or more; sometimes it takes three trees to get enough brush. When those little fish come, they lay eggs: they all go on [stick to] that brush. When salt water goes down, you see fish eggs now—just all white. Then they take them off; they make them dry. That's what they do. That's the place I'm born.

After my mamma died, my grandma raised me, my daddy's people. Lots of time people used to complain when people are "not high enough." That's why Paddy Duncan told me, "You're not cheap, my daughter. You come from a high place. I don't want somebody to laugh you down. No! High name, we got it. That's our daughter, you!" Coast Indian people call that "high-name people."

Me, they're going to call me [a new name]. Going to take me and put me on top! Yeah! I got lots of names, you know, me. Coast Indian names. That's what they do, Indians. My names—my own names—are these ones:

First, *K'algwách*—that's the time I'm born, my baby name. One old lady, she held my mamma; she helped [at the birth]. She said, "My name it's going to be, if it's a little girl." She gave me her name, that lady. That's her son's name—*Sagwaaye*—that my grandson Richard has—Coast Indian name. All my grandchild got Coast Indian names.

The next one, my next name, they made potlatch that time: *Kàdùhikh.* You see where Annie Ned lives alongside that mountain? Its name is *Kàdùhikh.* It belonged to somebody, used to be. They named me for it, and that's why they call me *Kàdùhikh.*

Another one, another of my names is *Téena. Téena: Ko'detéena.* White man uses that name now—"Tina." That's my namesake, my granddaughter Judy's daughter, "Tina." It's an Indian name. It's some kind of fancy thing—copper—about that big—they buy them from *Yaakwdáat*.[12] All kinds of pictures. They buy them at Dalton Post. Harry Joe's got one [copper]: used to be Big Jim owned it. When he died, Harry Joe took over; that's his people, you know. It's just like it's big money, see? That's why [they named me] *Téena*. Big money potlatch, that time. They put me on top of all that stuff—blankets, guns, everything. Then they called me . . . "*Téena*" . . . and they potlatched that thing now [the copper]. I'm a big girl, that time—ten, maybe. They wanted to make [the name] high, that's why they did that. It's just like you make a high name for your grandchild. That's why they threw stuff away, too, at the potlatch, the time they gave me a name. That happened at Dalton Post.

I've got no one behind me: my mother only had one girl. If she stayed alive, I would have brother and sister. She left because she didn't want her mother to feel bad. But my daddy's brothers, they can't let me go . . . I knew my mother when she left me. I was about five years old, that time, I guess—old enough to pick berries then. When she left, my daddy's people took me someplace.

So I've got no sisters. Pretty hard when I was a little kid—no brother, no sisters. My daddy's mother, my grandma, that's the one who raised me. Paddy Duncan, Pete Duncan, they stand for my clothes.

My grandpa, Scottie, was a policeman, used to be. His wife, my grandma, raised me at Dalton Post. We stayed down at the police camp, the customs house. When Skookum Jim found gold, white men just went that way. That time, lots of Indian policemen. Oh, talk about Indian policemen! Paddy Duncan, Pete Duncan, David Hume, Johnny Fraser—*lots* of people!

Grandpa, *he* knew white men: he'd been lots of times to Juneau. That time white men came, horses came. Lots of people were scared that time: "That's big dogs they're bringing," people think.

"I know horse!" my grandpa said. They look . . . they look . . . they're coming now. This Jack Dalton, now he's bringing packing horses. Working people, white men, go to Dawson. That's the time Jack Dalton brought cows to Dawson. Soon *everybody* brought cows that way. Another company brought cows in—sheep, pigs, too, they wanted to bring, but they died. Pigs are no good, but sheep can make it. Halfway down, they killed them—they sent the meat to Dawson.

Talk about cows! Cows coming now . . . crossing the creek . . . people watching. My grandpa ate it; Grandma, too. Some people were scared, though. But Grandma, she's not scared—she saw lots in Juneau. Some-

one kept cow there and got milk out of it. One man gave us pot of milk,
fresh milk. When they got too much, they give us one pot: "That little girl has to drink milk!" he told them. Gee, I don't like him!

I know [remember] when Jack Dalton first came in. I was raised at Dalton Post. Jack Dalton, he's got store there—that's why "Jack Dalton Post" they call it. He brought working people with him, Indians. Those people are Telegraph [Creek] Indians but they speak Tlingit. My grandma knows what they're saying: they told her where they came from. Jack Dalton was a bigshot: he had about twenty-five working people!

They built two buildings, one warehouse, one store: I used to buy raisins at his store. He married Indian woman—did you know that? He's got one kid, but that kid died. His wife died, too—she's Indian woman. After that, he went outside. Since that, he never came back. I guess he might come back someday.

They've got no money at Jack Dalton Post—just tickets: red one is one dollar, yellow is twenty-five cents—two bits—blue one is fifty cents. That's just how far they got—three.[13] In Haines they used real money, but not at Jack Dalton Post. Yes, I know the time Jack Dalton came, but that's all I know. I'm the oldest one. If I don't remember more, then nobody does. So other people shouldn't talk about what they don't know.

Weskatahéen is the same as Dalton Post.[14] Another one, Klukshu Creek. That's Crow water. That Weskatahéen, Wolf owns. Klukshu Yéił means Klukshu Crow. I'm Crow: can't fly, though!

When I was a little kid, I traveled lots—walked around on snowshoes. I've been down to Yaakwdáat, too, in summertime, by boat—down Dalton Post River. It goes to Yaakwdáat, that river. Klukshu Creek goes right clean to salt water, to Yaakwdáat, salt water, right there. Right there is that Indian city, Yaakwdáat.

Three boats went down, went to see Yaakwdáat. They fixed poplar tree boats—big ones: they cut out the inside; then they make hot water by putting hot rocks inside. When this boat tries to open a little bit this way, they [pry it open and] put in cross-pieces. My grandpa made that boat— Grandpa Scottie made that kind of boat. Used to be everybody made boats—Big Jim made one, too. And that's the kind of boat they used to go down.

I'm a little girl that time, but I'm big. I understood. Coast Indians talk a little different, though, Yaakwdáat Indians.

From Dalton Post, three boats went down. Big Jim and his wife [in one boat]; in another one, Grandpa's wife's sister was in the boat with my grandma. Lots of people went! There were lots in each boat, altogether more than ten people. My grandpa, my grandma, and me were three in one boat. Another had *Dàljini* and her daughter and her son—she's got no husband, that time.

That trip took about five days. Champagne River, *Nàlùdi* River, drops down a long way.[15] That glacier is way down there. They just go easy. They camped at *Noogaayík*.[16] Lots of people living there that time. *Tínx Kayaaní*, that's down that way, too.[17] We went down in summertime; Paddy Duncan shot a goat there. That's the time they told me stories about that place [see Section 6].

There's a big doctor there. That's why they wanted to see him, *Yaak-wdáat*. That's why they went down.[18]

Lake Arkell [Kusawa]: there's a long-time Indian trail that way.[19] Dalton trail is foot trail; it's been used long time, too, but Lake Arkell trail is shorter.

Then another time we went to see that first train to Whitehorse.[20] Not much white people in those days. When they hear train going to come, gee, everybody wants to see train. "Coming now, Carcross," they said. I guess Billy worked there. One man, right clean from Skagway, he started: "Stick Tom" they called him, that Indian. That's David Hume's uncle, his mother's brother. Right clean to Whitehorse, he did it; rock, he packed it. No machine, that time. Shovel, that's all—all hand work.

My grandpa was policeman that time. I'm a big girl, that time, not married, though. We came down, wanted to see that train. But it comes before us, that train: we came down late! Three days ago that train came. A train was coming every day now. We met one woman. "You going to see train?"

"Yes, that's why we come down," I tell her. Just a little house there, that's all.

Oh . . . it's coming now . . . Ding, ding, ding, ding . . . Some people get off there. One boat made it down to Whitehorse, too! After we saw that train, we walked back to Dalton Post. There's a walking road there, for a stage. Lots of mines there, lots of horses, so there's a walking road.

6 ✳ Stories from Childhood

"I've got no doctor, me, though—
Just stories.
When I'm kid, I ask them, 'Tell me story, tell me story,'
That's why they tell me.
That's the one I've got."

✳ *Nàlùdi:* The Lowell Glacier

One man lived down there, at *Yaakwdáat,*
"Yakutat," they call it, way down there: people lived at that place, near
   salt water.
Klukshu River goes down to that place.
From there, people came up to this Yukon.
One old man is coming and a little boy about so big.
When they got there, they met an old man, a Yukon Indian.
That old man has no hair on his head, nothing.
The little boy who came from *Yaakwdáat* told him,

"Ah, that old man!
The top of his head is just like the place where gopher plays—
A bare stump."
That kid laughed at him.

The old man who was with him said,
"Don't say that.
You don't know that old man!
Why do you say that?
That old man is your grandpa. When you're old, your hair is going to
   be that way, too!"

Well, that old man is from Yukon, you know.

After that, they went back.

Summertime, that old [Yukon] man went to *Nàlùdi.*
He's medicine man, you know, big doctor.

205

That ice was coming right down from the mountain.
At the end of the ice, a creek came down.
Right there, he sat down.

He said to himself,
"What am I going to do?"
His doctor talks to him.
"You think I'm going to bring that glacier to this mountain?
It's going to be flooded, that side."

His doctor told him,
"You try it. It's going to come."
That old man lay down, right there.
His doctor's working now on that glacier.

It comes down, comes down . . .
Glacier . . . glacier . . . comes down . . . comes down
Until it's all level with this mountain.

That's the first time it [Lowell Glacier] crossed.
That Indian doctor did that.

After he did that, it crossed another time.[21]
My grandma told me it was like that one time, in her time.
All flooded again, that 1016, Haines Junction, that way.[22]
Talk about gophers die! she said.
Before, that glacier didn't do that.
But after he did that, first time, from there it started.

That man stayed there on top of that glacier until that water is filled
    up.
Champagne Landing, everywhere is all full with that water.
There's a water place shows that yet.
"All full now," his doctor said.
"You know how far I'm going to clean them?
Pretty near to the middle of the mountain all I'm going to wash down."

"All right. Break it now," he said.
It broke down, that ice.
Water goes now.

People were staying at a flat place where Champagne Creek [Alsek]
    and Klukshu River [Tatshenshini River] meet—
Some kind of Coast Indian people.

They all died there, people—all washed down to salt water.
Just that one man was saved, that one who told the boy not to make
   fun.
That's the one he saved, that's all.
All cleaned right out.
They say they saw water coming halfway up the mountain.

That happened before my grandmother's time,
But in her time, that ice still goes, touches that mountain.
That time the water was still full.

I've been there, Nàlùdi.
That's the one that broke.
It's a long time since that ice met that mountain.

When my grandmother was a little girl, she stayed at Dalton Post all
   the time.
That's the time she said all the time when they cook they don't use
   cooking stick.
They boil food.
They don't let that soup run over, too, because there is danger in that
   ice.

If that ice smells grease, he doesn't like it.
Should be people just boil meat.
If he smells grease, that's the time he starts.

Just goats and sheep there, no caribou, no moose.

There was a flood in my grandmother's time, though,
But not as big as when that man did that: it's after him.
In his time, that ice came right up to that mountain—
That's why they call it Nàlùdi, "fish stop."
Right there, there is a big creek coming [Alsek River]
Bigger than the Klukshu River.
That creek came from the mountain.

That was before me, in my grandmother's time—
Maybe I was just born then.
August, they go to Kluane. Indians used to walk around like that.
Kluane people, Big Lake people—they're friends together.
They're going to Kluane, I guess.
They stay there, come back.
Flooded! Bear Creek is full of water! So they stayed on the other side.

No trees, I guess, just gravel, willows.
Just a little while, that flood: that flood was just a little while, just to
Bear Creek.
Then he broke down again—and then it's dry.

That's when one old lady told me,
"Talk about gophers!" she said, that flood.
Lots of gophers there. Dead ones. Just full of gophers!
They packed them in:
"Talk about gophers! I wish you were coming that time," she told me.
"That water dropped down in the morning when the glacier broke.
My husband packed in a big bag of gophers.
Then we started, dogs, everything, lots of gophers."

Since the doctor did that the first time, it happens again.
Some young people don't believe me when I say that.
But *I* don't say that: *people* say that.

✴ Moldy Head

Two years, one boy got drowned, stayed with fish.
But he doesn't marry fish, nothing—he just stayed.

He's just a little kid—he wants to snare seagull.
He's the same size as my little grandchild.

His mother gave him fish one winter.
"What for you give me this fish? It's moldy right here."
That boy threw away that fish—that's something wrong.

Next summer, when fish is coming,
That's the time he set snare for seagull. Got it!
"You got seagull. Quick, quick—
It's a deep place. It's going to go."
Just as soon as he's going to grab him, that boy fell in!
That seagull, too, he held him.

He fell in.
Did he drown? They don't know.
He goes down . . . can't do nothing.
He doesn't know where his home is now.

That seagull there is just like his partner.
He holds him—goes down.
He goes down that river—Klukshu River.

He's with those fish now.
They go down—past another city.
They talk about when they're going to break that war house—
That's people's fishtrap.

"We broke them already. We fight already."
That's what they say.
Other people are coming, other fish. All going the same place.
That's dogfish, I guess, that last fish:
Łùk, fish, they call them.
They go back now.

Go by a city.

Lots of people, lots of kids.
They've got nothing to eat. They've got nothing.

That seagull, though, he eats lots of fish eggs.
That boy wants to eat, too.
Seagull stomach is full.
That boy takes some, but he's ashamed.
He hides them someplace.
But someone sees him—

"Ahhhh, that boy, he eats dirty things."

That's just like the time he threw away dried fish!
They told him that was bad and he threw them away.
He got shame.

One of them came to him.
"Are you starving?"

He told them,
"Since I go away, I don't eat anything.
Just drink water."

"Come on, I'll show you."
He took him.
"See that little kid? You push him.
Then take him and cook him.
But be careful how you stick him, or he'll cry, that kid."

"All right."
He pushed that little boy.
Gee, a little king salmon fell in.
He hid him. His seagull is with him.
He made fire and ate him. He's full now!
Then he came back.
That little kid is playing yet!23
"See those people over there?" that little kid told him.
"They're drying fish. When they do it right those fish come back.
They don't kill them."

One old man looked like a chief.
That boy is lonesome sometimes.
That man tries to take him to that lake,
Sits down with him, puts his hand on his neck that [kindly] way.

"Come on, go with us."
That seagull is with him, too, all the time.
That big man sat with him beside that fish lake,
Holds his hand on that boy's neck.

Finally, he forgot his home.
He worries no more. He eats now, all the time.
He forgot it. He stays there.

One year, he stayed there.

Those boys told him,
"We're going to go with people. You come with us."

"Yes, I want to go."

"We're going to teach you."

They wait for the right time.
"Some people are going now, some people are going now.
We go now," they said.
They've got grub.
They feed him, too.
He eats.

They go . . . go . . . go . . . camp someplace . . . go . . . go.
Lots of people meet them, you know.

Already they cut them,
Make them dry when they come down.

"Don't know what that is they're making," he thinks about it.
He sits on the boat.
He doesn't work; just four boys work—they've got their own boat.
That seagull is with him, his partner all the time.

One place, water goes this way.
They're fishing here, too, you know, old people.

"Oh, we're going to throw some hook,
We're going to heave it.
Have you got hook?" [the fish hear people say.]

"Don't sit this way," they tell him.
"If you do, they're going to catch you tail side.
They're not going to get you. They're not going to kill you."

"Yes," he says, "that's what I'll do."
He goes himself, I guess, along there.
Right there . . . sees hook . . . yes . . . it goes across him.

"Pretty soon, fishtrap. Pretty soon that war house."
"Just in the morning, we're going to try it," they say.
They don't say "fishtrap," they say "war house."

In the morning the sun comes out. Up high.

"We're going to see it now, going to see that house!"
My goodness, right there he sees his mamma sitting down!
She's cutting fish.
His mamma.
He knows that someone is sitting down at the creek, at that fish water
   there.
They cut fish, sit down there.
He doesn't get worried. He just stays there.
Those boys are gone. They're gone to that house of war.

He stays there.
That lady hollers for her husband.
"Hah! King salmon there. Try to get it," she tells her husband.
He comes down, his daddy.
He hooks him. He clubs him. He's on the ground now.

He's got some kind of wire, that fish.
Copper wire, he's got it, you know.
That boy—it used to be all the time on his neck!

"Quick, cut him," he tells his wife.
"What's the matter?" he looks around.
He sees that one his son used to wear.
He runs home, that man, his daddy.
Skin. They wrap him in moose skin, take him home.
They go to his uncle's place.
He runs in there, his daddy.

"My brother-in-law! Our boy who got drowned.
That fish in here has got his copper wire.
We've got him home!"

"Bring him here."

His daddy brought him there.
They put him someplace up high and left him there.
They called all his people, that man, young people.

"We're not going to eat.
We're not going to drink water.
Four days like that.
We'll try to save that boy.
It might be he'll come back again."
That's what that man says.

"All right."

Everybody is in there now.
Men, some women.
They don't eat.
His mother, too, doesn't eat. No.
That boy knows that he's in the blanket.
He doesn't know he's a fish!

Three days, those people don't eat.
Sometimes they hold stick that way, just like Indian doctor.

Four days,
They hear a noise in the morning . . . "Ahh . . ."
Everybody wakes up. That man, his uncle says,
"Get up, get up. I hear something!"
People get up. Everybody sings!

"Take me down," that boy says.

Gee, there's a big boy inside. He's big doctor, that boy.

They're gone back, those fish.
The dry fish they cut up all go back home.
They've got a boat, I guess. Which way, I don't know.

But he came back a person.
He's doctor.
He knows everything.
He doesn't eat fish, though.

Shaatláax, they call him, "Moldy Head."

7 * Becoming a Woman

"Well, you're woman, so you want to learn everything.
They fix that hat.
Then you've got to learn everything.
My grandma teaches me. She knows everything."

When she's a woman that time, they put her away—put her under that hat. It's covered with little sticks—porcupine quills. They make a little place for her away from camp. No men are there, just women. They teach her to sew, sew for everyone. She sews skins—gopher-skin robe.

They take termite wood and they heat it up, put it on back of your hands so you'll be handy: you're going to be good at sewing then! They put string between your fingers. Yeah! So you're going to be handy—a good sewing lady. Whoever sews with porcupine quills is going to teach you to fix them. And you're going to learn Indians' own fishnet: they're going to show you, just like a doll's [a model].

They stay one month—high-tone people two months. I got four months, me. Then they took it off. That's why I'm old lady now, because I did that. I'm the last one, me.

You don't drink water. That means you'll be tough. Later you drink water only through a bone, not like this [indicating teacup]. Some kind of geese, swan's bone, like straw. You can't put your mouth [on a cup] or you won't talk good. You got to have that bone all the time on string around your neck.

No fresh meat, so you'll be tough: fresh meat is too soft. They give you what is good: dry one. No berries, or your head will shake when you get old. They brush crow feathers across your eyes so you'll get up early in the morning before crows. They give you goose feathers and you hold them in your hands and blow them in the air: then they make you get up and walk. That way, you won't get tired when you walk. And when you're going to stand up, you blow [indicates rubbing legs, then blowing into the air]: then you stand up. That's so you can't be heavy.

Around your neck, you wear a necklace with two sticks, with a bone shaped like pencil. You can't scratch your head except with a pencil bone or your hair falls out. My stepdaddy, he didn't want them, those sticks.

"How the hell you're going to have two of them?" he said. "Good enough she's got hat!"

Schoolgirls, me, I could fix them! Girls are no good now! They learn that at school, I guess. That's why they get old quick, this time, young people. I got it that way, see? You see I sew yet? Lots of young people are old ladies. Schoolgirls get *old!* They don't do this. Nothing!

I've got no teeth: that's why I walk around, then. But my teeth—if they stayed there, my leg would be no good. For one year I stayed in hospital. That's why doctor cleaned out my teeth. He told me, "No good. But if you got no teeth, you're going to have some kind of power again." That's why I did it.

They teach young men, too—tell them what they can't eat. But men don't have to go away like women. Woman, soon as they got it, they get away. Already her mamma has got hat for her when she's a big girl. Already they make her dress up that way, put stick [necklace] on. That water, she can't drink it from a cup. No! She's got swan bone. When you drink water you suck it that way [through swan-bone tube]. When you scratch your head, you've got two bones, do that way [scratch your head only with a bone]. Not with your fingers, or you lose your hair: I've got lots of hair.

They tie up here [below the knee], put ptarmigan foot [hanging from the tie]. Then, it's just like she's going to be ptarmigan when she's a woman: can't get tired. I used to be just like that, me. Look at me today, how much I'm old. Still I run around in the morning, cook hotcakes for my grandchild.

I'm Crow. When it's finished, Wolf people take off that hat and then Crow gives a potlatch. That's when Crow cuts up that hat and gives it out to Wolf. I was out four months. When they had that party, my grandma gave things to [Wolf] people: blankets, calico, food. That way I have lots of things in my life.

After they take off that hat, they plant a tree, so you grow straight. For me, they planted different tree each month: first one the same day they take off my hat. Then another one after one month. I got two, used to be, just two.

Then white man came. They quit it. Go to school. I started school, too, at Haines. But we fight too much, us girls. They scratched me one time. When he saw me do this [stick out my tongue], that's why my daddy got mad, Paddy Duncan. "Well, get off!" he said. "We lived before. We didn't read. We didn't go to school. We're living." That's what he said. He took me out of school. I didn't go to school long, but I saw lots of things. Same with my kids. They didn't go to school.

8 ✳ From Daughter to Wife

✳ Star Husband[24]

Those two girls are twins, sisters together, those girls.
Their mother and daddy are living yet.
But they don't get married, those girls, not yet.
They're women, so they get ready for marriage.

Nighttime, they sleep.
That's the time that oldest one says,
"Look, sister.
If I want to marry that star, do you think they're going to marry us?
That one, I like it, me.
That little bit gray one."

The younger sister said,
"Ah, no. Me that one."
That one she looks at has no gray, just bright.
"I want that one for a person."

They talk about it, talk about it.
They don't know if they're good hunting men.
When they married that way, those days,
They married sometimes lynx, sometimes wolverine, everything.
Used to be just like a person—wolf, lots of them, marten.
Person inside, they say.

They sleep now.

My goodness.
Somebody sleeps with them, with that oldest one!
She wakes up.
He's got gray hair—looks good, though.
She looks for her sister.
They're not home. Somebody sleeps with that sister.
216 She calls her, "Wake up."

"Yes, I wake up."
"Where we got this man from. Where are we?"

That younger sister, young fellow sleep with her.

"Well," those men say, "last night you talked about us.
You wanted to marry us. That's why we got you."
That's what they told them.

"Where's our daddy?"

"Well, he's down there.
Your daddy, your mamma, they can't come here."

Those girls got nothing to say.

"Well, what do you eat?" those men ask them.

"Well, we eat meat, fish, things like that."

"All right, we're going to get that for breakfast."
They go off to get gopher.

That oldest one doesn't like her husband.
He's a little bit old, you know.
Her sister, though, has a nice young fellow.

Just quick they come back, bring ten gophers.
The oldest one knows how to cook gopher, you know.
She singes them, skins them.
They cook gopher.

Well, her mother down there looked around.
Everything stays where it was. Nothing is moved.
They're just gone! Her daughters are gone!

That oldest girl tells her husband to bring lots of game,
Lots of caribou, lots of marten.

"Whatever you want for blanket,
I'm going to kill that animal for you," her husband told her.

"Yes, marten blanket."

He brings marten just like they were rabbits.
That girls skins them, makes good blanket.

That young girl said,
"What kind of blanket am I going to use?"

"Well, I'm going to bring you which one you want for your blanket.
Fox? Lynx? Marten, your sister has got already."

She wants lynx.
"Lynx, I want it," she said.

He got them.
She fixed them, that girl.
They're sewing, those girls.

Those fellows showed them the place they used to sleep.
"You know that place?
That's where we hear you say you like us.
Your daddy is still near there.
They moved down a little bit.
They miss you."

That oldest man said,
"We're going to go down.
We're going to kill game for them. Going to leave it.
What do they eat? What does your mamma like?"

"Well, that one."
They named them—caribou, sheep.
"You fellows kill marten, too, put them there.
Lynx for Mamma."

Those parents sleep.
They don't know.
That daddy gets up early to go hunting—the sun is not up yet.
My goodness, right there is a pile—marten, lynx!
Then meat already cut—fat—everything!
He wakes up his wife.

"Get up.
It's our daughters sent this for us.
Oh, just fat, meat, fur, everywhere."

Next those girls tell them,
"We eat fish. Bring them fish."

"All right, we'll bring them salmon."

Their daddy fixes the camp up.
He doesn't want to get away from camp there now.

Wants to stay for good.
He fixes Indian stick house, cuts the ground, puts food on top.
Big place they make.

That older star tells his wife,
"Your place is not so far away."

Talk about they kill game!
Those girls, they fix them. Those sisters talk together:
"You think we go down?
Which way we're going to go down?"
They sew lots of pants, lots of mitts.

"We're going to go down that way.
My old man said it's not so far—just our eye makes it look far."
That's what they say.
They make skin, dry skin, fix it this way [a tube].
They're going to leave it this way, put string down the middle,
Fix it up like saddle and sit on it, slide down.
This way they hold them: that's why they want lots of mitts.

It's good, you know.
They try it. They build a foot place—
They're pretty smart, fix it so they can sit down.
They've got lots of mitts.
They cover themselves all over with skin.

"How about we do it this way?"

"Yes, that's good."

"Well, I'm going to take my marten skin."

"Me, too, I'm going to take my blanket."

They try that rope down now.
They put big rock on and get ready to let it down to the ground.
Tie it at the top.

Their husbands said,
"We're going hunting two nights.
Two nights we camp and then we're going to come back."

Those girls get ready now, eh?
Who's going to be first?

"Me," the oldest one said.

"I'm going to go first behind you."

"All right."

They put on clothes now—it's hard work going down.
Not far apart, those sisters, the oldest one first.
They try it now.
Soon they started.
They go down, they go down, they go down . . .
When two mitts get holes, they put on another one.

Oh, my. They landed!

Her daddy fixes camp about one mile up that creek.
They walk around and find it.
"Ah, right there our camp used to be."

"Oh, my, Mamma takes all her blankets with her."
Nothing there.

They look around.
See their little sister about that big plays around that creek.
"Where's your mamma?"

"Where you fellows come from?" that little sister asks.

"Oh, we come back.
We wanted to see you."

"Mamma, right here!" that little one said.
"My sisters, they come!"
She's screaming, that little girl, runs to her mamma.

"We got husbands," they tell their mamma.
"We married that star!
That's where we've been. But we came down on a string."
Gee, she's surprised, that mamma.

They miss their wives up there—they know where they're gone.
They make these girls dream for their husbands.
Nighttime, they make them wake up.
They can't take them back anymore now.

"Why did you fellows run away?"

"Well, we're lonesome.
You think we're going to stay when we don't see our daddy?
When we don't see our mamma?
When we don't see our sister or brother?
It's pretty hard—you people up there stay just one place."

"Yes, you're right," those fellows say.
"Well, we're going to feed you.
We're going to give you what we've got.
Just right alongside of you,
We're going to pile them up there.
Anything you want, you say it when you go to sleep.
Call my name."

Gone. They're gone again.

"We can't stay here," they tell their wife.

Some people make this story a different way,
But this way is honest, you know.
Some people say they landed in a tree and they can't come down.
Then a man comes and says,
"I'm going to marry you," and packs them down.
No! They can't land in a tree; they land on the ground.

After that, just what those girls think, they pile up.
I don't know after that.
They married Indian, I think.
Wolverine, I guess.

✳ Wolf Helper

Long time ago, Wolf was just like a person.
People didn't know wolf at that time.

He came up to a woman and daughter who were making a cache.
This woman and her mamma were making a cache;
They were fishing when that Wolf man came that way.

"What are you doing?" he asked that young girl.

"We're fishing."

"Where are your people?"

"Me and Mamma, all the time we stay here, this fishing place.
We live on fish."

"You got no husband?" he asked that girl.

"No, everybody left us."

They fixed brush camp, that way—they put moss on top for warmth.

"All right. I'll come tonight," he tells that girl.
"Don't tell your mamma, though.
I'm going to come tonight.
I'll kill moose up there—I'm going to bring it for you people."

He's just a young fellow, you know.

She's fishing there at that big hole.
Fish are running. She hooks some on her spear.
She waits and her mamma comes down now.

"How many fish you got, daughter?"

"See right there?"

"Ahhh," she said.

Her mamma packed them up to the cache, piled them there, that way.
Came back.

"I cooked two fish, my daughter," she said,
"That way [roasted whole over the fire].
Fish eggs, too."

That time Wolf man came back and he started to eat that fish.
She watches him, that daughter.

"Who's that?" her mamma asked.

"I don't know."

"Looks like somebody.
He's a long way, your brother—he can't come.
After Christmas, he's going to come to see us.
After winter he's going to come down."

That young fellow came in, said hello.
"What you fellows doing here?
Hello, Grandma," he tells that lady.

"I don't know who's that, you," she says.
She moved her hand that way [gesturing to come in].
"Come in."

He brings in skin sleigh.
My, that lady is just surprised!
Skin sleigh, that man pulls right there.

"Open, Grandma. Lots of things inside.
I kill moose," he tells her.

She calls her daughter.
"Come on, come on now quick."
They open. My. Full of fat moosemeat!

They cook. After they eat, they sit down.

He said, "I'm going to go back again.
I've got a place.
I'm going to bring some more meat, Grandma.
I'm going to marry your daughter."

That lady said,
"All right, you're going to help us lots, grandchild.
Thank you."

"I'm going to hunt yet," that man said.
He took his skin sleigh, took it back.

Gee, they cook meat, those two.

"Well, he's going to marry you, that man," said her mamma.
"We're safe now! No more hard times!"

About two days after—three days, I guess—he came back.
He brought grizzly bear, fat, full inside that sleigh.

"Look," he said. "Do you want to see my snowshoes?"
He brought his snowshoes.
"Can you fix them right here? The string broke."

She tied them up again, that girl.
She fixed them, that broken string—he doesn't want them broken.
"That's good," he said.
"If my string is broken and I chase moose, he's going to run away.
It's going to hold me back.
That's why I need to fix it."

She does everything, that girl now, you know:
She makes skin—her mamma gives her skin.
"Make a skin shirt for him."

She fixes it. Nice.
Quills on. Sewed nice.
He doesn't come back yet, that man.
He hunts again.

He comes back.
He said,
"You know this kind of thing?
You make blanket," he tells his wife.
That woman's going to be his wife, see?
"You're going to make blanket."

Gee, that skin sleigh is just full up with marten.
So many skins!

Well, she fixes them—that girl fixes a marten-skin robe.
She uses it, that girl.
Got a rich man now!
They've got a big cache full.
Anything, they've got it.

That woman had a son, too; he's coming over at Christmas.
He looks around for where his mamma stays . . .
His mamma travels around.

Her son is coming:
"Hey, Mamma!"

"Ah," she tells her son.
"Your sister has got somebody.
We've got good living."

She's got marten-skin blanket, his sister;
Rich man, she married.

They cook moosemeat for him—oh, they cook everything.
They don't eat fish no more.
Just like a woodpile, grub!

When Wolf hunts, he's a good hunter, I guess, just like a person—
Used to be lots of stories like that, you know, just like a person.

When Wolf stayed, summertime, that old lady walked around with
    them.
She walked good, I guess.

"We've got to fix someplace for our camp," that Wolf said.
"Sheep here . . . caribou here . . . moose here.
All right," he said.

They made camp there now; they stayed for good.
People came by there.
Sure lots of meat, you know.

That old woman, his grandma, said,
"I'm getting old now.
You fellows stay together if I quit."
That young girl is sewing . . .
That's the way they tell this story.

Oh, my. People stop: some people stop when they come that way.

That man sees fire near a lake.
"I see fire," he said. "I guess it's somebody."
He said that to his wife.
"Do you want to go there with me?" he asked his wife.
"Might be they starve."

Those people are her mother's people.
They go there.
Gee, they're trying to fish, those people.
When they get one fish, they make soup from that fish meat.
They make big soup.

They're coming.
"We've got to pull some meat," that [Wolf] man said.
They put it inside moose[hide]—marrow, guts, everything.
Meat, fish, everything they load.
They pull . . . they pull.

226   Gee, some kids starve now.

Kitty
Smith Those people see two people coming on the lake—they look.
They're there fishing.

They're coming.

Her auntie, her mother's sister, gives her packsack.

Her husband gives meat to everybody—just empties up that skin
    sleigh.

My. That's the first time they see her husband!

They don't know she's got husband.

They know where they're staying, though.

That's why that woman's son comes all the time to see his mother.

They're fishing there, is why they stay there.

9 ✳ Marriage and Grandmothers

My first husband, I met at Dalton Post. One year after I became a woman, I stayed with him. Then we stayed at Canyon Creek—Canyon Johnny, they call that man. That's where my place used to be. We had a store there and we had house there. I met him from my grandma—well, that's old-fashioned way. We stayed down at Canyon.

He went to Kluane trapping, one time. My friend Frances was with me. I wanted to go trapping, too, me. "Come with me. Be partners," I tell her. No. She didn't want it. Going to trap alone.

So I go . . . go . . . down by that little creek. Stoneberries [Kinnikinick] all over there. I see little marks, little paws. Could be a pup, I think. Look . . . look . . . Then I see it. Little black fox. It just disappeared. Gone!

Well, I got tent. I pitched it there. I'm not in hurry that time. I know what I'm doing.

Next day, nothing. But I see those holes, fox holes—two. I set those snares, one at each place. Got little cage with me, a gunnysack. Wait . . . wait . . . Then, first one, I got it! Red fox. I caught it in that trap, tied it up in gunnysack, put it by my tent. Then next one, cross-fox, I catch. Same way! Wait . . . wait . . . Finally, I got black fox! That's the one.

I bring them back all. Gee, people are sure surprised. Shorty Chambers [the trader] is sure surprised. "I'm going to tell your husband when I see him!"

There's a man up there has horse and buggy—two horses. He wants to trade them for black fox.[25] Two horses, one buggy. Well, I want to keep red fox—I got five already. Cross-fox, too.

My friend came back, Frances. Got nothing! "Ah, my sister," she tells me when she sees it, what I got.

Well, they tell him now, my husband! He hears about it—hears about what I did! If he gets black fox, he wants that buggy—no roads that time. Well, that man comes to me, wants to trade that buggy. "I have to ask my husband," I tell him—I'm young yet. Well, sure. He wants me to do it. So we got that buggy and two horses for that one fox I got!

Then about one year later, I was fixing horses. That rope broke—all old—he should have fixed that one! They told him to fix it! Gee, what's wrong with that man! I fell down and the buggy turned over on me, fell   227 on my back and hurt my back. It got all swollen up. I got to go to hospital. Four days now, they're going to cut it [operate].

Just two days before I go to hospital, there was a dance at Champagne Landing. That Billy [Smith] came up to me, asked me to dance. "No," I tell him. "I've got to go to hospital. They're going to cut it, my back."

He put his hand on me, on my shoulder. "That's too bad, I'm sorry for you," he said that. Well, my husband sees that, watching, watching. He gets jealous, I guess.

That night after, I stayed with my uncle Albert Allen and his wife Jessie. That man [Canyon Johnny], he won't stay there—just wants to make trouble with me, calls Billy my "boyfriend." Well, he's not my boyfriend! He just said he's sorry about my back. Next morning, my auntie says to him, "What's wrong with you?" He slams the door, just feeds those horses. Then he came in, and he rolled up my bedroll. He took off! Leaves me with nothing! "He took your horses," they say.

"Well," I tell them, "I can't carry them with me if I die!"[26]

When I go to hospital, they asked for him, those doctors. Someone's got to sign for me. "Where's your husband?" Well, we wait . . . nothing. No, he's gone. My uncle Albert Allen, he's there, though. He signs for me, I guess. Sam Laberge is my mother's true brother. Albert Allen is her brother, too, but he had another mother.

So this time I came here for good! No more did I go back that way. Well, if I'd stayed with Canyon Johnny I would have stayed there yet. I moved to my uncle Albert Allen in Whitehorse: my grandma's son—my mother's mother's son—my mother's brother. "You've got no sense!" he told me. "You don't know nothing! Winter's coming now!"

"Well, you've got lots of dry meat, gopher, everything." I laugh. I don't think about nothing, that time!

"How you think you're going to sleep with no blanket?" he tells me.

"I'm going to sleep with my grandma!"

"Well, you beat me!" he told me.

"So long as my grandma is living, I don't care. I'm going to sleep at my grandma's back," I told him. "Grandma's my boss now." Dúshka, her name.

"What are you going to do? Are you trapping? Which way are you going to make a living up here?" he asks me.

"I'm trapping!" I said.

"Okay, I'll get traps for you."

He got me two traps. Oh, I shoot everything that time. We go to Fish Lake. I made $1,800 that winter with my grandma! I got him live—a live fox. I got him at Fish Lake, held him [by] two paws. Live fox, yet! Soft![27] I

put him in my packsack: I know what I'm doing, you know. Nighttime, I
came back. Women waiting at the tent, Emma [Burns], her mother Jessie,
my grandma. Emma is my mother's sister's daughter—I call her my sister.
They worry about me, I guess: "Ah, you came back. It's nighttime." They
think I'm hurt, see? I come close to Emma's mother [Jessie], Pelly Jim's
wife. "What you got?" they tell me.

"This is black fox," I tell them.

"My! She's got black fox!" They're satisfied!

Billy was staying at Robinson.[28] He heard about it, though, I guess.
He's Skookum Jim's nephew. He's been all over—been outside that time
his uncle got gold—Seattle, I guess. When he came back, people talked
about me, I guess. "That lady's a nice lady and they threw her away!"
When I got $1,800 for that silver fox, I sent my mother's brother, Charley
Brown, some rum. They were at Robinson: Billy [Smith] and Charley
Brown were partners, and John Joe was their partner, too. I sent it with a
young boy who was trapping there, too. "Where you get it?" they say.

"You know my auntie? Stays at Fish Lake? She got live fox. Got
$1,800!"

He holds that rum, Charley Brown: "$1,800. My!" I don't think any-
body makes that, this time. He came back to Billy and John Joe, by dog
team—tells them the story.

Christmas, we're going to come down; there's going to be a big party at
Jimmy Jackson's, at David Jackson's—his daddy used to be a captain on
the Yukon River, on a Taylor and Drury boat.[29] They told us to go down
to Whitehorse.

Well, I don't know. I don't care much. I don't know Christmas when I
stay at Champagne Landing. I asked Emma Burns's mother, Jessie, "You
fellows going to go downtown at Christmas?"

"If we get some foxes, we'll go down, I guess," they say.

I don't know. I tell them, "Grandma is boss." We've been there before
Christmas. We got money, bought grub. We've got a dog team—no cars,
that time.

There's just one car in Whitehorse: Camp Smith is his name, that one.
He wants to marry me, used to be, that one. But Grandma, she don't want
no white-man husband! Her daughter married white man [Kitty Henry].
Ten years she don't see her, from Dawson. That's why that kind she don't
like it . . . She don't like them, white man. "I don't like my grandchild
marry white man," she said. "No sir, not me."

John Joe tells her, "He's money man, Camp Smith. He's going to look
after you, give you a good home."

"No, I'm not going to give her to white man. That's my daughter's daughter, my grandchild. I'm going to give to Indian, not white man. I got one white-man son-in-law already: he don't help me."

Camp Smith is going to have a car. In March, he tells me, "Car's going to come today." Right there, Indian town used to be [at Lake Laberge]. He comes down, looking for me. "Soon as that car comes I'll look for you." There's a road then to Laberge—a "cat [caterpillar] road." It's going to come now, that car.

I tell Emma's mother, Jessie—my sister-in-law Jessie Burns—I tell her, "Gee! We're going to get ride from Laberge."

Jessie runs in: "Car's coming! It's stopping!" He gave us a ride all the way there—me, my girlfriends!

John Joe said, "You see that? If that man marries your grandchild, you're going to go in that kind of thing all the time."

"No! Just the same, no! I've got enough white men," Grandma said. "I think about it—maybe my daughter is going to come sometime . . . This year, maybe . . . But nothing! Just sends me a little money . . . 'Twenty dollars coming . . . I'm going to stay another year' . . . That's why I don't want it, white man, to take my grandchild this time. She's just the same as my wind, the air I breathe." My grandma didn't see highway. Before it, she died.

After I came to live with Grandma, Jessie Allen told her that Billy Smith wants to marry me. He wasn't married before me. He told Jessie Allen, "If she doesn't get her husband back, I'm going to marry her by Christmas."

We were going to Fish Lake, us, when we got a letter. It came to Jessie Allen. That's old time, old-fashioned way. Just like that, me, used to be. That's my uncle's wife, my mother's brother's wife.[30] She said, "Look! Champagne Landing letter." She teases me. "I'm going to tear up before I see you." She got letters all the time.

I got something at Taylor store, walked around for her, came back to meet her at post office. She has that paper, shows me. She opens . . . opens . . . opens that letter. She laughs, she laughs. "You know where comes from this letter?"

"No."

"It comes from Robinson." She opens. Hundred-dollar bill is in there. "That's your winter's grub," she tells me. "'I'm going to marry you at Christmas. I'm going to get you at Fish Lake to bring you to town.' That's what this letter says." When she came back, she showed it to her husband.

"Well, that's all right," he said, Albert Allen. "He's good man."

She sat down beside my grandma: that's my grandma's son's wife. Just like that, me, used to be! That's my uncle's wife, my mother's brother's wife. "Grandma, I'm going to read this letter to you." [Jessie Allen said.]

"Yes?"

"This Billy Smith, he's going to marry her."

"Hmm . . ." my grandma said. "Yes?"

"He says he's going to get you Christmas, before Christmas, at Fish Lake. Going to bring you to town. You hear me?"

"Yes." *Dän k'è* she talk, you know.

" 'I'm going to marry her,' he tells her."

"Well . . . I don't know . . . I don't know . . ."

"You got hundred dollars here for grub," Jessie tells her.

"Ah . . .!" [Mrs. Smith laughs, indicating negotiations were concluded.]

Yes, two white men wanted me—Camp Smith and one other. A big store man, his daddy used to be. I couldn't say anything: I'm not boss. But Grandma don't like it. He's not good enough. She gave one daughter to white man. Ten years, she don't come back from Dawson. "Who do they think looks after their mamma!?" That's why she doesn't want them. Billy says he wants to marry me. I told him, "Talk to Grandma."

"It's up to you," I told her.

"I'll build house for you, Robinson," [Billy said].

"Yeah? I don't see nothing yet."

Two days he stayed; then he goes back to Robinson to build house. "I'm going to build that house."

From there, I don't know: Grandma said yes. John Joe said yes. Whitehorse Billy said yes. All my mother's people said yes.

My grandma stayed with us all the time after that. This time, *any* way, girls go. But I don't want to do that to my grandma. I loved my grandma. What she tells, me, I believe it.

Billy bought lumber from Matthew Watson, built that house. Charlie Burns helped him build it. Billy was working at the mine, but his partner, Joe Jackie, told us about it.

After a while, maybe a month and a half, Joe Jackie came to get me— that's his partner, McIntosh's brother. He gave one hundred dollars to Grandma. And he gave two hundred dollars for grub. *Now* one hundred dollars is nothing, but that time, lots of money. This time [it buys] just two paper bags full! He gave me that money to get things for that house he's building—I got bed, stove, chairs, dishes, table, washtub. All! Then we took the train to Robinson, Grandma and me.

Trainman called out, "There's your house, Mrs. Billy Smith!" We've got heater, cook stove, bed, four chairs, couch.

And we stayed there now. I don't know my husband yet—he works! I don't know those Carcross people yet. That time Skookum Jim died, that's when I started to stay with Billy [1916]. We waited there one month while he's out working. Joe Jackie killed moose—he's just like brother to Billy. He's got a tent and he stays there with us, with Grandma and me.

Then . . . News coming! They're coming home! Billy got home early one morning, woke me up. "You're sleeping yet? Pretty soon sun comes out. Working people, we feed them." I had moose ribs ready, potatoes, four pies. I'm a good cook! Later, when my husband worked on hunting party, I worked at Carcross hotel four years, Dawson Charlie hotel.

10 ✳ The Resourceful Woman

"This is a story about a woman alone,
She's so smart she didn't even need a husband!"

✳ Mountain Man

There was one lady.
She walked around—young lady, you know.
They say she was stealing some kind of cache—nobody likes that.

One lady loved her, though—
Her auntie or her half-sister, I'm not sure.
She gave her lots of things—
Snare, some knife, sewing things, rabbit snare—
She gave it, you know, everything.

"They're going to throw away you!
You're going to go by yourself.
They talk about you all the time.
You steal, they say that you steal," she tells her.

"It's all right.
I'm going to try to live by myself anyhow.
Sometime somebody is going to find me, marry me," she says to that
    woman.

And they cut fish; she cut fish, too.
Then she packs them.
She went someplace.
People don't call her: used to be they call people when they're going to
    hunt.

"You're going to come with us?" they used to say.
But that time they don't say anything—just everybody gone.

But that woman told her,
"They're going to leave you right there."   233

"That's right."

And one man, just like a chief, said to her,
"What for you steal all the time?
Everything, you steal.
You can go anyplace you want to from here.
They're not going to take you anymore," that chief said.
He gives her matches, you know, that stone [flint]
He throws it to her.

"You keep this one."
And some kind of knife, don't know what kind of knife.

"Thank you."

That fish, they take it all away, I guess.

She catches some fish now—oh, she's got cache.
And she goes now herself.
She puts snare, catches gopher.
Strong woman.

One time she saw fire down there, on a lake.
She knows that's Indians, so she thinks she'll go there.
One old lady is getting water.

She's coming to the shore, that [young] lady.
That old lady sees her.
"Ahh . . . Where comes from that person who comes here?"

Her husband is coming, too.
"Where you come from?"

"Oh, I walk around—people left me.
I walk around. Anyplace I can die."
She says that.

"Well, come on. We're Indians. We're good.
Our son, used to be he killed game for us.
Bear killed him."
That's what they said.
"We're living now ourself. We do fishing here."

Lake fishing, I guess—little creek comes down—
Some kind of thing they put in the water:

The fish come in.
"One month ago our son got killed. Bear killed him.
We're just the same as you, too.
We pretty near die, us here."

He had bow and arrow, that young man.
They've got them:
"This one our son owned, look!"
They show that young lady.
"But he can't do it, your grandpa; he can't aim it."

"I'm going to try it, Grandma," she tells them.
Gee, it went a long way!

They go gopher hunting—that lady came with her.
Aha! Bull caribou walks around.
"I'm going to try it, Grandma."

"Yes, I'm going to watch you from here."

She sneaks up, that lady.
Just close, gee, that caribou jumps.
Another one comes same place—she aimed at that one, too.
That one just falls down there. She runs there.

"Grandma!" she said.
That old lady runs there. Gee, both two.
"What are we going to do, Grandma?"
They take off guts.

"We're going to see Grandpa. Show him!
That grandchild, she's got two!"
He's surprised at that.

They make dry meat there and then they give her that bow and arrow.
"Keep it, Grandchild. Keep it."

She carries it around all the time—she's got sack, you know.
She hunts around all the time.
She sees some kind of game—*xaas*, they call it [buffalo].
She goes there, just close.
She shoots him with bow and copper arrow.
That thing is going just that way till he falls down.
My . . .

They've got all winter grub now.

"Oh, my, I wish someone would help me turn this!
Too big!"
She stands up.
"I wish somebody would come to help me turn this game."

"Ah, I'm right there."

My, they don't know who that is cut them all up.
"Just give me liver," he said.
"I'm going to see you again sometime.
I've got a wife and lots of kids, long way," he said.
He's gone.

Well, she thinks about it.
Doesn't know who.
She brings her grandma there.
She tells her,
"Some kind of man, he helps me."
Well, they don't know. They walk around.

Gee, she sees lots of sheep up there in the mountain.
She can't climb up, though—she hunts around.
Gee, she'd like to get them now.

"What is that you see?" he asks her.

"Look at that sheep.
I can kill game with bow and arrow, but I can't climb up
    there."

He laughs at her now.
"I'm going to go up there.
I'm going to throw down there.
You get them, eh?"

"Yes," she says.

He's got nothing—no tools—that man.
She sits down, that lady.
Oh, my, those sheep just go that way,
Roll down . . . roll down . . . roll down.
I don't know how many sheep.

He goes there, finished.
My goodness—just that much pile of sheep!

They've got no marks on them—just like rabbit when you break the
    neck.
All same, that way.
She cuts off the head, that woman.
It's funny, she thinks . . .
Which way he kills them, that man?
She sits down.

He's coming, that man.

"Ha, ha, ha. You see I kill that game for you?
I don't use it, that game."
That's what he tells her.
He laughs.
"All, I broke their necks. All."

He lives inside that mountain, that man.
Some people inside, they say: *Shat'okaw,* they call them.
"Man inside."

And he talked to her.
He cut them for her, that sheep, cut the guts off, guts off.

"This one I'm going to pack.
I've got a grandma down there."

"Oh," he said.
"Where's your husband?" he tells her.

"No, I got no husband.
They throw me away," she tells him.
"I've got two grandpas down there, my grandma, my grandpa.
I found those people—that's who I stay with."

"Oh. You fellows come right here, see?
If that kind comes back,
I'm going to break his neck, throw down for you," he tells her.

"Yes," she said.
And she goes back. All guts cut off, those sheep.
He piles in one place, too. She goes back, shows them.

"Somebody kills sheep for me—
I don't know what kind of man, Grandma," she tells her.
"All just like rabbits which way he kills them.
Like gophers."
They get broken neck.
That's what he does, that time, that man.

"Ah," that grandpa said.
"I guess *Shat'okaw* does that."
That's what he says, that old man.
I guess he knows that kind of people, that old man, his story.
That's why he said,
"I guess *Shat'okaw*, he helps her."

My, they go there.
They don't bother that fish cache now!
They've got lots of grub all the time!

And two sheep roll down—she sees them, that woman.
She goes and she brings them, that time that man came.

"How about I marry you?" he tells them.

"What am I going to do about my grandma?"

"Well, they're going to stay there.
They're going to stay there for good. We'll feed them."

"Well, I'm going to tell them."
She tells them.
She brings that two sheep just close.
She comes back, tells her grandma:

"You stay here for good.
You think you fellows are good?" ·

"Oh, yes, so long as we eat."

"We're going to bring wood for you, too;
He tells me, that man."

Well, they stay there—don't know for how long,
Everything is coming there.
That woman comes to see them all the time.

Good story, eh? That's the end.

✳ The Woman Who Was Thrown Away

One lady used to stay in Teslin, but they gave her trouble.
They chased her—they don't want her, that lady.
Some people say she bothers somebody's husband—
Just jealous, I guess.

So she goes away—stays herself.
She knows how to do it.
Winter is coming now.

"Don't know what I'm going to do.
Don't know which way I'm going to make a living."

Well, she goes, keeps going somewhere.
My, she sees somebody's track. Looks like a trail.
Keeps going, keeps going.

She finds some kind of camp. People have made fire there.
She goes on that trail—
She's pretty smart, that woman.

Those are Telegraph [Creek] people she finds.

"My goodness," she looks in creek. "Gee, lots of fish there.
I don't know which way I'm going to get them."
She's got one fish already. She cooked that fish.

"Ahh," somebody's boat's coming.

"Aye . . . Who's that?" they call.

She can hear that talk.
Pretty near Telegraph way, we talk; she can understand it.
That lady sat down.

"Where do you come from?"

"Oh, long way. Come from long way.
People don't like me.
I bother somebody's husband, they say.
My husband is gone a long time, and they don't like me.
That's why I go away for good. I want to die someplace."
That's what she said.

"You want to come with us?
Lots of people up here," they tell her.
"Lots of women. Lots of people. City there."

"All right."
She's got dog, too—one dog.
She takes her dog pack and gets in that boat.
Goes back with them.

"There's a chief here.
We're going to take you to that chief."

They're coming there.
"Come in," one man tells her.
She hears them talk their language.

"We found this lady.
She went away from her people—
They don't like her, that's what she says.
She wants to die someplace, wants to get away.
If she gets killed, she doesn't mind."

"She's got no people where she comes from?"

"I don't know . . . I'll ask her . . .
You got people there? Where do you come from?"

"No. Come from long way, down this way.
Used to be my mother married to that place.
Then after she dies, my auntie raised me.
That's all one, me. I'm alone now.
That's why they don't like me much," she said.

"All right. You stay here.
When you're married, it's going to be all right here.
You don't want to be dead in the woods," that chief tells her.
"Up there is a man with no wife.
You take her there," he tells them.

"Yes, pretty soon lots of fish going to come."

She's got a place now,
Fish come, they cut lots of fish—do anything.

That woman was Liard Tom's mother, but she didn't come back to
    Teslin.

Liard knows she is from Teslin, from salt water.
Liard Tom has lots of daughters, but Teslin can't take them back.
They told me that.
Just like they throw them away.

✳ The Stolen Woman

A man and a woman had a bark boat.
They make dry meat.

One day he said, "Look. Our boat is cracked.
We'll have to fix another one."

Somebody did that to their boat.
"Looks like somebody cut it, see?" that woman said.

They had a camp on shore.
The husband kept hunting; all the time he hunts.
She fixed a skin, tanned a skin.

Boat is coming.
They see her—two men.
"You've got a husband?"

"Yes, I've got a husband."

"We're going to take you for our wife."

"What are you talking about?
I don't want to leave my husband!"

Two men.
She tried to stop them. No.

"We're going to kill you if you don't go with us.
Get in our boat!"

She took her sewing bag.
Puts away her husband's moccasins, tied up his blanket.
Everything—put some kind of light there, matches, I guess.

They wait for that husband to come back.

"What are you doing with my wife?"

"We're taking her. We're taking your wife."

Bad people, eh?

"Where do you come from? I want to know." he tells them.

"You know that sky?
You see that sky?
We're going through that way, the way daylight broke, the time the sky
   lifted from salt water.
We go the other way: other-side people are us," they say.
"Your wife we pay for," they say.
They shoot squirrel tail to him on bow and arrow.
Then they shoot owl foot to him.

He called to his wife:
"Don't be too sorry.
Used to be I got lots of people, you know.
Don't be sorry too much, but think about me sometimes."
Gone now.

From there, he went to his country.
He has lots of people, that man.
They make ready for war. They are going to take back that woman.
They fix everything, that way, war stuff.
Bow and arrow, horn, sharp stick for spear, club.
They go now.

Those men told them where they come from.
They keep going, keep going.
They see an island—round island.

"I guess that's the place," that man said.
Soon, daylight.
That sky lifts [vertically] and they go in.

The other side is winter: this side is summer.
They are lucky they took their snowshoes. Ice here.
They see just where the boat landed there, so they put away their boat.

There is an old trail up there.
They keep going on that trail, big trail—snow on top.
They keep going, keep going.
Big lake in there, though.

On the other side is a camp—brush camp.
At night they are going to sneak down there.

They see two old ladies. They've got fish there, hanging up.
They're sitting outdoors.
One tells her partner,
"Bring that wood so we can cook that fish quick."
She pulls and pulls . . . Gee, what's the matter . . .
Those men push that lady and she falls down.
The other one laughs.

The other one [who fell] whispers,
"Don't say anything. Somebody did that to me."

Those war people are coming.
Gee, those women get scared.

"You know my wife they took this way?" the man asked.

"Yes, we know," they said.
"They went to summer side and took a woman.
This place, though, is all the time winter: no summer here.
As many years old as I am, I don't know that summer place.
I don't know where that place is they got that woman.
Summer place, that place.
No snow. That's what they said.
She's got two husbands here," those women said.
"We're going to tell you how to get there.

"You're going to go this way.
Trail is going to split here: one is going to be a big trail; other trail
    same, too.
You fellows got to go this trail [to the right].
All the time they do that way, hunt."

They see that trail now, and they follow this one [on the right].
They see some people watching from the top of the hill:
See fire . . . See Indians' camp . . . That camp is full.
They are going to sneak there.

That lady's husbands are gone.
It's dark—no daytime there either, I guess.
Somebody cut wood.

That lady camps behind all the time with her husbands.
People camp on ahead—she doesn't want to get mixed up with those
  people.
Just all the time [lags] behind.

Somebody cut wood.
They sneak up . . .
That's his wife, that man. That's the one they take away.
They are coming to her. They help her cut wood.

"Where's your husbands?"

"They hunt, all the men. Just women here."

"We're starved," they tell her.
"You got meat?"

"Yes."

She broke her stone ax: her husbands' mother is in there.

"This ax broke. Look," she tells her.

"Oh, my," she said. "I'm going to tie it up."

While her mother-in-law is fixing it,
That girl put fat, grub, under her clothes.
She kept walking around, packing wood.
She packs wood in, and she packs food out to the men.
I don't know how many times.

She came back: "That stone ax is broken again."

That time she cleaned off all that skin sleigh of dry meat.
She feeds them lots.
"I'm packing my wood," she says. "Packing wood."

It's getting darker.
That night is going to be war, now, going to fight.

They tell her, "You try to get away."

"I'm going to run this road."

Her husbands come back with skin sleigh.
Another one comes back. He's got wolf-skin blanket.

All night she said, "Too hot this wolf-skin blanket.
Too hot, I can't breathe.
That's why I feel sick all the time."

"All right."
They give her marten-skin robe, her husbands.

Her husbands sleep right there, another one right there,
One on each side of her.
Soon she has a stick right ready—club, you know.
Puts it beside her, listens all the time.

They start to fight now.

Her husbands, she clubs them right away.
Pretty soon, she gets up. She runs out the door, see people going that
    way.
She goes on that road, her.
All those people get killed. Nothing left.

Those people come back. Going home now.
Those two old ladies are sleeping.
They are frozen there—I guess they gave up.

They got in the boat again.
They waited for the sky to lift up.
I don't know what place that is . . . I guess that moon is on the other
    side.

11 ✳ Life at Robinson

"My roots grow in jackpine roots.
I'm born here. I branch here."

When I was going to have my first child from Billy, he told me,
"You should go to hospital. It's a better way." But we were way out
hunting. No train there!

I told him not to worry. "I know how to have a baby! I got two already."
Some women helped me—Daisy's [Daisy Smith's] mother, my auntie
Mrs. Carmack, Mrs. Patsy Henderson . . . Ida was that baby.

Billy still wanted me to go to hospital. I didn't like it, but I didn't say
anything. I had that baby when he was out hunting. When he came back
his auntie met him: "You've got a little baby girl." My!

When they have a baby, they put a belt on the lady's stomach. When
you're going to have your first baby, you get up in the morning. You rub
some kind of feathers—rub your stomach and then blow in the air. Then
that baby is going to be easy born. I didn't do that, but my grandma told
me about it.

I had two kids from my first husband. I had friends at Champagne
Landing help me. They put two sticks [upright and parallel, in the
ground]. I hold them. Then somebody holds my back; somebody holds
my knees [in an upright position]. I had none of my babies at that doctor
place, but my daughter did. Both those babies died—they were walking
by that time—one died in Champagne, one in Whitehorse. Pneumonia
or flu or something . . .

I had six children with Billy. Only two still living—my daughter, May,
and my son, Johnny.

First was Ida . . . she died from TB when she was grown up.

Then Sam . . . he had an accident, hunting, and that powder stayed in
his leg [blood poisoning]. He died from that.

The next one was Willie: he was young man, too, when he died. We
were in Teslin and they couldn't get plane into Teslin to get him to
hospital. He died from sickness.

Then Johnny: he's Whitehorse chief now.[31]

One more is Grace. She died when she was just a little girl. I don't
know the name of that sickness . . .

Then my daughter May is the youngest. She's with me yet. Of all my

eight babies, only two are living yet . . .

I handled my daughter's first child. Her husband wanted her to go to hospital, but we were way down at Nazarene Lake. She got sick and she had that baby in just one hour. Her husband came back and my grandson, Vines, ran out. "Dick, I got little brother! Baby!" Oh, my, Dick ran in.

"Gee, how you know how to handle baby?" he tells me.

"I know," I tell him. "I know."

I helped with Daisy Smith's baby, too. I sat at her back. Kate Carmack was just like my husband's mother; she said to me, "You know everything!" I learned all that by watching when I lived at Champagne Landing. I learned it by watching when I was a young woman. You think young girls going to do that this time? Just doctor!

After I stay with Billy, I broke my leg one time. I fell down on the ice: that's my leg, that one. It broke here [cracked lengthwise], but Indian medicine people fix it. Indian doctor fixed it, and after just two days, three days, I walk around. He fixed it with moose bone, put it this way [like a splint]—that goes right to my bone, I guess. But it didn't grow right; that's why I've got this one [a cane]. Just a little while ago, they found out. They took a picture.

When I started to stay with my husband, Billy Smith, we stayed in Carcross and Robinson. *Ddhäl Nàdhäda*—Robinson mountain—we hunted there. Used to be big meat hunts there. Lots of people—Slim Jim, Laberge Bill, John Joe—on top of that mountain. There's a pass at the head of Grey Mountain—they used to go there to hunt moose, to the other side of the mountain. Lots of people used to hunt there with him— they all died out now—Big Salmon Jim, Slim Jim, Charlie Burns—it's Jim Boss's country down at Laberge, though.

So I learned this people's language. I talk Coast Indian language, too. One time in Carcross, a Tlingit man came in from Juneau: he's sitting with his wife, talking to his wife. He sees us: "I guess they've got skin [moosehide]," he tells his wife. "Should be you ask for skin. They belong to Whitehorse people." Me and Susie and Kitty Walker—we were there. There used to be excursion to Whitehorse, train. Lots of people come. They talk their own way: "Moose skin, you should ask those ladies. They got some to sell, I guess." He tells his wife, but I hear him, me. "ANYBODY . . . GOT . . . SKIN?" they tell us, really loud, really slow. I answer him in Tlingit. He looks at me! "Ah, where you come from?"

"You know Paddy Duncan?"

"Yes."

"That's my daddy's people. That one is his brother. *Should* be I talk that way," I tell him. They grab me! Gee, they're surprised.

Another time Ida and Dora were walking downtown—they know Coast Indian talk, those girls. But Coast Indians think these Yukon Indians don't know coast language. John Adamson was there. Those girls talk Tlingit: "Look, he's got skin moccasins. It's raining. He can't know anything!" Those girls say that.

John Adamson, he heard that. He comes from coast. "I know that, just the same I wear them," he said.

Gee, they get shame when they hear him. "We got nothing to say," they said. "Where you come from?"

"I come from coast."

"You know Paddy Duncan? That's my mother's daddy, my grandpa," Ida says.

"Well, that's my uncle," he said, John Adamson.

One time we're in Wheaton [River]. Ida saw that poplar tree. "Look, Mamma!" I think about it all night. Next day, I went to get it.[32] That's the time I carved those things, poplar. My own daddy made silver [jewelry]. Talk about fancy job! Jewel stuff. That's why I guess I carve, me. I did that when we were living at Robinson.

We lived there long time. After that, we looked for gold. We got gold mine up there, "Shininook," they call it: "he gets up." My husband's uncle was Skookum Jim, so I guess he's got to look for gold. My sons worked it with him. They worked the creek. We got a big house. We got hydraulic . . . But that main creek is no good.

I don't know how many years we stayed at that mine. Pretty near ten years, I guess. Four of my kids died there: Sam, he was hunting beaver. There was accident—that bullet went in his foot and he got poison from that. Then Ida got TB. Nobody goes outside for TB that time; this time, you got TB, you go to Edmonton.[33]

We were trapping at Robinson when the Alaska Highway went through. We were going trapping. I had one of my girls with me, May. We stayed there—nobody else there. We got little home there. My son Johnny works in town: he and Ned Boss worked there. Sometimes he came to see us.

One man came and told us, "They're going to build highway." There's an old road there, government's own. One car going, that's all [a wagon road]. Well, he started to talk highway. "Well," he said, "they start from way down. 'Start City,' they call it—Edmonton. From there, they're going to start, two days more. The working people are going to come by plane.

You're going to see them here. They're going to make a road. They're

going to just cut tree, just cut tree." Well, that's what they say. We don't
believe it, you know. He don't believe it, too, that man. "Oh, I don't
know," he said. "Going to be our own road, going to be, I guess. It goes
fast, road, you know." And, they talk about it, talk about it. They're going
to start tomorrow for here. And some people, they're going to start *from*
here—Indian guides. One from Watson Lake. One man is going to leave
from Whitehorse. And they're going to go to meet him from Teslin.³⁴

My old man, Billy Smith, went to Watson Lake as the guide. From here,
he went to Watson Lake. From Watson Lake, somebody meets him. He
just walks. He knows the route . . . Billy knows. "I'm going to cross up
there . . ." You know that creek where bridge crosses? "And this side, I'm
going to cross McClintock. Then to *Dasgwaanga*, from there that way . . ."
They put on paper which way he's going to go: some bigshot put it on
paper. It's just like we don't believe it! Too hard work, we think! They're
not going to make it. Well, we don't know bulldozers!

They're coming now. They started! Well, Billy's going to go tomorrow:
"Tomorrow I'm going to go," he said. Somebody with him, white man.
And they met him there at Watson Lake.

They walk, walk, blaze, blaze. Two men behind them. The guide just
walks. This side, one man blazes; other side, another man blazes. Keep
going, keep going, that guide keeps going, you know. They end up
someplace—Billy knows the name of that place. And, they make it to
Teslin. From there, he starts to Watson Lake. Some Teslin Indians go with
him. That man, white man, has radio—you know that kind? "Billy, he left
this morning from Teslin. Frank Johnson goes with him." That's what he
said. "Teslin men: three, four, five, six people going now from there."
They don't rest. White man coming now. "You know, Mrs. Smith," he tells
me, "pretty near to hot springs, they make it. Two days more they're going
to make it to Liard hot springs."

Well, I know. I've been traveling that way, used to be—just walking. One time I walked from Teslin—me and another woman, Laberge
Harry's wife. From Tagish to *Dasgwaanga*, there is a foot trail. Billy took
the boat with all our stuff: he goes by water; me, I go straight. Billy fixed a
map for me, the way the trail is. You see that Teslin bridge? Mrs. Geddes
met me halfway—she had kids in school at Carcross. She came from
Teslin but she made dry meat all summer at Nisutlin bridge.

From Teslin Lake, we took off: we loaded from Teslin. From there, the
dogs packed: another trip . . . another trip . . . another trip. Three trips;
we kept going that way. I've got five dogs, me, and Harry's wife had four.
She's got two boys and one girl; I've got my son Sam and my daughter Ida.

Way down by Liard River is that Nazarene Lake: that's where we go to trap. This time do you think schoolgirls are going to do that way!? Look how much I did on those trips with dog pack.

So I knew that way—knew where Billy was going. [While he was gone] we stayed at Robinson, hunted tree squirrels. Just *quick* they fixed that road. There was a big camp at Robinson—over one hundred working people. But the highway came quick. "They make it to Watson Lake now," that white man tells me.

Some soldiers are good, you know. Christian. They don't use drink. They wear a cross—Negro people—all full that kind. They're nice people, believing people. One time my grandchild saw them. "Mamma! Some kind of man. He's got a black face." She runs to her mamma. "What kind of man?"

"Oh, just some kind of white man. He won't bother you." Then she wasn't scared.

Then, they were just going . . . coming now . . . small little cars, you know. Then big ones . . . just about one month, wide road. Well, they just go that way—bulldoze trees. They go fast! Next time we go to our trapping ground, at Nazarene Lake, we go in big truck.

You know how we bought that truck? Sewing! One pair of moccasins is worth twenty-five dollars. I got hundred muskrat skins. I wanted to make blanket for myself, but I made mitts. Fur mitts! Soldiers buy them for twenty-five dollars. Mukluks sometimes fifty dollars!

Everybody helped sew. Then my son-in-law, Dick Craft, takes a boxful to the airport. He sells to soldiers when they're leaving. He takes three boxes full, and my gopher coat, my own. Dick Craft, he put it on. When he came back, he's got a thick sweater. "What did you do with Mamma's coat?"

"They pay eighty dollars!" he said.

I made my husband a coat one time from skin of a young caribou, trimmed that one with beaver. Soldiers came one night and asked to buy it. "How much?"

"Five hundred dollars," that's what Dick Craft said. Those soldiers gave him five one-hundred-dollar bills.

My husband and my son-in-law took those things we made to the airport. When we finish, we've got a boxful. *Lots* of them! May, she sewed porcupine-quill moccasins—five pairs one time. Soldiers pay a high price!

So Dick Craft went to town. He drove back in that truck! Well, men made money, too! Oh, just like that, money, that time. My!

Sure we're glad about that highway! Everybody, car, they got it. But some girls got kids, and then the soldiers left. Well, government helped, gave canned milk. Then lots of people died from sickness. My daughter, May, it spoiled her: she got TB—four years in hospital, May, Edmonton. Sickness, they don't know much about sickness, that time . . . I don't think they had TB before. Then after, lots of that sickness. Everything changed after that highway. No more dog packs—no more snowshoes.

From there, my daughter got sick. I looked after her kids when she was in hospital. We lost one of her kids with measles . . . When she came back from Edmonton, my daddy, Paddy Duncan, told me, "I don't want her sick again. I don't want her to go away again, my grandchild. I've got some kind of dope I'm going to fix her. Before sun comes up in morning, put this on your body."

That's what he told her. See? She's not sick now. With that kind of medicine, you can't eat fish eggs or that sickness comes back. Don't eat red berries—just black ones and blueberries. But no soapberries, cranberries, fish eggs. You have to quit red things!

I went out to Little Atlin, one time, with my grandson Richard, his wife, my little grandchild. We go hunting out there, you know. That's the time of year moose are running, Little Atlin.

A big truck pulled up . . . stopped—it had its house on top. It's bigshot government man. My grandson Richard knows him.[35] I don't know him, me, but Richard knows that car with its house on. That man comes to me. "Got to take care of that, your fire," he tells me. I don't say nothing. I don't know he's bigshot, that man.

After he finished talking, I tell him, "Look, you fellows spoil Yukon," I tell him. "Yeah! That time my grandpa burned tree when he hunts moose. He makes fire. He don't burn anything. What do you fellows do? This time you throw away cigarette stumps. Big fire. You spoil Yukon, all. Should be where your grandpa country, you stay in. Where's your grandpa's country? Your grandma? Where?" I tell him.

"Well, outside, long way," he said.

"How the hell you're coming here, then? Nobody called you to come here."

"Well, you're right, Missus," he tell me.

"Me, my grandpa's country, here. My grandma's. My roots grow in jackpine roots all. That's why I stay here. I don't go to your grandpa's country and make fire. No. My grandma's country I make fire. Don't burn. If I be near your grandma's country, it's all right you tell me."

"Oh, you beat me!" he said. He walks away.

After, my grandson came back. "What you tell him, that man. You know that man is bigshot?"

"Well, that's all right," I tell him. "I'm bigshot, too. I belong to Yukon. I never go to his country. I'm born here. I branch here! The government got all this country, how big it is. He don't pay five cents, he got him all. Nobody kicks me out. No, sir! My roots grow in jackpine roots."

He laughs, my grandson. "You're a bad woman, Grandma."

Billy was sick for six years before he died. He was blind then, so I hunted. I looked after him. When he was sick, before he died, he told me, "Should be you find someone to look after you. When I'm gone, you should find a new husband. If one of them asks you, go with him, my nephew."[36]

I tell him, no. "I can't take men no more. I can make my own living." Should be you're on your own. Nobody can boss you around then. You do what you want. My grandchild can look after me. Before, I wanted a husband, wanted kids. I lost six of those kids—six of mine. After I'm past that, though, I don't want to be bothered with men. One *Dakl'aweidí* man used to bring me meat and fish after Billy died—we raised him when he's a kid. One time I asked him to stay with me, but he said no. "Too much it's like you're my mother."

When Billy died, he told me, "I'm going to come back. If I'm still around after I die, I'm going to come back. I'll knock at the window so my grandchild can let me in."

One time we were sitting here: we heard three knocks at door—but that time it was just a dog. I dreamed about it, though. I talked with Susie [Fred], too. She says, "Your old man can't come back that way. He's going to turn into baby. He's going to be *nedlin*."[37] I know it's true.

I miss all my sisters-in-law:[38] Mrs. Whitehorse Billy . . . Mrs. Charlie Burns . . . Jessie Burns . . . Jessie Walker . . . Jenny McKenzie . . . Jenny Laberge . . . Kitty Walker . . . Susie Sam . . . Might be I'm going to catch them yet. I don't know which way they're gone. All Wolf ladies I talk about—I don't know which way they're gone. I sure loved them all, used to be. Best friend of mine, Jessie Walker, used to be. All Wolf women, all. They don't think about me anymore, when they're gone.

I made song for them [she sings and then translates]:

> Where are they gone?
> How tough to sing alone.
> They all left me.
> Where are they gone now, all?

How much power do you people think I have?
You left me.
You don't think about me, back this way.
All my friends, where are they gone?
I'm going to be there someday.

When I go, I'm going to say goodbye. I'm not going to look back. Just one way I'm going to go.

12 ✳ Grandmothers and Grandsons

"When I was a kid that time, one old lady, like me now, she had stick [crutch] like this one.

'Don't touch that, my grandchild.' She called that stick her grandchild. That stick does everything for her! That's why she called it 'grandchild.'"

✳ The First Time They Knew *K'och'èn*, White Man

You know my grandson, Kenneth?
He looks after me, takes care of me.
They're that way, Indians, long time ago, I guess.

Where they get meat, long time ago,
One Indian boy got meat for his grandma.
All the time he does that, that boy.
No white man that time—they don't know white man.

I'm going to tell you a story about this one, that boy.
He looked after his grandma—he took care.
Where they kill meat, he goes, that boy.
He gets meat. They've got two dogs—
No dogs long time ago, they say; just a little while ago, that dog.

They kill two caribou.
His uncle killed them.
"You get meat: your uncle killed caribou.
Are you going to go?"

He says, "Yes."

They say,
"You take your dog."
He took his dog. Goes.
He told his grandma,
"Don't get wood, Grandma.
I'll come back. I'm going to get wood.
254 My uncle killed caribou."

People go to get meat.
Everybody packed him: everybody went to that meat place.
That boy, he looked for bones someplace, after people go—
Looks around to see if he finds something: he takes them.
He's got two dogs to pack them, too.

People are gone already.
He goes back. He's the same big as my grandchild Kenneth.
This is a *story*, you know, not "story." It's *true* story.

He sees a rainbow, about same big as this tent.
He stood up about this far from it, and somebody talked to him.

"Go through." He doesn't see who said that.
"Go through."

He comes, his dogs behind. Goes through.
Other side, little bit long way, he stands back.
Big sack falls down there.

"Don't eat that meat anymore!
You're going to eat this grub.
This one in the sack.
Don't drink water from this ground for one week!
That many days, don't take water from this ground.
You're going to use this one, from inside your grub here,
Or else we're going to come, going to get you."

He took that sack.
Put it on top of his pack.
He doesn't see that man who talks to him, but he sees that rainbow.
But he talked to him.

His grandma cooked already—
That's what I do with Kenneth here—cook soup, everything.
So when he comes back, he runs here,
"What you cooking, Grandma, soup?"

"Yes."

Last night he cooked, him. Fed me here.

"I cook some gopher. I kill two, grandchild," she said, that old lady.
"I cook that one."

"No, Grandma, I'm not going to eat.
I've got something to eat," he said.

She looked.
Something's wrong, she thinks.

"I'm not going to eat anymore, Grandma.
I've got my grub here, my sack."

That one who talked to him told him,
"Tell those people to fix some things for you."

He told his grandma,
"Tell those boys they got to come,
Their uncle, too, has got to come here."

Grandma goes to tell them,
"He wants you . . . Don't know what's the matter.
He said it."

They come there and the boys sit down.

"I want you to fix that high bed for me," he said.
"I want to lay down on top."
Just quick they fix him.
"And two bridges, I want you to fix this way."
Bridge goes right there, right here, that far.
"Well, thank you," he said.
"Somebody talked to me; that's why I say that.
You come tonight before you eat: you come to this bridge.
Then I'm going to tell you.
You hold your wife's hand when you come on that bridge.
I'm going to tell you."

His grandma got scared, you know.

"Don't think about it, Grandma. Eat. You eat good."

They fix already that bed for him. On top.
He opens his sack—he doesn't know this kind of grub.
He eats something from there.
Water in there, too. He drinks water.

And he said,
"They're coming now."

He sings some kind of song,
    "Come on, come on, my friends."

"You hold your wife's hand.
Go down, turn that way."
He tells them, "I'm going to be white man."
Nobody knows *K'och'èn* that time. That boy called them *K'och'èn*.
Right today they use it.
He said, "*K'och'èn* you, *K'och'èn* that one."
Turn that way, turn that way.
All that camp.

"You fellows are going to be white." That's what he said.
They don't know what he means.

"I'm not going to eat anymore for seven days," he said.
"One day, this ground going to be full of *K'och'èn*.
You're going to be *K'och'èn*, you people."
Nobody knows.
"Going to turn white man."
How many white-man grandchild have I got now?
That time, look!
I talk white-man way, too, now.
He's honest, that boy, isn't he?

Seven days he stayed there.
And he told his grandma.
He gave her a big sack, that big one—don't know where it came
    from—
Anything, Indian grub, dried fish, everything is in that sack.

"Right here your grub is going to stay, Grandma.
Anything you want stays there.
It's not gone till you're gone.
That sack is all full of grease, everything.
No more you're going to look for grub.
Anything—fresh meat, you want it—
It's going to stay there—inside.

"You want ribs? It's there.
What you wish for before you open, you say you want that one—
Right there it is.
Until you're gone, I leave this sack for you.

I'm going to stay here two days more, Grandma," he told her.
"Then gone.
Don't be sorry, nothing."

Him, he called them K'och'èn.
That's why this time Indians, nothing.
Right today, everybody calls them K'och'èn.

That time he gave them bread, nobody knows that.
"This kind of grub you fellows are going to eat."

It's true, this one.
That boy, he's gone—nobody knows where.
Now I sit down on top of that bed,
You sit on bed.
Before that, bed was on ground.

"You're going to be that way and you're going to turn to white man."
What white man?
That time nobody knows it.

✻ Owl Story

This is a story about that owl they burned.
It happened down at Noogaayík.

Lots of people were staying down there.
They dance, sometimes; Indians dance just for fun.
They were doing that.

One lady said, "Where's my kid?"

One kid missing. They run around—nothing.

That time one man said,
"What is that track I see down there?
It's just like one big grouse track on the sand.
Big," he said. People went there.

Yes, they saw them.
Big tracks there—like grouse tracks.
Ah, well.
Something came and took that little kid, little girl.
They don't know what.

Well, he's coming now—two owls.
They talk just like people. They come in here.

"One little kid.
Give me one little kid or I'm going to eat you all," he said.

"Where do you come from?"

"We come from that place," they said.
There used to be a glacier there, that place.[39]
That owl came from a little glacier in there.
That glacier hasn't melted yet—
It's about the same size as Fish Lake Mountain. Big place.
I guess Owl lived inside there—he melted it down a little bit.

They gave him dog:
They can't kill owl, can't kill him anyway. Too big, you know.

One old lady couldn't walk around.
She crawled around, but her hands are strong.
She got paralyzed, I guess.

"What are we going to do now?
We gave them all our dogs."
Nobody's got dogs that time, just a few men.

They got one slave—somebody had him.
They gave that one to the owls:
Those owls didn't come back for four days.

People say: "Maybe they're not going to come back.
They're gone. They took that slave.
We can't do anything now."
Well, that old lady, she can't walk.
"We might as well throw her away," they think.

Her grandchild is just a little boy.
He doesn't want to let his grandma go.

"Just as well I die if my grandma dies."
No, his daddy doesn't want it; his mamma cries.
"No." He won't leave his grandma.
"Just as well you kill me right there," he said.

They let him go now, that kid.
Well, they built a brush camp that way—

260   I guess it was her own brush camp, I don't know—
Kitty   It was big.
Smith   I guess she can still make good brush camps.
       His grandmother brought him those things.
       Then she dug a hole [tunnel], that lady, out the back way—
       I guess they crawled around that way—a long way.

That ground was frozen now, on top.
Her grandchild packed that grub.
Then they packed in branches and filled that brush camp up.
They got ready now:
They fixed some kind of grease, gopher grease.
They put on rags, anything.
Then they tied it up, wrapped it around sticks.
They gathered up pitch—her son-in-law had brought it to them to
   start fire.

He's coming now, one Owl Man.
His wife is not with him.

"Where have these people gone?" he asked.
I wonder how he can talk that way?

"Well, they've gone to another city," that old lady told him.
"They threw us away so you can eat us.
That's why they threw us away."

"Heh. You're an old lady. I guess your heart is good."
He doesn't know that little grandchild is in the ground, that way.
She's got something she is going to close off that tunnel with, too.

"Gee, I'm an old lady.
If you eat me, you're going to be sick.
Where's your wife?"

"She ate a dog bone.
She got choked," he said. "She died."

"All right. You might as well get warm, dry yourself.
I'm just an old lady.
Not good to eat."

"All right."

That old lady made a dry fire.

"Gee, your back is wet."

He turned around that way. His back to her.

That old lady put grease on the fire.
It started to burn.
She threw on pitch.
Everything she threw on. Wood, too.
Then she rolled down that big rock,
Rolled it away from the mouth of the tunnel.
She closed it right back.

She's gone with her grandchild out there.
I guess there's fresh air in there—that ground is not thick.

They hear him . . . That house started to burn.
"Hunh. My eyes start to burn.
What's the matter with that old lady?
She talks too much.
Should be I killed her already."

He starts to burn.
Then it's quiet. Quiet now.
They guess they can get away now.
But they stay there, stay there.

Well, it's a long time now.
That's when the old lady pushed away the rock.
She came up. That big owl is all burned.
He lies on his side, all burned.

He told his grandmother,
"We killed him already.
Where's your house?" No house there.

They made a fire.
I guess they put away their own grub.
That owl is pretty near half-cooked. They eat now.

Then—it's funny, you know—that old lady got up!
She got up with two walking sticks!
Hey! She just walks that far [twenty feet].
She doesn't feel anything—just goes that way.

"What's the matter, Grandma? You walk!"

"Well, I don't know, my grandchild."

Yes, those claws are long.
They chop them, tie them up that way in a little sack.
That owl is dead, now.
Her grandchild is going to pack it—they have skin sled, too.
She walked that way.
The little boy is strong now, I guess. He went.

They go, go, go.
Someplace he pulls his grandma, you know—does that.

Gee, they see that open space—fire, smoke.
People living there right in that open place.
They're coming there. That's her daughter.

"What's the matter? They're coming, them.
My mamma looks like she is in skin sleigh."

"Run there," she tells her husband.

Yes, he pulled his grandma. I guess he's big.

"Where's your owl?"

"We killed him."

"How did you fellows kill that owl?"

"We killed him anyway."

"They say they killed owl!" [people say]

"No! Which way?"

"We burned him."

"My goodness," say lots of people.

Same time they started to go back with that old lady.
Gee, right there, owl is burned.
They explain that owl's wife got choked—she's dead.
They look around that way. He's dead, anyway. Burned.

I saw that place.
It's a rock now.
It looks just like burned bones right there at *Noogaayík*.

✳

PART THREE

Old-Style Words Are

✳

✳ # Just Like School

✳ ANNIE NED

✳

✳

✳ ## Introduction

Mrs. Annie Ned was born sometime during.the 1890s near the old settlement of Hutshi in the southern Yukon Territory.[1] Her mother, *Tùtaɬmą*, was a woman of the Crow moiety from the Dalton Post area, and her mother's parents were *Kàkhnokh* [Big Jim] and his wife *Dakwa'äl*. Mrs. Ned's father was *Sakuni*; he was one of six sons of the man known as Hutshi Chief, a central figure in Athapaskan-Tlingit trade. Hutshi Chief had both an Athapaskan name, *Kàkhah*, and a Tlingit name, *Kaajoolaaxí*. He also had two wives, a Tlingit wife, *Däk'äläma*, who was Mrs. Ned's paternal grandmother, and an Athapaskan wife, *K'edäma* (figure 4); these marriages ensured his position in the trade network.

The child was given the name *Ntthenada* and the English name Annie. She had a younger brother, Frankie, and a younger sister. Their mother died when Annie was five or six years old, and her father followed the custom of taking his wife's half-sister, *Gàch'ema*, as his second wife. But although *Gàch'ema* was also the daughter of Big Jim, or *Kàkhnokh*, she had a different mother, and Annie's "true" grandmother on her mother's side, *Dakwa'äl*, insisted on raising the little girl. Periodically, she also lived with her other grandmother, *Däk'äläma*. Raised by women who were probably born in the 1850s or even earlier, it is not surprising that Annie developed a conservative understanding of the "old ways."

Mrs. Ned spent her earliest years around Hutshi and recalls both her first potlatch and her emotional reactions to that event. Her child's-eye account comes from a time when potlatch participants could distinguish where other visitors had traveled from by the clothing they wore and by the songs and dances they performed. As a young woman, she was secluded for a respectable three months, and she attributes her long life to

the care with which her grandmother attended to the details. She was courted by Skookum Jim, who had recently made the discovery setting off the Klondike gold rush, but rejected him because his life was already taking a direction generated by unexpected wealth and attention. Instead, she married Paddy Smith, and during their life together they had eight children.

Mrs. Ned describes her early adult life in her father-in-law's country at Kusawa Lake and along the upper Takhini River. Paddy Smith spent each autumn working for big-game guides in the western Yukon, and while he was away, Mrs. Ned provisioned the family with fish and small game. From his employment, he sent money to buy flour, tea, sugar, and tobacco from the trader, and when he returned he went out to hunt their winter's meat: "he hunts for me, I fish for him." Paddy's younger brother, Johnny Ned, came to live with them at one point and later, appropriately, became Mrs. Ned's second husband.

Mrs. Ned is an extremely competent woman who hunted extensively both with her husbands and on her own. She has also made some very fine moosehide clothing decorated with exquisite beadwork from old patterns. Her father and her second husband were both well-known shamans, or "doctors," and Mrs. Ned herself has long been recognized as a woman having special powers. But, as she takes pains to point out, anyone so foolish as to discuss his or her power publicly could lose it; hence her references to her own powers are all circumscribed.

Of the accounts in this volume, Mrs. Ned's is the one least likely to approximate Western notions of a life history. Although she states that it is important for her to record a life story, her culturally distinctive view of her life is in no way circumscribed by personal experience. She insists that she wants to talk only about "important things," and she rejects as trivial her memories of the time she was almost blinded when a gun backfired, the time her leg was broken in an accident, the time her home burned with all her belongings inside. She even passes over her thirty-year marriage to her third husband, a "white man," as unsuitable for inclusion in her life story. Instead, her statements about her experiences focus on what she learned as a child and what she can teach as an elder.

Now in her mid-nineties, Mrs. Ned is a remarkably independent woman with a wry sense of humor. She has never been ill a day in her life, she maintains, until January 1984, when she underwent major abdominal surgery. Some members of her family and her medical doctor expected her to be hospitalized for some time, possibly for the rest of her

Mrs. Annie Ned, photographed near her home in 1987. Photo by Norma McBean.

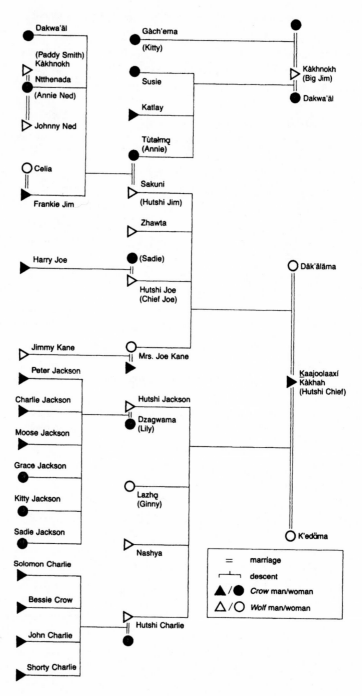

Figure 4. Partial family tree of ancestors of Mrs. Annie Ned

life. She, in turn, referred to her doctor in the third person as "the little guy" and made it clear to him and to everyone else that she had no intention of languishing in a hospital bed or in Whitehorse when she could be at home. By spring, she was back in her cabin on the Takhini River, thirty miles from town. Although her daughter, a son, a son-in-law, and grandchildren all lived nearby, she remained resolutely self-sufficient there in the summer of 1988.

✳ Narrative Text as Collaboration

I first met Mrs. Ned in 1970, when one of her sons took me to meet her at her home in Takhini Crossing. She impressed me as a forthright and perceptive woman who took some time out of her busy day to sit and visit with me before returning to her work. My recollection of that visit is that she was the one asking the questions, most of them amused queries about my limited contributions as a potential daughter-in-law.

We began working together recording oral history ten years later in 1980 with funding from the Yukon Native Languages Project, and in the years since then our collaboration has been a continuing source of delight for both of us. She takes our work extremely seriously, but, never able to resist an opportunity to make a joke at my expense about our comparative life experience, she now speculates about the potential collaboration we could have as co-wives for some unsuspecting man, she as the senior, knowledgeable partner, and I as the younger, stronger, and trainable one.

Most of her training, though, is directed at ensuring that I learn to "get the words right." The central idea shaping Mrs. Ned's account is that spoken words are infused with power that increases in value with repetition. We agree that my role is to record those words accurately for her and to make them comprehensible for a wider audience. This involves more than exotic stenography, because an intermediary adds a layer of interpretation. Her own words best describe her view of our work: "You are looking for words, so I'll teach you the words, and you can write it down. I do this with just one person, to keep it straight. Maybe we get mixed up, other way." During the time we have worked together she has frequently explained her motivation for recording her words so they can be written down: "Long time ago, what they know, what they see, that's the one they talk about, I guess. Tell stories—which way you learn things. You think about that one your grandma tells you. You've got to believe it, what Grandma said. . . . Old-style words are just like school!"

Mrs. Ned's approach to telling her story is similar to that of other narrators in this volume, except that she is more likely to use speeches and songs than traditional stories to explain events. Her virtuosity is often bewildering to listeners unfamiliar with this idiom. The narrative conventions she uses are grounded in her optimistic assumption that listeners share her context for understanding what she is saying. Although this would undoubtedly be true for an audience of her contemporaries, her speeches are sometimes obscure for a Western audience and even for younger Native people who have been educated in government schools. A formal speech may plunge an unfamiliar listener into a dense, incomprehensible world without the leavening of context; however, given that context, her "old-style words" become infused with enormous power.

Her expectation of a shared context has two consequences for a written account. First, I try to introduce her account by providing some of the basic knowledge she expects her listeners to have, juxtaposing her words with my own commentary. Second, I have chosen to edit her account more than the others—not by changing her words, but by rearranging them to meet the grammatical demands of English where such reorganization seems to make her meaning clearer.

Mrs. Ned sees herself as one of the last elders and therefore as a particularly important teacher. She knows that, in her own childhood, instruction came directly from "long-time people," who taught with stories. Her primary concern is that now "schoolkids learn from paper," and so her continuing objective has been to prepare a book they can read. "Kids used to do jobs for old people—get wood, water. They paid us with stories! We bring wood: now! Time like school! We stayed there—we listened." Her recurring theme is that authority to speak about the past comes not from originality but from accurate repetition. In all her teaching she insists on naming her source, and she differentiates between two kinds of authority. First, and most important, is the received wisdom from elders: "I know what I tell. This is not just my story—lots of people tell that story. Just like now they go to school, old time we come to our grandpa. Whoever is old tells the same way. That's why we put this on paper." The second kind of authority comes from direct experience—from having witnessed a particular event. "That one story my grandpa tells me. But this time, myself, this time I'm telling you the story." She is careful not to speculate when I ask her questions outside her experience: "I don't know that one. That's what they say, but I don't see it. Whoever tells you this, ask him." And she challenges the authority of anyone younger than herself. Referring to someone ten years her junior, she comments: "[That person] is too young. [That person] didn't see it. Just a kid. Old people, that's the ones I tell you."

During the summers of 1985 and 1986 much of our work involved traveling by car to visit places she remembered. Our drives in the summer of 1985 had a particularly evocative quality because the Alaska Highway was undergoing massive reconstruction cross-cutting an area Mrs. Ned knew intimately as a young woman. Using her cane to hoist herself into my car (which she refers to as a "white-man rig") on a typical day in summer 1985, she smiled cheerily and announced, "Chicago, here we come!" At which point we launched ourselves into a particularly crater-like zone of construction along the highway.

Flanked by enormous equipment, we passed the hill *Sankàlà* where she lived with her second husband; she explained that it was owned by *Ajàngàkh,* her second husband's paternal grandfather, who belonged to the Wolf moiety. Then she pointed out *Nichàlà,* where she and her second husband used to hunt on horseback, and another hill where she went as a child with an old woman hunting "gophers" (ground squirrels). As we drove, she sang several old songs made by people at *Sankàlà;* when we reached an open valley, *Kosàndagà,* she abruptly switched to a particular song she made long ago when she and her classificatory sister came here to hunt gophers. "I feel bad when I think about it. That's why I sing."

As we traveled in the bright, dusty afternoon, she commented on changes in poplar growth, on periods when people noticed either an increase or a decline in the caribou population in the southern Yukon. The tape recordings from each of these drives are marred by the drone of motors from nearby equipment and from our car but are densely packed with context. The need to dodge construction vehicles, some of them piloted by her grandsons, who wave at us as we pass, lends a particular irony to our conversation.

When I ask her *how* people learned from the stories and names, she replies: "You know old people, long time, they call this country where they [the places] are. That's from this man, he tells it—next one, he tells it—that's the way we got it. Just like you read. Just like when we go to school for that old man. We bring some wood, bring some water to old people to tell us this story. We don't pick it up for nothing!"

Mrs. Ned's account is shorter than the others, but it has a compelling density. The length is less a reflection of the amount of time we have spent working together than of her sense that repetition confers value on words and my editorial decision to combine accounts she tells more than once rather than to present several parallel versions of each event. Mrs. Ned imposes clear editorial rules herself, deciding what should remain and what should be eliminated. She is very sensitive to the role of the tape recorder and regularly advises me when it should be turned on and when our discussion should remain unrecorded. We have had longer informal conversations about her life which she explicitly does not want included in her account, so those materials are omitted.

✳ Narrative as Explanation

As noted above, sections of Mrs. Ned's account often appear to be formal speeches, delivered to a tacit audience. Although they contain very little information we would recognize as personal, they are entirely consistent with her view of what constitutes an authoritative account of a life. In the overall arrangement of her written text, I have tried to maintain her sense of how these elements should be combined and at the same time respect her desire that people outside her community should be able to understand her story. Again, family history and secular personal accounts are presented in odd-numbered sections (1, 3, 5, 7) and the stories, songs, and oratory that constitute her "explanations" for these events appear in even-numbered sections (2, 4, 6, 8). Section 9 shows how she more typically combines them herself.

Section 1 locates her *Shagóon* at Hutshi. She begins by establishing her undisputed authority to speak about the past, identifying the time when she first "got smart" at the age of ten and started to understand and think about the narratives she heard from old people who "told their story all the time." She insists that the correct way to tell stories involves reliable repetition: "you don't put it yourself and tell a little more," because you aren't actually the person telling the story, only a conduit from the original narrator. From the outset, then, it is clear that this set of rules for recounting oral tradition works against any possibility of a highly personal narrative.

The genealogy Mrs. Ned dictates is centered on her "father's people," unusual in the southern Yukon, where descent is traced through one's mother's line. However, her own mother died when she was a child and none of her mother's brothers or sisters seems to have had children who survived, whereas her father's family was a large and important one at Hutshi, where she grew up. She underscores the stature of her paternal grandfather, Hutshi Chief, by pointing out that she and her brother have maintained the grave of his Tlingit trading partner, *Gasłeeni,* as a sign of esteem for that partnership.

She goes on to identify the significance of moiety affiliations and the control of particular salmon streams by *Kajìt* (Crow) and *Ägunda* (Wolf) moieties. She refers to her own *Gaanaxteidí* clan in her account, the chief Crow clan among the Southern Tutchone, but says that her father's Wolf, or *Ägunda*, people did not have a separate clan. The Southern Tutchone clan system seems to have come from the coastal Tlingit: Hutshi was at the northern edge of the territory where membership in Tlingit-named clans was considered important. A distinction conventionally made by anthropologists between moiety and clan is that moiety members have no shared history whereas the clans within a moiety claim ownership of specific histories, crests, songs, and dances. In Mrs. Ned's account the differences between clan and moiety is sometimes blurred.

Her interpretation of Tlingit-Athapaskan trade is unorthodox. Standard sources on trade between coastal and interior Indians suggest that Tlingits initiated and dominated trading encounters in the Yukon, at least during the era of European fur trade. Many southern Yukon elders acknowledge this power imbalance by emphasizing any Tlingit ancestry they may have. Mrs. Ned, however, identifies exclusively with her interior Athapaskan origins. According to her interpretation, when Athapaskans and Tlingits first met, Athapaskans had both rich resources and ingenious technology, whereas Tlingits were relatively impoverished "poor cousins." She underscores this view of her own ethnicity by drawing parallels between the dependence of Tlingits and later of white men on Athapaskans, especially Athapaskan women: "When Coast Indians came, they wanted Yukon woman. White man, too, they wanted Indian woman. Without it, they can't survive. Me, I'm Yukon woman!"

Mrs. Ned goes even further. According to her grandfather, Hutshi Chief, Tlingits at *Noogaayík* on the Alsek River first discovered that there were upriver people when they saw chips floating down the Alsek. They followed the river to its source that winter and encountered Athapaskans dressed in beautifully decorated clothing. The indigent Tlingit, she says, greatly admired the Athapaskans they met: "They've got *nothing*, those Tlingit people, just cloth clothes, groundhog clothes. Nothing!" By contrast, Athapaskans had "ready-made moccasins, buckskin parky, silver-fox, red fox, caribou-skin parky sewed up with porcupine quills." The Tlingits, she says, were eager to have these things, so "these Yukon people *told* Coast Indians to come back in summertime" (my emphasis).

All this happened before her time, when her grandmother was young; she indicates the antiquity of this trade using the common convention "about one thousand years ago, about two thousand years ago" to mean simply "long ago." Indeed, De Laguna did learn from Yakutat Tlingit at the mouth of the Alsek River how much they admired the moosehide clothing made by inland Athapaskans.[2] Eventually, Mrs. Ned says, Tlingits achieved the upper hand because they had direct access to trade goods—sugar, tea, tobacco, guns, knives, and axes, and the Yukon people "got crazy for it." By the time she was born, she continues, all this was changing, the real watershed coming "when Skookum Jim found gold."

If Section 1 sets out a genealogical framework for understanding history, Mrs. Ned gives another dimension to the past when she tells one of her grandfather's stories about "how first this Yukon came to be." The story tells how Beaverman (*Äsùya*) and Crow (*Ts'ürk'i*) rid the world of giant man-eating animals at the beginning of time and made it safe for human beings. Stories about Crow and about Beaverman are widely told in the southern Yukon; in most versions, though, Crow stories and Beaver narratives are told separately. Mrs. Ned's version is distinctive because Crow and Beaverman worked together, rather than independently. When they finished their work, she says, Crow went to the Coast and Beaverman remained in the Yukon.

When she tells this story, she continues to make confident assumptions about her audience's knowledge. To follow the dialogue, one must understand that in myth time the sky came down to the earth at the horizon and it was possible for people to be stolen away to the "far side," where everything was perpetual darkness and winter. "When the people went from home, all the far side they go. All got eaten by Wolverine. That's what the old people tell . . ." One must also recognize the signs that immediately identify a stranger as a nonhuman masquerading as a human being, signs that guide *Äsùya* in his task of "cleaning up" the Yukon River. First, such an individual inevitably refuses human food, but if he can be tricked into eating it, he will become human. Second, a nonhuman pretender distinguishes himself by sleeping on the opposite side of the fire from human beings. Mrs. Ned speculates about what motivated *Äsùya* and Crow to undertake this journey and stresses the complementarity of their talents; for example, Crow can fly around to provide *Äsùya* with the perspective necessary for his work. Crow is also verbally adroit: "Talk, talk, talk . . . you know that Crow." Other conversational points are more obscure: in one section Beaver (the man) and beaver (the animal) negotiate concerns jointly shared by human beings and beavers.

The family history Mrs. Ned presents for her first husband, Paddy Smith, is largely a listing of personal names and place names associated with that phase of her married life (Section 3). The setting is the lake now officially known as Kusawa, but she uses three names interchangeably when referring to it—the Tlingit name *Koosawu Áa*, the Athapaskan name *Nakhų*, and the earlier English name, Lake Arkell. This long, winding lake served as one of the earliest trade routes between coast and interior.[3]

Paddy Smith's paternal grandfather, *Nùlatà*, made his headquarters at the narrows one-third of the way down the lake, at the place called *Nakhu*, meaning "raft crossing." The lake was very shallow at the narrows, making it possible to run a fishnet across its entire width and intercept large quantities of fish. So important was this constriction to the lake fishery that the Athapaskan speakers who came here gave the name *Nakhu* to the entire lake.

Just east of the narrows was a mountain, and between the mountain and the lake a narrow strip of land provided an ideal location for entrapping caribou. Prior to 1910, when large herds of porcupine caribou were still plentiful in the southern Yukon, they could be driven through the slot between these two natural barriers and trapped in a corral, a long fence made from brush. *Nùlatà's* control of the corral and the narrows on behalf of the Wolf moiety made him a significant figure in this region. As she explains, "owning" the lake did not mean that *Nùlatà* or his Wolf kinsmen made exclusive use of the lake, but rather that he was in a position to invite others to come to hunt and fish there.

Section 4 presents formal narratives associated with Kusawa Lake and relies heavily on context Mrs. Ned has already provided. The central question in each of these stories is whether people risk abandonment and isolation when they travel in unfamiliar territory. The first concerns *Nùlatà*, himself. As an important headman, he arranged for each of his daughters to marry a man in a different Yukon village and celebrated the event by having each woman walk to her husband across moosehide blankets decorated with moose hoofs, abalone "mother of pearl" buttons, or dentalium shells. In this way he was following the example of important coastal Tlingit traders who established social and economic linkages with the interior by choosing inland husbands for their daughters. The second story concerns a Tlingit man traveling in unfamiliar territory with in-laws who leave him behind when he becomes trapped on a mountain, *Gäh Ddhäl*, above Kusawa Lake. The action in this account occurs over several hundred kilometers: it begins at Dalton Post and involves a trip across country to Kusawa Lake, then down the Takhini River to the Yukon River, then all the way to Lake Laberge, and ultimately to Tagish. A third tells of the near-death of a Tlingit man who fell into a glacial crevasse on his trip home from a trading expedition to the interior; her various retellings and her commentary on this story suggest that it explores the issue of uncertain ethnic boundaries between Athapaskan and Tlingit territory.

In Section 5 Mrs. Ned brings her own childhood into the narrative for the first time. She begins by giving her name, her clan, and a genealogy of the household in which she was raised. Her goal here is to establish how children were expected to behave during her youth. Frequently, she shifts from the personal, "I did this," to the impersonal, "Girls should do this," juxtaposing normative statements with descriptions of actual events. She repeatedly refers to nine or ten years as the age of awareness, "when I got smart," the age when youngsters began to have some cultural context for understanding what was happening around them and could be relatively self-sufficient.

Her most emotional description is that of the potlatch she witnessed as a young child. It was held by her grandfather for her deceased mother, and she remembers the white crow they put on the grave, a crow that "looks like seagull," representing Crow before he was blackened trying to escape through a smokehole. She describes the activities—the invitations, the arrivals, the clothing, the colored blankets, the dances. From the perspective of a child, who could not fully understand what was happening, she conveys her own alternating terror and relief when her grandfather, dressed in a "gunnysack," blackened his face and held her while he sang his song and people began to dance. "I thought, 'What's he doing that for?'" A canvas was hung in front of the dancers, and when it was taken down, each group began to dance in turn.

She recounts her own puberty seclusion impersonally, suggesting that it was of proper length and her instruction of suitable quality to protect her to her present age. She lists the preparations that were made for a young woman—the bone drinking tube, the scratching stick, the swan's down, the rules governing sitting position, food consumption, and work, and concludes, "All those things I did. That's why I'm old woman and still I'm good yet."

Most of my questions about her youth are met with formal oratory, with speeches she offers as a demonstration of how she actually learned as a child. Whenever possible, in fact, she shifts the ground from discussion of her own life to a speech, using this form to discuss "what kids should know." Three such speeches are included in Section 6; they reaffirm themes that are now becoming familiar—the power of words, the skills needed to survive, the importance of learning from one's grandmother. She follows them with a discussion of the correct way to tan hides, but its rhetorical value comes from the ways she uses the words rather than from any clear set of steps about how to perform this task. Once again, she talks about trade. Prior to Athapaskan/Tlingit trade, she says, people hunted furs for their own use. Then they began trapping furs to exchange. When whites arrived, trappers began negotiating directly with traders. She repeats that Athapaskans treated first Tlingits and later white men as equals, but that in each case the tables eventually turned as the visitors took control of the economy, of women, of land.

Section 7 describes her two marriages and some of her activities as a mature woman. She points out that marriage bonds used to represent a contract between groups; now that marriage is viewed as an alliance between individuals, those bonds are more tenuous. Her account of her marriage to her first husband, Paddy Smith, is centered in the Kusawa Lake–Takhini River region. She talks of this part of her life mainly in terms of the work she did while he was away hunting or working as a big-game guide. She stayed with her grandmother, raised her eight children, sewed skin clothing that she sold in Whitehorse. She hunted moose with her uncles, cut and dried the winter's supply of meat, then went fishing at Klukshu to put up the winter's supply of fish, "maybe five hundred fish so we won't go short."

She contrasts her own hard work and abilities with her observations about young women today and applies the metaphor of "words" to "behavior": "It's *true*, I think, what old people did!" If words can be true or false, then behavior, too, can be true or false.

She gave birth to her children "Indian way," but as with puberty seclusion, her account is phrased in terms of "old Grandma words" rather than in terms of her own experience. When I questioned her more specifically, she remarked that this was not one of the subjects she wanted to discuss on tape; it comes too close to issues surrounding women's power. She describes the sickness that came with the 1920s worldwide influenza epidemic, particularly the deaths of old people. The police tried unsuccessfully to quarantine Hutshi, but she insisted on going back to help. Police brought in soup so people could be fed, but still many died.

Discussing her marriage to her second husband, Johnny Ned, she reiterates moiety rules: "Later they gave me Johnny Ned. That's how they did it, old days. We don't let it go; just have to take it. . . . Indians are like that. You can't let it go. That's why my husbands' people keep me company now that I'm alone." Annie and Johnny made their headquarters close to what is now called "Stoney Creek," near the Mendenhall River.

While Mrs. Ned is careful to ensure that events she defines as "trivial" are excluded from this account, she is equally concerned that certain "important" issues not be included. Critical here are the details of *how* people in her family, including her second husband, obtained spiritual powers. One of the fundamental rules about spiritual power is that it should not be discussed casually. The best way to talk about it is indirectly, through stories. Her most straightforward reference to her own powers is her regret that she did not yet have them when her daughter became ill: "I got no doctor power that time: that came later. You know it when you get it: game teaches man." Speaking openly about sources of power on tape would be quite inappropriate because the words, once captured, might be used out of context. Such indiscretion could certainly result in loss of one's powers. Again, the guiding principle here is that words have power simply by being spoken, and they must be used carefully.

Johnny Ned became a very powerful shaman in the southern Yukon, much to the consternation of local missionaries. Although Mrs. Ned is willing to discuss his powers obliquely, she demonstrates her thorough understanding of power in her explanation of why she cannot specify how he actually acquired it:

> I can't talk about Johnny: It might be we make mistake. I can't speak for other people. I can't show my husband's song [on tape]. I can tell you what happened, though. To start with, he got Indian song. That man doesn't know anything [about English], doesn't talk. How come he talks that time? [He began speaking and reading English]. . . . My husband took control all over: Carmacks, Dawson, all over. He took it around, that control.

She refers to a "Mr. Young," who was a missionary in 1917. An unsigned letter on file in the Anglican Church records, possibly written by the same Mr. Young, advised an incoming missionary about the delicacy of the situation:

> There is a cult in existence in the Champagne district under the leadership of Johnny Ned. For the most part, his teaching is all right. However, he has some fantastic ideas and has mixed on some native superstition to Christianity. I think that it is better to recognize everything that is good in his teaching than to attempt to antagonize him. After a while when you get to know him you may be able to steer him along the right lines. A great many Indians throughout the country have been more or less worked up over his teachings and some of them believe his story regarding visions that he has had. Mr. Swanson and I talked over the subject and agreed that it was better to approve of his teachings so far as they agreed with Christian and to emphasize the fact that what he is teaching is the religion of Christ as practised and taught for hundreds of years.[4]

Mrs. Ned and I have discussed the letter, and she explicitly rejects this interpretation: "It didn't come from God! He got it himself!"

If Mrs. Ned's narratives are distinctively formal and emphasize the importance of "old-style words," the songs she sings capture the emotions, the humor, the affectionate personal relationships of everyday life. Songs form a significant part of her discussions of her adult life, and Section 8 provides transcripts of only five of the many she sings. She is one of the very finest singers in the southern Yukon. Her repertoire is large, and she is careful to explain who "made" each song, the occasion when each was composed, and why it was sung. Despite her ninety-some years, her voice remains deep and powerful.[5]

Songs orient people to place. As we drive through the southern Yukon, Mrs. Ned often interrupts our conversation to make a statement such as, "You don't know this place, so I will sing this song to you to tell you where you're going. This is Big Jim's song. It's just like he cries with this song."

A final section presents two accounts about land and landscape which blend Mrs. Ned's own observations with traditions passed on from grandparents. The first discusses glaciers and refers to the Lowell Glacier, in the southwest Yukon, which has surged in historic times. Older people regularly assert that glacial surges are caused by careless human beings cooking with grease near glaciers. If one does accidently burn grease near a glacier, as in this story, it is possible to reverse the damage by throwing a blanket on the fire. A second story provides oral testimony about questions still puzzling biologists—the major shifts in the caribou population which occurred in the southern Yukon sometime during the first decade of this century.

Increasingly, these days, Mrs. Ned makes reference to the two grandmothers who raised her and how she thinks about their words now that she is old herself: "[When] somebody is going to be old, they're going to feel it. That time, I'm young, I go anyplace. . . . Now that I'm old lady, I think about how those people feel. Even when my grandma was blind, she still taught us how to snare, how to make spring trap. I wish she were here now . . . I'd give her tea. My grandma is the one who raised me."

1 ✳ Our *Shagóon*, Our Family History

*"Since I was ten, that's when I got smart.
I started to know some things."*

I'm going to put it down who we are. This is our *Shagóon*—our history. Lots of people in those days, they told their story all the time. This story comes from old people, not just from one person—from my grandpa, Hutshi Chief; from Laberge Chief; from Dalton Post Chief. Well, they told the story of how first this Yukon came to be.

You don't put it yourself, one story. You don't put it yourself and then tell a little more. You put what they tell you, older people. You've got to tell it right. Not *you* are telling it: it's the person who told you that's telling that story.

My grandpa, one man, was Hutshi Chief. He's got two wives: one from Selkirk, one from Carcross; his name is Ḵaajoolaax̱í: that's Tlingit. Oh, call him a different one: Kàkhak—that's *dän k'è* [Southern Tutchone]—that's an easy one. His Coast Indian name comes from a long time ago: it was from trading they call him that way. You see, long-time Coast Indians, they go through that way to Selkirk, all over.[6]

We'll start off with Hutshi Chief first. We'll do the women next time. He married first my grandma from Carcross: *Däk'äläma*. His Selkirk wife was *K'edäma*: she's the one they call Mrs. Hutshi Chief.

My daddy's name was Hutshi Jim: my daddy, Hutshi Jim, is the oldest. Another brother is Chief Joe—Hutshi Joe—he had the same mother. One grandpa we've got, and I've got lots of cousins up at 1016[7] from this lady, *Däk'äläma*. Jimmy Kane was her grandchild, too: Jimmy Kane's mother, Mrs. Joe Kane, is her daughter.

These kids are all born around Hutshi. Hutshi is a coast name: Coast Indians call it *Hóoch'i Áayi*—means "Last Time Lake." That's when they go back. Then after white man came, they didn't come back [to Hutshi]. The *dän k'è* name is *Chùinagha*. Lots of people used to live at Hutshi. My grandpa had a big house at Hutshi . . . all rotten now. Oh, it used to be good fishing spot! King salmon came that way, too. Everybody came there together. *Kajìt* [Crow] owns that place, but they're not stingy with it.

Dalton Post, too—just free come fish![8] But this time [it's] no good, they say.

Wintertime, people hunted fur, used dog team. After they came [back] from Dalton Post, they hunted dry meat, put up food, berries. They put

them in birch bark, they freeze them and put them away. They put stoneberries in moose grease—that's just like cheese. And roots are like potatoes: they clean them up and cut them and put them in grease, for the kids. There's no hard times. There used to be caribou there all the time. I remember big herds of caribou. But now no more.[9]

My daddy, my uncles, they all stayed around Hutshi Lake. But when they got married, the woman maybe wants to go someplace [with her family]. That's the way.[10] Now Indian woman when she marries white man, he takes *her* home . . .

My grandpa's house is there yet, though, all fallen down, rotten. Lots of houses there, used to be. But at Hutshi, nobody is there yet. You see [the cemetery] where there's lots of dead people there? My grandpa died at Hutshi, and his two wives are buried there with him.

My mother's name is *Tùtaɬmą* and she was from Hutshi. Her daddy was Big Jim. There's another Coast Indian man from Dalton Post they call Big Jim, but that one's different—this one is Big Jim from Hutshi. I don't know his dad, though. My grandpa was too old [to tell me] by the time I got smart.

Big Jim's Indian name is *Kàkhnokh*. He married *Dakwa'äl*, and they had a daughter, *Tùtaɬmą*. That woman was my mother. My grandfather, Big Jim, has an old house at Jojo Lake—it's an old house that fell down already.

Long-time people, anyplace they go round. [People] come from Dalton Post—go see everybody from the next country when you've got time. They see them. They talk. Then they go back in time to put up groceries for themselves in winter. They're trapping, and they hunt for fur.

This is our *Shagóon*. *Kajìt*, me—that's Crow: *Ts'ürk'i*. Wolf people they call *Ägunda;* wolf [the animal] is *ägay*. Hutshi Chief was *Kajìt*, and Big Jim was *Ägunda*. That Big Jim from Dalton Post was Crow.

My mamma's people are Crow—*Ǥaanaxteidí*. My daddy is different; they're Wolf, *Ägunda*. That Crow started with our side. Crow claims Frog. All Crows, we claim it, used to be. But this time, nothing [people don't know about this].

Now I'm going to tell a story about long time ago. This is my two grandpas' story, Big Jim's and Hutshi Chief's. I'm telling this story not from myself, but because everybody [old] knows this story. This is not just my story—lots of old people tell it! Just like now they go to school, old time we come to our grandpa. Whoever is old tells it the same way. That's why we put this on paper. I tell what I know.

This time people talk way under me, not my age. They say they know! What I see, I tell it, me. This story is my grandpa's, Hutshi Chief.

Well, Coast Indians came in here a long time before white people. People had fur, and they used it for everything themselves. Nobody knows alcohol, nobody knows sugar before those Coast Indians came. They brought guns, too. No white man here, nothing.

At *Noogaayík*, Tlingit people first saw chips coming down from up-river.[11] People making rafts, I guess, and the chips floated down.

"Where did this one come from?" they asked. So that time Coast Indians wintertime to Dalton Post. That's the way they met these Yukon Indians. Yukon people are hunting, and they've got nice skin clothes—Oh, gee, porcupine quills, moose skins, moccasins! Everything nice.

Coast Indians saw those clothes and they wanted them! That's the way they found out about these Yukon people. Right then, they found where we hunted. Coast Indians traded them knives, axes, and they got clothes, babiche, fish skin from the Yukon. They've got *nothing*, those Tlingit people, just cloth clothes, groundhog clothes. Nothing! Goat and ground-hog, that's all.

But people here had lots of fur and they used it in everything them-selves—ready-made moccasins, buckskin parky, silverfox, red fox, caribou-skin parky sewed up with porcupine quills. You can't see it, this time [anymore], that kind. I saw it, that time. My grandma got it . . . so pretty . . .

So that's how they got it! Coast Indians got snowshoes and moose-skin clothes—all warm—parky, caribou parky, caribou blanket, caribou mat-tress. Anything like that they want to use. Those people wanted clothes from here in Yukon . . . Skin clothes, sheepskin, warm mitts . . . So they traded. They did it for a purpose. Our grandpas make different snow-shoes [from Tlingit style] in this Yukon. They fixed them with caribou-skin babiche, nice snowshoes. Coast Indians traded for snowshoes, traded for clothes. They traded for snowshoe string, for babiche, for sinew, for tanned skin—all soft.

I don't know the time Coast Indians came to this Yukon. My grand-mother, my grandpa, *they* told me that's the way.

These Yukon people told Coast Indians to come back in summertime. So they did, next summer. Yukon people had lots of furs. That time they don't know money—they don't know where to sell them. So Coast Indians brought in guns. Well, they're surprised about that, Yukon people! They've been using bow and arrow! So they traded.

Coast Indians got guns, knives, axes. They came on snowshoes. They packed sugar, tea, tobacco, cloth to sew. Rich people would have eight packers each! They brought shells, they brought anything to trade. They traded for clothes. Coast Indians brought sugar, tea. At first these Yukon people didn't want it. But pretty soon, they went to Klukwan. They took their fur. They knew where to sell it now. They would go down wintertime with toboggan, Dalton Post way or by Lake Arkell.

But people here got crazy for it [trade goods]. They traded for knives, they traded for anything, they say—shells, guns, needles. When you buy that gun, you've got to pile up furs how long is that gun, same as that gun, how tall! Then you get that gun.[12]

I don't know those guns—that's before me. I don't see it. But my grandpa had that kind at Hutshi. I saw what they've been buying, though—blankets, not so thick, you know, quite light. You could pack maybe fifty blankets, I guess, from the coast. They would bring all that. Everybody bought their grandpa, their grandma a knife that time!

My grandpa, Hutshi Chief, had a trading partner, *Gasłeeni.* We fixed up his grave, my brother and myself. Old people were satisfied with Coast Indians, what they used to bring—cloth, guns, and matches. They used flint before, and birch bark. Coast Indians taught people to chew [tobacco]—I never used it, me. I never used to use sugar, either.

Well, Coast Indians would rest there and then they could go anyplace, see? They go hunting; then they go back. Then these people would go down to see them.

Dalton Post people are all our people, and Burwash people—all ours. Some from Carcross, too. This time just where they stay, they stay; that's what it looks like to me.[13] It was my grandpa, my grandma who told me about that, about before.

I never saw *those* ones—I know lots of Coast Indians, but they didn't bring anything in my time: I didn't see Coast Indians packing. It was before me, I guess, when my grandma was young—about one thousand years ago, about two thousand years ago, now!

When Skookum Jim found gold, that's the time everything changed. This time we can't do it now, can't travel around. People stay where they stay.

2 ✳ How First This Yukon Came to Be

"Some people tell stories Coast Indian way.
Me, I tell it Yukon way."

✳ Crow and Beaverman[14]

Well, I know lots of people, old people, long time.
They tell the same stories, old people
That's the ones I know,
[About] first when this land comes,
When this ground was fixed.

One time, lots of people camped at one place.
People go one way [in one direction], one way they go.
Other people don't know which way they went.
They don't come back, don't come back, don't come back home.
They just go.

Crow and Beaver—they call Beaver *Äsùya*—that means Smart Man,
The two of them [go together], that's all.
They figure they want to go the way those people go.
Somebody tells them to go because people don't come back.
They go . . . they follow—they follow the track.
They go . . . go . . . go.

Pretty soon they come to a mountain, a mountain.
They climb to the top of the mountain:
It goes downhill, bad place.
From here they slide down, those people [who disappeared].
Then, Wolverine stays down there:
He's got something to kill people when they slide down—
Dry something—little dry tree, you know;
They slide down,
And it's just like they're poked inside [impaled] with that one,
Get killed.

282   In those days that Wolverine, he's big, big!

Long time ago, they're big, they say, Wolverines.
They eat those people.
His wife, too, is big.
As soon as they get people there, they eat them.

I said that old people tell me this story.
Not one man told me, but ten people, old people.
My grandpa and my grandmother,
They're all with me when they died.
Other old people, too, they told me.

So Crow and *Äsùya* killed him.
They come to that Wolverine place, to the slides.
They know that down there something is killing the people.
Those Wolverines put water down there to [make a] slide down.
Then it froze, and you can slide down fast.
Just then, they're poked inside.

Crow and Beaver take off their shirt.
They put the branches inside and make it [look] like a leg, too.
Then they push it down.
Pretty soon, a man is down there on the bottom
And he pokes at the branches they put in the shirt, filled up like a person.
They see him.
Then he pulls it—it's light, that one.
He's got a camp there.
His wife is there, his family is there.
He comes down.
He started poking a stick into them.
So Crow and *Äsùya* think about it theirself, and they killed him with
    bow and arrow.

They've got a sharp rock, I guess, a long time ago—a bone.
And when it hits him, it comes out.
It goes right through and kills him.

"That was not a person, that one, Wolverine."

Oh, big. They're big!
So they kill him.
They ran down one side [of the slide] and they killed that Wolverine.
    Big one.
They poked him with that bow and arrow.

284   His wife stays there, too; she's big, too, that one.

Annie   Fat.

Ned   They eat lots of people, I guess.

Then they come to his wife.
"What for you eat people?
What for your husband eats people, you too?" they tell her.
"I suppose you got to be game, you."

Just like they lesson people, teach people, that Crow and Beaver.

Well, they talk.
"We got to kill her."

"Yes, we got to kill her, too."

That one's got pups, that woman.
They kill her, kill with bow and arrow, same.
After that, they cut her open.

Those pups climb up trees like this. Wolverine.
They're alive then,
As soon as they kill her, Crow and Beaver run to the tree.

"What are we going to do [with them]?"

"Well, when they grow how big they are now [that's enough]."

They don't want [them to be] big.
It's just like they hit them.

"So, we've got to kill them.
Save two, one female and one man."
They saved two; the rest they want to kill them.

That Beaver wants to climb up to where they got in the tree.
But they pee on him!
He comes back.

Then Crow does that: he flies there and kills them.
He asks each, "Are you a girl?"

"Yes."

"And you?"

"Yes, a boy."

That's all. Two only, they save.

Then he tells them,
"You've got to be the same big. Don't eat anybody!
It's no good!"

See? Lots of people, I guess, they eat.

Long time, first this land is mud, I guess, that time.
Then from there, this story comes . . .
They tell next man, next man, next man.
Now it comes to the last.
But these schoolkids don't know, this time, this story, see?

Then they say,
"We're going to give you feed, what you're going to eat."

They give them ptarmigan.
They kill ptarmigan with bow and arrow, bring a bunch over there.

"You could get it yourself, after.
Don't eat persons again.
You're going to be game, you," they tell him.

When the people went from home
All the far side they go.[15]
All got eaten by Wolverine.
That's what the old people tell. That's lots of people.

From there, they give feed.

Then they tell them, "You eat dried meat cache."

What for they say that!!!

"Somebody's cache, and gopher, too, you've got to eat it.
You kill for yourself."
Then they tell them:
"Same big as Wolverine," they tell them.
[I.e., wolverines must never grow larger than these pups.]

Then they go from there.

II

They walk around . . . walk around.
Then they camp someplace like this. Snow.

They've got to eat something, I guess, themselves.
They came to a camp.

So they camp.
Pretty soon, one man comes.
Around this land, this ground, first they see him.
First everybody they bring it on this land.
He looks the same as a person.

Then they give this: moose nose they cooked.
They cut it for him:
"Right there, that's what we eat."
That man picks it up; he smells it, puts it back.
Now they found out! That's no good.[16]

They tried to give him something to eat.
If he eats that now, he will turn to person.
Yeah! That man could turn to person like them.
That's why they showed him that one.

He won't take it, what people eat.
He knows it.
He leaves it.

[This is how] they know how true is person:
They got it, that one—they fix up that ptarmigan and they cook it,
That one, too, they give it.
He smells it. He leaves it.

"How come you're not hungry?" they tell him.

Already they know.
Both of them know what he eats: he eats person!
It's for that reason they go round this ocean, I guess,
But this is Yukon story, this one.

Then Äsùya said,
"That thing's no good," he said.
"Which way did he come [from]?"
He follows; he's going to watch it here.

You know Crow . . . he flies around.

Äsùya follows his tracks and finds his sack—
Moose-skin packsack, used to be, they say, long time—

He opens it.
Here it's kids feet there! Indians!

> He looks same as a man, too, [like an] Indian.
> They call him *Kojel*. Yeah. Long time.

He opens that. Crow. Hangs it up again.
He brings moosemeat to his partner.
They got moosemeat, too; cook moosemeat.
They try to show people, too.

Then they camp.
"We've got big place here. You sleep right here, my friend."
They call him *shǫ'ǖr*, "my friend," long time.

Now people are coming. Lots of them.
And they camp this side, other side of the fire!

Then they want to dry their moccasins;
They put up pole, those people.
That's why they do that, I guess.
And they fixed it there; they dry moccasins on the fire.

So he sleeps.
They sleep. Two men (Crow and Beaver).
And they bring this along: green club from a tree.
They cut it there, put it there.
They've got bow and arrow, too.

> I don't know who put it [caused it],
> That Smart Man to go round,
> To clean up that kind of people.
> Just like somebody tells him who's no good.
> That's why *Äsùya*, they call him.
> *Ts'ürk'i* [Crow] helps, too.

They went to sleep.

Pretty soon, he gets up, that man. He gets up.
Those moccasins, which one is pretty, he moved it in place of his
    moccasin.
He thought he's going to kill those two.

They know it.
They watch it.

288　　One sleeps one way, one sleeps this [the other] way.
Annie　Their feet reach like this [touching].
Ned　　Soon as that man gets up [they kick each other].
　　　　That's why they sleep that way.

Pretty soon he gets up.
How he thinks he's going to kill two men?

They snore.
"Get up, get up!"
They jumped on that man. One of them hit him.
The other one got up and he hit the back.
And they killed him: they clubbed him down!

In the morning, his shoes were there.
He thought he was going to kill those people,
So he's got good mukluks; he put them in place of his moccasins.

So they picked the moccasins up again;
They put them on.
They leave his mukluks there.
They go.
Then they know where he comes from.

Got to go that way, they say.

III

They walk, walk.
Pretty soon, they're by the lake, where people stay.
A man—that's another man—comes from that camp by the
　　lake.
They call him shą'ÿr.

"What are you doing?"

　　Well, I don't know how they understand.
　　They understand anything, those two!
　　That's how they're built, I guess.

"So what are you doing, Shą'ÿr?"

"Well, I'm fishing here."
He wants to push those two men [Crow and Beaver] in the airhole in
　　that lake, that man.
That's the way people go, I guess, people before.

So they've got to play with him [delay him] by that airhole.
They see fire back there [at his camp].
The river runs for him.

"Say, Shą'ųr, take off your clothes and stuff them in that airhole.
We've got better kind."

   How crazy to say that!

So he took off his clothes and put them in the airhole.
No clothes, pretty soon.

Then they run around.

   They should kill him right away! What for . . . !

Pretty soon, he's cold.
That's the time they run, they run.
When they got to a big stump, they went inside, Ts'ürk'i and Äsùya.
Must be getting beat, I guess.
Ts'ürk'i and Äsùya, they just run inside.
Without clothes, he's getting cold.

They've got sheshel [stone ax].
He did that. He took it like this [swung it].
Oh, he put his head up. They watched it.

In that airhole are his clothes.

From there, they run.

What they think, I guess, is how tough!
Should be easy to kill him.
I don't know why they do that.

So they go inside that big wood.
He comes: he's going to kill them.
No, they can't hit him!

[Claps] They kill him! Push him in airhole!

Then they go to that place where they see smoke.
That's all the people living there, only that man they got.

Just a woman there.
They give her the same thing:
Moose nose cooked, ptarmigan cooked, everything.

"You want to eat?"

"No," she smells it, puts it down.
"I don't know what kind that one [is]."

So he said, "What do you people eat?"

They could hear anything, I guess, that one.
Right there, somebody talks to them.
"No good . . . Not a true person."
So they killed her.

That's the bad people.
They eat people, too, like *Kojel.*

A long time ago, first it was night.
I don't know what it could be, me, too . . .

IV

Then, they go from there.
People got smoke there, under the mountain.
There's a lake there.

[Crow and Beaver discuss]:
"He's a person, all right, that man."

"No, it's just like that Wolverine."

They went to where an old man stays with his wife.
They've got a young girl.

"Ho," the old man says, "I can't climb up to that sheep up there.
You see him?
I can't climb up there anymore.
My leg is no good.
You're going to be my son-in-law [if you kill him]."

He said that to that young man, Beaver.
He'd like that Beaver for his son-in-law.

Well, fourteen years old, she's got a hat, that girl,[17]
Stays a long time away when that happens.
Then he says that, that old man [to *Äsùya*].

[Beaverman says,] "Oh, my moccasins are no good, all torn."

"Well, I'm going to give it to my daughter quick [to sew].
You take it off."

That, his daughter, he put on [dressed up] like sheep.
Right there, walking around there, that's his daughter.

Äsùya wants to kill those two.

So that old man said,
"I've come this way, and I'll kill him from here."

"All right. All right."

Now he [the old man] sewed it up himself [pretending his daughter
     did the work].
Then he said, "All right, we go. I'll go, too," that old man said.

Äsùya has got sharp bow and arrow under his hair.
They go there.

[The old man tells Äsùya to push the sheep down the mountain but
     really intends to push Äsùya.]

[Äsùya] pushed him down.
That old man's wife was there, has that shęshęl.
They see her: Crow, he can see that [by flying around overhead].

Äsùya asks, "Where from? Show me where to step."

That mountain is hard. It's wintertime.
He does that, then. Crow pushes him over.
Here, his own wife kills him at the bottom.

Yeah!

Then Crow, he flies and Äsùya goes down again.
That's his wife, there.

"What does your daddy do? [they ask the daughter].
Are you a person?
What are you?
You want to be saved?"

That Crow comes back.

"Go home."
She's just fourteen years old.
They brought her back to the house.

"What are you?" [they ask her].

"Bear. Bear we are."

"Well, what do you want to do, killing people?
If you're going to keep on, we're going to kill you."

She said, "No more."

They give her food and she eats it, so they let her go.
They let her go.

V

Then after that, they came to a regular bear.
Must be springtime now.
They go around yet, that bear family.
Regular bear. Big bear. They come.

Bear says, "Yeah! We want to get that Äsùya—Beaver there."
They want to kill that beaver, bear.18
They want to eat him.

Well, beaver is his people:
[Äsùya asks bear,] "What you been doing?"
[I.e., How have you been trying to catch beaver?]

"Well, we tried to kill him.
He goes right in the middle of that place, open place.
We set out fishnet."
Beaver wears a row of teeth around his neck.

Then Ts'ürk'i said, "I think they're no good, these people."
He goes around, he flies.
Sometimes when they get stuck he flies around to find out what it is.

Those bears really want to kill beaver.
Then they caught him.
That's beaver there. Oh, he knows now, Beaver.

He says, "Right close to there, they set a fishnet for me.
They're going to eat people, shür, bear.
They eat people. How about you?"

"Oh, bad one, that people.
I've got no place to go, wintertime.
They pretty near got me," [the beaver said].

Well, they killed bear.
They set a beaver net and he chews that one, that beaver.
That's why they don't get him, see?
Then they kill that bear.

One beaver, he goes on the water.
Just Crow alone.
"You've got enough food?" he tells beaver.

"Yeah. Got a little bit now."

So they bring poplar tree, throw in there.

Well, that beaver says,
"We want fur. People are going to get fur."
That's why people now get skin, fur, from beaver.

And that's why bear, he can't kill people.

Grizzly bear, though, he kills people this time, see?
They don't get after him. He passes [escapes] them.

Then they [Crow and Beaver] go from there.
They do everything in springtime there.
Go round, round,
Which way bad people stay.

"Don't kill nobody. Don't bother people.
That's game, you, for people to eat you. Don't do that."

And they go on . . . got boat now . . . float down . . . float down . . .
They come to ghost—*ts'in.*
They're lying there.

So, he said, "All full dry meat."
They don't see anybody.
You know Crow! He wants to eat dry meat, anything.

Beaver says, "No, you don't want to eat it. Don't bother."

Just the same, Crow, he picks it up from nobody,
Loads up that boat with dry meat.
Pretty soon, they float from there.
Hhhht, hhht—under boat, that's ghost!
From where they take that meat, it goes back again.
It goes back in that boat!

That meat is all hung up again!
He does that just the same, that Crow. He wants to find out, see?

That Beaver, though, he just watches.
He says, "No people? What kind of people is that?
What kind of people do you think are here?
How come that boat comes back here?"

Crow eats it anyway.
That Crow does everything!
Here it comes straight through him, that meat!

Well, they can't do anything.
They can't see who it is.
He loads up again. He goes.
It got back up there, all that meat hangs up again.

And they talk about it.
"Well, I got beat here now! What do you think?"

Then *Ts'ürk'i* talks,
"Well, just show up for your meat!
Because nobody's there, that's why we take it.
Why don't you show?"

Talk . . . talk . . . talk . . . you know that Crow!

Äsùya can't do nothing, too.

"Oh!" somebody says. "We don't bother nobody.
We don't bother you."
Somebody said that, finally.
Talk! They can't talk for nothing!

Then Beaver said,
"What kind of people you?"

"Ghost. *Ts'in*. We don't bother anybody.
Why do you take our grub? Yeah!
We're the same people as you were before we die.
We can't do nothing to you. We don't bother people."

That's ghost country I think they've been to, see?

So Beaver said,
"You're going to do nothing to people? To our people? You?"

"No, we bother nobody. We are a different place.
We come from you people who died.
We died.
We got our own groceries. No way we bother people."

So they let it go, that one. Can't do nothing.
Not going to bother anybody, not doing harm.
So they let them go.

VI

After that, they go, go.
They're close to salt water now.
They come to fishing.

Deer. Long time ago is like person, I guess.
That one killed people, too.
Something wrong, I guess. It grows big.
So Crow calls him,
"My auntie's husband! Let's fish. I'd like to see fishing."

He goes with a boat, goes with a boat.
Then he gets on with it.

"What kind of bait you got?"
That's hook bait for fish.
They're coming to salt water.

Cháatl [halibut] they want. *Cháatl.*
That's the one he throws on.
Pretty soon he killed it, that auntie.

So pretty soon Crow comes back to that man's wife.

"Where's your auntie's husband?" says that woman.

"Oh, he's coming. He's got lots of fish—saltwater fish.
We're going to give you halibut bellies."

He gives her rocks, hot ones!

"These are halibut bellies which my auntie's husband [i.e, your
    husband] gives you.
I've got them, my auntie."

She eats it like that, that lady, those rocks.
She got killed right there.

So he was married to a lady who was no good, I guess, that one.
That's why they did that.
Just funny how they can kill them.

Then, after that, they got on the boat.
Whenever they see that kind, they give them what a person eats.

"You're not going to grow anymore.
Just the same big you stay."

From there, they split.
Ts'ürk'i goes to Coast Indian side.
Beaver goes to Yukon side.
They're going to straighten up this world.
No more danger, they say.

"So I'm going to be Yukon" [Beaver said].

"Well, I'll come back" [Crow said].
I'm going to saltwater side."

That's what I know of this story.

VII

That's why that Crow don't want fish to come from salt water, this way,
     see?[19]
Must be that's why.

That time he put his hand [wing] like that at Klukshu, [pointing
     toward the coast].
At Klukshu, they've got saltwater fish.

He should leave it alone!
Then those fish would come up there, Champagne.

You see that Dezadeash Lake?
About three miles [separates the two drainages].
But he makes Dezadeash come out other side [flowing north].
King salmon, the other side; silver salmon.
He did it there, too.
His hand he put up like that.
That's what they say, old people, see?

Then he did that to this place, too, Kusawa Lake.
Other side water ran down to Klukwan,

Fish came there, too.
What for Crow do that that way?
Glacier on top there, that's what he did!

He *could* have made fish go this way!
Just to Haines summit, fish go.
That Lake Arkell, a mountain goes like that.
From the other side, big river goes down to Klukwan.

3 ✳ My Husbands' *Shagóon*

"We learn from Grandma, Grandpa, what they do and they explain to us. I think everybody knows that, but I know what they say!"

Now I'm going to tell my husband's history, Paddy Smith. My first husband was Paddy Smith, *Kàkhnokh*. His grandmother married from Coast Indians to this Yukon.

My husband's father had Coast Indian name—*Goonxaktsáy*. Coast Indians gave him that one when they came to trade. White man gave him a name, too—Johnson. Indian way, *dän k'è*, his name was *K'ayędatà*.

Those days one man had one partner. First time Coast Indians trade, they brought in different colored blankets—red blankets, yellow blankets, blue blankets. No duty that time they pack![20] My grandma gave me one of those blankets, but I put it up with my daughter when she died.

Later they gave me Paddy Smith's brother, Johnny Ned: Paddy's mother and Johnny's mother are sisters, so it's just like they are brothers, Indian way. Johnny's mother and father are both from Yukon: his father's name was *Tsenedhäta*, Frank Slim's namesake. That's how they do it in the old days. We don't let it go—just have to take it.[21]

My father-in-law's country, Paddy's father's country, is right here. Steamboat Landing—*Dùuchùgà*, "driftwood creek." It's just like a bridge there where the driftwood builds up. Two rivers meet there—Lake Arkell River [Takhini River], *Dùu Chù*, and Mendenhall River, *Chènk'äla Chù*. It comes from Ten Mile Lake [Taye Lake], *Chènk'äla*. Long time ago, king salmon used to go up *Chènk'äla Chù* to Ten Mile Lake, but in my time there were too many beaver and king salmon didn't go through. My father-in-law moved here when he married Paddy Smith's mother. He lived this side [north side] of Mendenhall River, *Chènk'äla Chù*. After I stayed with my husband, Paddy Smith, we had house other [south] side of the river.

Long time ago, Coast Indians used to come to here—to *Dùuchùgà*—to trade. This is my father-in-law's country: he stayed here all the time. There's a graveyard up above there: my father-in-law's mother is buried there—*Shotk'e*—and also my mother's brother, *Katlay*, Charlie.

That Lake Arkell they call Kusawa. That's *Koosawu Áa*, "long lake"; in *dän k'è* it's *Nakhų Chù*, "raft crossing." They call that narrow place *Nakhų*, but the lake takes its name from that narrow place.

Now I'm going to talk about *Nakhu*, the narrows at Lake Arkell. My husband's people own that Lake Arkell. One man owned it: *Nùlatà* was his name, my husband's father's father. He stayed there all the time. All that lake belonged to them, *Ägunda*, Wolf.

Before Coast Indians—before guns—they had a ranch for moose at Lake Arkell. They've got a corral there where they set snares. I never saw caribou snared—that's before my time—but I knew that kind [of snare]. *Everybody* came there—lots of meat, lots of fish. Everybody helped together. Sometimes they go to Klukshu, to get fish—sometimes they want a different kind of fish, I guess.

That corral was down at Lake Arkell, at *Nakhu*, at the narrows. You can't see them [corrals] this time . . . Even *I* didn't see them when I was young, when I went there. This land, he comes out, grows anything.

That narrow place just goes across there. They put fishnet there—that's why they got it there. They made sinew themselves, early days. When Coast Indians came that time they got [string] fishnet. Before that, they just tied up sinew like thread. Then you get lots of fish, they say.

To get there, you go to head of river, cross that lake, then maybe fifteen miles—old people don't know "miles" those days—maybe ten, maybe more. They put snares between the lake and mountain, then run the caribou through.

Nùlatà owned *Nakhu*, but he's not there alone. Lots of people came to him, from all over. He stayed there, but everyone came there—my father-in-law, Laberge Chief, all Carcross people come there. All Hutshi—all go there, have a good time. Everybody is satisfied with him, *Nùlatà*. Everybody! He's not stingy with it. It's that narrow place. That's where they cross with rafts, there. It's not too far to go there. Yeah. They all enjoy.

Then *Nùlatà* and his people travel round—to Klukshu, to Dezadeash, to Hutshi. That's what they do, long ago. If they want to trap, nobody stops them. They're free to go.

There used to be lots of caribou, even in my time. When caribou came, it was just like horses. You could hear it [hooves] making noise on the ice. Way back I went around with my grandpa; he shot fifty caribou. Long time ago, people made caribou summer parky. Summertime skin has short hair; it doesn't come off. [They decorate it with] all porcupine quills, pretty. Moose were getting short when caribou came; not too long ago, they came back again. But people bother them too much, I guess. They're dying off, I hear.

Coast Indians come to this Yukon in April. They would start off from Klukwan. That [Kusawa] River comes down behind that mountain like this, way down to Klukwan. Well, they came up. They walked this way.

They pulled things on the ice. They've got a trail from Klukwan, see? Where the river comes down. Glacier is there, too, at the head of the lake, on the top of the mountain. Then they come here by Lake Arkell, down this way. Now this time you can't go that way. Only one way now. There's car trail now.

They don't call it right, Lake Arkell—*Koosawu Áa*, they call it, "long ways lake." At the head of Lake Arkell there's lots of wood where the river comes in. Coast Indians made rafts, not boats. Rafts work better than boats on Lake Arkell: when waves come, boats have to pull out. But when they make rafts, nothing is wrong with them. They take out tree roots, split them, put them in water. Then they twist willows, tie up green trees. Then they tie every log together, tie up, tie up. Then they come on this Takhini River, on rafts. Then they go to Lake Laberge: the [Tlingit] man who trades there stays there; the others go on to Fort Selkirk. That's as far as they go.

I saw one man from Haines [who used to trade here]. His name was *Lootáax*. He said when he saw smoke fire [on Yukon River], that's the time he used to like. Then he knew people were there. That's the time he's satisfied.

There's another way Coast Indians used to go to Hutshi: they went by Dezadeash Lake, on foot trail [Chilkat Trail]. They made birch tobog-gan—no nails. It's strong! They tied it up with moose skin; then they came to Aishihik, to Hutshi. People there know Coast Indians are coming when they hear guns.

Yukon people have gray silver fox; they use that to buy guns. They buy their outfit—sugar—nobody knows sugar. People start singing, "They're coming now!" Everybody's happy when they hear it! My grandpas Hutshi Chief, Hutshi Big Jim told me that.

From Hutshi they go to *Lù Shäw*—Fifty-Two Mile—they call that lake. I've got a home there: that's where I raised my kids. Not too far from Hutshi—one day's walking. Lots of fish there, whitefish. Then they go down to Selkirk. Everybody has got what they bring. At first these Yukon people don't want it . . . But they learned, they learned Coast Indian talk.

Coast Indians pack their own food when they come. They kill some-thing when they are traveling. They've got one hook for fish, big trout. They don't get stuck. White man gets stuck! Indian, if he's got something, sinew, anything, he sets it. He gets it! He gets rabbit; he gets anything!

When Coast Indians came, they wanted Yukon woman. White man, too, they wanted Indian woman. Without it, they can't survive. Me, I'm Yukon woman![22]

Coast Indians used rafts, but in Yukon they made moosehide boats. I made one. Down at Snag we were ratting.[23] Just nothing but lakes down there, Snag! My husband got two bull moose skins. You've got to join them this way, hind leg side. You sew it with babiche. Then you put it meat side up so it will dry tight. You could make a frame out of little trees—birch—no nails, just tree roots to tie it up, and moose-skin rope, babiche. We used nails, though, that time. It was a big boat! About six people sit on it. *Kanday dhù nàlàt*: "moose-skin boat." They're strong enough to jump in! Coast Indians never made it, though; they've got no moose; they can't kill moose up there. They just make rafts: they came down to Selkirk the long way, and then they walked back.

4 ✳ Stories from Kusawa Lake

"I think about Coast Indians a long time ago.
That's the one I'm telling
What I know, I tell."

✳ *Nakhu̧*: Kusawa Lake Narrows

I'm going to talk about *Nùlatà,* yeah.
My grandmother told me the story about him.

Well, down at Lake Arkell, narrow place,
They call it *Nakhu̧.*
Nakhu̧—narrow place—that's where rafts cross.
From there, he's got corral for moose long time ago.
He stayed there all the time.
He snared moose, caribou, sheep—they've got someplace for sheep,
    too—
Well, he got it.
Lots of fish there, too, *Nakhu̧.*

People come around to him all the time,
To visit, to get meat.
Then that *Nùlatà,* he's got daughters.
People come from Carcross, anyplace,
To marry his daughters.

The first girl got married to Carcross.
Her name is *Gúnxaadaakeit.*
That time, after Coast Indians came across to this Yukon,
That time, I guess, some kinds of things they've got:
Gúnxaa, Gúnxaa.[24]
It's high [expensive] that time from Coast Indians.
Those ones, he threw away that time his daughter is going to marry
    that man.
He threw them on the ground,
Then she goes on top of them to get married with this man.

302

Then after, another daughter is going to get married somewhere, too.
Aatthándlaya—that one there, he put bead—
Beads, but they look like bone [dentalium shells?]—
He threw that one.
On top, she walked to her husband.
Now she got married.

Next one, *Aakegántth'at.*
From that place, *Nakhụ,* that narrow place at Lake Arkell,
He threw moose skin in there, too—big moose skin.
That's the one, moose-hoof blanket,
And she goes on top of that skin when she's going to be married.

That's all *Nùlatà dunyèn ke,* for his children.
His daughters married that way from that *Nakhụ.*
He's the one that's got that moose corral.

Now finished, this story.

✳ *Kwǎnshalta*

Well, those people were a big family from Dalton Post.
They were packing fish to the head of Lake Arkell.[25]
They come there, to the head of Lake Arkell—
Packing that fish over to the lake.
Then they came by raft—they're going to make a raft.
One of those men who is coming has a wife from Laberge—her name
    is *Shuwuteen.*

When they came to the head of the lake, they made a raft.
There was lots of game that time—sheep, goats, moose,
Standing right on the shore.

    This is before me—I don't know that man.
    But the rest of them I knew when I got smart.

They killed lots of moose and they killed lots of sheep
And they had that fish they packed from Dalton Post.
Moose . . . moose . . . moose . . . sheep . . . sheep . . . sheep.

    Finally, they came to that place that's narrow at Lake Arkell—
    Nakhụ

Right there, they stayed.
They dried a little meat.

Then they started with a raft down Lake Arkell River [Takhini River].
When they got to that canyon a little before Steamboat Landing,
Right there they towed their boats through.[26]
Must be strong people, see?
They took the load off—it's too heavy—
And they towed the raft.
Then they had no trouble from there to Laberge.

So they go there, and end of this lake, they camp.
From there that man saw sheep.
"Why should people go?" he thinks. Gee.
In the morning he tells people,
"I'm going to climb up that hill,
Lots of sheep."
That man is Albert Allen's namesake.
This was long time ago, but people had guns that time,
Coast guns.

He climbed up.
Oh, that sheep, he shot him—he shot one.
Then he followed one up that mountain.
Oh, it's bad, that mountain—
Gäh Ddhäl, they call it—"rabbit mountain."

Now! He got stuck right there.
He's got no way to turn. It's bad, that mountain!
You should not go there for sheep!

He stayed there: he held on like this [with one hand].
Rock on one side.
He's got gun, but he can't do anything.
Way down, there's a good landing, but he held that rock, one hand.
He stayed there one night.

Next day, oh, he's getting weak.
He's going to fall down any time.
Then he said,
"Which way am I going to be saved?"

That's the time those rafts all go.
He *sees* them down there—he's not too far from there.

He sees them—lots of rafts go down.
He tries to holler, tries to holler.
But no . . . nobody.

Where do those people think that man is?
Crazy, eh?

The last boat went.
That's the time he sang—but I don't know that song.
Used to be I know, but I can't sing:

"Which way am I going to get help here?
I'm all in now."

He sang that in his song—that's half of it, I know.

Oh, he feels bad, feels bad.
Nobody with him . . .
So he talks, talks.
"They go, they go . . ."

Then, just like somebody said,
"We're going to save you;
We're going to save you.
You jump on that place."

Yes, this is how old people believe, long time.
I guess that's how he got help.

He held up his gun.
He put it up this way.
"I'm going to try now."
Just like that. He can't stand any more.
"If I fall down, that's all right, too," he thinks.

Just with one hand he's holding on.
He looked down. He finished his talk.

"Who's going to help me from here?
How am I going to get off?
I think I'm just done now, just done now."
Oh, he sang a long time that song.
"Help me. My time [to die] is now."

He jumped!
The rock stands up—willows come this far.

Annie
Ned

[Claps] He pretty near fell back.
Just like they put it [helped him].

He stayed right there.
He had lunch, though.
Next day afternoon he lay down there,
Water running through there from the mountain.
It's a good place there—he lay down.
After a while he took water.
It must be a long time he lay there.

It gets dark, gets dark.
Then he looked for his packsack.
He got that lunch, got that water, chew.
He falls asleep.

Well, the sun comes up.
It must be twelve o'clock, I guess. Daytime.
He knows everybody is gone.
Then he ate his lunch.
He got up that time, sat down good.
It feels good to chew.
There's something [some power] there, too.

Two nights, he was just about going to fall off there.
That's the time he jumped.
His name is *Kwǎnshalta.*

   This is long time ago.
   I don't know the man in this story.

He felt good in the morning.
He ate his lunch. That's all the lunch he's got—he's good now.
He's good to walk down the side of that mountain.
He made it!

Gee, how close! He sees them land.
He should try.
His wife is with them, too!
Those people stay at Steamboat Landing.
"Oh, that man will go to Laberge, I guess," they said.
They start off from Steamboat Landing.
"I guess he took off."

So he came along.
He's got nothing to eat. He walked down slowly.
He's hungry, hungry.

He was nearly all in—nothing to eat.
He hollered across there at Steamboat Landing.

There's nobody.
No raft there.
He hollered . . . Nobody.

Then he thought about it.
He's got gopher snare in his pocket, I guess,
Two or three snares—men are always like that when they go hunting—
So he figured he's played out now.
But there are lots of gophers, so he set his snares—
He caught two or three gophers.

"Might as well I sleep here."
Two nights in the mountain he held to that rock:
He's got to be weak that time he jumped!
He lay like that a long time, saw that last raft leave.
He can't shoot, too, because he left his gun above him.

So, he eats now: he eats two gophers.
He's got to go to the other side,
But he's got no way to cross that Takhini . . .
He comes down, comes down:
At Thirty-One Mile, he crosses.

He's getting strong now, but it's a long way.

Must be people wait for him over there.
He shouts . . . No answer.

　Crazy people, eh?

He figures that they go down to Laberge
He figures they've come down already to Laberge.
Then he stayed there till afternoon.
He set it, that snare:
He got it, got gopher.

Then shortcut, this way.
He gets two or three gophers and he gets tough.
Now he goes down.

Now he gets to mouth of Takhini—nobody there.
He figures he can cross that river on a log.
Nothing, no rope. He gets on, hold it with his leg, goes across.

Those people go to Laberge.
No man—nothing.
Oh, everybody cries.

Three nights later, right here he comes.
He's not had much to eat.

That time he said he's not going to take back his wife, *Shuwuteen*,
That Mrs. Henry, at Laberge, that's her namesake.

So he went away from there to Tagish.

That's bad rock there! *Gäh Ddhäl.*
You can't climb up, can't go that way!
You have to go around.

That song he sang says:

"Who's going to help me here?
I keep on this rock.
Might as well be I jump.
Man is man."

That's what I know of that song.

He never came back to his people.
He stayed someplace, way out.

I've been up there [*Gäh Ddhäl*], but not that way;
[There's a safe route up the] back way.
My old man killed caribou.
It's a nice place up on top.

✳ The Man Who Fell through a Glacier

At the head of Lake Arkell [Kusawa] they've got that ice—glacier, you
   know.
That's the place that Coast Indian fell in, when he's going back to
   Haines.

They should do it the same time; they should get him!
But they didn't.
They went on.

He fell through to a little island there—a dry place—and he stayed.
He's got lunch in his pack, some grease.
They've got no rope, I guess; that's why they go.
Well, he's gone already, I guess they think—he went through a crack.
He should holler there!

So, they went back now.
They put up potlatch in Klukwan.
Everybody cried.
He hears them . . . he's cold![27]
They should have tried to get him!
Ah, people are crazy!

Just pretty soon, now, he's feeling cold.
Don't know how many days it is now.
He's got moose skin in his pack and he put it on.
When it gets wet, he gets another one.
He put beaver skin—you know how it can't get wet through—
He put it on.
Big place, they say that is: more water than sand.
He sleeps and eats. He's cold, though.

Oh, he's strong.
He eats his last grease now.

So then they came back with that rope and they put it down.
They send one [person] in—they had to get that body, I guess.
So that man slid in that way, too.

Pretty soon something came down.
Ice. A big chunk of ice.
Something is coming down—he touched it.
"Ahhhh. Oh, my!"

Well, that man is just about all in!
He moved his head.
Over ten days by now.

He [the man who went down the crevasse] told them,
"If I've got his pack, got his body, I'll do this," he said [pulling the rope].

310   Everybody cried.

Annie   They should have done that the same time [that he fell in],

Ned   Cut up moose skin [to make a rope to rescue him].

They've got lots of moose skin.

But they just let him go.

But that man saved himself, wrapped himself in moose skin, in gopher
robe.

They pulled him out.

His head went just like that [limp].

They make fire already.

They covered him up.

They gave him something hot.

They took off his wet clothes.

They put up camp there.

He ate lots of grease, started to get stronger.

He moved.

Already they had the potlatch!

He told them that he saw that potlatch.

    Why? Did they see the body? What for they want a potlatch!

    They should have taken the body out first!

    Awful, eh?

They started there maybe two days; they fed him.

So, he started to go, he started to get strong and go.

They carried him halfway there in a moose skin.

About halfway there, he got strong and he started to walk.

People were coming.

They were coming to help, I guess.

Here that man is walking around. Goodness!

This happened at the other end of Lake Arkell.

I've been there, but I've never seen that glacier.

5 ✳ Childhood

"Just like you're learning things
Just like you're going to school
[They tell stories] to make your mind strong."

My name is *Ntthenada.* I was born at Hutshi—that's what my father, Hutshi Jim, told me.

My mamma died when I was six years old. After she died, Hutshi Jim married her sister, my auntie: she took it over. That was my mother's sister, my stepmother—Kitty, they call her—Mrs. Hutshi Jim. *Gàch'ema.* She was Big Jim's daughter, too, but she had a different mother. My father and my stepmother wanted to raise me, but she won't let us go, Grandma. After my mamma died, then my mamma's mamma, Mrs. Big Jim, raised me, *Dakwa'äl.* And sometimes I stayed with my other grandma, *Däk'äl-äma.*

I'm the oldest—I've got two behind me, one sister and my brother, Frankie Jim. Frankie was next to me. My sister was the youngest.

After I was six years old, I stayed with Grandma. Girls that age play all the time—play dolls, play with friends. By eight or nine, you should know something about your own people. After that, ten or eleven, they tell us how to go round, set snares with Grandma. No gun, but we get along.

Pretty soon, I knew my way, I started to sew. Then we gave to my uncles what I made. Then they paid me with furs.[28] That's when people heard about Taylor and Drury [traders], so they started saving fur. Before that, kids used it for blankets. I'm ten years old, what I'm telling now.

Then my auntie married Jack Pringle, Dalton Post policeman, and I stayed with them. I went to Klukshu when they put up fish. After that, Peter Anderson married my mamma's mamma's sister. I stayed with them and went to school in Whitehorse for one year. I called him Dad. Then my grandma took me back; she took me out of school.

My daddy was a big doctor, but I can't talk about that. Might be it won't go right. Might be no good to us. He didn't drink or smoke or chew—it just came to him.

I'm going to tell you a story about what I saw that time at Hutshi. This is a special story about which ways they did things a long time ago. We learned from our grandma, from our grandpa. Whatever they do, they explain it to us. I think everyone knows that, but I know what they *say.*   311

My grandpa was going to fix up his mother's grave that first time I remember. He called Carcross people; he called Dalton Post people; he called Hutshi people. He called them. Nobody was staying at Little Salmon that time—just Big Salmon, Little Salmon people were all together.[29] Two men he sent down to Carcross, two to Aishihik.

If Crow person dies, Crow people make a party and they invite Wolf. The first time I saw that, my grandpa put on a gunnysack. Then he put coal on his face. Gee, *lots* of people were there, dancing. Gee, I held on to him [in fright]. He started to sing. Then people started to dance. I let him go then—I didn't cry—but he made me scared. I was a little girl. I thought, "What's he doing that for?" They came from a long ways—from Dalton Post, Champagne, Selkirk, Kluane Lake. They walked there.

Then when I was ten years old, they put up my mamma's grave. Big Jim did it for his daughter, my mother. I remember *that*; I'm big that time. I see and I remember; that's how I learned.

That time all the people came. First came Aishihik people. Then Dalton Post people. These ones don't come quick [because they are farther away]: Little Salmon, Big Salmon. Then comes Carcross.

That time I saw it—old-fashioned. They danced with old-fashioned clothes, blankets, button blankets, moose-hoof blankets—I've got that kind, too; I made it myself. What I've seen, I fixed it the right way. I don't use new-style cloth—just old-style beaver cloth. It costs too much now! Eighteen dollars a yard. I made that one myself; we used it!

They've got a big canvas there; they put it on the other side.[30] [When they are dressed] they're going to go inside the house now; that's where they're going to dance. The rest of the visitors haven't showed up yet.

Grandpa cut a gunnysack like this—holes for his arms. Then he made his face black. Gee, I'm afraid they're going to kill him. I was frightened when I saw that. Me, I held him; I hung on to that grandpa. Then people started dancing and I let go of him, watched them. People ate. They danced. They sang their songs. I still know those songs, even how long ago that is.

Grandma goes first; then another wife comes behind. I hang on to Grandpa. I don't know what they're going to do! "Are they going to kill him or what?" I think.

As soon as he goes outdoors, he starts to sing. Then people took down that canvas and started to dance. Gee! *Lots* of people. Lots of women, too. They called them all in: *Kajit* [Crow] called them in. They ate an early supper; they went in. Oh, they'd fixed it up for people already.

Me, I laughed! Why do they do that? It's funny to me, I tell you.[31] So many people came in that I got scared. "Come on, Grandpa." After I see it,

I let go and I looked at people dancing. Blue! Blue blankets. Coast Indians keep a big cache [of blankets], all blue! Guns shoot: those late people are not too far now across the lake. Big raft, they put in there. They bring everybody across there and then they stop.

Now I know it's no use holding my grandpa. The same thing happens again. First they feed them, then the dance is going on and they go into the house.

Pretty soon, again we hear guns, the same kind. This time Little Salmon people come. There are lots of people—it's a big place, a meadow, a good place. They leave their packs there. And the guns shoot: when people come, they shoot. These next visitors start to dance, too. Aishihik people dance, too. All big place. There are some good dancers. They all go in.

Carcross people come next day, I guess. Ah . . . one lady's got looking glass—my, she danced good. A big fat woman! She danced in backwards—Hu, Hu, Hu, that way. It's a big house, my grandpa's house.

What [gifts] do you think they're going to get, those people?! Porcupine quills, moccasins, caribou skins. Gee, nice. And the blankets! Gee, you ought to see the dancing! This Carcross song, I got it—I know it.

Those Klukshu people wear red blankets—those Klukshu people. Humpback fish, little red fish come to that Klukshu: that's the dance they're making. That's the story I told you one time. People were dancing just like little fish!

People came from Carcross, from Dalton Post, from Aishihik. I know [remember] but I didn't know [understand] what is going on. People all have different dances: Klukwan dance, Hutshi dance, Ayan dance.[32]

They put white Crow on my mamma's grave. It doesn't look much like Crow: it looks like seagull. It's from long time, from the first time, before it got it that way [blackened] that time Crow got trapped in smokehole. That's the time he turned black. Before that, he was all white.[33] Everybody knows that story. Crow must be a partner with Jesus!

When kids played, after that, we did just like those people. It was fun for us, that's why we did it. We don't know. Us kids learned those songs, those dances from watching at potlatches. That's the way I learned.

Kids used to do jobs for old people—get wood, water. They paid us with stories! We bring wood: now! Time like school! We stayed there—we listened.

One time we got wood for one old man. He's smoking his pipe, wants to finish his pipe first. Us kids wait, wait . . . Then finally, my brother

Frankie Jim, he took that wood back to where we got it! It's gone now! He goes home. "Why you're back?" my grandma asked.

"Oh, that man is too slow."

That old man was mad when he found out: "Why you do that?" Next day we work like hell, us.

Now that I'm old lady, I think about how those people feel. Even when my grandma was blind, she still taught us how to snare, how to make spring trap. I wish she were here now . . . I'd give her tea. My grandma is the one who raised me.

From way back, old ladies tell us stories about what they see. That's how they teach kids. By ten years, they can go by themselves, help their mothers. That's the way we learned from our grandma. I think about it after. I think what they talk about. I believe it!

When I became woman, they put me away for three months. Still I've got my teeth! My grandma helped me then, my mother's mother. When a girl turns to woman, that time they teach you lots of things. When you're wearing long hat first, lots of things you have to do.

You don't scratch your head with your hand: you've got something to scratch it with—a special stick. You take off that hat at night to sleep but you wear it daytime, all the time. You can't drink from a cup full of tea. They give you swan feathers: you put them on your hand and blow them. When the feathers rise, it means you put your hand on someone and you help them. When you stand up, you can't use your hands to help you.

You can't talk to your brothers—only to your younger brothers, not to your older brothers. You eat only dry meat, not fresh meat: don't eat too much of it—young girls should be careful what they eat. These ones, now, don't. You put beaver teeth in your mouth, so your teeth will last. Look how young girls now have false teeth! Me, I've got my own teeth. You wash your hair with nunch'ru [?], "soap from the ground."

All those things I did. That's why I'm old woman and still I'm good yet. Do you think these young girls going to learn something?[34] This time they go in bush, can't get anything.

This tattoo I got when I'm fourteen years old: my name Annie here, then a cross on my other arm. My brother-in-law made it when first I stayed with my husband. He made it with needle and thread [saturated with charcoal]. One mistake here, though: it says ANИIE, and on my other arm a cross—+.

6 ✳ "Since I Got Smart"

"Old-style words are just like school . . .
Since I know, old people tell us stories;
That's the ones I show you."

I

I want these people, all friends of mine to listen to me,
What I've been doing since I was girl.[35]

When I'm a baby, I don't know it.
But since I got smart
I want to say something for you to hear me.

These grandchildren are all over.
All over, white people's kids, Indian kids.
All over, grandchildren now.
I'm their grandma.
Sit down.

I don't know my age.
I've been born before white man came around,
That's why I don't know.

Well, thank you very much, [for asking me] to tell you.

This time, I stay in Takhini.
This house I stay inside, I enjoy.
I say thank you very much for it.

My grandmother told me everything.
That's the one I tell you this time, all this.

Used to be people loved each other—
Your cousins, your uncles, all your sisters.
You learned how to keep your old man [husband];
You learned what Grandma said.

So, I'm all alone now, this time.

When I hunted, I hunted in the bush, way up the mountain.
I had snowshoes on.

I packed my babies.
I didn't want them to get hurt at home, so I took them.

Then my son, Roddy Smith, when he knew his age—
That's the time I kept them at home—
He looked after his sister and his brother.
So I don't worry, go hunting, go trapping.

My grandpa, Hutshi Big Jim,
That's the one who helped me.
So I would go with him, trapline, camp out,
Yeah.

We got everything.
When he got caribou, we put down a mattress—
We got good mattress of moose skin—
That's enough for your bedding.
It's not cold when you stay out.
This time, I stay here.

It must be pretty close, my age.
This time, I can't walk.
But I don't feel sorry for that! More friends!
No more snowshoes, me.
When I go, I get on white-man rig. Car!
I go.

Well, I say thank you for that,
I say thank you for that.
I love good people,
No matter who, I love.

[When] somebody is going to be old, they're going to feel it.
That time, I'm young, I go anyplace, go anyplace.
Hunt. I hunt for my kids and what they want to get.

[Now] from the store, buy anything
For my kids.

When I stayed at Steamboat Landing,
I put my fishnet,
That time, I get lots of fish and dry, dry.
I do it for winter.

Well, my kids are not with me that time,
Out hunting, out working.
When they come back, I do this for my sons.
Hunt gophers, rabbits with a snare.
Put up what they need.

They've got a song for those rabbits.
Rabbits made this song because they're satisfied for people.
I'm going to show you:

Old people long time, they know this song.
Old people, when they go hunting, they sing.
That's for good luck.
Everything has got a song.
They want to get something—they get it.
They've got no gun this time: bow and arrow.
They're satisfied.

I remember an eclipse, one time.
I'm a woman, that time, trapping with my grandpa.
People have song for that, too.
They go outdoors and sing.
I just saw night eclipse, myself,
But I hear about others, before my time.
That time people sang to make the sun come out.
The one I remember people sing makes the moon come out.
Old-style words are just like school!
This song is what Indians think about long time,
So you got to think about it!36

Since I know, old people, they tell us stories.
That's the ones I'm showing you.

Everything has got a song, for Indian people. Everything.
Long time ago, they know it.
Same as this time, we've got radio, tape.
They've got no tape, that time, and still they sing.
I know those songs from old people.
That's the best I could tell you, what I know.

Long time ago, what they know, what they see
That's the one they talk about, I guess.
Tell stories—which way you learn things.

318	You think about that one your grandma tells you.
Annie	You've got to believe it, what Grandma said.
Ned	That's why we've got it.
	It's true, too, I guess—
	Which way they work at moccasins . . .
	Which way they make sinew . . .
	Which way to fix that fishnet . . .
	Some lazy women don't know how to work,
	Don't believe what old people tell them.
	And so . . . short net!

II

Well, long-time people—
My grandfather, some old grandmothers—they told me this story.
They told me.
They teach us.
They teach us how to make moccasins, how to make sinew.
We sew with sinew—I've got that kind here.

You cut the skin with a knife—show Grandma.
Same thickness, you measure there.
Right here, at the knee, you make it even;
Then you fix it. That's why it's so much thick.
Kendhät, they call that board.[37]

Then after you clean it, you wash the skin for blood—blood comes
    out.
Then you dry it,
Put on smoke, keep on smoking it.

Then you put in moose brains:
Four times I put it under water, my own skins.[38]
Then I start to sew moccasins,
I make some sinew.
That's what Grandma used to do long time ago.

And that gopher skin—they hunt gopher in the bush.
We wash it, clean it up good, nice.
That's the one I use in dance this time, use it for a blanket.[39]

Caribou skin, you fix it all over.
It's tough, though.

Oh, my, it's hard to clean it!
My old man helped me; we fixed three in one day.

What Grandma does, you do:
You tan, you smoke.
[You make] what color you like—light brown, dark brown.
Not much smoke, it comes out light;
It looks good, that time they work.
This time, I don't think these girls know it.

You make gopher snare, spring snare.
You've got little stick, like this.
Where gophers live, you've got to move it,
Fix it back this way.[40]

Lots of things: snowshoes—
But I didn't make that one, me.
Old Man made them all the time.
But we worked on babiche, and that skin you fill it with—
Babiche, caribou skin. Snowshoes.
You make little holes around [the frame], then fill it up.
Looks nice.[41]

Then you make fishnet.
Use long sinew from the back of moose.
That was before me, but they've got it still, in my time.
I saw my grandmother, my grandfather.
Coast Indian stuff I saw, too.

Toboggans, they make from their own birch.[42]
They fix skin toboggans, too.
Everything good—strong.
Then you put one moose in it.
My brother, Solomon Charlie, pulled one moose uphill that way.[43]
Sometimes they have two.
The woman handles one, the husband handles the other.

III

I want to talk only about proper things, old time[44]—
How they work for their own life.
They work by themselves to get their game.
That time no guns, no knife.

320 How is it that white people don't believe [understand] this?
Annie So long as you've got your sinew in your pocket
Ned You'll get it [game]
If you know the right way.

You sew; if you don't, you'll get no moccasins.
But they do fine. Buy groceries with what they catch.
They've got sharp knife made of rock.
When it gets dull, they sharpen it.
No matches! Can white men figure this out?
Who told them how to do that?

This story that I tell
Lots of people tell it.
Same story, same story,
That's the one I use,
What they get taught from Grandma, Grandpa,
That's right, too.

Old people have been here before me.
I know their names.
My grandmother told us the story about these people, so I know.
My father-in-law was *Goonxaktsáy*, Johnson.

From there, these people come—
From Dezadeash, from Klukshu, from Dalton Post.
All the families, Wolf, Crow, enjoy themselves.
This time, no people now—
Just schoolkids.
They don't know what I'm talking about, this time.
These old grandma words, old grandpa words.
Hutshi Chief is my grandpa, my dad's side.
My mother's side, Hutshi Big Jim.

Just here [indicating mountains]
Just covered up with sheep, caribou.
When they've got enough meat,
Enough fish from Klukshu,
All go home.
Then wintertime they go trapping, since those Coast Indians came.

Before Coast Indians came,
They didn't care [about trapping furs to trade].

They skinned them and kept the fur—
They used it for themselves.
Then, when winter comes,
The families come here
[To] my father-in-law's ground, my mother-in-law's [i.e, at the junction
    of the Mendenhall and Takhini rivers].
We travel here for fur,
Put up dry meat.

When people first saw stores in Whitehorse, saw trains—
Taylor and Drury got a store first time—
Then we got something from there,
Then we stay here.

When we want to go, we go to Hutshi, to my grandpa.
We can trap there, too, if we want to.
This time all over with trapline now.
I finished mine now.
But two many grandchildren,
Too many young people [for everyone to have a trapline].

They [white men] wanted Indian women when they first struck
    [gold].
Same time, they married Indian women. Yeah!
[We treated them] just like our people, white man.
But it's a little too much—now we can't get game.
When ducks come from outside, we don't get it.
We don't get lots of things.[45]
So I don't think about it too much, me.
But now there are too many kids, schoolkids.
I don't think they can go into the bush and get something to eat . . .

Long time [ago] though, a ten-year-old kid gets his own living.
But this time it's pretty hard for kids.
They can't hunt in the bush.
Pretty near all halfbreeds.
Long time ago, though, your grandpa teaches you, "Do this."
You go. That's how they teach them.
When you get married, you look after your grandma—
All your family.

That's what we do.

[Then she begins talking about *Nakhụ*, the Kusawa Lake narrows:]

Annie
Ned

That wintertime it's open, that place,
That narrow place.
That's the place you set your fishnet, old people.
Long time before me.

Sinew fishnet—
They've got everything good.
That old man has got corral for moose.
He snares them; everybody comes.
He gives it away, that moose
That's a long time ago, they say.
I didn't see it, but I know my father-in-law traveled there.
Laberge Chief is his cousin.
They all come, want to go to Hutshi
All come like that, long-time people.

7 ✳ Marriage

"I want to talk only about proper things, old time."

Long-time people, when you get married, they do it this way. If a man wants you, he sends his mother: his mother and his father come to your mother, your father. They bring lots of stuff. They've got to pay.[46] If your mother, your father say they want him, all right. It's not only *me*, long time. *She* knows that, too [indicating an older woman friend].

Then your mamma talks to you: "You got to treat right your husband." And his mamma says, "Your wife doesn't like something, you've got to take her word. See how much we've done for you? You have to believe your mother and father." Your mamma says, "Your husband doesn't like what you do? You've got to take his word."

This is a love song: you listen. Long-time Indians had the same thing, old people. This is their song, their song to their boyfriend or girlfriend, long time. When they're going to get married, they sing. That means that after they get married, they don't quit! Stay with him. You love your husband; must be that man loves his wife, too, long time. This time girls, they hear song . . . they like that man . . . but after a while they go to another one. Long time ago, it's not like now. Their mother teaches them. Dad says yes, yes. [Then] they go. Then they're married. They get along.

You've got to do some cooking for your husband. You've got to give two moccasins, two warm socks. You give mukluks when he goes to the mountain, so your husband's feet won't get cold. That's what they've been doing, long-time people. I gave my husband two [pair of] moccasins; when it gets wet, he comes back and puts on dry ones. This time, nothing, I don't think.

That's why we get along good, everybody, long time ago. My grandmother and my grandpa stayed together till they died—my grandpa and everybody's grandpa, long time. They go like that. No quit. No run away. Yeah!

This is a long-time old song they sing together—a wife and her husband. Crow and Wolf are married, [so there was] no trouble, long time. You've got to explain right that song, see? You've got to say it to the right person . . . Not like radio! [See songs, Section 8.]

Before I got married, Skookum Jim wants to marry me. But he drinks   323 too much. Who's going to stand for that? I'm a girl then. Soon I got engaged to my husband.

My first husband was Paddy Smith, *Kàkhnokh*. His mother came; his father came. They brought blankets, money. My mother died and so my grandma raised me. After we're married we came back all the time to look after Grandma, Grandpa. That's what Indians do: we don't let it go. Now Indian woman when she marries white man, he takes her home.

But this time they turn to Grandma's side, this time, women. You hear about that? I don't know how come. That way is good, too.[47]

First I left my grandma here. My grandpa, Big Jim, and my grandma. And I go with my husband. That's the first time—just married. We went down to Fifty-Two Mile. My husband was trapping there, Paddy Smith. That's near that lake, *Lù Shäw*. We would go back to Hutshi all the time. We've got to go back to look after my grandma and grandpa. Yeah, Hutshi Chief. We brought them everything—food . . . meat. When my daddy got old, we looked after him, we kept him. That's what we did. We didn't let them go.

After we were married, my husband, Paddy Smith, worked all the time. But I don't know about his work: I don't check on him! I don't want to follow around! He worked on train trail to Pueblo [mine]. Then he was interpreter for police, when hard case comes. After that, my husband goes to work for big-game hunters, for Eugene Jacquot. He worked in Alaska, too.

I stayed with Grandma at Jojo [Mendenhall River]. I stayed home, looked after kids. I sold sewing to Sewell's store and in Taylor and Drury's store—moccasins, mitts, coats.

When moose are fat, I go hunting with my uncles: I cut meat, dry meat, make tallow, make grease. When you kill moose, you got to pack baby up the hill. These young ladies, I don't think they could make it: "I'm tired . . . got to get the car . . ." It's *true*, I think, what old people did! Then I would go fishing at Klukshu—put up maybe five hundred fish so we won't go short. Some people put up one thousand fish!

My husband sends money to Shorty's store.[48] When he comes back in October, pretty near everything I've got before he's back. When it gets to be wintertime, he comes and kills moose. Then people settle at Hutshi, or Fifty-Two Mile, or Laberge. Winter camp. They enjoy themselves. Do nothing! Talk about themselves—which way they're going to be. Then more hunting. He hunts for me, I fish for him!

Sometimes we go to Steamboat Landing, *Dùuchùgà*, summertime. That's his father's home, my father-in-law. That's my father-in-law's country. He stayed there all the time. Taylor and Drury boat used to come there—bring groceries. People cut wood for that boat, to buy their

groceries.

We got eight kids. They're lots, my sons: Roddy, Elijah, Percy, Matthew, Walter. My daughters are Lydia, Mary, Stella. I had lots of adopted kids, too. When their mothers die, I take them—Annie Broeren, Grady Smith, I raised them.

When you have babies Indian way, it's easy. You do what Grandma tells you: keep moving around, don't sit down. I had mine quick. You have two sticks, sit up. My daughters had theirs in hospital. It's harder that way.

Fifty-Two Mile is up Dawson Road. We had a house there. My son Elijah keeps it now. My sons went to Carcross school, but they got sick. Nobody told us, so when we found out, we took them out. Their daddy said, "No use to send them. We'll try another place." My daughter Mary got sick one time, her liver. Nothing I could do—I got no doctor power that time: that came later. You know it when you get it: game teaches man.

Flu came in with Charlie Baxter's hunters, big-game hunters—1920. Paddy Smith, my husband, got it because he went on the hunt. Just like somebody shoot them, people died. I was at Champagne alone. I went down to Ten Mile Lake with my two kids. Old people were with us, too.

Then Charlie Jackson came and told me my husband is just about all in. I took all that food we dried, put it in dog pack. When I got there, he didn't know me . . . I tried Indian medicine and next morning he's all right. But old John Jack died . . . and his wife . . . and then my grandma . . . then my grandma's brother "Canyon" . . . and his wife.

I thought my grandpa was safe in Hutshi, me. I started to worry about him. Two more people died at Ten Mile Lake: Hutshi Bill—that's Charley Bill's daddy—they pull him back in sled. Both my grandmas died at Hutshi with that flu . . . Then my uncle and auntie, Charley Jackson's parents, died. And then my grandpa died.

Police came then: they tried to keep people away from Hutshi. But I went there anyway. Police brought in beef so we could make soup for sick people. But not just Hutshi—people got sick everywhere: Champagne, Canyon, Hutshi, Dalton Post—all. I didn't get sick. Not so many kids got sick. Mostly old people died.

My second husband was Johnny Ned. My first husband and I raised that kid, Johnny Ned, because his mother died. After she died, Paddy brought him to stay with us—well, that's his younger brother—their mothers are sisters. We looked after him, raised him up. Later they gave me Johnny Ned. That's how they did it, old days. We don't let it go; just have to take it. Paddy died, so I stayed with Johnny Ned.

Paddy Smith died after a hunt. He worked too much—he's older than me. Well, your brother's wife, you can't let it go. You've got to get his brother. All over, us Indians [did this]. You can't marry another man. Johnny Ned was younger. He was good, though, looks after kids. We married, too. Indians are like that. You can't let it go. That's why my husbands' people keep me company now that I'm alone.

Then we moved to Stony Creek, next to *Sankàlà,* near *Nichàlà.* His grandpa is *Ajàngàkh,* his daddy's daddy. That's Wolf: he's the one who owned that *Sankàlà.* After I stayed with Johnny Ned we used to hunt on that [next] hill, right there, *Nichàlà.*

Lots of people lived at this Jojo [Mendenhall River] that time: my uncle, Hutshi Jackson; his wife, *Dzagwama;* my father, *Sakuni;* my grandpa, Hutshi Big Jim, *Kàkhnokh*—that's my mamma's daddy. Then there was Hutshi Charlie, and Takhini John and his wife, my auntie *Lqzhq.* That valley next to there [east of Mendenhall] is *Kosàndagà.*

I can't talk about Johnny: it might be we make mistake. I can't speak for other people. I can't show my husband's song [on tape]. I can tell you what happened, though. To start with, he got Indian song.[49] That man doesn't know anything, doesn't talk. How come he talks that time? He started to talk. I thought he's gone crazy! So I got Mr. Young [the missionary], and he said, "Don't bother, Annie. I think he's going to go somewhere. He's believing." My husband took control all over: Carmacks, Dawson, all over. He took it around, that control. It didn't come from God! He got it himself!

After he got his power he can heal people. But he can't cut moose! He can kill it, but someone else has to cut it for him. Then one time he cut it, and he died from that. I told him, "Don't! We've got lots of grub."

Still, he did it. "I'm not going to stay very long." That's when he's gone.

I think he came back. One little baby came to me *nedlin.*[50] When they're like that, they've got a mark. When a kid comes like that, he says he knows you. But when he grows, he forgets. That *nedlin* [means] "come back."

When war came, my son was in the army, overseas. I was going with Red Cross, that time. I stayed with it, Red Cross. Sometimes those army socks we fixed. You've got to go and pray for your son. I would go there and work at socks—just white people there. Every time I went to Whitehorse, I would go Red Cross. To her: Taylor and Drury.[51]

I'm going to talk about one time when I went to Whitehorse. That's the time the army comes. My son is out! We got letters all the time; policeman used to bring them to me. That time policeman comes to where we were living. "American soldiers are going to come to Whitehorse. You've got to come." Red Cross lady, Mrs. Taylor, is there. I stood right alongside those

white ladies.

After that we moved to Takhini. My husband Johnny had the trapline from Stony Creek to Lake Arkell. I want my grandchildren to have that one, but too many grandchildren!

My last husband, Henry Dakota, is a Frenchman. I'm married to him for more than thirty years. He's a good man. But we're not talking about that.

8 ✳ Getting the Words Right

"This song is what Indians think about, long time
So you've got to think about it."

Song #1

This song belongs to Wolf people. A Wolf man is singing to his girlfriend:

My girlfriend cannot look at me
I wish you could fly to see me.

Transcription and translation

Lines 1 and 3:

dzedze	*dadǫ*	*nadäla*	*ts'ezha*	*kuna*
I wish to fly	this way	she is coming	it happens	

dän	*łąya*	*dan*	*k'anutaya*
person's	friends	person	he/she looks after him/her

Lines 2 and 4:

dzedze	*dadǫ*	*nadäla*	*ts'ezha*	*kuna*
I wish to fly	this way	she is coming	it happens	

dän	*zųǫ*	*dän*	*k'anutaya*
person's	sweetheart	person	he/she looks after him/her

Free translation:
I hope (my girlfriend) would come back this way.
I want to look after my friend, my sweetheart.

Song #2

This is another song made by a Wolf man, Casey Fred, for his girlfriend. He was at one end of Dezadeash Lake, and she was at the other end. The wind came up, making it too dangerous to cross the lake. He wanted to see her, and he could see her fire, so he sang:

328

Pretty soon, I'm going to make it to the other side,
My *zuą*, my sweetheart.

Transcription and translation

Jeneda	*nerts'eni*	*kwäna*	*Titl'at*
		[*no-a*]	
she feels bad	they say of you	it happened at the same time	Dezadeash Lake

kwäts'an	*ninghą*	*kwädura*	*le-hi-e-haya*
from	over you	they make a story	

łutla	*na*	*nets'eduni*	*no-a*
truly (question)	(question)	are they telling	

ninghą	*kwädura*	*le-hi-a-haya*
		[*zuą*]
over you	they make a story	

(Mrs. Ned sometimes substitutes the *no-a* question form for *kwäna*, and *zuą* [sweetheart] for *le-hi-a*.)

Free translation:
They say that you are feeling badly at Dezadeash Lake.
Is this story they are telling about you really true?

Song #3: Jimmy Johnson

This song was made by Copper Lily Johnson, for her husband, Jimmy Johnson. She was Crow, and she made this song as a kind of joke that people hugely enjoy. This is probably one of the most popular songs in the southern Yukon. Mrs. Ned comments: "They were just married. She should sing love song to him! Instead she calls him down in this love song":

> Jimmy Johnson-ah
> I cook for you
> I boil meat for you.
> Your legs are crooked!

Annie
Ned

Verses 1, 2, and 3:

Jimmy Johnson	Jimmy Johnson	*mekeshäna**	*deghwäda*
		[*weẕat k'aya*]	
Jimmy Johnson	Jimmy Johnson	your foot bones	are crooked
		[shin bones]	

nidaw	*iẕhura*	*a-ha-ya-a-hi-ya*
for you	I did it	

Jimmy Johnson	Jimmy Johnson	*dadǫ*	*nintläla*
Jimmy Johnson	Jimmy Johnson	you come back	you are hopping
		toward us	along

Verse 4:

Naghaya	*lach'ia*	(o) *wekeshäna**	*daghwäda*
Wolverine	looks like	foot bones	crooked

Song #4: *Nadaya* song

This song was made for *Nadaya*, Fred Boss's namesake, Jimmy Johnson's father. He had two wives. One time he went trapping and left his wives at Aishihik. He was supposed to be gone for only two days, but he didn't come back for a month. His wives felt badly; they were running out of food and were sure that he had died. They made a song about him and went looking for him, singing it. On the way, they met him:

> He's got skin toboggan loaded with fur—fifty fur!
> That's the time that old man got mad!
> "What's the matter? Do you wish me to die?
> When I stayed alone I had hard time.
> Nobody cooked. Nobody helped me."
>
> Those women ran to him:
> "What's the matter, *Nadaya*?

---

*m and *n* are interchangeable with *w* in Southern Tutchone, so "foot bones" can be pronounced either *mekeshäna* or *wekeshäna.*

You get married in the bush?
We missed you. That's why we made song for you.
We're glad to see you!"

Transcription and translation

Seku	dazı̨ą̨ [ghadeya]	lach'e	natläla
comes back	our sweetheart [our nephew, opposite moiety]	seems like	hopping along

Nadaya	lach'ea	natläla
lynx (his name)	looks like	hopping back

Song #5

This song was made at Dalton Post. In the days before there was a road, people used to travel to Haines, Alaska, by toboggan trail. When they got above tree line, they would sing a south-wind song:

> You need wind? You start song.
> Old people's song.
> Then south wind blows.

Transcription and translation

Nı̨ts'i	dhäl	tl'e]
		] (repeated throughout)
wind blows	warm	]

Nı̨ghra	ke	kwätü	däjela]
			] (repeated)
your sons	(plural)	summit	they went]

Nikaghwa	kudejela
for you	they are traveling

9 ✳ Changes in the Land

"This land, he comes out. Grows anything."

✳ Glaciers

This is the story about that Bear Creek—
My grandpa—Frankie Jim's namesake—he told me this story.
Lots of people tell it, too.

That time, they say, the water raised in this Yukon, long time ago.
You heard about it?
That time, the water raised, they say.[52]

He said this happened at Bear Creek, when my grandpa is young.
They put up gophers for wintertime.
Meat, too, they dried.
He's pretty old, that time he died, Grandpa.

So, him, his wife, and *lots* of people hunt—
You know, put up food for winter, everything.
That time they worked, water's getting high!
They didn't know it until that water came to the meadow where they
  stayed.

So he said to his wife,
"We've got to pull out those snares."
And they went halfway up that hill—it's high, there, Bear Creek.

Then what are they going to do after?
Well, glacier, he opened, I guess.
Then, they went on top of there, halfway up that hill, above that lake.
Just like a wave, halfway, that water.

Well, they thought about believing that:
That's Coast Indian, he told them that, long-time people.

Well, they stayed there.
As soon as it comes up halfway,

It's just like a wave, they say.
Everybody feels bad:
They don't know what they're going to do.

In the morning, Grandpa got up, measured that water:
They're going to go to the mountain if that animal comes out.[53]

But that water doesn't come out quick.
You can see waves on the hill, this time still.[54]

So he tells his wife,
"That water's going down!"
He measures that water with a stick.
"It goes two sticks down," he said, where he measured.

Gee! Then they stay, they stay.
Someone got raft—they want to go to the mountain.
But then it went down quick, that water.
Then, meadow again! Oh, gosh!
He goes down to that meadow: talk about gophers!
Dead gophers!

He was packing dog pack, him.
Now people don't go [anywhere]! Got to stay one place.
But Grandpa, he walked around.
Bunch of gophers; everybody is just packing gophers.

From then on, those gophers are gone.
How many years it took those gophers to come back!
That's what they say.[55]

When you fry grease by fire,
That's the time it cracks, that glacier.
Then lots of water comes—that's what they say.
Then the water is all full.

One man did not believe that—Frank Stick, his name.
He didn't believe it.
He put goat grease, thick like that.
He burned it.
Then that glacier started.
When he threw a blanket in the fire, that made it stop again.
Well, there's something inside that glacier: he smells it.
Then it quiets down.
I don't know myself what is going on that time.

That one story my grandpa tells me, Bear Creek glacier.

Annie
Ned

But this time, myself, this one *I'm* telling you the story.

We had it, one time, head of Lake Arkell with my first husband.
Old Man tells me,
"Don't put grease. It spoils everything," he tells me. "It's no good."

We wanted to meet my husband's mother from Dalton Post.
We've got kids that time.
That glacier, that head of Lake Arkell,
We got *njäl* there, his daddy.
Njäl, long-time people.[56]
[Near] where they dry meat is *njäl*.
Inside, it's good: you dry your meat there.

He says he killed three caribou there close to that glacier, that
     mountain,
Close to that place that man fell through the ice [Section 4].

We got in there—just small kids with us,
Johnny is with us, too: he's a man, though, that time.
We got to those caribou, three bulls. Fat.
We got little tent.

I don't know what for he wants to hunt, hunt, hunt, my old man.
My old man, I tell him not to go that way (toward the glacier).
"Around here, lots of caribou," I tell him.
Just willows, no trees there; just little trees on top of mountain.
That's the ones we burn them.

Then *he's* the one put grease [another hunter, Jack Smith].
He's Indian! He knows!
I don't know what for he did that!

We just came out from down there.
Then Old Man, he wants to go hunt.
I don't know, me, too: pretty dangerous, that way.

So pretty soon, we brought in meat.
Johnny wants to take meat down where boat is.
Pretty steep hill down.
I tell him, "Don't go that way!
You come where your brother is going to come this way.
You go down and look for him."

He goes that way.
Gee! Well, we start to eat now.
Ha! Big wind!
Just first time he comes out, that rain put the fire out.
All wet.

It gets dark.
Johnny, he cut those little trees on the mountain.
They made fire.
Then we tried to put strong way that tent.

Just like that! Rain.
Gee, I worry about Old Man.
"Shoot!" I tell Johnny. "Shoot!" [to signal him]

It's alongside that glacier, it happened.
He's got slicker coat, though.
Gosh, nothing.

Then I heard something break.
You know he carries around blanket in bush.
I smell something burning: that man burned up his blanket.
He stopped that rain!
But dark, though.

Gee, we holler, we holler.
How come my husband goes that long way, near that glacier?
He doesn't know where to go:
He started fire under that kind of bushy little tree in mountain.
He put light there, but it's raining.
He goes there under that little tree.
Thick.
He stays there, underneath.

Then pretty soon that rain stops.
He knows, he says, which way that rain goes.
Gee, that glacier is close!

That time he brought that, Johnny,
He talked.
"He's going to come back," he tells me.

Then he heard that gun. Right!
Goes right through.

Annie
Ned

"Shoot some more."
Little longer he shoots.
Then he found out his way.
Pretty soon we hear shot—then we shot.
Just soaking wet!
Hole in his blanket he threw in the fire.

Jack Smith is pretty old; just the same he burned grease.
When Old Man came back, he said,
"There's no kids here! Who did that?" he said to us.
Well, we don't know, us, he did that.
Gee, Jack Smith got mad at himself.
"That's me, I did that," he say after he burns that grease, fat.

There used to be lots more thunder than now:
Thunder comes from cracking glaciers.
That glacier makes big noise when he wants to do something.

✶ Caribou

Already moose were getting short when caribou came.
Lots of caribou around here when I got my kids,
Used to be [1910–15].[57]

When lake froze in winter,
When caribou came,
It was just like horses, same.
You could hear their feet making noise,
Making noise [imitates hoofs on ice].
Lots of caribou covered up these hills.

I want to talk about this story:
Old people tell this story.

One time, caribou took people.
That man had a little bit of doctor, I guess;
Well, caribou took him.

Everybody felt bad: he was gone.
His wife was left alone.

Right in the middle of the lake, they heard caribou singing his
song.[58]

People don't know what to do—
They tried to get him.

One man said, "Well, let's go. We're going to try."
Yeah!

They've got bow and arrow, that's all—they have no gun yet.
It was a long time ago, I guess.
They heard that man's song.
I think it was wintertime.
Wintertime.

That caribou just lay down in the middle of that ice.
All the time he stayed in the middle.
For a long time, they watched him.
Whenever they tried to come to that caribou, all the time he watched
    them.
He looked from person to person,
And all the time he didn't sleep.

One man told them he was going to do it.
Then he sneaked in. [She shows how he wrestled with the caribou and
    held it down.]

The caribou spoke:
"You smell," he told people.

Well, that man knew how to talk to caribou.
"What about your kids?" they asked him.
"Your kids are crying for you," his own brother told him.
"What's wrong with you?"

He couldn't help it.
So they brought him. They brought him home.
They took him home!
I guess his wife is glad: he's got kids, too!
His wife came, and his kids.
He held his kids' hands, but for his wife, nothing.
He doesn't know her yet.

Well, they took him back.
They told him.
Then they watched him.
They made a camp for it [away from the human camp].

338	Somebody watched him there.
Annie	He wanted to go!
Ned	He doesn't eat their food—he only eats willows.
	You know what that means!
	But they kept him the other side of the fire.

Then he came back to person.
But he can't hunt caribou anymore.[59]

This was way before my time, but I saw lots of caribou.
They came back, caribou.
All this mountain was covered by caribou.
Used to be we had caribou not too long ago when my kids were
    growing up.

One time lots of caribou fell through the ice, one lake:
I called my husband back to get the meat.
My mother-in-law came to get the skins.
She got enough that time: she had her son with her.
But they are hard to clean when they fall in that way.
That's the last time caribou came this way.
That's the last time we saw caribou come.

But they didn't come back. How come?
That man came back to person.
Then he knew where moose are, where caribou are.
He tells them, but he can't hunt them.

That's the last time caribou came this way.
Since then, nothing.

After Skookum Jim found gold, everything changed.
White people came to this country.
White people learned everything from Indians.
Now they want the whole thing, the *land!*
I've got sixty-four grandchildren in this Yukon.
I worry about them, what's going to happen?
White people, where's *their* grandpa? *their* grandma?
Indians should have their own land.

Cultural Constructions of
Individual Experience

A distinctive feature of the life stories told by Mrs. Sidney, Mrs. Smith, and Mrs. Ned is the way each narrator includes recognizable, formulaic narratives as essential components. Some of the stories they tell are familiar from other parts of North America: numerous versions of the Star Husband story, the Dog Husband story, the Lynx Husband story, and other Animal Husband stories have been recorded and analyzed by scholars. The adventures of the protagonist often seem to follow a regular sequence, such as, the Magic Flight or Transformation Flight.[1]

More interesting, though, is the persistence of these stories over time. Virtually every aspect of Yukon Native economy, social organization, and style of life has changed during this century. The brief but turbulent influx of prospectors during the Klondike gold rush, the establishment of ecclesiastical residential schools, the involvement of Native trappers in an international fur market—all these processes undermined the subsistence economy and called into question longstanding cultural traditions. Construction of the Alaska Highway by the U.S. military in 1942–43 brought another unexpected burst of activity: the resulting road system contributed to the development of an unstable mining economy and an expanding government infrastructure. The slow progress of land-claims negotiations during the 1970s and 1980s brought further disruptions. Yet despite these changes, stories persist. Many narratives told by these women since 1974 were recorded in some form in Alaska in 1883 and in 1904 and in northern British Columbia in 1915.[2] Each ethnographer believed that he was working with the last storytellers familiar with old traditions. Although details may have changed in stories told in the 1980s, plots and motifs are easily recognizable. Why have these stories persisted when so much else has changed? How do women continue to use them to explain events in their lives?

The enduring tradition of storytelling in the southern Yukon Territory suggests that narratives continue to address important questions during a period of industrial and government expansion and social upheaval. Older Athapaskan/Tlingit women also insist that stories are instructive, though never in any simple or didactic way. They repeatedly state that young girls should be learning from the stories. Until recently, every Athapaskan Indian learned either through direct experience or from   339 verbal descriptions or instruction. An ultimate value of oral tradition was to recreate a situation for someone who had not lived through it so that the listener could benefit directly from the narrator's experience.[3] Mrs. Ned notes emphatically that "old-style words are just like school!" Mrs. Smith regularly punctuates her account with the comment, "Young girls, I could teach them!" And Mrs. Sidney points to the value of story models in her compelling statement that she has tried to live her life "just like a story." The persistence of stories and storytelling suggests that oral narrative is central to an indigenous intellectual tradition and provides the core of an educational model.

❋ Educational Strategies in Oral Narrative: The Stolen Woman

If we want to understand how narrators make connections between stories and experience, we must first be familiar with assumptions every storyteller and listener would have shared when these women were growing up. Everyone understood that human beings and animals were born into a world suffused with and animated by power; at the beginning of time, animals and humans shared certain attributes, such as language. The dilemma northern hunters faced was their simultaneous dependence on the goodwill of powerful animals and the necessity of killing and eating them in order to survive: resolving this issue posed a major intellectual preoccupation for all adults living in the western subarctic. Animals appear in these stories as thinking beings, able to adopt human disguise. Such an animal might "show" himself to a human being and offer formal permission to hunt his species and instruction about how to accomplish this correctly. A listener would know how important it was to be prepared for such encounters, since they were both valuable and inescapable.

One genre of transformation story is particularly intriguing because women so often use it when explaining some aspect of their lives or when talking about what they would like to "teach young girls." In such a story the protagonist meets a superhuman being (usually an animal disguised as a person) and is taken on a journey from the secular, material, temporal world of everyday life to a supernatural, timeless domain. The two domains—ordinary reality and the unfamiliar realm—are marked off in some physical way: the protagonist may pass under a log, into a cave, beyond the horizon, or may be given a "slap" causing temporary amnesia. The physical characteristics of this new domain are the reverse of those found in the more familiar world. It may be a "winter world" where everything is white, including people and animals; usually the customs, food, and behavior of human beings are offensive to the inhabitants. Often the central organizing principle is a refraction of the human world from the perspective of animals. This view of human social order is not a mirror image, but one that (like myth itself) simultaneously unbalances and reorients the protagonist, revealing the ordinary in new ways.

Journeys taken by male protagonists do not seem to be quite the same as those taken by women. The dramatic action surrounding a male hero explores his separation from the familiar world, his transformation as a result of his journey, and his eventual return to the human community with a spirit helper and with new understandings that will benefit everyone. Male protagonists rely on supernatural intervention to acquire knowledge and on the efforts of the community to socialize that knowledge. (See, for example, the story of Moldy Head, pp. 75–78, 208–13.) Narratives with a female protagonist are different. A woman is accosted by a (male) stranger who "steals" her and spirits her away to another world. Instead of acquiring an animal helper, as a man would, she concentrates her mental energies on actively escaping to her human community. In most stories she manages to out-think her captors and to get free on her own, often actually assisting would-be rescuers. Inevitably, she deals with superhuman power by using a range of skills taught to women at puberty, skills demonstrating her general competence as a human being. Ultimately, she relies on her powers of reasoning rather than on supernatural assistance.

Why do narrators find in these stories such cogent metaphors for explaining their experience? Even when different narrators tell the "same" story, each gives her own distinctive version. Each teller emphasizes difficult choices faced by a protagonist similar to those she, or someone in her family, has had to make at marriage, after a death, or in a crisis. A narrator is also likely to expand on skills she shares with the protagonist, both tangible, practical abilities and less tangible knowledge about women's power. The way the story makes its "point" or gains its meaning depends on the particular situation it is used to clarify. Traditional Athapaskan narratives are powerful because they are constructions rooted in general social concerns, even though they are refracted through individual tellers by the time we hear them. Like all good stories, they contain multiple messages: they explore social contradictions women have faced, but they also dramatize a cultural ideal women recognize.

Structuralists have argued convincingly that myth arises in contradiction, not as a straightforward projection of ideal behavior. They advise us to look for explanations of narrative in areas of social life that seem troublesome. In narrative, contradictions can be made clearer by exaggerating examples of birth, death, heroism, and treachery in order to explore the less dramatic but equally complicated issues arising in everyday life. Stories with a variety of dramatic outcomes enable listeners to weigh alternative approaches to problems they confront as young people, as mature adults, as grandparents.

A particularly difficult issue for aboriginal hunters in this part of the world was the question of how to maintain the integrity of social groups in the face of ongoing ecological pressures to reorganize households in different seasons and in times of scarcity. One way this was done was by recruiting new members, especially adult males, by arranging marriages between individuals from widely scattered groups. A woman traced her descent through her mother's line, and ideally she could expect to marry a man who would come to live with her people, become partners with her brother, and support her aging parents. But for a range of practical reasons, this did not always happen. A woman might have to move to her husband's family at marriage to stabilize trading relationships or to balance the number of able-bodied adults to dependents in a group. Furthermore, a woman always faced the risk of being "stolen" in a feud or war.[4] There was the additional possibility of being abandoned for antisocial activity and having to fend for oneself.

Numerous stories dramatize such conflicts. Two girls stolen by Star husbands struggle with the conflicting loyalties they feel to parents and spouses (pp. 105–7, 216–21); ultimately, their commitment to parents motivates them to return to matrilineal kin. A married woman kidnapped by a lynx is able to escape once she discovers his identity (pp. 117–19). A stolen woman not only outwits her captors but also helps her rescuers by stealing food for them and helping attack her abductors (pp. 119–25, 241–45). Another story recounts the journey of a Tagish woman who married to a distant group but escaped and traveled home when she was abused by her in-laws (pp. 125–27). Two narratives told by Mrs. Smith dramatize potential and real-life conflicting loyalties she, her mother, and her husband's aunt all had to face in their marriages: one looks at the risks involved in marrying a stranger and moving to a distant group away from the protection of kinsmen (pp. 190–93); another explores the opposite theme, in which a woman's loyalty to her husband outweighs her obligations to treacherous brothers (pp. 193–200).

Nonetheless, an explanation rooted exclusively in social contradiction ignores the issue of individual talents and certainly does not fully account for the way narrators actually *use* the symbol of the stolen woman as a model. Although it is clearly important to steer away from surface meanings of oral narrative, it is equally critical not to dismiss or ignore narrators' claims about the social significance of their stories. Mrs. Sidney,

Mrs. Smith, and Mrs. Ned regularly reflect on the educational importance of the written record they are making as a legacy for young people. No matter how fabulous the plot or incredible the adventures of the protagonist, myth provides an allegory of social interaction, interaction that takes place in the *story* of the myth rather than in its underlying structural oppositions.

The content of stories we read in this volume may deal with excursions to unfamiliar worlds, but success is demonstrated with reference to familiar skills. For both male and female protagonists, the sequence involves a separation, an initiation, and an eventual return to normal life. The gender differences define the way the sequence is accomplished. An important sequence in "stolen woman" stories is the heroine's inevitable goal to escape and return home to her familiar setting. She accomplishes this by demonstrating her discretion in dealings with power and her competence in a range of skills taught to women at puberty. Male protagonists seem more likely to submit to and learn from the spiritual, supernatural aspect of their voyage, and their success is demonstrated when they return with an animal helper. Women who try to confront power individually suffer tragic consequences, usually death. Women who rely on learned, shared, "practical" knowledge to achieve their ends eventually succeed. In stories the stolen woman seems to exemplify the qualities of an ideal woman, just as the power bringer does for men.

The *way* women make the journey home is important. For example, when the two sisters decide to leave their Star husbands, the young women engineer their escape by manufacturing lengths of babiche and pairs of protective mittens and pants. They puncture a hole in the sky and climb down to earth, where they are reunited with their parents (pp. 105–7, 216–21). A young woman stolen from her puberty hut outwits her captors by rubbing cranberry juice on her legs to feign menstruation (reminding them of women's powers to spoil men's hunting) and by refusing to cross a bridge that might transport her to a different dimension (pp. 108–10). Three other stories tell of abandoned women who fend for themselves so successfully that they are welcome additions to the groups that eventually take them in (pp. 233–41, 258–62). Commenting on one of those protagonists, Mrs. Smith remarked, "She's so smart she didn't even need a husband." On the other hand, a young girl who tries to confront power directly, as a man would, brings serious consequences both to herself and to her family (pp. 102–5).[5]

These stories tackle worrisome issues, but they also reflect a cultural ideal in which acquisition of superhuman power was largely the domain of men, and women relied more on their ingenuity in daily life. Men's power was contingent on access to supernatural understanding that translated into hunting success; women's status was more likely to depend on empirically based knowledge and competence as a hard worker and on discretion in responding to power. In stories male protagonists cross to the supernatural domain, identify with a captor to the extent of taking on his physical characteristics, acquire a new name to symbolize new status, and return to the social world with the assistance of a supernatural helper. Female protagonists more often perfect their ability to live by their wits and escape to the human community using ingenuity and practical abilities to outsmart captors.

A basic tenet of anthropology is that interaction between individuals is structured by the institutions of society. In "traditional" societies there is usually a fairly close fit between values and institutions, a shared body of mutual understandings about how to behave. In "modern" societies longstanding values regularly come into conflict with institutional changes. Because narratives follow a culturally specific sequence moving through a series of conflicts to some resolution, they are structurally equipped to address dilemmas accompanying change.[6]

* Behavioral Models in Narrative

Looking at the behavior of protagonists in these stories raises intriguing questions about gender models in narrative, the association of men with one kind of knowledge and of women with another kind. Successful male protagonists return with what appears to an outsider to be spiritual knowledge; successful female protagonists seem more often to return by demonstrating their learned, shared, practical abilities. This distinction, though, may be largely a Western one. There is no evidence that an Athapaskan storyteller would distinguish between these two kinds of knowledge. A narrator would see nothing inherently more "practical" in such a woman's behavior than in the entirely practical male vision quest that, if successful, could result in a mutually supportive relationship between hunters and game. Stories about stolen women seem rooted equally in an understanding of power and in the practical, empirical domain of observable, transferable knowledge all women are expected to master by the time they become adults. In other words, practical and spiritual knowledge are inextricably enmeshed: women used the same sets of abilities to confront transcendent beings and to survive in everyday life.

Examination of possible connections between story models and behavior directs us to cross-cultural interpretations of gender. Athapaskan stories come from a cultural tradition very different from contemporary Western society; yet from a Western perspective, behavior of female protagonists is guided by demonstrably practical skills. Female protagonists seem to make choices and to act in ways congruent with contemporary Western expectations about "responsible" women; behavior of male protagonists sometimes seems rather ethereal, as they search for a kind of knowledge devalued in the industrial north.

This difference has obvious implications in a setting like the Yukon, where Natives, accounting for one-third of the territory's population, have to contend with both Western institutions and Western interpretations of their behavior. In this cross-cultural setting there is greater consistency between narrative models and normative expectations for women's roles than there is for men's roles. Younger Native women whose behavior wins approval from their elders are precisely those rewarded by Western institutions, particularly by social agencies that define women as being "more practical," "more adaptable," and "more flexible" in coping with change than men.

Usually Western economic and social explanations are offered to account for this perceived adaptability of women: the greater number of service jobs available for women, the tendency of girls to remain in school longer than boys, the greater continuity women experience in their role as child-bearers, and so on. But weight should also be given to indigenous models of explanation embedded in stories. The story models work today as in the past, though in an entirely different context. Contemporary Athapaskan/Tlingit women are likely to be rewarded by Western institutions for behavior consistent with their traditional roles, whereas the decline in land-based activities has forced men to make more dramatic adjustments. Women who are influential in political organizations, for example, have usually been able to achieve this without leaving the community. Many women simultaneously raise a family, hold a regular job outside the home, and become active in community affairs.

Narrative models may also influence men. Men holding positions of visible economic and political influence in Native organizations often are those individuals who at one point left the community to study at universities or colleges or to receive technical training in southern Canada. In other words, they have made the physical equivalent of a narrative journey, have returned to the Yukon with new knowledge, and have moved directly into prestigious careers or political positions. They seem to have converted the quest for spiritual knowledge into a quest for the kind of practical knowledge that will help them cope with Westerners, knowledge that is in part about the larger world and in part about the immediate world of culture contact. Native artists and musicians in the Yukon are often men whose art requires solitary creative activity; more women describe themselves as storytellers, an art practiced with other people, particularly children. At a more tragic level the majority of alcohol-related deaths and suicides involve men, often men recognized as having particular creative talent. Women also may face serious social crises, but they seem more able to cope with emergencies within a framework of familial and social responsibilities.

* Oral Tradition and Oral History: Getting the Words Right

Orally narrated accounts have been central to another controversy in northern Canada during the last decade: specifically, how researchers can draw on Native oral traditions to reconstruct a more balanced picture of the past. For several reasons, northwestern Canada seems to offer attractive opportunities for oral history research. Reliable records rarely exist before the twentieth century; even when they are available, they reflect the views of short-term visitors. Many historians and scientists doing research in the north would welcome perspectives of indigenous people on questions they are asking. Perhaps most important is the commitment of aboriginal people to record oral accounts from elders which will allow them to document their own past in their own voice using their own oral records.

These factors give oral history rather elastic promise; however, well-intentioned but uncritical use of oral traditions developed in one cultural context as though they can be equated with tangible historical evidence may lead to misinterpretation of more complex messages in narrative. Attempts to sift oral accounts for "facts" may actually minimize the value of spoken testimonies by asserting positivistic standards for assessing "truth value" or "distortions." Similarly, the idea of recording oral accounts to store in archives for future analysis ignores the way their social meaning is linked to how they are actually used to discuss contemporary events.

To interpret any account, written or oral, a student of the past must evaluate the context in which the document was recorded. Researchers working with archival documents share a general framework for interpreting the circumstances influencing the production of government records, log books, diaries, personal papers, and newspapers. But these same criteria may be quite inappropriate when applied to cultural documents from an unfamiliar tradition. Oral storytellers seem well equipped to correlate seemingly unrelated ideas and show their interconnections; researchers who try to winnow "facts" from oral accounts and relate them to documented "facts" may be less successful.

An alternative approach treats oral tradition not as evidence but as a window on the ways the past is culturally constituted and discussed in different contexts.[7] For example, named places and landscape features figure prominently in the accounts in this volume; again, it is instructive to look at how place names are actually *used*. When I asked women to talk about the past, they used traditional stories—particularly stories having a strong competent woman as the central protagonist—to explain specific events in their lives. When we turned our attention to language documentation and I asked them to teach me Athapaskan and Tlingit names for landscape features, they did so by recounting events from the past to explain the names. In other words, only by asking about named topographic features did I finally begin to hear accounts approximating my original expectations about oral history. By imbuing place with meaning through story, narrators seemed to be using locations in physical space to talk about events in chronological time.

An element common to narratives about named places and stories about stolen women is their attention to travel. If the "stolen woman" stories, discussed above, all involve journeys to an unfamiliar world, accounts of the recent past suggest a focus on travel in *this* world. Toponyms and descriptions of travel become mnemonic devices linking segments of life experience. Because names play such a significant role in the three accounts, it is worth looking at how each woman uses them.

Mrs. Angela Sidney

On the day we began working together Mrs. Sidney made it absolutely clear that the proper way to talk about the past is to begin with clan history. Clan history is narrated as a travelogue. She locates each clan at a specific place and traces a journey to other named places and an eventual fresh beginning in new territory. Although the chronology may be ambiguous, the named locations are not.

Her own *Deisheetaan* clan traces its history to coastal Angoon, the Tlingit village from which four *Deisheetaan* sisters married inland. One went to Tagish, one to Teslin, one to Telegraph Creek, and one to Ross River. But despite this dispersal, members of this entire matrilineal clan share bonds of kinship, an origin story, songs, crests, and a claim to the land. "One nation owns it, not one person alone: we all own it," she points out, indicating examples of *Deisheetaan* lands by naming them in English, in Tagish, and in Tlingit. For example, the village of Carcross (called *Naataase Héen* in Tlingit, and *Todezáané* in Tagish), located at the junction of Nares Lake and Bennett Lake, belongs to her *Deisheetaan* clan.

Her father's *Dakl'aweidí* history, by contrast, begins inland, at *Taltan* (near Telegraph Creek, British Columbia), and involves travel down the Stikine River toward the coast, including a terrifying trip under a glacier, where clan members composed a song to celebrate their survival. When they reached Wrangell safely, "that's when they got their name, *Dakl'aweidí*," so that even selection of a clan name is linked with a particular location: a second song was sung there. Then they split into three groups, two remaining on the coast and one heading back to the interior via the Chilkat River; from there, members of the third group traveled over the mountain pass to Kusawa Lake, then east along the Watson River, and finally up Bear Creek Pass to Tagish, where they remained. Some intermarried with inland people they met on the upper Yukon; others went overland to Ross River.

The third *Shagóon* she tells is that of her husband's *Yanyeidí* clan. These ancestors separated from others on the Taku River, traveled down that river, and stopped at a point of land where their leader sang a commemorative song. Then they moved on to the mouth of the river, where they built a little cabin, or *yan*, and chose a new name. "We're going to change that name. We're going to be *Yanyeidí* from now on." This group traveled back from the coast and inland to Teslin.

As Mrs. Sidney moves closer to a time period that is recognizably historical, place names seem to take on clear mnemonic significance (Section 3). Even though she never met her grandparents, her references to them are linked with named places, specific locations where they were born and where they were traveling when they died. Her mother's mother, for example, was born at a place named *Men Ch'ile Táh* (Tagish) or *Héen Kas'el'ti Xoo* (Tlingit)—both translated as "among the ragged lakes"—now known by the English name Log Cabin. She died not far away on a mountain pass:

> She died when my mother was six or seven. . . . going through that pass from Millhaven, going through to West Arm. There's a little creek comes down—they call it Rosebud Creek—that's where they climbed up right on top of the mountain. She was carrying her baby, my mother's sister. Here that baby died five days after her mother—that baby must have starved herself, my mother said. . . . Well, of

course, they burned people that time I'm talking about, and they brought her ashes back to Carcross.

Mrs. Sidney refers to her mother's stepmother in much the same way: "*Stóow* is the one that died at Indian Point, *Ta Tígi.*" Likewise, she notes that her father's father, *Tl'úku*, died at Quiet Lake, as did her father's brother, and that her father's mother, *Guná*, died at Bennett. When she discusses her parents' childhood experiences, the emphasis is always on where they traveled, her mother's trip down the Taku River as a child, her father's journeys to Quiet Lake as a child and regularly to the coast when he was older.

It is when she talks about her own life that we see segments of experience clearly articulated by named places and associated with specific years. Identifying 1910, when she was eight years old, as the first year she remembers clearly, Mrs. Sidney begins by providing a named location as the setting for her story. "The earliest time I'm talking about is 1910—I can't remember when I was much younger. I remember when we were staying across Ten Mile on that island—they used to call that island 'Tagish John Island' . . . it's right straight across Ten Mile. I remember that time: that's year 1910."

By 1912 she is even more specific about connecting time with place (Section 7). She describes moving with her parents and her older brother from Tagish to Carcross, then to *Taaghahi*, then to Millhaven Bay, then back to *T'ooch'Áayi*. The following year, 1913, she met her Marsh Lake cousins for the first time, and they traveled from the foot of McClintock River at Marsh Lake to Judas Creek, to *Kooshdaa Xágu*, and then on to Whitehorse. In 1914 she went from Whitehorse to *Tsuxx'aayí*, then back to Marsh Lake and up the McClintock River. "I remember I just felt like I was home while I was there."

Her account of her courtship is also embedded in discussions of travel (Section 13). George Sidney was from Teslin, but he was working in Whitehorse as a longshoreman in 1916. Angela's father sent word that George should stop at Marsh Lake sometime when he traveled past to visit his parents at the head of Teslin River; the invitation was formally delivered in Whitehorse by "my father's niece, my aunt, Mrs. Whitehorse Billy." Everyone understood that this was more than just a casual invitation: George's father told him, "Maybe he wants to give you his daughter or something like that. . . . Go. Whatever he wants you to do, just do it. It's okay." So George made arrangements to leave immediately, catching a ride by boat with Pelly Jim. Understanding his obligations, he built a meat cache at *Chookanshaa* shortly after he arrived and spent that winter drying meat for Tagish John's family. After some time, the union was formalized, with a "nice big dinner . . . on the mountain . . . *Tl'ó K'aa' Dzéłe'* " (the Tagish name for *Chookanshaa*).

In 1917, the year following their marriage, Mrs. Sidney stayed at Carcross while her husband worked on the White Pass Railway for the summer. That fall, he hunted in the mountains and at *Skwáan Taasłéyi*, Skwaan Lake, while she took care of her sick mother and played with her little brother: "I was still a kid yet." Her first son, Peter, was born at Tagish, and hence he "put a claim on that Tagish John Rock," *Ḵaajinéek' Teiyí*, so named because *Ḵaajinéek'* once gave away all the fish he caught there. Four months later, they traveled a hundred kilometers south to Teslin, where they spent a year living with her husband's family. And so her account continues, incorporating most of the 230 named places she has mapped.[8]

The sense of place that permeates Mrs. Sidney's life account is equally important in the traditional stories she tells. When Game Mother made animals at the beginning of time, she hung her trampoline to four named mountains surrounding Carcross (Section 2). The stories of Fox Helper and Wolf Helper are set at named places on the Tagish Lake system (Section 8). Mrs. Sidney has remarked that when she tells some of these stories, she follows the narrative "like a map," a comment I have heard from other storytellers.

Toponyms may also contain pragmatic information of interest to students of oral history. There are names referring to fauna: *Óondáa Tóo'e'* identifies a creek where a particular species of whitefish spawns. *Nústséhé Mene'*, "fox lake," names a spot where foxes came to get spawning fish. *Éleish Tóo'e'*, "moose-lick creek," is a good location for hunting. Other names provide hints about changing vegetation: *Tséi Chó Desdél Ní*, "big red rock," was once a navigational beacon visible from Tagish Lake but is now obliterated by poplar; *K'ayé Desdél Ní*, "red willow point," has been submerged since a dam was built in the 1960s. Still other names are associated with material culture—"big fishnet place," "moose-corral point," "place for packing skin boats over."

Since 1978 Mrs. Sidney has traveled extensively—to the Philippines; to Vancouver; to Toronto, where she was a major performer at a storytelling festival in 1983; to Ottawa, where she received the Order of Canada in 1986; to Fairbanks; and to Angoon, Alaska (Section 17). Her account of her trip to Angoon in 1984 is perhaps the richest of her many travel narratives, because it so clearly emphasizes the continuing importance of linking her *Shagóon*—her family history—to place.

Mrs. Kitty Smith

Mrs. Smith frequently begins an account by asserting that names are intrinsically part of *any* description about how people used to live, that stories give meaning to the landscape. She may introduce her discussion with comments such as, "I'm going to tell you how Indians lived and what way this ground we call it," or, "These stories are true stories, how this ground came to be."

She names the place where she was born, *Ǵaax'w áa yéi daanune yé*, and describes her travels down the Tatshenshini and Alsek rivers as a child from her family's headquarters near *Neskatahéen*, past *Noogaayík* and *Tínx Kayaaní* and on to *Yaakwddát* (Section 5). At the same time, she tells stories associated with surging glaciers, such as the Lowell Glacier—*Nàlùdi* (Section 6). If Mrs. Sidney's names for places incorporate historical observations about changes in landscape, Mrs. Smith's stories about glaciers and the catastrophic emptying of ice-dammed lakes are of interest to glaciologists working in the southwest Yukon. The Lowell surged in 1852 and again sometime after the turn of the century; her translation for *Nàlùdi* is "fish stop," suggesting that salmon may once have migrated up the Alsek River.

Her narratives, too, emphasize the cultural importance of travel. When the two sisters leave their Star husbands (Section 8), they cite their need to travel as a legitimate excuse: "It's pretty hard—you people up there just stay one place."

The extent to which Mrs. Smith's account of her own life is embedded in named places and travel became clear when we began recording toponyms in her language around Marsh Lake and Fish Lake. Until that point, the life history she narrated was almost exclusively concerned with her childhood on the Tatshenshini River, a branch of the upper Alsek. As we began making regular visits to Marsh Lake, the focus of her life account shifted to named places associated with this area, two hundred and fifty kilometers to the east, where her mother's people made their headquarters and where she moved after she met and married her second husband, Billy Smith (Section 9).

She traveled widely as a married woman and describes a trip she made with a woman friend from Teslin east as far as the Liard River. When her husband was hired as a guide along this same trail during the construction of the Alaska Highway, she mentally followed his route because she had already made the trip herself (Section 11).

As I transcribe her tapes later, it becomes apparent that what she has recorded is not just a list of names. The inward eye of memory collaborates with images of landscape, and these names summon up layers of association. Our conversations include discussions of the nature of land ownership by Crow and Wolf moieties, how they made their claim to the land, and the Southern Tutchone and Tlingit names for all the people and places involved. She gives a painful account of deaths in her mother's family. She points out the location where she and her husband Billy Smith made their headquarters and the area where they hunted after their marriage. This leads her to comment on changes in salmon migrations since the construction of a nearby dam in the early 1960s. Naming individual glaciers in her Southern Tutchone language, she recalls how they were once dens of giant animals that emerged to terrorize human beings whenever they smelled burning grease. As we drive, she sings songs associated with places we pass and tells why and how the songs were "made." Our conversations remind her of the puzzling dilemma that all this is "getting weaker since white men came." She states her belief that perhaps some of the power can be restored to the names if they are written, because otherwise they seem to fall into disuse.

Mrs. Annie Ned

In Mrs. Ned's account, names are often so deeply embedded in context that it is difficult to understand whether the travel described is occurring in the world of familiar reality or in a transcendent sphere. She asserts the importance of travel early and often, expressing a sense of disappointment that people no longer understand its value: "Long-ago people, anyplace they go round. . . . go see everybody from next country. . . . This time just where they stay, they stay; that's what it looks like to me. . . . This time we can't do it now, can't travel around. People stay where they stay. . . . That time, I'm young, I go anyplace—go anyplace. Hunt. . . . [But now] no more snowshoes, me. When I go, I get on whiteman rig. Car! I go."

Although she insists that her *Shagóon* is centered at Hutshi, in the central Yukon, her actual account begins as a narrative about the travel involved in trade between coast and interior, beginning with Tlingit curiosity about the people living upriver from *Noogaayík* and culminating in their eventual meeting with inland Athapaskans. Tlingits began making annual trading trips to Hutshi, or *Hóoch'i Áayi*, which she translates as a Tlingit word meaning "last time lake," adding "that's when they go back" (Section 1).

Like Mrs. Smith, Mrs. Ned makes a distinction between the hunting territories of her first husband and those of her second. The two men were brothers by the Southern Tutchone system of kinship reckoning, because their mothers were sisters. Each had the same hunting territory as his father's father, that is, the grandfather of his own clan (Section 3).[9] She names those two grandfathers, describes the territories each controlled, and then discusses where she traveled with each of her two husbands.

The *Shagóon* she tells for her first husband, Paddy Smith, is centered partly at Kusawa Lake and partly at *Dùuchùghà*, where the Mendenhall River (*Chènk'äla*) empties into the Takhini River (*Dùu Chù*). The names she uses for the lake suggest something of its use. She translates the Tlingit name *Koosawu Áa* as "long way" (or "skinny lake"), referring to the lengthy travel route from coast to interior. But if the Tlingit orientation to this lake was longitudinal, Southern Tutchone interest was focused on a particular spot, *Nakhụ Chù*, "raft crossing." The name identifies the narrows where Athapaskans converged from Dalton Post, from Carcross, and from Hutshi for the excellent winter fishery and nearby caribou hunting.

Her second husband, Johnny Ned, had a paternal grandfather named *Ajängàkh*, who owned the hills *Sankàlà* and *Nichàlà* standing just north of the Alaska Highway at Stony Creek; later she and Johnny Ned made their headquarters there. Just as the names around "Steamboat Landing" or *Dùuchùgà* on the Takhini River tend to be associated with her first marriage, references to place names around Stony Creek tend to be linked with her second. In other words, her account of her lineage and her marriages is told with reference to particular landscape features. After talking about her second husband for a while, she concludes, "That's all Stony Creek, what I said." The stories and events become an intrinsic part of each toponym.

Her stories, too, are set at named places and explore questions about particular landscape features. Her Crow and Beaver narrative concludes with reference to a puzzle that has long preoccupied people in the southwest Yukon. Klukshu, Dezadeash, and Aishihik lakes drain to the nearby Pacific, whereas the surrounding lakes—Kusawa, Hutshi, and Kluane—all drain north to the Yukon River and then flow some three thousand kilometers to the Bering Sea. The major significance for Native people is that different kinds of salmon migrate up the different drainages, the rich sockeye only ascending the shorter Alsek/Tatshenshini. Mrs. Ned's narrative credits Crow with establishing these drainages as he moved to the coast after he and Beaverman had completed their work.

The toponyms these three women include in their narratives do much more than identify places. They bring together varieties of information in one small word: familiar landscape features allow people to use points in space to talk about time, and symbols from nature to talk about culture. Such connections can be made particularly clearly in the metaphor of named places. When Annie Ned instructs me, as she does all the time, "we've got to get the words *right*," she is absolutely correct. Through words the landscape is fashioned into a world of manageable, human proportions. If, as Rosaldo advises, "doing oral history involves telling stories about the stories people tell about themselves,"[10] place names may provide a point of entry to the past.

This volume has tried to explore the critical intelligence embedded in narrative by showing how narrators use stories to talk about their lives. By incorporating traditional narrative into their discussion of past and present, Angela Sidney, Kitty Smith, and Annie Ned raise an issue significant for anthropology. The distinction social sciences conventionally make between what we call "expressive forms" and what we characterize as "adaptive strategies" may be totally inappropriate in situations where people see storytelling as central to their culture. Some anthropologists and historians are investigating the extent to which social structure and literature share a common ground. For example, historians with an interest in cultural history have recently shown how sixteenth- and seventeenth-century Europeans used stories to think about and interpret the changing social and economic order.[11]

The narrators whose stories appear in this volume examine questions about social change in various ways. Sometimes their use of narrative is explicit, as when Angela Sidney refers to her attempt to live her life "like a story"; other times their use of narrative is more indirect, when they respond to my questions about their lives by *telling* a story that initially seems to come from a very different period of time.

Mrs. Smith's life description, for example, suggests remarkably autonomous behavior: she left an unsatisfactory marriage sometime in the 1920s and decided to support herself by trapping. Her striking success trapping live foxes that she could sell to fox farms made her unusually independent for a woman in her society during this era. Younger women, living today in a different social context, are inclined to regard her as an early feminist. Yet she insists that she was entirely "old-fashioned" in all her decisions during that period and makes much of her deference to maternal uncles, to their wives, and to her maternal grandmother. The stories she tells mediate this apparent contradiction: repeatedly, her female protagonists demonstrate exceptional independence, but their reward is a stable place in an extended family setting, grounded in social context. Individual autonomy is only a means to an end for these protagonists; their goal is reconnection with community.

Outwardly, Mrs. Sidney has lived a conservative Tagish life. Yet her account shows how she has accomplished this by reflecting on ideas from other cultures, adapting them (usually by thinking about how they relate to "old stories" she knows), and making them part of her repertoire of ideas. Frequently, when she has faced an unfamiliar situation, she has searched for explanation in a story her mother or an aunt told her. For much of her adult life, people have come to ask her for advice because she can usually find an appropriate narrative or song to broaden their framework for thinking about their question. She continues to do this, in her mid-eighties, both when she wants to explain some past decision she has made and when she encounters ideas new to her. Her intellectual drive to formulate consistent links between "old ways" and "new ways" permeates her entire account.

Mrs. Ned remains a powerful figure in southern Yukon society, where she has lived for almost a century. She is recognized throughout the Yukon as having special knowledge about spiritual power. Underlying her account is her emphasis on the power of words, on the value of discretion, on being able to differentiate between information that should be shared and information that is essentially related to power and therefore not openly discussed. The stories she tells reflect her understanding that only a fool speaks indiscriminately; the inappropriate use of words can bring serious consequences to both speaker and listener.

A comment by Mrs. Ned emphasizes parallels between narrative explanation and academic storytelling. Of the elders I know, Mrs. Ned is the one most interested in what scientists are doing in the southwest Yukon. In 1982 the Yukon Historical and Museums Association sponsored a conference in the community of Haines Junction, in the southern Yukon. The laudable aim of the conference was to have archaeologists from across Canada meet with local elders to exchange ideas about Yukon prehistory in a relatively informal setting. Not surprisingly, the archaeologists did most of the talking. Mrs. Ned, already in her nineties, sat all day listening patiently while one archaeologist after another presented papers describing current research. Finally, late in the day, she stood up and asked,

Where do these people come from, outside?
You tell different stories from us people.
You people talk from paper—
Me, I want to talk from Grandpa.

In a very real sense she has identified what seems to be the central issue,
for social science is a form of storytelling, and the way we tell stories
largely determines who will hear them.

Notes

Preface

1. White, "Autobiography of an Acoma Indian" (1943), 377.
2. Crapanzano, "Life Histories" (1984), 958.
3. It has since been renamed the Yukon Native Language Centre.

Introduction: Life History and Life Stories

1. Cited by Harbsmeier, "Beyond Anthropology" (1986), 47.

2. For critiques from within anthropology see Rabinow, *Reflections on Fieldwork in Morocco* (1977); Said, *Orientalism* (1978); Michelle Rosaldo, *Knowledge and Passion* (1980); Ellen, *Ethnographic Research* (1984); Whittaker, *Mainland Haole* (1985); Clifford and Marcus, *Writing Culture* (1986); Marcus and Fischer, *Anthropology as Cultural Critique* (1986). Some of the thoughtful life histories appearing in the last few years include Kelly, *Yaqui Women* (1978); Freeman, *Untouchable* (1979); Crapanzano, *Tuhami* (1980); Dyk and Dyk, *Left Handed* (1980); Savala and Sands, *Autobiography of a Yaqui Poet* (1980); Shaw, *My Country of the Pelican Dreaming* (1981); and Shostak, *Nisa* (1981). Over the years, various surveys have been made of the use of life history in anthropology: Dollard, *Criteria for the Life History* (1935); Kluckhohn, "Personal Document in Anthropological Science" (1945); Shaw, "Life History Writing in Anthropology" (1980); Langness and Frank, *Lives* (1981); Crapanzano, "Life Histories" (1984); Bertaux and Kohli, "Life Story Approach" (1984); and Watson and Watson-Franke, *Interpreting Life Histories* (1985). European studies of life history are particularly interesting because they look at how narrators use the experience of telling their story as a way of symbolically transforming the past: see Paul Thompson, "Life Histories in Poland" (1979) and "New Oral History in France" (1980); Bertaux-Wiame, "Life Story Approach to the Study of Internal Migration" (1979); Morin, "Anthropological Praxis and Life History" (1982); and especially Passerini, *Fascism in Popular Memory* (1987).

3. There is no universally accepted term to refer to indigenous populations of Canada. Many indigenous people prefer to use the term in their own language denoting "the people"; however, in the Yukon there are seven distinct Athapaskan languages spoken, as well as Tlingit, and terms for self-designation may differ. When Angela Sidney, Kitty Smith, and Annie Ned use a word from their own language like *den* (Tagish) or *dän* (Southern Tutchone), the terms for "person, Indian," I follow their usage. In everyday unself-conscious discourse in the Yukon, people refer to themselves as "Indian" or "Native"; I follow that usage when speaking more generally.

4. Bataille and Sands, *American Indian Women* (1984).

5. Jelinek, *Women's Autobiography* (1980), 17–19.

6. Sidonie Smith, *Poetics of Women's Autobiography* (1987), 50–51; Carby, *Reconstructing Womanhood* (1987), 6; Foster, *Witnessing Slavery* (1979), 132.

7. See, for example, Barrett, *Geronimo's Story* (1906); Radin, *Crashing Thunder* (1926); Neihardt, *Black Elk Speaks* (1932); Ford, *Smoke from Their Fires* (1941); Simmons, *Sun Chief* (1942); Dyk, *Son of Old Man Hat* (1938); Kroeber, *Ishi* (1961); Spradley, *Guests Never Leave Hungry* (1969); Wallace, *Handsome Lake* (1970).

8. See Reichard, *Dezba* (1939); Marriott, *Maria* (1948); Lurie, *Mountain Wolf Woman* (1961); Scott, *Karnee* (1966); and accounts recorded by Michelson, "Autobiography of a Fox Indian Woman" (1925), "Narrative of a Southern Cheyenne Woman" (1932), and "Narrative of an Apache Woman" (1933); by Underhill, *Autobiography of a Papago Woman* (1936); and by Kelly, *Yaqui Women* (1978).

9. Malinowski, for example, argued that what people said about their past was largely irrelevant: narrative accounts had little intrinsic value and served primarily as charters to justify the present social order as old traditions were modified to meet new needs (*Magic, Science and Religion* [1954]). Vansina countered that historians should be using oral accounts as well as colonial records to reconstruct the past; however, others have objected to his criteria for "truth" or "falsity" and to his search for "distortions" and "original versions." See, for example, Vansina, *Oral Tradition* (1965); Beidelman, "Myth, Tradition and Oral History" (1965); and Miller, "Listening for the African Past" (1980).

10. For a fuller discussion of this, see Leach, *Structural Study of Myth* (1967), especially his introduction, and LeRoy, *Fabricated World* (1985), chapter 1.

11. See Frank, "Finding the Common Denominator" (1979), 74.

12. The reference here is to the all-encompassing titles of these works rather than to their contents. See Osgood, "Distribution of the Northern Athapaskan Indians" (1936a), *Han Indians* (1971), *Contributions to the Ethnography of the Kutchin* (1936b); Honigmann, *Kaska Indians* (1954); McKennan, *Upper Tanana Indians* (1959).

13. The initial position about hunting territories was put forward in 1915 by Speck, "Family Hunting Band." Years later, responses came from Leacock, *Montagnais "Hunting Territory"* (1954); from Helm, "Arctic Drainage Dene" (1965); from Knight, "Re-examination of Hunting, Trapping and Territoriality" (1965); it has continued in Damas, "Band Societies" (1969); in Dyen and Aberle, *Lexical Reconstruction* (1974); and in Helm, ed., *Handbook of North American Indians*, vol. 6, *Subarctic* (1981).

14. See McClellan, *My Old People Say* (1975a), and her papers on "Intercultural Relations" (1981b), "Inland Tlingit" (1981c), "Tagish" (1981d), and "Tutchone" (1981e) in the *Handbook*, vol. 6, *Subarctic*, and McClellan et al., *Part of the Land* (1987). The ethnographic overview in this section incorporates her research.

15. Yukon Indians use "Crow" to refer to the large northern raven (*Corvus corax principalis Ridgway*) rather than to the smaller crow (*Corvus caurinus Baird*), and they use it in the same way coastal Tlingit people use "Raven"—to refer both to the moiety name and to the trickster who created the world at the beginning of time. The moiety names, though, differ from the animal names: *Kajìt* refers to the Crow moiety, but *Ts'ürk'i* is the name for the bird and for the

character in Crow stories. *Ägunda* is the name for the Wolf moiety, whereas wolf,
the animal, is *ägay*.

16. It is generally acknowledged that sequestering of daughters confers status on families who have resources to do so, but retrospectively these narrators refer to the high status of the secluded woman herself.

17. See Urquhart, ed., *Historical Statistics of Canada* (1965), 14.

18. See Cruikshank, "Gravel Magnet" (1985).

19. See, for example, Balikci, *Vunta Kutchin Social Change* (1963); Chance, "Social Organization, Acculturation and Integration Among the Eskimo and the Cree" (1963); Honigmann, "Social Disintegration in Five Northern Canadian Communities" (1966); Hoseley, "Factionalism and Acculturation in an Alaskan Athapaskan Community" (1966); VanStone, *Changing Culture of the Snowdrift Chipewyan* (1965).

20. For perspectives from Native people see excerpts included in Berger, *Northern Frontier, Northern Homeland* (1977); Lysyk et al., *Alaska Highway Pipeline Inquiry* (1977); and Brody, *Living Arctic* (1987). Scholarly analyses of the same process come from Asch, "Dene Self-Determination" (1982), and Feit, "Future of Hunters" (1982).

21. Passerini, *Fascism in Popular Memory* (1987), 17.

22. See, for example, Tom, *Duts'üm Edhó Ts'ètsi Yū Dän K'i* (1981) and *Èkeyi/My Country* (1987); Tlen, *Speaking Out* (1986); Easterson, "Traditional Ways to Preserve Indian Culture" (1987); Geddes, *Three Elder Storytellers* (1986); Penikett, *Potlatch Conference Report* (1986).

23. Cruikshank, "Becoming a Woman in Athapaskan Society" (1975b), *Athapaskan Women* (1979), *Stolen Woman* (1983), and "Tagish and Tlingit Place Names" (1984).

24. Rosaldo, "Doing Oral History" (1980), 16.

25. Boas made this point explicitly in his "Mythology and Folk Tales of the North American Indian" (1914), 375, and it has been reiterated by linguists ever since.

26. Tlen, *Speaking Out* (1986), 7.

27. Nora and Richard Dauenhauer discuss this problem in their volume of Tlingit oral literature, *Haa Shuká/Our Ancestors* (1987), 7–8. They point out that, when stories are translated from original languages to standard English, we lose the idiomatic way the storyteller puts words together in his or her own language to create a unique performance.

28. Copies of the tapes as well as archive sheets describing the content of each are on file in the Yukon Native Language Centre and the Yukon Archives; however, corrections or alterations suggested by narrators when we check my transcript mean that there are sometimes differences between the taped accounts and the written text.

29. See Hymes, "Discovering Oral Performance" (1977), and *In Vain I Tried to Tell You* (1981); Tedlock, "On the Translation of Style in Oral Narrative" (1971), "Toward an Oral Poetics" (1977), and *Spoken Word and the Work of Interpretation* (1983); Toelken, "'Pretty Language(s)' of Yellowman" (1969); and Toelken and Scott, "Poetic Retranslation" (1981). Toelken, though, does mention the problems of this format for representing tonal languages like Athapaskan. Tedlock argues that *all* spoken language should be written in this form, that prose paragraphs are a convention developed from writing rather than from speaking.

30. Louise Profeit-LeBlanc, for example, is a younger woman widely acknowledged as an extremely talented storyteller, both within and beyond the Yukon. In the late 1980s, she has paid particular attention to ways stories can be used to help people resolve social issues in their communities.

I. My Stories Are My Wealth

1. Maria had a second name, Ḵaax'anshee, and Tagish John was also sometimes called by his other name, Haandeyéil.
2. In 1948 Mrs. Sidney met Catharine McClellan, and their association has continued during four decades. More recently, linguists Victor Golla, Jeff Leer, and John Ritter have all worked with her.
3. The position of Governor General is largely a ceremonial one in Canada: Madame Sauvé's gender is quite irrelevant to the appropriateness of the metaphor.
4. Sidney and others, My Stories (1977), and Sidney, Tagish Tlaagú (1982).
5. Sidney, Place Names (1980).
6. Sidney, Haa Shagóon (1983).
7. For detailed description of various traditions associated with Deisheetaan clan history see McClellan, Old People (1975a), 468–74, and De Laguna, Story of a Tlingit Community (1960), 133–35. For Daḵl'aweidí traditions see McClellan, 446–57, and for those associated with the Yanyeidí clan, McClellan, 457–68. A trip under a glacier is a theme in both Wolf and Raven clan histories, but there is also evidence that glaciers were surging in this region during the time she discusses; see Tarr and Martin, Alaska Glacier Studies (1914).
8. Berton, Klondike (1972), 41.
9. In October 1988 Mrs. Sidney was invited to take part in the official ceremony to open the newly built Yukon College in Whitehorse. As her contribution, she again sang the Ḵaax'achgóok song. Later she told me, "The reason I sang this song is because that Yukon College is going to be like a sun for those students. Instead of going to Vancouver, or Victoria, they're going to be able to stay here and go to school here. We're not going to lose our kids anymore. It's just going to be like the sun for them!"
10. Both these references signify the wealth and high status of a family who could afford such a magnificent gesture: the slaves were killed to commemorate the event.
11. This point may seem minor to an outsider, but it has continued to be a source of intense irritation for elders. The man involved in the discovery of Klondike gold with Skookum Jim was his nephew, Ḵáa Ǥoox, a member of the Daḵl'aweidí clan, who was nicknamed "Dawson Charlie" by his friends and relatives after the discovery because the gold rush led to the creation of Dawson City. However, because he came from Tagish, he is often called "Tagish Charlie" in written accounts of the gold rush (for example, in Pierre Berton's popular account, Klondike). This causes confusion because an entirely different man, Yéiłdoogú, (also known as Xóonk'i Éesh), from the Deisheetaan clan already had the name "Tagish Charlie" (see Mrs. Sidney's genealogy, figure 1). To clarify this distinction, two headstones, prominently displaying their different crests, have been placed on each man's grave in the Carcross cemetery—a Wolf for Dawson Charlie and a Crow for Tagish Charlie.

12. In a version recorded by McClellan, *Old People* (1975a), 446, the Thunderbird feathers exploded.

13. Mrs. Sidney is referring here to discussions she has had with anthropologist Catharine (Kitty) McClellan during their long association. McClellan identified two groups of *Yanyeidí*: a group originally on the Taku River was pushed north to the Nisutlin River when a second *Yanyeidí* group moved in from the coast. She designates the original group "Old *Yanyeidí*" and the newer group "New *Yanyeidí*."

14. See McClellan, *Old People* (1975a), 117–18, for a discussion of this story among Tagish and Inland Tlingit speakers, and Teit, "Tahltan Tales" (1919), 230–32, for a Tahltan version.

15. *Tudech'ade* was a man of the *Dakl'aweidí* clan who watched the process and learned the songs, so that today Tagish *Dakl'aweidí* have the right to sing them.

16. The marriage of Angela's parents, Maria and Tagish John, was thoroughly conventional because they were double cross-cousins. Maria's maternal grandmother, *Sa.éek'*, had a brother named *Tl'úku*, who was Tagish John's father. But Tagish John's mother, *Guná*, had a brother named *Shaakóon*, who was Maria's father. Such an alliance reinforced existing ties between the *Deisheetaan* Crow clan and the *Dakl'aweidí* Wolf clan.

17. As the genealogies show, it is quite common to have more than one name, but this sometimes makes the narrative difficult to follow. Annie Atlin had two names, *Sakinyáa* and *Sa.éek'*. *Aandaax'w* is referred to by several different "whiteman names" in this account—sometimes "Grandma Hammond" and sometimes "Mrs. Dyea John" or "Mary John."

18. Mrs. Sidney says that this was a preferred marriage pattern in the old days and that there is a Tlingit expression for it, translated as "on top of her mother." Again, the custom emphasizes the overriding importance of maintaining clan linkages previously established by a marriage.

19. The custom of naming a parent after a child, as "father of ———" or "mother of ———," is common in the southern Yukon. *Tláa* means "mother of" in Tlingit; the corresponding Tagish and Southern Tutchone word is *Ma* (see Linguistic Note). *Tashooch Tláa* also had a second name, *Kaa.ítdesadu.áxch*.

20. Mrs. Sidney is referring to meetings held in the 1980s to involve elders in Yukon land-claims discussions and is drawing an explicit parallel between the high-status *Deisheetaan* sisters who married inland and these Tagish women who married even farther into the interior.

21. See also McClellan's analysis of these same narratives about Skookum Jim, recorded with Tagish people a generation older than Mrs. Sidney, in McClellan, "Wealth Woman" (1963).

22. Swan's down has transformative properties and is associated with shamans and with curing, making it a suitable gift for an animal spirit helper.

23. There was a later, smaller gold rush at Atlin, British Columbia.

24. Ideally, a woman would be assisted at childbirth by someone from the opposite moiety, but in practice any woman available would have helped.

25. McClellan, *Old People* (1975a), 377, identifies various ways women prepared their daughters for easy delivery while they were still children. An older female relative might drop a newborn puppy or a porcupine fetus down a girl's dress in such a way that it did not touch her body. She also points out that some women believed this was a dangerous practice because it might cause babies to be born too quickly.

26. *Hedysarum alpinum,* or "bear roots," can be eaten either raw or roasted.

27. See Teit, "Kaska Tales" (1917), 443, for another version of the same narrative.

28. All unused parts of the fish must be returned to the water so that fish will continuously regenerate and return. By handling the fish carelessly, the boy loses the same part of his own body that he mistreated in the fish. When he corrects his behavior, his body, like that of the fish, becomes complete again.

29. They were cousins, classified as "sisters" (*nishemb'e',* second-person possessive of *eshemb'e'*) because they had the same maternal great-grandmother (see Mrs. Sidney's *Deisheetaan* genealogy, figure 1).

30. McClellan, *Old People* (1975a), 37, notes that the use of uncomplimentary nicknames was one way of controlling children's behavior.

31. Patsy Henderson was her father's classificatory nephew (see Mrs. Sidney's *Daḵl'aweidí* genealogy, figure 2), but Angela always refers to him using the "uncle" term *eshtáa* because in Tagish the terms for "father's brother" and "father's [classificatory] sister's son" are identical, making them sociological equivalents.

32. Fish Lake is in the hills above Whitehorse, at considerably higher elevation than the town. Because temperature inversions cause cold air to sink into the valley in winter, it is often much warmer in the mountains. Fish Lake is mentioned as one such favorable winter camping spot in both Mrs. Sidney's and Mrs. Smith's accounts.

33. McClellan, *Old People* (1975a), 449, notes that in Carcross the houses of Skookum Jim and of his nephew Dawson Charlie were also sometimes called *Ḵéet hít,* or "Killer Whale House."

34. Button blankets made of red, black, and navy wool cloth and decorated with small pearl-colored buttons were modeled on coastal style and were made in the interior once these items became available through trade.

35. She refers here to Mrs. Annie Ned, one of the other narrators in this volume, who already had two children when Mrs. Sidney was still a child.

36. She is referring to the custom of giving potlatch names, which are bestowed by a man of the same clan as the recipient, but two generations senior. She phrases it as, "You have to name your great-grandchildren on your same side," but the ideal person to name a child seems to be one's father's father, who would be of one's own moiety. Daisy Jim belonged to the *Ǥaanaxteidí* clan; "Bill Bone's wife" (her Tlingit name was *Ḵaadzaasxée*) belonged to the *Ǥaanax.ádi* clan; and Skookum Jim's daughter Daisy Mason belonged to the *Lukaax.ádi* clan (all Crow clans). Unfortunately for Angela, whose father's father, *Tl'ùku,* had died some years earlier, there was no living *Deisheetaan* male elder genealogically distant enough to name her.

37. McClellan, *Old People* (1975a), 181–82, says that this is originally a Southern Tutchone *Ǥaanaxteidí* (Crow) clan tradition, brought to Tagish by a Southern Tutchone woman who married a *Daḵl'aweidí* man.

38. Because songs are usually addressed to members of the opposite moiety, everyone is entitled to use them because they belong to either the "side" who made the song or the "side" for whom the song was made. A singer must begin by naming the singer and the circumstances under which the song was first sung.

39. This was really her mother's aunt (her mother's mother's sister), referred to sometimes as *Aandaax'w,* sometimes as "Grandma Hammond," and other times as "Mrs. Dyea John." Ideally, a woman of the opposite moiety in the relation of

"aunt"—specifically, someone in the category of "father's sister"—would be in charge, but her family was traveling and only women of her own moiety were present, so they prepared her hood. The girl could eat nothing until she was "under the bonnet."

40. McClellan, *Old People* (1975a), 360, notes that the woman bringing water to the girl would spill it twice before offering it to her so that the trainee would not be greedy later in life.

41. After seclusion the "long hat" was cut up and distributed to appropriate relatives from the opposite moiety, and the tent was also given away to the "other side." The people who received Angela's tent were from the correct clan; in fact, they were her future husband's older brother and his wife, but they were genealogically distant, and here she is naming women who, in her opinion, had a better claim to it.

42. Mrs. Sidney's description was so emphatic that I asked her whether she felt cheated, and she replied, "Yes, yes, yes!" In fact, all the women who discuss their life histories here agree that a lengthy seclusion conferred high status on a young woman. Aunt Susie, *Ḵaałaa*, was a *Daḵl'ushdáa* cousin of Angela's father and therefore a person from the appropriate clan to remove the bonnet.

43. Once back in camp, a woman had to maintain respectful avoidance toward older brothers and all older males of her own moiety.

44. After Skookum Jim found gold, he sent his daughter, Daisy, to Seattle to school. She studied acting briefly in California and made periodic trips back to Carcross, especially when her father became ill at the end of his life, but she was ambivalent about her place, or lack of it, in Carcross. She died in 1937 (Phelps papers, Yukon Archives).

45. Skookum Jim married a coastal Tlingit woman from the Łukaax̱.ádi Raven clan, so Daisy, like her mother, had a Łukaax̱.ádi name; again, Angela Sidney is emphasizing the clear boundaries that govern who is entitled to use particular names.

46. This story is told widely in other parts of North America by Inuit in Alaska and Canada (and Greenland) and by Native Americans in the Mackenzie region, and on the Plains, Plateau, and Northwest Coast. For other versions see Teit, "Kaska Tales" (1917), 463–64; Swanton, *Tlingit Myths and Texts* (1909), 22–24; Habgood, "Indian Legends" (1970); and Sheppard, "Dog Husband" (1983).

47. See Stith Thompson, "Star Husband" (1953), for a comparison of eighty-six versions told north of Mexico; also Levi-Strauss, *Origin of Table Manners* (1968), 200–203; and *Naked Man* (1971), 387.

48. George Sidney's father and Angela's aunt *Sadusgé* were both *Deisheetaan* and were classificatory brother and sister; consequently, *Sadusgé* would use the nephew term meaning "my brother's son" when she spoke to George, and when he spoke to her he would address her by the aunt term meaning "my father's sister." (The other nephew and aunt reciprocal terms, "sister's son" and "mother's sister," are entirely different because they refer to individuals of one's own moiety.) Because the system of kinship reckoning merges generations on the male side, Angela would use the same nephew term to address her future husband as would *Sadusgé*, and he in turn would refer to his future wife as "my aunt."

49. She is using Tagish kinship terms here when she explains how she addressed him, and Tlingit terms by which he addressed her (because his language was Inland Tlingit).

50. This aunt was the adopted daughter of *Gunaatdk'*, the Marsh Lake Chief, and his wife, *Tashooch Tláa*—Angela's father's sister. In other words, she had the same sociological relationship to Angela—a cousin Angela called "father's sister"—that *Sadusgé* had to George. An opposite-moiety aunt in the relationship of "father's sister" had a privileged role in marriage negotiations.

51. In earlier days a prospective husband would be expected to work for his parents-in-law for at least a year before marriage. Her father considered himself a progressive man, "not old-fashioned," as he states in his speech further along.

52. "W.A." refers to the Woman's Auxiliary of the Anglican Church.

53. George Sidney worked for the White Pass and Yukon Route on a regular seasonal basis for years, on their railway between Skagway and Carcross; during these periods, he and Angela based themselves in Carcross.

54. Mrs. Watson taught at the Chooutla residential school when Angela was in first grade.

55. Ideally, brothers-in-law worked together as "partners" in this way. Her comment "they're the boss" refers to her parents: her husband and brother gave them food, which was then her parents' to redistribute.

56. See Teit, "Kaska Tales" (1917), 464, for a version of the narrative told by Albert Dease at Dease Lake in 1915. In Dease's version the dramatic action focused on the husband's pursuit of his wife and the supernatural assistance he received from an eagle.

57. "Tagish John Rock" (or *Kaajinéek' Teiyí* in Tlingit), located at the head of Tagish Narrows, is submerged when water levels are high. Angela's father, Tagish John, originally claimed this rock for Wolf people, and from that time on, his name was linked with it: whenever he caught fish from this rock he would "potlatch it" away to other people. Because Tagish John's grandson, Pete, was born near here, he later claimed that particular rock.

58. Later Mrs. Sidney commented that, on the coast and farther in the interior, women remained upright, in a crouching position, at childbirth. See also McClellan, *Old People* (1975a), 351, 379.

59. Before the arrival of missionaries, Tagish people practiced cremation. By the late nineteenth century, they were wrapping the ashes in cloth, placing them in a box or container, and putting them in a grave house called a "spirit house," along with such personal possessions of the deceased as utensils, drinking vessels, tools, clothing, blankets, and pictures. See McClellan, *Old People* (1975a), 249.

60. See McClellan, "Indian Stories About the First Whites" (1970b), 126, for Edgar Sidney's own account of his experiences after he moved from the Pacific coast to the interior high country.

61. The Yukon and British Columbia had different laws governing hunting and trapping and different "opening" and "closing" dates for hunting specific animals: this caused particular confusion for Indian people living close to the territorial/provincial boundary.

62. The worldwide influenza epidemic that began in 1918 had a devastating effect on the Yukon, where it began to take a toll by the spring of 1920.

63. During the construction of the Alaska Highway, Indian people near the route came into contact with a number of illnesses for which they had no immunities. A medical doctor stationed with the U.S. Army near Teslin reported that Indian people in that community were overwhelmed serially by measles,

dysentery, jaundice, whooping cough, mumps, tonsillitis, and meningitis. See Marchand, "Tribal Epidemics" (1943), 1019–20.

64. Mrs. Sidney's description of how her clan acquired the right to use that song and her reasons for making a gift of the song to her son form an integral part of the story. Patsy Henderson, a senior man of the *Daḵl'aweidí* clan, complained to Angela's mother that Angela hadn't the right to use that song because it belonged to another clan. She explains here how she demonstrated to him that the song had been given to *Deisheetaan* by the *Kiks.ádi* clan as part of a settlement after a dispute, and that she was actually using it in an appropriate way.

65. Originally, houses of *Daḵl'aweidí* clan members and *Deisheetaan* clan members were spatially separated; this changed when the federal government became involved in constructing housing for Indian bands and chose the locations where houses would be built.

66. Mrs. Sidney is referring to the *Kwänlin Dän* band (formerly the Whitehorse Indian band), which was moved to a site within the city boundaries of Whitehorse during the 1920s. Only in 1987 was that particular community relocated to an area of town where running water and other services are available. In 1984 the band officially changed its name to *Kwänlin Dän*, meaning "people of the rapids." The Carcross meeting she describes here probably took place sometime in the 1950s.

67. For a version of this narrative written in Tlingit with an English translation, see Dauenhauer and Dauenhauer, *Haa Shuká* (1987), 82–107.

68. Some versions of clan history suggest that dispersal of *Deisheetaan* resulted from internal clan differences, a common theme in coastal Tlingit narratives; from the perspective of the visitors at this meeting, the emphasis was on *Deisheetaan* unity, and younger people, particularly, wanted to eliminate any references suggesting the contrary.

69. Mrs. Sidney had with her a photo taken by Catharine McClellan during her fieldwork in Angoon.

70. The original name, *Xutsnoowu*, means "Brown Bear Fort" and reflects the large population of grizzlies on Admiralty Island. See De Laguna, *Story of a Tlingit Community* (1960), 25.

71. According to De Laguna's informants, *Deisheetaan* was once a branch of the *Gaanax̱.ádi* clan. A dispute arose when a *Gaanax̱.ádi* man discovered that his wife had a *Deisheetaan* lover; the husband killed the man, causing a breach between the two clans. In one version of the story the decision about which clan would leave and which one would stay was settled by a "hockey game" between *Gaanax̱.ádi* and *Deisheetaan* women, and the *Deisheetaan* victors stayed in Angoon. See De Laguna, *Story of a Tlingit Community* (1960), 133–35.

72. Mrs. Sidney has this *Deisheetaan* crest beaded on her vest and painted on her drum—a beaver with two front paws, four hind legs, and two tails; she says that it represents beaver as a shaman or "doctor" sitting behind his dam and holding back the water.

73. De Laguna, *Story of a Tlingit Community* (1960), 27, says that Dog Salmon People are another distinct Raven sib [clan] that is recognized as having originated from one of the *Deisheetaan* lineages.

74. Raven represents the same moiety that people in the interior call Crow; similarly, Eagle is the coastal Tlingit equivalent of the inland Wolf moiety. Hence, Raven could be referred to as "Eagle's wife."

75. Austin Hammond is a senior Tlingit man of the *Deisheetaan* clan who lives in Haines, Alaska. When Mrs. Sidney asked him for advice about appropriate behavior, he responded with a narrative, which she repeats here.

76. This Pelly River shaman was one of the most famous in remembered Yukon history. McClellan describes how shamans borrowed enough of the trappings of Christianity (shamanistic performances on Sunday, representations of crosses) to appear to ally themselves with the missionaries, but not in any way that undermined their own influence (see McClellan, "Shamanistic Syncretism," 1956).

77. Frequently, older people identify a time when they were very ill in this way: a golden ladder comes down from the sky and they have an intense desire to climb it, but they are stopped by someone who insists that it is "not your time (to die)." The pattern follows that of a shamanic voyage to another dimension.

II. My Roots Grow in Jackpine Roots

1. Sidney and others, *My Stories* (1977), and Smith, *Nindal Kwädindür* (1982).

2. Each narrator in this volume traces her ancestry to a coastal Tlingit woman. In Mrs. Sidney's case the four sisters were *Deisheetaan* Crow women. Although Mrs. Smith is also Crow, the sisters she names were *Dakl'aweidí* Wolf women because she was raised by a *Dakl'aweidí* grandmother. Mrs. Ned gives a similar account of her first husband's lineage.

3. For a comparison of oral traditions and written documents associated with both the Marsh Lake deaths and Skookum Jim's discovery of gold, see Cruikshank, "Life" (1987), 233–59.

4. McClellan, *Old People* (1975a), 494–96, suggests that this was one way of demonstrating how a man's economic strength could complement the woman's role in transmitting social position.

5. A Northwest Mounted Police officer, Inspector A. M. Jarvis, wrote in his annual report from Dalton Post in 1899, p. 58, "We were fortunate in securing the services of two of the best Indians of the Stick tribe as special constables. . . . One of them, 'Doctor Scottie,' is a medicine man and the most respected and feared amongst all the natives."

6. Mrs. Smith says that she married Billy Smith shortly before his uncle Skookum Jim died (1916), so the year she earned $1,800 trapping was probably 1914 or 1915.

7. A copy of this photograph is in the Yukon Archives, Territorial Archives, Whitehorse, Yukon, and is number 807 in the photograph collection.

8. This symbolizes the high status of the child whose birth will be honored by a wealthy family.

9. Mrs. Smith tells a lengthy version of this story in Sidney, Smith, and Dawson, *My Stories* (1977), 85–89. Here I include only her commentary about its continuing significance. For Tahltan versions of this story see Teit, "Tahltan Tales" (1919), 216–18, 230–32; for Tagish and Inland Tlingit versions see McClellan, *Old People* (1975a).

10. In Mrs. Smith's version of the story, Game Mother was given a food box that contained a live goat whose meat could be taken without harming the goat.

11. *Ǥaax'w áa yéi daadune yé* may refer to a fishcamp at the mouth of the Alsek, near Dry Bay. Frederica De Laguna, *Mount St. Elias* (1972), 85, notes that

on the lower Alsek River the Dry Bay-Akwe River area used to be excellent for fishing.

12. *Yaakwdáat* refers to present-day Yakutat, though Mrs. Smith may actually mean Dry Bay, where Yakutat Indians lived when she visited Dry Bay as a child. The name *Téena* is related to the Tlingit word for "copper." Beaten coppers made by coastal Tlingit were highly valued articles of trade and were occasionally purchased by Southern Tutchone Indians living at Dalton Post. She indicates that the size was roughly six inches by nine inches.

13. Throughout the Yukon, independent traders used their own systems of tokens rather than money, a policy that continued well into this century.

14. *Neskatahéen* and *Weskatahéen* are used interchangeably in conversation because the distinction between a nasal (n/m) and w is not significant in the Southern Tutchone language. Official maps seem to use both spellings. It is the name of the original trading center where Southern Tutchone met Chilkat Tlingits; when Dalton arrived, he built his post only a short distance away.

15. "*Nàlùdi*" refers to the Lowell Glacier; it flows into and has periodically blocked the Alsek River (see Section 6).

16. *Noogaayík* (McClellan's *Nuqwa'ik'*) was a community established by coastal people who came to the Alsek during the last century to trade. Their numbers were depleted by sickness, and by the time McClellan visited Champagne during the early 1950s, *Noogaayík* had been abandoned for some years; see McClellan, *Old People* (1975a), 28.

17. *Tínx Kayaaní* was another settlement on the Alsek. De Laguna, *Mount St. Elias* (1972), 87, translates it "Kinnikinik Leaves."

18. This may have been the famous Dry Bay shaman, Wolf Weasel, mentioned by De Laguna, *Mount St. Elias* (1972), 90. According to people who spoke with her and with Catharine McClellan at Champagne in 1954, this man had died forty years earlier.

19. Before the Chilkat Pass became a regular trail for aboriginal trade, Chilkat Indians crossed to the interior over mountains at the head of Kusawa Lake. Mrs. Annie Ned discusses the importance of this old route at length in her account. Both she and Mrs. Smith refer to Kusawa Lake as "Lake Arkell," its official name for a brief period at the turn of the century.

20. The White Pass and Yukon Railway from Skagway to Whitehorse was completed in 1900.

21. There is clear scientific evidence that the Lowell Glacier did surge in 1852, building an ice dam across the Alsek River to a height of two hundred meters and creating glacial Lake Alsek behind the dam. When the pressure of the lake broke the ice dam, the water discharged in a catastrophic flood, drowning Tlingit people downriver at the junction of the Tatshenshini and Alsek rivers. The event is clearly preserved in the oral history of Tlingit people living at Yakutat, Alaska. De Laguna heard about it from Yakutat Tlingit informants on the coast and was able to date the event at 1852; see *Mount St. Elias* (1972), 276. McClellan also heard about the more recent flooding shortly after Mrs. Smith's birth; see McClellan, *Old People* (1975a), 71–72. Elsewhere I have compared various oral and scientific accounts about surging glaciers in this region (Cruikshank, "Legend and Landscape" [1981], 74–78).

22. Until Canada underwent metric conversion, numbered mileposts marked the full 1,500-mile length of the Alaska Highway from its beginning in Fort St.

John, British Columbia, to its terminus in Fairbanks, Alaska. "1016" is the old milepost number marking the location of the community of Haines Junction and is still used as a place name by older people.

23. By killing the fish in the way he has been taught, he ensures that each salmon will be reconstituted as before.

24. See Stith Thompson, "Star Husband" (1953) for a comparison of eighty-six versions told north of Mexico. In his analysis Thompson identifies the Wolverine episode as optional, not part of what he calls the "core story." Mrs. Smith refers to this episode, explicitly stating that it is not part of her story; Mrs. Sidney includes the episode in her version.

25. In the early part of this century a fine black fox might be worth two thousand dollars; see McClellan et al., *Part of the Land* (1987), 37.

26. This version was recorded July 15, 1985. Ten years earlier, in 1975, Mrs. Smith recounted a slightly different version; though the spirit is essentially the same, a comparison of the two suggests that the emphasis may be shifting in her explanations as she gets older:

> I got two kids from him, but he wanted two wives, I guess. I don't care for that. One time we came to a dance, a white-man dance. I danced with somebody.
>
> "How you learn to dance? You dance good," they tell me.
>
> "Oh, sometimes they dance there, at Champagne. We're mixed up with white people there now," I tell him. When we dance, we talk. And when my husband sees that, he got mad and quit me. Crazy man, eh? When he left, he took all my stuff—my two suitcases. After one month, he wanted to come back to me. I tell him, "Go to hell. Don't come back no more!"

27. Live foxes, like the one Mrs. Smith caught, were particularly valuable because they could be sold to fox farmers for breeding purposes.

28. Robinson was a station stop on the White Pass and Yukon Railway, between Carcross and Whitehorse.

29. The traders Taylor and Drury operated a number of posts in the Yukon Territory in the early part of the century and serviced many of them with their own riverboats.

30. As Mrs. Smith's mother's brother's wife, an opposite-moiety aunt who was a member of the same clan as the prospective husband, Jessie Allen was an appropriate person to act in the marriage negotiations. (See also Mrs. Sidney's account, Section 13.) In the account that follows, Mrs. Smith is emphasizing that she was entirely deferential to her grandmother and to her aunt in these discussions, repeating, "Just like that, me, used to be."

31. Her son, Johnny Smith, was chief of the *Kwänlin Dän* band during the 1970s and from 1981 to 1988.

32. Mrs. Smith became well known as a carver during these years. Her carvings were of mythological themes, and whenever she begins talking about how she carved, she shifts almost immediately to tell a story from which she made a carving. On this occasion, she told me about a carving she made of two snakes trying to climb a tree during the world flood at the beginning of time.

33. In the 1950s, when tuberculosis became a major risk for Yukon Native people, those identified as ill were evacuated to the Charles Camsell Hospital, in Edmonton, for treatment; many of them had to stay there several years.

34. Three regiments of soldiers reached Whitehorse in April 1942. From there, one worked north to Alaska while another worked south toward Teslin. A third regiment was sent to Teslin by boat and worked south to Watson Lake. Elsewhere I have discussed retrospective accounts recorded with Indian people who lived along the highway during the construction period and have compared them with government documents available in the Yukon Archives; see Cruikshank, "Gravel Magnet" (1985).

35. Here Mrs. Smith is referring to a former commissioner of the Yukon Territory.

36. The appropriate person to marry her when her husband died would be someone of his own clan, Daḵl'aweidí, preferably his nephew, his sister's son, or someone in a socially equivalent relationship to him.

37. Nedlin refers to a deceased person's rebirth as a new baby. Such a child will give a sign at an early age to an appropriate person that he or she remembers incidents from his or her former life. Often the details the child reveals are ones that could be known only by the deceased and the person the child tells. The child is always someone of the same moiety or clan as the deceased person. As the child grows older, he or she forgets this former life.

38. Mrs. Smith is naming women of the Wolf clan or moiety who can all be classified as "sister-in-law." As one of the oldest living people in the Yukon, she sometimes finds it sad that all her friends have gone before her.

39. Glaciologists have identified a number of surging glaciers in the area just west of Dalton Post (personal communication, G. K. C. Clarke).

III. Old-Style Words Are Just Like School

1. In Native oral tradition, Hutshi has a prominent place as a major trading center, one of the farthest inland centers visited by Tlingit traders on their annual trip from the coast.

2. De Laguna, Mount St. Elias (1972), 214.

3. The route appears on the early map made by the Tlingit chief Kohklux; see Davidson, "Explanation of an Indian Map" (1901). The German ethnographer Aurel Krause noted in his 1885 account, The Tlingit Indians (1956), 136, that the north end of Kusawa Lake was a trade rendezvous used by Chilkats and Athapaskans. Writing in 1887, Canadian geologist George Dawson commented that the use of this route by Tlingit traders was declining by then because the journey from the coast to the head of the Takhini was so difficult. The Chilkat trail took longer, but it was less dangerous. See Dawson, Report on an Exploration (1898), 160.

4. This letter is on file in the Anglican Church records, Yukon Territorial Archives, and is dated April 25, 1917.

5. For musical notation see Cruikshank, "Life" (1987), 697–706. Tones are not marked on Southern Tutchone words in these songs because tones change when sung.

6. Fort Selkirk on the Yukon River was another longstanding center for Tlingit/Athapaskan trade. In 1848 the Hudson's Bay Company tried to build its own post there, but Tlingits were unwilling to tolerate the competition and destroyed it.

7. Haines Junction. See Part II, note 22.

8. King salmon arriving at Hutshi would have made the long journey from the Bering Sea up the Yukon River, then up the Nordenskiold River to Hutshi. People living near Dalton Post occupied a different river drainage and had access to the richer sockeye salmon coming from the Pacific via the shorter Alsek and Tatshenshini route. When E. J. Glave reported on his travels to this region in 1892, he noted that people from Hutshi went to Neskatahin (the original name for the village near Dalton Post) each year to "recuperate on the fatted fish" available there; see Glave, "Pioneer Packhorses" (1892a), 869. Mrs. Ned's comment about Dalton Post's being "no good" now refers to recent government restrictions placed on Indian fishing there.

9. There is evidence that moose and caribou habitats have shifted during the last one hundred and fifty years. Biologists are still not sure of the reasons for their disappearance and reappearance. Two subspecies of barren-ground caribou formerly ranged in the southern Yukon—the large herds of Stone Caribou (*Rangifer arcticus stonei*) and the less gregarious Osborn Caribou (*Rangifer arcticus osborni*). Herds of Stone Caribou have been seen in historic times around Whitehorse, Carcross (short for "Caribou Crossing"), and near the upper regions of the Alsek River. Indian tradition's description of them as blackening the ice at Kluane Lake and Aishihik Lake has been confirmed in the archaeological record, though they have not been seen in recent memory; see Workman, *Prehistory* (1978), 16, and McClellan, *Old People* (1975a), 108.

10. Ideally, in the "old way" a couple stayed with the wife's family for at least a year after marriage, though it is unclear to me how often this actually occurred. By custom, a man then contributed to his wife's parents' household for the rest of their lives. A common reference to this tradition comes in the way a woman may still refer to a new son-in-law: "he's working for me, now."

11. According to McClellan, *Old People* (1975a), 28, *Noogaayík* was an important fishing village on the Tatshenshini River in the nineteenth century. The village was established by Tlingits who had moved into the interior, probably from the Chilkat area, after striking up a trade in furs with people farther inland. From *Noogaayík* a trail led directly to Klukwan, a Chilkat Tlingit headquarters close to the coast.

12. Tlingit traders reputedly used this practice in their trade with interior Athapaskans, relying on their middleman position to charge high prices and to maintain a trade monopoly with their inland neighbors.

13. By naming communities that are now widely dispersed, Mrs. Ned is contrasting present-day, permanent villages with settlement patterns in former times, when mobility was essential to a sense of community.

14. As Mrs. Ned tells this story, she sometimes adds her own commentary, and I have set these reflections off from the narrative by indenting them.

15. Her comment refers to the time at the beginning of the world when the sky came down to the earth at the horizon and it was possible for people to be stolen away to the "far side," where everything was perpetual darkness and winter.

16. *Äsùya* recognizes two indicators that this individual is not human. First, he will not eat human food. Second, beings who disguise themselves as humans characteristically sleep on the opposite side of the fire from people.

17. She is secluded at puberty, under the conventional "long hat."

18. "Beaver" (capitalized) refers to *Äsùya;* "beaver" (lower case) refers to the

animal. There is some interplay here between concerns that beavers and humans share in the following dialogue.

19. After Crow went to the coast, he established drainage patterns so that Klukshu drains to the nearby Pacific coast, while Dezadeash and Kusawa lakes drain north to the Yukon and ultimately to the Bering Sea.

20. The international boundary separating the Yukon Territory from the state of Alaska cross-cuts this old trade trail, and all goods transported across are now subject to a tariff.

21. All three narrators make regular reference to the idea that, when they were young, a marriage was viewed as a contract between kin groups, not between individuals. At the death of a spouse, someone in an appropriate category (usually a sibling of the first spouse, or in the case of a man's death, a maternal nephew) was expected to "take over" the widow or widower.

22. Mrs. Ned's account confirms many of the points in Van Kirk's analysis of the role women played in the fur trade; see her *Many Tender Ties* (1980).

23. They were trapping muskrats on the small lakes near Snag, some three hundred kilometers northwest of Kusawa Lake.

24. *Gúnχaa* means "abalone" or "mother of pearl" and refers to special buttons used by Tlingits when they traded with inland people.

25. This trip would have been made by the overland trail joining Dalton Post with Kusawa Lake. They would be carrying dried sockeye salmon, not available in Kusawa Lake.

26. The junction of the Mendenhall and Takhini was named "Steamboat Landing" when traders Taylor and Drury began to bring their riverboat there to deliver supplies and to buy furs. A few miles upstream the river is particularly treacherous during high water.

27. In his liminal state he was able to "hear" them; in some versions the food they destroy at the potlatch goes directly to him and saves his life.

28. Mrs. Ned is referring here to her opposite-moiety uncles, her father's brothers, who would be expected to "pay her with furs" because they were Wolf and she was Crow.

29. Big Salmon and Little Salmon were two Northern Tutchone communities on the Yukon River; most of the residents moved to Carmacks or to Whitehorse after the road was built from Whitehorse to Dawson in 1952 and steamboats were taken off the Yukon River.

30. The canvas was hung as a curtain while people prepared their costumes behind it. When everyone was ready, it was taken down and people began to dance.

31. Here Mrs. Ned imitates the sounds of guns shooting and sings the welcoming song. Rifles were fired into the air to welcome visitors as they arrived from different parts of the Yukon.

32. By "Klukwan dance" Mrs. Ned is referring to Tlingit-style dancing; "Hutshi dance" would be that of her own Southern Tutchone people; "Ayan" is a term meaning "people downriver," in this case referring to Northern Tutchone people.

33. Mrs. Ned is referring to a well-known Crow story that tells how Crow, once white, was blackened by smoke when he tried to escape through the smokehole at the top of the tent.

34. As she says this, she makes handwriting motions with a scathing gesture, implying that is all young women do now. Like Mrs. Smith's remarks, though,

Mrs. Ned's comment is more an expression of concern than a criticism of behavior. Older women sometimes feel that younger women who have not experienced seclusion and the associated instruction remain at risk and unprotected.

35. Mrs. Ned regularly shifts to formal oratory when she is talking about "what young people should know." Because this narrative form is so characteristic of the way she instructs younger people, I include in this section three examples of her oratory about the time "since I got smart." In her oratory the rhythm often seems as important as the words; hence I have retained the style used elsewhere in this volume for traditional narratives.

36. At this point in her story, Mrs. Ned began to sing, and a friend who was present joined her; normally, this song is used only at funerals, she says.

37. This *kendhät* is a smooth, flat piece of wood over which the skin is draped while the woman scrapes it (with a two-handled knife) to remove the flesh and make the skin uniformly thick.

38. The process of soaking the skin in water in which the brains have been immersed, then scraping it, and then smoking it is repeated several times to give the skins the special soft "tan" that seems impossible to reproduce commercially. (See McClellan, *Old People* [1975a], 256–66, for a detailed discussion of skin tanning.)

39. For a number of years now, Mrs. Ned has trained a group of young people—many of them her grandchildren—to dance the "old-style" dances. Her own costume includes the gopher-skin blanket she mentions here.

40. She indicates the construction of a gopher (ground squirrel) snare by hand movements. The actual snare, made of eagle feathers, is tied to a supple "spring stick" and poked into a gopher hole with a sharp stick. When the gopher disturbs the snare, a trigger is released; this causes the stick to bounce back to its upright position and traps the gopher in its burrow.

41. Babiche (made from thin strips of soaked moose or caribou hide) and sinew (made from the back legs of large animals) were used for all aboriginal lashing, netting, and sewing and are still employed by women who place special value on working with handmade materials (see McClellan, *Old People* [1975a], 256–57).

42. Birch toboggans were probably made downriver from Fort Selkirk on the Yukon River where birch was plentiful; upriver, birch was almost absent and skin toboggans were more common.

43. Solomon Charlie was her classificatory brother because they had the same paternal grandfather; that is, their fathers had the same father but different mothers.

44. This third talk was given on a day when we traveled to Kusawa Lake. We were going to visit two archaeologists, Sheila Greer and her assistant, Brenda Kennett, who had invited us to their camp so they could talk with Mrs. Ned about their work in this region. They had visited Mrs. Ned at her home, and she was quite interested in learning what they were doing. She recorded the formal introduction to her "talk" at her home, before we left, and then continued it as a formal speech to four of us at Kusawa Lake: myself, the two archaeologists, and a wildlife officer. We all had lunch together; afterward, while we were drinking tea, Mrs. Ned began speaking. She covers much of the material she had already presented less formally above (in Sections 1–5), but she considers this particular presentation important because she was talking near the setting where the events occurred.

45. Mrs. Ned is expressing a concern repeated by Native people throughout the Yukon, that hunting and trapping are still economically and socially important to Yukon Natives despite the presence of modern conveniences. Nevertheless, imposed legislation governing registration of traplines, hunting, fishing, and migratory birds makes it increasingly difficult for Native people to continue those activities.

46. It was customary for the prospective groom's parents to bring a gift to the mother of the bride—blankets or hides, or more recently, money. The girl's mother had the final say, depending on whether she accepted or rejected the gift.

47. Mrs. Ned is referring first to the preferred pattern of initial matrilocal residence after marriage. Her comment about "turning to Grandma's side" refers to the recent repeal of a controversial section of the Indian Act (Section 12[1][b]) which formerly compelled an Indian woman who married a non-Indian man (or a man not defined as Indian under the act) to forfeit Indian status for herself and her heirs. "Status" Indians are those registered as Indians under the terms of the Indian Act. This particular section of the act was judged to discriminate on the basis of gender and to contravene the new Canadian Constitution; it was repealed in April 1985. Subsequently, many women who had lost their Indian status in that way have been able to recover it.

48. Shorty Chambers was the trader at Champagne Landing.

49. An essential component of a shaman's power was his song, which came to him as a result of his contact with an animal spirit helper. Earlier, Mrs. Ned made a similar statement about her father's power. She has sung her husband's song for me several times, but it would be entirely inappropriate to make a tape recording of it.

50. *Nedlin* refers to a deceased person's rebirth as a new baby (see Part II, note 37).

51. They met at the home of Mrs. Taylor, the wife of one of the traders.

52. Mrs. Ned is referring to flooding that has occurred periodically when the Lowell Glacier surges, damming the Alsek River and creating a lake upstream. See also Mrs. Kitty Smith's account, Section 6.

53. Older people understood that glaciers are dens of giant animals and that if "something inside" a glacier smells grease cooking, it may emerge, triggering a glacial surge. This region is of particular interest to geophysicists because of the high concentration of surging glaciers.

54. The hills in this area show clear beaches, marking levels reached by different lake fillings.

55. Arctic ground squirrels, or "gophers," are extremely numerous in this area and are especially relished in the spring when they are fat after the winter hibernation. The population is subject to cyclical fluctuation, but a flood destroying all the burrows in an area would significantly influence population recovery.

56. *Njäl* refers to the common aboriginal house type in the southern Yukon, the double lean-to, constructed of poles and covered with moss and brush.

57. See note 9.

58. When a caribou began singing the song belonging to the doctor, people realized that the man had become a caribou.

59. This outcome corresponds with the experience of Mrs. Ned's own (second) husband, who was unable to hunt large game animals after he acquired his powers.

1. See Stith Thompson, *Tales of the North American Indians* (1929) and *Motif-Index of Folk Literature* (1955).

2. Versions were recorded by Krause, *Tlingit Indians* (1956); by Swanton, *Tlingit Myths and Texts* (1909); and by Teit, "Kaska Tales" (1917) and "Tahltan Tales" (1919, 1921).

3. See McClellan, *Old People* (1975a), 66–67, and Ridington, "Technology, World View and Adaptive Strategy" (1982), as well as his "Knowledge, Power and the Individual"(1988).

4. See McClellan, "Feuding and Warfare"(1975b), 181–258, for a discussion of the "stealing" of women, and also Slobodin, "Without Fire" (1975), 260–301, for comments on the "prize woman" in Kutchin stories.

5. For a more detailed analysis of these stories see Cruikshank, "Myth and Tradition as Narrative Framework" (1988).

6. For a careful elaboration of this argument see Will Wright, *Six Guns and Society* (1975), 192.

7. See Basso, " 'Stalking with Stories' " (1984), for a seminal paper on this topic.

8. Sidney, *Place Names* (1980).

9. Since one's father is by definition a member of the opposite moiety, *his* father (one's paternal grandfather) necessarily belongs to one's own "side" or moiety.

10. Rosaldo, "Doing Oral History" (1980), 89.

11. See, for example, Ginzberg, *Cheese and the Worms* (1976), and Darnton, *Great Cat Massacre* (1984). Despite his alleged disinterest in narrative content or social meaning of narrative, one of Levi-Strauss's major contributions was to unite the two categories of "myth" and "social organization" and to show that they could be analyzed by the same method and thus could possibly be seen as phenomena of the same order.

Glossary of Native Terms

Language is designated as follows:
Southern Tutchone = (ST), Tagish = (T), Tlingit = (Tl)

áa – "lake" (possessed form, *áayi*) (Tl)

Aagé – personal name (Tl)

Aakegántth'at – personal name (?)

Aandaax'w – personal name (Tl)

Aatthandláya – personal name (?)

(ax)aat – "(my) auntie" (Tl)

ägay – "wolf" (ST)

Ägunda – name for Wolf moiety (ST)

Ajàngàkh – personal name (ST)

akeyí – "trampoline-like swing made by Game Mother" (Tl or T)

Äsùya – "Beaverman" (ST)

cháatl – "halibut" (Tl)

Chènk'äla – place name (ST)

Chènk'äla Chù – place name (ST)

Chílíh Dzéłe' – place name (T)

Chookanshaa – place name (Tl)

Chooneit Shaayí – place name (Tl)

Chooneit Wusi.axu Yé – place name (Tl)

Chùinagha – place name (ST)

Ch'óonehte' Má – personal name (T) (note high tone on *Má* only in this context)

Däk'äläma – personal name (ST)

Dakl'aweidí – Tlingit-named Wolf clan (Tl)

Dakl'usháa – "woman of the *Dakl'aweidí* clan" (Tl)

Dakwa'äl – personal name (ST)

Dàljini – personal name (ST)

dän k'è – "Southern Tutchone language" (ST)

Dasgwaanga – place name (Tl)

Ddhäl Nàdhäda – place name (ST)

Deisheetaan – Tlingit-named Crow clan (Tl)

Deishuhít – "end-of-the-trail house" (Tl)

den k'e – "Tagish language" (T)

Dǫ' – character in story (ST)

dunyèn – "children" (ST)

Dúshka – personal name (T)

Dùu Chù – place name (ST)

Dùuchùgà – place name (ST)

Dzagwáa – personal name (T)

375

Dzagwama – personal name (ST)
dzéƚe' – "hill, mountain" (T)
Éleish Tóo'e' – place name (T)
(esh)dezhä – "(my) younger sister" (T)
(esh)embe'e' – "(my) father's sister" (T)
(esh)idaa – "(my) nephew" (T)
(esh)táa – "(my) father's brother" (T)
Gáanuulą́ą – place name (T)
Gàch'ema – personal name (ST)
Gäh Ddhäl – place name (ST)
Gasƚeeni – personal name (Tl or ST)
Goonxaktsáy—personal name (Tl or ST)
Guná – personal name (T)
gúnxaa – "abalone, mother of pearl" (Tl)
Gúnxaadaakeit – personal name (Tl)
Gaanaxteidí – Tlingit-named Crow clan (Tl)
Gaanax.ádi – Tlingit-named Crow clan (Tl)
Gaax'w áa yéi daadune yé – place name (Tl)
Gooch Ooxú – personal name (Tl)
Gooch Tláa – personal name (Tl)
Gunaaták' – personal name (Tl)
Haandeyéiƚ – personal name (Tl)
Héen Kas'eƚ'ti Xoo – place name (Tl)
hít – "house" (Tl)
Hóoch'i Áayi – place name (Tl)
Hunxu.aat – personal name (Tl)
Hunyís – personal name (Tl)
Jamalooga – place name (T)
Jikaak'w – personal name (T)
Kaagwaantaan – Tlingit-named Wolf clan (Tl)
Kaa.ítdesadu.áxch – personal name (Tl)
Kàdùhikh – personal name (ST)
Kajìt – name for Crow moiety (ST)
Kàkhah – personal name (ST)
Kàkhnokh – personal name (ST?)
kanday dhù – "moose skin" (ST)
Kashadandá – personal name (T)
Katlay – personal name (ST?)
Kàt'et – personal name (ST)
Kat'oà – personal name (ST?)
ke – "for" (ST)
Kéet hít – "Killer Whale House" (Tl)
Keikandagán – personal name (Tl)
Keish – personal name (Tl)
kendhät – "board for working hide" (ST)
Kídéeténe' – place name (T)
Kiks.ádi – Tlingit-named Crow clan (Tl)
Kojel – personal name (ST)
Koosawu Áa – place name (Tl)

ḵooshdaa – "otter" (Tl)
Kooshdaa Xágu – place name (Tl)
Kosándagà – place name (ST)
Kwákah Dzéłe' – place name (T)
Kwǎnsha – personal name (ST)
Kwänlin Dän – "people of the rapids" (ST)
Kwǎnshalta – personal name (ST)
Ḵaachgaawáa – personal name (Tl)
Ḵaach.ádi – Tlingit-named Crow clan (Tl)
Ḵaadzaasx̱ee – personal name (Tl)
Ḵáa Ǥoox – personal name (Tl)
Ḵaajinéek' – personal name (Tl)
Ḵaajinéek' Teiyí – place name (Tl)
Ḵaajoolaaxí – personal name (Tl)
Ḵaałaa – personal name (Tl)
Ḵaatułak'é – personal name (Tl)
ḵaax̱ – "sawbill duck" (Tl)
Ḵaax̱ Teiyí – place name (Tl)
Ḵaax̱'achgóok – personal name (Tl)
Ḵaax̱'anshi – personal name (Tl)
Ḵaneegweik – personal name (Tl)
Ḵudeinahaa – personal name (Tl)
Ḵudewoogoot – personal name (Tl)
K'aa' Deitl'óoní – place name (T)
K'asmbáa Dzéłe' – place name (T)
K'ayę̜datà – personal name (ST)
K'ayé Desdéł Ní – place name (T)
K'edäma – personal name (ST)
k'o – "cloud" (ST)
K'och'èn – "white man" (ST)
K'odetéena – personal name (Tl or ST)
Ḵ'ałgwách – personal name (Tl?)
Lą̜zhą̜ – personal name (ST)
La.oos – personal name (Tl)
La.oos Tláa – personal name (Tl)
Łḵóot – place name (Tl)
Lootáax – personal name (Tl or ST)
łù (or łùk) – "fish" (ST)
Lù Shäw – place name (ST)
Łukaax̱.ádi – Tlingit-named Crow clan (Tl)
-ma – "mother of" (ST, T, Tl)
Małal – personal name (T?)
Mandasaa (varies with Wandasaa) – personal name (Tl)
Médzíh Dzéłe' – place name (T)
Men Ch'ile Táh – place name (T)
Métáatl'e Shéch'ée – place name (T)
Naaḵw – "Octopus" (character in a story) (Tl)
Naasgas'éi Shaayí – place name (Tl)
Naataase Héen – place name (Tl)

Nadagáat' – personal name (Tl)

Nahóowu – personal name (Tl)

Naɣhu – place name (ST)

Naɣhu Chù – place name (ST)

nàlàt – "boat" (ST)

Nàłùdi – place name (ST)

nedlin – "reincarnated" (T)

Neskatahéen – place name (Tl)

Nichàlà – place name (ST)

njäl – "aboriginal house type" (ST)

Noogaayík – place name (Tl)

Ntthenada – personal name (ST)

Nùłatà – personal name (ST)

Núhstséhé Dzéłe' – place name (T)

Núhstséhé Mene' – place name (T)

Óonáa Tóo'e' – place name (T)

Saayna.aat – personal name (Tl)

Sadusgé – personal name (Tl?)

Sagwaaye – personal name (ST? Tl?)

Sakinyáa – personal name (Tl)

Sakuni – personal name (ST)

Sankàlà – place name (ST)

Sa.éek' – personal name (Tl)

(du) séek' – "his daughter" (Tl)

shaa – "hill, mountain" (Tl)

sháa – "woman" (Tl)

Shaakóon – personal name (Tl)

Shaashuhídi – "mountain house" (Tl)

Shaatláax – "Moldy Head" (character in story; place name) (Tl)

Shaaw Tláa – personal name (Tl)

Shadanaak – personal name (Tl?)

Shagóon – "family history" (Tl)

shal – "fishtrap" (ST)

shär – "bear" (ST, T)

Shásh Zéitígí – place name (T)

Shat'okaw – character in story ("Mountain Man") (ST)

shą'ür – "my friend" (ST)

shęshęl – "stone ax" (T)

Shotk'e – personal name (ST)

Shuwuteen – personal name (Tl)

Skwáan – personal name (Tl)

Skwáan Taasłéyi – place name (T)

Stóow – personal name (Tl)

Taaghahi – place name (T)

Taagish Héeni – place name (Tl)

Taagish Tóo'e' – place name (T)

Taxaadí T'ooch' – place name (Tl)

Tàkàtà – personal name (ST)

Takàyeta – personal name (ST)

Taɬtan – place name (T)

tangwat – "bone tool for fleshing meat" (T)

Tashooch – personal name (Tl)

Ta Tígi – place name (T)

Tatl'èrma – personal name (T)

Téhzáa Chó Sáye' – place name (T)

teiyí – "rock" (Tl)

Tínx Kayaaní – place name (?)

Tláa – "mother of" (Tl)

Tlaagóo – "Surprise!" (Tl)

tlaagú – "stories" (Tl)

Tlákwshaan – personal name (Tl)

tlein – "big" (Tl)

Tloox – place name (Tl)

Todezáané – place name (T)

Tséi Chó Desdéɬ Ní – place name (T)

tsei'e' – "rock" (T)

Tsenedhäta – personal name (ST)

tsós – "sawbill duck" (T)

Tsuxx'aayí – place name (Tl)

Tudech'ade – personal name (T)

Tukyeidí – Tlingit-named Crow clan (Tl)

Tùtaɬmą – personal name (ST)

Tl'anaxéedákw – "Wealth Woman" (Tl)

Tl'ó K'aa' Dzéɬe' – place name (T)

Tl'úku – personal name (Tl)

ts'in – "ghost" (ST)

Ts'ürk'i – "Crow" (both the bird and the hero of Crow stories) (ST)

T'ooch' Áayi – place name (Tl)

T'ooch' Lutú – place name (Tl)

Weskatahéen – place name (used interchangeably with *Neskatahéen*) (Tl)

xaas – "wood buffalo" (Tl)

Xóonk'i Éesh – personal name (Tl)

Xúts Tláa Ta.eetí – place name (Tl)

Xutsnoowu – place name (Tl)

(Ax) Xúx – "(my) husband" (Tl) (term of reference)

X'eis'awaa Shaayí – place name (Tl)

Yaakwdáat – place name (Yakutat) (Tl)

yádi (pl. *yátx'i*) – "child of" (with reference to a clan) (Tl)

Yanhít – name for *Yanyeidí* [clan] House (Tl)

Yanyeidí – Tlingit-named Wolf clan (Tl)

(Ax) Yéet(k') – "(my) son" (Tl)

yéiɬ – "crow" (Tl)

Yéiɬdoogú – personal name (Tl)

Yéiɬs'aagi – personal name (Tl)

Yéiɬshaan – personal name (Tl)

Bibliography

Asch, Michael
   1982 "Dene Self-Determination and the Study of Hunter-Gatherers in the
      Modern World." In *Politics and History in Band Societies,* ed. Eleanor
      Leacock and Richard Lee. Cambridge: Cambridge University Press,
      pp. 347–71.
Balikci, Asen
   1963 *Vunta Kutchin Social Change: A Study of the People of Old Crow, Northern
      Yukon Territory (NCRC 63–3).* Ottawa: Department of Northern Affairs
      and National Resources. Northern Co-ordination and Research Centre.
Barrett, S. M.
   1906 *Geronimo's Story of His Life.* New York: Duffield and Co.
Basso, Keith
   1984 " 'Stalking with Stories': Names, Places and Moral Narratives Among
      the Western Apache." In *Text, Play and Story: The Construction and
      Reconstruction of Self and Society,* ed. Stuart Plattner. Washington, D.C.:
      Proceedings of the American Ethnological Society.
Bataille, Gretchen M., and Kathleen M. Sands
   1984 *American Indian Women: Telling Their Lives.* Lincoln: University of
      Nebraska Press.
Beidelman, T. O.
   1965 "Myth, Tradition and Oral History." *Anthropos* 65(5–6): 74–97.
Berger, Thomas R.
   1977 *Northern Frontier, Northern Homeland: The Report of the Mackenzie
      Valley Pipeline Inquiry.* 2 vols. Ottawa: Minister of Supply and Services.
Bertaux, Daniel, and Martin Kohli
   1984 "The Life Story Approach: A Continental View." *Annual Review of
      Sociology* 10:215–37.
Bertaux-Wiame, Isabelle
   1979 "The Life Story Approach to the Study of Internal Migration." *Oral
      History* 7(1): 26–32.
Berton, Pierre
   1972 *Klondike: The Life and Death of the Last Great Goldrush.* Rev. ed.
      Toronto: McClelland and Stewart.
Boas, Franz
   1914 "Mythology and Folk Tales of the North American Indian." *Journal of
      American Folklore* 27:374–410.
   1916 "Tsimshian Mythology." *31st Annual Report of the Bureau of American
      Ethnology, 1909–10.* Washington, D.C.
Brody, Hugh
   1981 *Maps and Dreams.* Toronto: Douglas and McIntyre.
   1987 *Living Arctic: Hunters of the Canadian North.* London: Faber and Faber.   381

Brumble, H. David III

1988 *American Indian Autobiography.* Berkeley and Los Angeles:University of California Press.

Bruss, Elizabeth

1976 *Autobiographical Acts: The Changing Situation of a Literary Genre.* Baltimore: Johns Hopkins University Press.

Bullen, Edward L.

1968 "An Historical Study of the Education of Indians of Teslin, Yukon Territory." Master's thesis, University of Alberta.

Carby, Hazel V.

1987 *Reconstructing Womanhood: The Emergence of the Afro-American Woman Novelist.* New York and Oxford: Oxford University Press.

Chance, Norman

1963 "Social Organization, Acculturation and Integration Among the Eskimo and the Cree: A Comparative Study." *Anthropologica,* n.s. 5(1): 47–56.

Clifford, James

1983 "On Ethnographic Authority." *Representations* 1(2): 118–46.

Clifford, James, and George E. Marcus

1986 *Writing Culture.* Berkeley and Los Angeles: University of California Press.

Coates, Kenneth S.

1984 "Best Left as Indians: Native-White Relations in the Yukon Territory, 1840–1950." Ph.D. dissertation, University of British Columbia.

Crapanzano, Vincent

1980 *Tuhami: Portrait of a Moroccan.* Chicago: University of Chicago Press.

1984 "Life Histories: A Review Article." *American Anthropologist* 86(4): 953–60.

Cruikshank, Julie

1974 *Through the Eyes of Strangers.* Whitehorse: Yukon Territorial Government and Yukon Archives.

1975a *Their Own Yukon: A Photographic History by Yukon Indian People.* Photographs collected by Jim Robb. Whitehorse: Yukon Native Brotherhood.

1975b "Becoming a Woman in Athapaskan Society: Changing Traditions on the Upper Yukon River." *Western Canadian Journal of Anthropology* 5(2): 1–14.

1978 *When the World Began.* Whitehorse: Yukon Territorial Government, Department of Education.

1979 *Athapaskan Women: Lives and Legends.* National Museum of Man Mercury Series, Paper No. 57. Ottawa: National Museums of Canada.

1981 "Legend and Landscape: Convergence of Oral and Scientific Traditions in the Yukon Territory." *Arctic Anthropology* 18(2): 67–93.

1983 *The Stolen Woman: Female Journeys in Tagish and Tutchone Narrative.* National Museum of Man Mercury Series, Paper No. 87. Ottawa: National Museums of Canada.

1984 "Tagish and Tlingit Place Names in the Southern Lakes Region, Yukon Territory." *Canoma* 10(1): 30–35.

1985 "The Gravel Magnet: Some Social Impacts of the Alaska Highway on Yukon Indians." In *The Alaska Highway: Papers of the Fortieth Anniversary Symposium*, ed. Kenneth Coates. Vancouver: University of British Columbia Press.

1987 "Life Lived Like a Story: Cultural Constructions of Life History by Tagish and Tutchone Women." Ph.D. dissertation, University of British Columbia.

1988 "Myth and Tradition as Narrative Framework: Oral Histories from Northern Canada." *International Journal of Oral History* 9(3): 198–214.

Cruikshank, Julie, and Catharine McClellan

1975 *Preliminary Investigation of the Social Impact of the Alaska Highway on Yukon Indians: Probable Parallels to the Impact of Pipeline Construction.* Testimony for the Mackenzie Valley Pipeline Inquiry, 5 May 1975.

Damas, David

1969 "Contributions to Anthropology: Band Societies." *Proceedings of the Conference on Band Organization.* Ottawa: Anthropological Series 84, National Museum of Canada Bulletin 228.

Darnell, Regna

1974 "Correlates of Cree Narrative Performance." In *Explorations in the Ethnography of Speaking*, ed. Richard Bauman and Joel Scherzer. Cambridge: Cambridge University Press.

Darnton, Robert

1984 *The Great Cat Massacre and Other Episodes in French Cultural History.* New York: Basic Books.

Dauenhauer, Nora Marks, and Richard Dauenhauer

1987 *Haa Shuká/Our Ancestors: Tlingit Oral Narratives.* Seattle:University of Washington Press; Juneau: Sealaska Foundation.

Davidson, George

1901 "Explanation of an Indian Map of the Rivers, Lakes, Trails and Mountains from the Chilkaht to the Yukon drawn by the Chilkaht Chief, Kohklux in 1869." *Mazama* 2(2): 75–82.

Dawson, George M.

1888 "Notes on the Indian Tribes of the Yukon District and Adjacent Northern Portion of British Columbia, 1887." *Annual Report of the Geological Survey of Canada*, n.s. 3(2): 191B–213B.

1898 *Report on an Exploration in the Yukon District, Northwest Territories and Adjacent Northern Portion of British Columbia, 1887.* Ottawa: Geological Survey of Canada.

De Laguna, Frederica

1960 *The Story of a Tlingit Community: A Problem in the Archaeological, Ethnological and Historical Methods.* Washington, D.C.: Bureau of American Ethnology Bulletin 172.

1972 *Under Mount St. Elias: The History and Culture of the Yakutat Tlingit.* 3 vols. Washington, D.C.: Smithsonian Contributions to Anthropology 7.

1975 "Matrilineal Kin Groups in Northwestern North America." In *Proceedings: Northern Athapaskan Conference, 1971*, ed. A. McFadyen Clark, 1:17–145. Ottawa: National Museum of Man Mercury Series, Canadian Ethnology Society Paper No. 27.

Dollard, John

1935 *Criteria for the Life History.* New Haven: Yale University Press.

Dyen, Isadore, and David F. Aberle

1974 *Lexical Reconstruction: The Case of the Pro-Athapaskan Kinship System.* London and New York: Cambridge University Press.

Dyk, Walter

1938 *Son of Old Man Hat: A Navaho Autobiography.* New York: Harcourt, Brace.

1947 *A Navaho Autobiography.* Viking Fund Publications in Anthropology No. 8. New York: Wenner-Gren Foundation.

Dyk, Walter, and Ruth Dyk

1980 *Left Handed: A Navaho Autobiography.* New York: Columbia University Press.

Easterson, Mary

1987 "Traditional Ways Preserve Indian Culture." 2 parts. *Dän Sha* 14(1): 15, and 14(2): 14.

Ellen, R. F. (ed.)

1984 *Ethnographic Research: A Guide to General Conduct.* London: Academic Press.

Emmons, G. T.

1911 *The Tahltan Indians.* Philadelphia: University of Pennsylvania Publications in Anthropology 4(1).

Feit, Harvey

1982 "The Future of Hunters within Nation States: Anthropology and the James Bay Cree." In *Politics and History in Band Societies,* ed. Eleanor Leacock and Richard Lee. Cambridge: Cambridge University Press, pp. 373–411.

Ford, Clellan

1941 *Smoke from Their Fires: The Life of a Kwakiutl Chief.* New Haven: Yale University Press.

Foster, Frances Smith

1979 *Witnessing Slavery: The Development of Ante-Bellum Slave Narratives.* Westport, Conn: Greenwood Press.

Frank, Gelya

1979 "Finding the Common Denominator: A Phenomenological Critique of Life History Method." *Ethos* 7(1): 68–94.

Freeman, James

1979 *Untouchable: An Indian Life History.* Stanford: Stanford University Press.

Geddes, Carol

1986 *Three Elder Storytellers.* 16-mm film footage. Whitehorse, Yukon.

Geertz, Clifford

1983 " 'From the Native's Point of View': On the Nature of Anthropological Understanding." In *Local Knowledge,* ed. Clifford Geertz. New York: Basic Books.

Ginzberg, Carlo

1976 *The Cheese and the Worms: The Cosmos of a Sixteenth-Century Miller.* Trans. John and Anne Tedeschi. Baltimore: Johns Hopkins University Press.

Glave, E. J.
    1890 "Our Alaska Expedition." *Frank Leslie's Illustrated Newspaper* 70:
        June 28, July 12, July 19, Aug. 9, Aug. 16, Sept. 6, Nov. 15, Nov. 22,
        Nov. 29, Dec. 6, Dec. 13, Dec. 20, Dec. 27.
    1891 "Our Alaska Expedition." *Frank Leslie's Illustrated Newspaper* 71: Jan. 3,
        Jan. 10.
    1892a "Pioneer Packhorses in Alaska. 1. The Advance." *Century Illustrated
        Monthly Magazine* 44(5): 671–82.
    1892b "Pioneer Packhorses in Alaska. 2. The Return to the Coast." *Century
        Illustrated Monthly Magazine* 44(6): 869–81.
Goody, Jack
    1977 *The Domestication of the Savage Mind.* Cambridge: Cambridge
        University Press.
Habgood, Thelma
    1970 "Indian Legends of Northwestern Canada by Emile Petitot." *Western
        Canadian Journal of Anthropology* 2(2): 94–129.
Hallowell, A. Irving
    1960 "Ojibwa Ontology, Behavior and World View." In *Essays in Honour of Paul
        Radin,* ed. Stanley Diamond. New York: Columbia University Press.
Harbsmeier, Michael
    1986 "Beyond Anthropology." *Folk* 28:33–59.
Harwood, Frances
    1976 "Myth, Memory and Oral Tradition: Cicero in the Trobriands."
        American Anthropologist 78(4): 783–96.
Helm, June
    1965 "Bi-laterality in the Socio-territorial Organization of the Arctic
        Drainage Dene." *Ethnology* 4(4): 361–85.
Helm, June (ed.)
    1981 *Handbook of North American Indians,* vol. 6, *Subarctic.* Washington,
        D.C.: Smithsonian Institution.
Henderson, Patsy
    1950 *Early Days at Caribou Crossing and the Discovery of Gold in the Klondike.*
        Ed. J. M. Boyer. Bremerton, Wash.: privately printed.
Honigmann, John J.
    1949 *Culture and Ethos of Kaska Society.* New Haven: Yale University
        Publications in Anthropology No. 40.
    1954 *The Kaska Indians: An Ethnographic Reconstruction.* New Haven: Yale
        University Publications in Anthropology No. 51.
    1966 "Social Disintegration in Five Northern Canadian Communities."
        Canadian Review of Sociology and Anthropology 2(4): 199–214.
Hoseley, Edward H.
    1966 "Factionalism and Acculturation in an Alaskan Athapaskan
        Community." Ph.D. dissertation, University of California, Los Angeles.
Hymes, Del
    1977 "Discovering Oral Performance and Measured Verse in American
        Indian Narrative." *New Literary History* 7:431–57.
Hymes, Del (ed.)
    1981 *In Vain I Tried to Tell You.* Philadelphia: University of Pennsylvania
        Press.

Jarvis, A. M.
1900 "Annual Report of Inspector A. M. Jarvis, Dalton Trail, 1899." *Annual Report of the Northwest Mounted Police*, 1900, 58–59.

Jelinek, Estelle C.
1980 *Women's Autobiography: Essays in Criticism*. Bloomington: Indiana University Press.

Kelly, Jane Holden
1978 *Yaqui Women: Contemporary Life Histories*. Lincoln: University of Nebraska Press.

Kluckhohn, Clyde
1945 "The Personal Document in Anthropological Science." In *The Use of Personal Documents in History, Anthropology, and Sociology*, ed. Louis Gottschalk, Clyde Kluckhohn, and Robert Angell. New York: Social Science Research Council.

Knight, Rolf
1965 "A Re-examination of Hunting, Trapping and Territoriality Among the Northeastern Algonkian Indians." In *Man, Culture and Animals: The Role of Animals in Human Ecological Adjustment*, ed. Anthony Leeds and Andrew P. Vayda. Washington, D.C.: American Association for the Advancement of Science, pp. 27–42.

Krause, Aurel
1956 *The Tlingit Indians*. 2d ed. Trans. Erna Gunther. Seattle: University of Washington Press. (Originally published in German in 1885)

Kroeber, Alfred
1908 "Black Wolf's Narrative." In *Ethnology of the Gros Ventre. Anthropological Papers of the American Museum of Natural History* 1(4): 197–204.

Kroeber, Theodora
1961 *Ishi in Two Worlds: A Biography of the Last Wild Indian of North America*. Berkeley and Los Angeles: University of California Press.

Krupat, Arnold
1981 "The Indian Autobiography: Origins, Type and Function." *American Literature* 53(1): 22–42.

Lakoff, G., and M. Johnson
1980 *Metaphors We Live By*. Chicago: University of Chicago Press.

Langness, L. L., and Gelya Frank
1981 *Lives: An Anthropological Approach to Biography*. Novato, Calif.: Chandler and Sharp.

LaViolette, Forrest E.
1961 *The Struggle for Survival: Indian Cultures and the Protestant Ethic in British Columbia*. Toronto: University of Toronto Press.

Leach, Edmund (ed.)
1967 *The Structural Study of Myth and Totemism*. London: Tavistock.

Leacock, Eleanor
1954 *The Montaignais "Hunting Territory" and the Fur Trade*. American Anthropological Association Memoir 78, 56(5).

Lee, Dorothy
1959 "The Conception of Self Among the Wintu Indians." In *Freedom and Culture*. Englewood Cliffs, N.J.: Prentice-Hall, pp. 131–40.

Legros, Dominique
    1981 "Structure socio-culturelle et rapports de domination chez les
        Tutchone Septentrionaux du Yukon au XIXe siècle." Ph.D. dissertation,
        University of British Columbia.
LeRoy, John
    1985 *Fabricated World: An Interpretation of Kewa Tales.* Vancouver: University
        of British Columbia Press.
Levi-Strauss, Claude
    1968 *The Origin of Table Manners.* London: Jonathon Cape.
    1971 *The Naked Man.* New York: Harper and Row.
Lurie, Nancy Oestrich
    1961 *Mountain Wolf Woman, Sister of Crashing Thunder: The Autobiography of
        a Winnebago Woman.* Ann Arbor: University of Michigan Press.
Lysyk, Kenneth M., Edith Bohmer, and Willard Phelps
    1977 *Alaska Highway Pipeline Inquiry.* Ottawa: Minister of Supply and
        Services.
McCandless, Robert
    1985 *Yukon Wildlife: A Social History.* Edmonton: University of Alberta Press.
McClellan, Catharine
    1950 "Culture Change and Native Trade in the Southern Yukon Territory."
        Ph.D. dissertation, University of California, Berkeley.
    1956 "Shamanistic Syncretism in Southern Yukon Territory." *Transactions of
        the New York Academy of Sciences,* series 2, 19(2): 130–37.
    1963 "Wealth Woman and Frogs Among the Tagish Indians." *Anthropos*
        58:121–28.
    1964 "Culture Contacts in the Early Historic Period in Northwestern North
        America." *Arctic Anthropology* 2(2): 3–15.
    1970a *The Girl Who Married the Bear.* Ottawa: National Museum
        Publications in Ethnology 2.
    1970b "Indian Stories About the First Whites in Northwestern North
        America." In *Ethnohistory in Southwestern Alaska and the Southern Yukon:
        Method and Content,* ed. Margaret Lantis. Lexington: University Press of
        Kentucky.
    1975a *My Old People Say: An Ethnographic Survey of Southern Yukon Territory.*
        2 vols. Publications in Ethnology 6 (1 & 2). Ottawa: National
        Museums of Canada.
    1975b "Feuding and Warfare Among Northwestern Athapaskans." In
        Proceedings, Northern Athapaskan Conference, 1971, ed. A. McFadyan
        Clark. Canadian Ethnology Service Paper No. 27, 1:181–258. National
        Museum of Man Mercury Series. Ottawa: National Museums of
        Canada.
    1981a "History of Research in the Subarctic Cordillera." In *Handbook of
        North American Indians,* vol. 6, *Subarctic,* ed. June Helm. Washington,
        D.C.: Smithsonian Institution, pp. 35–42.
    1981b "Intercultural Relations and Cultural Change in the Cordillera." In
        Handbook of North American Indians, vol. 6, *Subarctic,* ed. June Helm.
        Washington, D.C.: Smithsonian Institution, pp. 387–401.
    1981c "Inland Tlingit." In *Handbook of North American Indians,* vol. 6,

Subarctic, ed. June Helm. Washington, D.C.: Smithsonian Institution, pp. 469–80.

1981d "Tagish." In *Handbook of North American Indians*, vol. 6, *Subarctic*, ed. June Helm. Washington, D.C.: Smithsonian Institution, pp. 481–92.

1981e "Tutchone." In *Handbook of North American Indians*, vol. 6, *Subarctic*, ed. June Helm. Washington, D.C.: Smithsonian Institution, pp. 493–505.

1985 "Travel." Unpublished manuscript.

McClellan, Catharine, with Lucie Birckel, Robert Bringhurst, James A. Fall, Carol McCarthy, and Janice Sheppard

1987 *Part of the Land, Part of the Winter: A History of the Yukon Indians.* Vancouver: Douglas and McIntyre.

McDonnell, Roger

1975 "Kasini Society: Some Aspects of the Social Organization of an Athapaskan Culture Between 1900–1950." Ph.D. dissertation, University of British Columbia.

McKennan, Robert

1959 *The Upper Tanana Indians.* New Haven: Yale University Publications in Anthropology No. 55.

Malinowski, Bronislaw.

1954 *Magic, Science and Religion.* Garden City, N.Y.: Doubleday, Anchor Books.

Mandelbaum, David

1973 "The Study of Life History: Gandhi." *Current Anthropology* 14(3): 177–206.

Marchand, John

1943 "Tribal Epidemics in the Yukon." *Journal of the American Medical Association* 123:1019–20.

Marcus, George E., and Micheal M. J. Fischer

1986 *Anthropology as Cultural Critique.* Chicago and London: University of Chicago Press.

Marriott, Alice

1948 *María: The Potter of San Ildefonso.* Norman: University of Oklahoma Press.

Michelson, Truman

1925 "The Autobiography of a Fox Indian Woman." *Fortieth Annual Report of the Bureau of American Ethnology, 1918–19,* 291–349.

1932 "The Narrative of a Southern Cheyenne Woman." *Smithsonian Misc. Collections* 87(5).

1933 "Narrative of an Apache Woman." *American Anthropologist* 35:595–610.

Miller, Joseph C.

1980 "Introduction: Listening for the African Past." In *The African Past Speaks: Essays on Oral Tradition and History,* ed. Joseph C. Miller. Kent, England, and Hamden, Conn.: Dawson, Archon.

Morin, Françoise

1982 "Anthropological Praxis and Life History." *International Journal of Oral History* 3(1): 5–30.

Murie, Olaus J.

1935 *Alaska-Yukon Caribou.* Washington, D.C.: U.S. Department of Agriculture.

Ned, Annie
1984 *Old People in Those Days, They Told Their Story All the Time.* Compiled by Julie Cruikshank. Whitehorse: Yukon Native Languages Project.

Neihardt, John G.
1932 *Black Elk Speaks, Being a Life Story of a Holy Man of the Oglala Sioux.* New York: William Morrow.

Osgood, Cornelius
1936a "The Distribution of the Northern Athapaskan Indians." *Yale University Publications in Anthropology* 7:3–23.
1936b *Contributions to the Ethnography of the Kutchin.* New Haven: Yale University Publications in Anthropology No. 14.
1971 *The Han Indians: A Compilation of Ethnographic and Historical Data on the Alaska Yukon Boundary Area.* New Haven: Yale University Publications in Anthropology No. 74.

Parsons, Elsie Clews
1919 "Waiyauitiea of Zuni, New Mexico." *Scientific Monthly* 9:443–57.
1921 "A Narrative Tale of the Ten'a of Anvik, Alaska." *Anthropos* 16:51–71.
1922 *American Indian Life.* New York: B. W. Huebsch.

Passerini, Luisa
1987 *Fascism in Popular Memory: The Cultural Experience of the Turin Working Class.* Trans. Robert Lumley and Jude Bloomfield. Cambridge: Cambridge University Press.

Penikett, Lu Johns
1986 *Potlatch Conference Report.* Whitehorse: Champagne-Aishihik Band and Yukon Historical and Museums Association.

Preston, Richard J.
1966 "Edward Sapir's Anthropology: Style, Structure and Method." *American Anthropologist* 68(6): 1105–28.
1972 "The Anthropology of Sapir." In *The Meaning of Culture,* ed. Morris Freilich. Lexington, Ky.: Xerox College Publishing.
1975 *Cree Narrative: Expressing the Personal Meaning of Events.* National Museum of Man Mercury Series, Paper No. 30. Ottawa: National Museums of Canada.

Rabinow, Paul
1977 *Reflections on Fieldwork in Morocco.* Berkeley and Los Angeles: University of California Press.

Radin, Paul
1913 "Personal Reminiscences of a Winnebago Indian." *Journal of American Folklore* 26:293–318.
1920 "The Autobiography of a Winnebago Indian." *University of California Publications in American Archeology and Ethnology* 16(7): 381–473.
1926 *Crashing Thunder: The Autobiography of an American Indian.* New York: Appleton.

Reichard, Gladys
1934 *Spider Woman: A Story of Navaho Weavers and Chanters.* New York: Macmillan.
1939 *Dezba: Woman of the Desert.* New York: J. J. Augustin.

Ridington, Robin
1982 "Technology, World View and Adaptive Strategy in a Northern

Hunting Society." *Canadian Review of Sociology and Anthropology* 19(4): 460–67.

1988 "Knowledge, Power and the Individual in Subarctic Hunting Societies." *American Anthropologist* 90(1): 98–110.

Rosaldo, Michelle

1980 *Knowledge and Passion: Ilongot Notions of Self and Social Life.* New York: Cambridge University Press.

Rosaldo, Renato

1976 "The Story of Tukbaw: 'They Listen as He Orates.'" In *The Biographical Process: Studies in the History and Psychology of Religion,* ed. Frank E. Reynolds and Donald Capps. The Hague: Mouton.

1980a "Doing Oral History." *Social Analysis* 4:89–99.

1980b *Ilongot Headhunting, 1883–1974: A Study in Society and History.* Stanford: Stanford University Press.

Said, Edward

1978 *Orientalism.* New York: Pantheon.

Sapir, Edward

1922 "Sayach'apis, A Nootka Trader." In *American Indian Life,* ed. Elsie Clews Parsons. New York: B. W. Huebsch.

1924 "Culture, Genuine and Spurious." *American Journal of Sociology* 29:401–29.

1927 "The Unconscious Patterning of Behavior in Society." In *Selected Writings of Edward Sapir,* ed. David Mandelbaum. Berkeley and Los Angeles: University of California Press, 1949, pp. 544–59.

1932a "Group." In *Selected Writings of Edward Sapir,* ed. David Mandelbaum. Berkeley and Los Angeles: University of California Press, 1949, pp. 357–64.

1932b "Cultural Anthropology and Psychiatry." In *Selected Writings of Edward Sapir,* ed. David Mandelbaum. Berkeley and Los Angeles: University of California Press, 1949, pp. 509–21.

1938 "Introduction." In *Son of Old Man Hat: A Navaho Autobiography,* recorded by Walter Dyk. New York: Harcourt, Brace.

Savala, Refugio, and Kathleen M. Sands

1980 *The Autobiography of a Yaqui Poet.* Tucson: University of Arizona Press.

Scott, Lalla

1966 *Karnee: A Paiute Narrative, the Story of Annie Lowry.* Reno: University of Nevada Press.

Shaw, Bruce

1980 "Life History Writing in Anthropology: A Methodological Review." *Mankind* 12(3): 226–33.

1981 *My Country of the Pelican Dreaming: The Life of an Australian Aborigine of the Gadjerong, Grant Ngabidj, 1904–1977.* Canberra: Australian Institute of Aboriginal Studies.

Sheppard, Janice

1983 "The Dog Husband: Structural Identity and Emotional Specificity in Northern Athapaskan Narrative." *Arctic Anthropology* 20(1): 89–101.

Shostak, Marjorie
　　1981 *Nisa: The Life and Words of a !Kung Woman*. Cambridge: Harvard
　　　　University Press.
Sidney, Angela
　　1980 *Place Names of the Tagish Region, Southern Yukon*. Whitehorse: Yukon
　　　　Native Languages Project.
　　1982 *Tagish Tlaagú/Tagish Stories*. Recorded by Julie Cruikshank.
　　　　Whitehorse: Council for Yukon Indians and Government of Yukon.
　　1983 *Haa Shagóon/Our Family History*. Compiled by Julie Cruikshank.
　　　　Whitehorse: Yukon Native Languages Project.
Sidney, Angela, Kitty Smith, and Rachel Dawson
　　1977 *My Stories Are My Wealth*. Recorded by Julie Cruikshank. Whitehorse:
　　　　Council for Yukon Indians.
Simmons, Leo
　　1942 *Sun Chief: The Autobiography of a Hopi Indian*. New Haven: Yale
　　　　University Press.
Slobodin, Richard
　　1975 "Without Fire: A Kutchin Tale of Warfare, Survival and Vengeance." In
　　　　Proceedings, Northern Athapaskan Conference, ed. A. McFadyen Clark.
　　　　Canadian Ethnology Service Paper No. 27, 1:259–301. Ottawa:
　　　　National Museums of Canada.
Smith, Kitty
　　1982 *Nindal Kwädindür/I'm Going to Tell You a Story*. Recorded by Julie
　　　　Cruikshank. Whitehorse: Council for Yukon Indians and Government
　　　　of Yukon.
Smith, Sidonie
　　1987 *The Poetics of Women's Autobiography: Marginality and the Fictions of Self-
　　　　Representation*. Bloomington: Indiana University Press.
Speck, Frank
　　1915 "The Family Hunting Band as the Basis of Algonkian Social
　　　　Organization." *American Anthropologist* 17(2): 289–305.
　　1935 *Naskapi: The Savage Hunters of the Labrador Peninsula*. Norman:
　　　　University of Oklahoma Press.
Spradley, James P.
　　1969 *Guests Never Leave Hungry: The Autobiography of James Sewid, a
　　　　Kwakiutl Indian*. New Haven: Yale University Press.
Stanton, Donna
　　1984 *The Female Autograph: Theory and Practice of Autobiography From the
　　　　Tenth to the Twentieth Century*. Chicago and London: University of
　　　　Chicago Press.
Steward, Julian
　　1934 "Two Paiute Autobiographies." *University of California Publications in
　　　　American Archeology and Ethnology* 33:423–38.
　　1938 "Panatubiui, An Owens Valley Paiute." *Bureau of American Ethnology
　　　　Bulletin* 33:423–38.
Swanton, J. R.
　　1909 *Tlingit Myths and Texts*. Washington, D.C.: Bureau of American
　　　　Ethnology Bulletin 39.

Tanner, Adrian

1965 "The Structure of Fur Trade Relations." Master's thesis, University of British Columbia.

1979 *Bringing Home Animals: Religious Ideology and Mode of Production of the Mistassini Cree Hunters*. New York: St. Martin's Press.

Tarr, Ralph Stockman, and Lawrence Martin

1914 *Alaska Glacier Studies*. Washington, D.C.: National Geographic Society.

Tedlock, Dennis

1971 "On the Translation of Style in Oral Narrative." In *Toward New Perspectives in Folklore,* ed. Americo Parades and Richard Bauman. Austin: University of Texas Press, pp. 114–33.

1977 "Toward an Oral Poetics." *New Literary History* 8(3): 507–19.

1983 *The Spoken Word and the Work of Interpretation*. Philadelphia: University of Pennsylvania Press.

Teit, James

1909 "Two Tahltan Traditions." *Journal of American Folklore* 22(85): 314–18.

1917 "Kaska Tales." *Journal of American Folklore* 30(118): 427–73.

1919 "Tahltan Tales." *Journal of American Folklore* 32(123): 198–250.

1921 "Tahltan Tales." *Journal of American Folklore* 43(133): 223–53.

1956 "Field Notes on the Tahltan and Kaska Indians, 1912–1915." *Anthropologica* 3:39–171.

Thompson, Paul

1979 "The Humanistic Tradition and Life Histories in Poland." *Oral History* 7(2): 21–25.

1980 "The New Oral History in France." *Oral History* 8(1): 14–20.

Thompson, Stith

1929 *Tales of the North American Indians*. Cambridge: Harvard University Press. Reprint. Bloomington: Indiana University Press, 1967.

1953 "The Star Husband." Reprinted in *The Study of Folklore,* ed. Alan Dundes. Englewood Cliffs, N.J.: Prentice-Hall, 1965, pp. 414–74.

1955 *Motif-Index of Folk Literature*. 6 vols. Rosenkilde and Bagger: Copenhagen.

Tlen, Daniel L.

1986 *Speaking Out: Consultations and Survey of Yukon Native Languages Planning, Visibility and Growth*. Whitehorse: Yukon Native Language Centre.

Toelken, Barre

1969 "The 'Pretty Language(s)' of Yellowman: Genre, Mode and Texture in Navaho Coyote Narratives." *Genre* 2(3): 211–35.

Toelken, Barre, and Tacheeni Scott

1981 "Poetic Retranslation and the 'Pretty Languages' of Yellowman." In *Traditional Literatures of the American Indian,* ed. Karl Kroeber. Lincoln: University of Nebraska Press.

Tom, Gertie

1981 *Duts'úm Edhó Ts'ètsi Yū Dän K'i/How to Tan Hides in the Native Way*. Whitehorse: Yukon Native Languages Project.

1987 *Èkeyi: Gyò Cho Chú/My Country: Big Salmon River*. Whitehorse: Yukon Native Language Centre.

Underhill, Ruth
  1936 *The Autobiography of a Papago Woman.* Memoirs of the American
      Anthropological Association, No. 46. Menasha, Wis.: American
      Anthropological Association.
Urquhart, M. C. (ed.)
  1965 *Historical Statistics of Canada.* Toronto: Macmillan.
Van Kirk, Sylvia
  1980 *Many Tender Ties: Women in Fur Trade Society in Western Canada.*
      Winnipeg: Watson and Dwyer.
Vansina, Jan
  1965 *Oral Tradition: A Study in Historical Methodology.* Chicago: Aldine.
  1985 *Oral Tradition as History.* Madison: University of Wisconsin Press.
VanStone, James
  1965 *The Changing Culture of the Snowdrift Chipewyan.* Ottawa:
      Anthropological Series 74, National Museum of Canada Bulletin 209.
Wallace, Anthony
  1961 *Culture and Personality.* New York: Random House.
  1970 *Handsome Lake: The Death and Rebirth of the Seneca.* New York: Knopf.
Watson, Lawrence C., and Maria-Barbara Watson-Franke
  1985 *Interpreting Life Histories: An Anthropological Inquiry.* New Brunswick,
      N.J.: Rutgers University Press.
White, Leslie
  1943 "Autobiography of an Acoma Indian." In *New Material from Acoma.*
      Bureau of American Ethnology 136:326–37.
Whittaker, Elvi
  1985 *The Mainland Haole.* New York: Columbia University Press.
Wood, Z. T.
  1899 "Annual Report of Superintendent Wood, Tagish, Upper Yukon, 1898."
      Annual Report of the Northwest Mounted Police, 1899, 42–43.
Workman, William
  1978 *Prehistory of the Aishihik-Kluane Area. Southwest Yukon Territory.* Ottawa:
      National Museum of Man Mercury Series, Archeological Survey Paper
      74.
Wright, Ronald
  1988 "Beyond Words." *Saturday Night,* April, 38–48.
Wright, Will
  1975 *Six Guns and Society: A Structural Study of the Western.* Berkeley and Los
      Angeles: University of California Press.

INDEX

In the American Indian Lives series

DATE DUE